The Armenian Experience

The Armenian Experience

From Ancient Times to Independence

Gaïdz Minassian

Translated by Peter Gillespie

I.B. TAURIS

LONDON • NEW YORK • OXFORD • NEW DELHI • SYDNEY

I.B. TAURIS
Bloomsbury Publishing Plc
50 Bedford Square, London, WC1B 3DP, UK
1385 Broadway, New York, NY 10018, USA

BLOOMSBURY, I.B. TAURIS and the I.B. Tauris logo are trademarks of
Bloomsbury Publishing Plc

First published in Great Britain 2020

Arméniens: Le temps de la délivrance by Gaïdz Minassian
Original copyright © CNRS Editions, 2015

Cover design by Alice Marwick
Cover image: *The Artist and his Mother*, c.1926–1936, by Arshile Gorky (1904–1948),
20th Century, Whitney Museum of American Art, New York, USA.
(© De Agostini Picture Library/Bridgeman Images/ARS, NY/DACS, London 2018)

Bloomsbury Publishing Plc does not have any control over, or responsibility for, any
third-party websites referred to or in this book. All internet addresses given in this
book were correct at the time of going to press. The author and publisher regret
any inconvenience caused if addresses have changed or sites have ceased to
exist, but can accept no responsibility for any such changes.

A catalogue record for this book is available from the British Library.

A catalogue record for this book is available from the Library of Congress.

ISBN: HB: 978-1-7883-1224-0
       PB: 978-0-7556-0074-8
       ePDF: 978-1-7867-3561-4
       eBook: 978-1-7867-2561-5

Typeset by RefineCatch Limited, Bungay, Suffolk

To find out more about our authors and books visit www.bloomsbury.com
and sign up for our newsletters.

Contents

Acknowledgements

I would especially like to thank all the members of my family for their continued support, especially my brother Vrej Minassian, my sisters Aznive Minassian and Elisabeth Koutzouzian, as well as my friends Ariane Chemin, Armand Thomassian, Daniel Findikian, Frédéric Bureau, André Manoukian, Francisco Barros, Eric Collier, without forgetting my girlfriend Delphine Goulmy. My thanks also go to my colleagues from Le Monde, Christophe Ayad, Raphaëlle Bacqué, Alain Frachon, Jean Birnbaum, Nicolas Weill and Franck Johannès.

My thanks also to Professors Jean-Pierre Mahé, Krikor Beledian, Claude Mutafian, Aram Mardirossian, Bertrand Badie, Bui Xuan Quang and Vincent Duclert for their advice. Special mention for Professors Taner Akçam and Richard G. Hovannisian who have contributed to the construction of this book; let them be thanked.

In addition, I would like to warmly thank Mr. and Mrs. Daron Bogossian (Paris), Raffi Krikorian and Hemera Intel Trade Comm. Consulting Lyon, Manuel Manoug Pamokdjian for their generosity in making the translation of this book into English possible. The Muscari company also contributed financially to this project. My warm thanks to them. Finally, this book would not have been possible without the support of several philanthropic foundations known for their investment in the dissemination of knowledge, their solidarity with the book and their commitment to the development of publication on the Armenian identity in the world. They are the Calouste Gulbenkian Foundation in Lisbon, Portugal, the Lea and Napoleon Bullukian Foundation in Lyon, France, and the Boghossian Foundation in Brussels, Belgium.

Finally, this book would not have been possible without the support of Christelle Voisin, Martine Bertea and Blandine Genthon, Executive Director of CNRS Editions.

MUSCARI   BOGHOSSIAN FOUNDATION   FONDATION BULLUKIAN

CALOUSTE GULBENKIAN FOUNDATION

Introduction

Two years ago, the Armenians overthrew Serzh Sargsyan's regime in the Republic of Armenia and launched the so-called 'Velvet Revolution' without any acts of violence or vandalism. Since this Armenian Spring, a new power has been set up in the Armenian capital with the aim of freeing the Republic from post-Sovietism and of giving hope to the Armenian people, especially the young, who are the true spearhead of the Revolution. Between 23 April and 9 December 2018, the Velvet Revolution under the leadership of Nikol Pashinyan, drove Serzh Sargsyan out of office. Pashinyan won the Yerevan mayoral election, dissolved the Parliament and won early parliamentary elections in December. The joy that lit up the faces of the young protestors who took to the streets of Yerevan concealed a number of legitimate concerns. While there is no doubt that the 'New Armenia' they were celebrating made a clean break from 27 years of injustice and impunity, Armenians are keenly aware that the 2018 Velvet Revolution is still fragile. The inhabitants of Armenia, an old nation but a young state, know there is a chance they may not taste the fruits of their revolution unless they rise to three main challenges.

The first challenge addresses the following question: Has Armenia broken away from post-Sovietism? Is this a 'colour revolution', similar to events which took place in Georgia in 2003 and in Ukraine in 2014? Post-Sovietism is a transition phase experienced by ex-Soviet states which is dominated by part-conservative, part-liberal thinking and breaks away from communism and traditional Soviet methods.

These elements combine in Armenia's post-patrimonial and authoritarian regime which demonstrates loyalty to Russia: corruption is endemic, social inequality runs deep, an oligarchic system thrives and there is a high level of emigration.

Similar to the Georgian and Ukrainian models, the Armenian revolution is led by an opposition leader, in this case member of parliament Nikol Pashinyan. Just like its other revolutionary cousins, the Velvet Revolution was born out of distrust between leaders and a civil society which has become increasingly independent.

Armenia's young generation wants to live under the rule of law. It wants mindsets to change and to open up to the world and it no longer accepts the traditional setup of the country's political parties. In that sense, the Armenian revolution follows closely in the footsteps of the colour revolutions. While there are similarities, the context in Armenia differs widely. The country stands out from Georgia and Ukraine in several ways: its geography (the country is enclaved), its past and the memory of the genocide, its pro-Russian stance and security issues.

While security is a major concern in Georgia and Ukraine, it is not such an existential issue in those countries as it is in Armenia. The social discontent that eventually led to the overthrow of pro-Russian regimes in Tbilisi and Kiev was predictable. However, in Yerevan in April 2018, two months before Sargsyan was ousted, nothing seemed to indicate that his leadership would end in a matter of weeks. In Armenia, the proponents of change had a different strategy, which consisted of differentiating their 'revolution' from the other post-Soviet revolutions, especially with regard to violence which they wanted to avoid at all costs along with the risk of civil war and tension with Russia.

In an effort not to make their movement geopolitical, the instigators of the revolution chose not to attach a pro-Western or anti-Russian stance to their protest. Their goal first and foremost was to restore the dignity of the Armenian people who had been trampled on by history and humiliated by their leaders.

The absence of a diplomatic agenda highlights a more profound issue, which is how Armenians regard the concept of sovereignty. On this point, two processes have historically lived side-by-side. One is an extension of what is currently happening in Russia and the other is related to Armenia's independence.

This two-fold dynamic is at the root of what is pushing people out onto the streets of Yerevan today. On the one hand, pro-Russians believe that Armenians should be loyal to Russia in the name of strategic tradition. For them, the reunification of both territories is more important than independence. On the other hand, those who are for independence are striving for Armenia to free itself from foreign intervention to fight against all forms of domination in the name of an historic tradition. It follows that independence is their number one priority.

The pro-Russian point of view takes a functionalist and instrumental approach. Here, Armenia is perceived as being a product of its own history: in other words, what is good for Russia is good for Armenia. Conversely, the structuralist and fundamental 'pro-independence' approach is that favoured by Nikol Pashinyan when he describes his politics as being 'neither pro- or anti-Russian nor Western, but pro-Armenian'. Pashinyan has often said that the Armenian Republic must respect all its diplomatic engagements and reinforce its alliance with Russia to balance out its bilateral relationship as, he points out, Moscow needs Yerevan in the region just as much as Armenia needs Russia. However, Armenia has also been busy building multilateral ties, especially following the success of the Francophone summit in Yerevan in 2018. Armenia is a member of the Eurasian Union and is a signatory the Comprehensive and Enhanced Partnership Agreement with the European Union. The Armenian Republic hopes to be a bridge between both markets and to open itself up to wider economic opportunities.

This leads us onto the second challenge. Will the Velvet Revolution boost Armenia's economy? Pashinyan is well aware that if it does not yield any economic benefits, it will stagnate before fizzling out. For that reason, he has called for an 'economic revolution'. To achieve this, the regime needs to break down Armenia's monopolies, revive small trade, provide guarantees to investors that the Armenian market is transparent and reassure businesses from the Armenian diaspora that investing in the country is safe. It must also open up the country by reinforcing its ties with Georgia and Iran on the North–South corridor. Ambitious regional co-operation projects are on the table, but it is too early to tell if there is the necessary will to make them happen, with the priority being the reinforcement of peace in the area.

Next comes the third challenge: will the Velvet Revolution succeed in promoting peace between Armenia and Azerbaijan? Both are involved in a dispute over Nagorno-Karabakh (Artsakh Republic in Armenian), an Armenian province which Stalin attached to Azerbaijan in 1921. Following Armenia's victory after a four-year war, Armenia, Azerbaijan and Nagorno-Karabakh signed a ceasefire. The OSCE Minsk group, co-chaired by the US, France and Russia, has been overseeing a negotiations process with all parties, but since 1996, Yerevan has been carrying out negotiations directly with Baku.

Just after he became prime minister, Pashinyan declared that all parties involved in the dispute over Nagorno-Karabakh should return to the negotiating table. He argued that since Armenians from this province have their own representatives and do not take part in Armenian elections, he was, therefore, not their legitimate representative. Baku did not take up his suggestion and since then, nothing has evolved on the ground.

Beyond these three challenges, studying the Velvet Revolution offers a very good opportunity to delve back into the history the Armenian people. Thus, a New Armenia was created in 2018, the year of the anniversary of the centenary of the founding of the First Republic in 1918. Indeed, 100 years ago, on 28 May 1918, Armenians proclaimed their independence as a Republic, becoming a sovereign state after six centuries of foreign domination. Yet this fledgling republic, formed only three years after the first genocide of the twentieth century in 1915, was soon to collapse, following the collusion in 1920 between Kemal's Turkey and Lenin's Russia.

A century later, the Republic of Armenia, free of Russian control since the fall of the Soviet Union and the end of the Cold War, marks the centenary of its independence and looks to the future.

In the United States, successive administrations have refused to recognize the massacre as a 'genocide' out of respect for their NATO commitments and defence partnership with Turkey, which has always displayed resistance to the use of the word, maintaining the official position that the deaths, terrible as they were, occurred during the chaos of warfare and were not sanctioned by the central government in Istanbul. On both sides of the Atlantic and elsewhere in the world, when the genocide is raised in political debate, all sides fall back to their established positions, effectively amounting to a stand off. Turkey categorically opposes international recognition of the terminology and threatens the disruption of diplomatic relations should any country seriously challenge its position, one it has held officially for decades. Armenians, whether in Armenia or the diaspora, are adamant that the enormity of the 1915 events was genocide pure and simple and that it is wrong to raise legalistic points about the correct use of terminology.

The nebulous Armenian question

There has never been so much talk as there is today of the 'Armenian Cause', yet a clear definition of the 'Armenian Question' remains elusive (haï tad in Armenian, hence the neologism, Haitadism). Why do the issues provoke so much passion? As the stepchild of the old Eastern Question, the Armenian Question is inevitably complex: one cannot possibly understand the emotional dimension of the exchanges between the various sides without teasing out these complexities. Firstly the geographical and temporal distances (Armenia, a mountainous territory located between Turkey, Georgia, Azerbaijan and Iran, is physically and historically far removed from most of the West) underscore the difficulties.

Secondly, how we view the events of 1915 – as a series of massacres or genocide, lies at the core of the issue – is a matter of international importance. Achieving and maintaining peace in this area between Anatolia and the Caucasus, at the crossroads of Europe and Asia, has global repercussions. Since the collapse of the Soviet Union, Armenia has regained its independence and joined the international community which, since the Second World War and despite numerous failures, has striven for peace in the world. But the Armenian Question, whether raised by the Republic of Armenia itself or by its widespread diaspora, remains a festering sore which is liable to be easily inflamed. An unresolved Armenian Question could, at any time, tip into crisis in a region already burdened with instability, confrontation and conflict. Antagonism involving a range of different local and world powers – Turkey, Iran, Azerbaijan, Georgia, Russia, the United States – can easily be fed by ongoing difficulties between Armenia and Turkey. Despite potential connections to pressing global problems, the Armenian Question fails to appear on the international agenda and, when examined, is considered in terms of Turkish relations with Russia, the United States or the European Union. In other words, the issue is invariably viewed as a by-product of strategic factors extending from Turkey's multi-dimensional interests. In reality, the more the Turkish Republic gains on the world stage or goes through major political or economic crises, the greater the importance of the Armenian Question.

It would be imprudent, however, to attribute the reasons for such dismissive treatment exclusively to the rigidities of the international system and superpower rivalries. Which brings us to the third complexity in attempting to understand the Armenian Question. This relates to a set of issues which arise in the domestic Armenian sphere: the weight of popular memory in Armenian perceptions of national identity. As Elie Wiesel said 'the Armenians are passionate about memory: they excel in the commemoration of events and tributes to the victims of this or that national tragedy, or to historical figures'. To find a way out of this labyrinth of real and imaginary, all actors in the Armenian Question need to free themselves from the shackles of memory and to recognize that identity does not emerge from this psychosocial divide of the real and imagined.

The complexities of the question

Before addressing the many peculiarities of the Armenian Question, as an Armenian myself, I am conscious that we must first rid ourselves of certain preconceived ideas associated with Armenian identity. For too long, some have attributed the fate of the Armenians to their land being a crossroads, a never-ending exchange between East and West; yet other nations, too, can lay claim to such spatial and cultural dichotomies.

Nor is suffering through genocide peculiar to Armenians. Another exclusivist idea that should be dismissed is that Armenian identity was born of a diaspora provoked by the massacres of 1915. Not only did the Armenian diaspora begin long before the genocide – the first waves of migration began with the fall of the Bagratid Kingdom during the eleventh century – but other national groups have experienced these forms of migration and subsequent shifting relationships between home country and receiving country. Moreover, with the advent of globalization, the concept of diaspora has expanded exponentially: today, we can even go so far as to speak of a European diaspora.

So, we need to look elsewhere for the specific, defining features of the Armenian Question and explore new avenues of investigation. Analysis of the historical sources, both Armenian and non-Armenian, reveals six possible identity markers. The first, namely the weight of memory, is largely the result of a long process of identities being constructed around specific readings of history. Armenians see their history, their national story, as a collective tragedy which singles them out from the rest of humanity. From the time of Tigranes the Great, leader of the Armenian Empire in the first century BC, until the Armenian victory in the Nagorno-Karabakh war against the Azerbaijanis following the collapse of the Soviet Union, the history of Armenia is that of a long and inexorable decline and collective failure, interspersed with episodes of national sovereignty and hope. Armenian history is nothing if not a story of consolation and resilience.

The second defining feature of Armenian identity is its unique position in response to the denial by Turkey of crimes committed. Modern Turkey has encouraged a genuine 'denial industry' of the facts of the 1915 genocide, as attested to by Turkish historian Taner Akçam. Falling in line with the official line in Turkish history and the rationalizations of Kemalism, a collective amnesia permeates the Turkish state, institutions and society. Wherever organized and whoever the initiators, every demonstration which honours the victims' memory comes up against the political, diplomatic, economic and cultural arsenal of the Turkish state. This has made the denial of what today would be labelled 'crimes against humanity' a cornerstone of its foreign policy. In more recent years, however, Turkish society has begun to consider the need for historical revision. Despite the government's persistence in pursuing its policy of denial, some elements of Turkish civil society have begun to recognize the unthinkable – Turkish culpability in the events of 1915. This conciliatory approach goes beyond material issues such as reparations for the victims and descendants of the survivors of 1915; instead, it turns the Armenian Question into a more complex, Armenian–Turkish issue.

The third marker of Armenian identity simply acknowledges the fact that the basic elements of Armenian 'nationhood' were formed long before similar developments in Europe. Indeed, in the space of only 100 years, from the beginning of the fourth century to the beginning of the fifth century AD, an Armenian territory was established with a distinct ethnic identity, language, religion and historiography. This transitional period between Antiquity and the Middle Ages thus remains at the heart of Armenians' national identity, embedded deep in their collective psyche. While European nation-state building was beginning to take shape as the Middle Ages waned, Armenians were experiencing a slow decline that lasted until the eighteenth century, following which they sought to restore their past grandeur and heritage going back three millennia. With its romantic concept of the nation, articulated before the advent of the concept of the 'nation-state', the Armenian experience is unique in that it enshrines a deep and ancient sense of group belonging.

Another – fourth – defining identity marker is that the Armenians have no tradition of sovereign statehood. In almost 3,000 years of history, Armenia experienced only two periods of real independence: first under Tigranes the Great (95–55 BC) and then in the High Middle Ages, under the Armenian Kingdom of Cilicia, between the eleventh and fourteenth centuries. In other periods, Armenia was merely a client state under Persian, Roman or Arab rule. In the modern era, the First Republic of 1918–1920, which arose in the aftermath of the First World War and the Bolshevik Revolution, was too ephemeral to be considered an example of sovereignty, although these two years did feed into the image of Greater Armenia held up to the world by US President Woodrow Wilson in 1920 when creating the Treaty of Sèvres. It is this image that remains, to this day, the driving force behind Armenian nationalism.

This brings us to the fifth Armenian trait: the representation of territory and its relationship to modernity. With the national awakening of nineteenth-century continental Europe, 'land' became identified as national territory, a defining element of nationhood. In Armenia, from the Early Middle Ages onwards, geography was considered by chroniclers such as Movses Khorenatsi (c. 410–490) and Anania Shirakatsi (610–685) to be part of a master narrative for tracing Armenian national identity. Presentations of the historical geography of Armenia veer between an historical space which is part real and part an imagined reality, both revolving around a shared concept – the land of Armenia.

Domination

Armenians have yet to free themselves from the mindset of being a dominated culture. They are never the subject of their own destiny, but objects produced through various processes of domination. They are not exempt from this system of dependence and servitude, even when Armenia recovers a form of sovereignty. As state institutions are still weak, Armenian society has not seen its demands enacted by the national elites who, in any event, do not seem to feel they are accountable for their actions. Since the collapse of Communist totalitarianism and the beginning of post-Soviet liberalization, Armenian society at the beginning of the twenty-first century, is split between those who would rather follow the old stereotype and those who are willing to behave and think differently and who are still struggling to be heard. Speaking of the diaspora, it would be awkward to speak of 'Armenian societies' – although we might reasonably refer to Armenian communities when speaking of the 'ghettoisation' in the Near East or in some Western cities. Whether integrated or assimilated into their respective States, these communities are diluted in modern societies and each individual enjoys the same rights and freedoms as his fellow citizens. In this respect, the Armenians established in France or in United States of America over four generations have become citizens and represent an example of successful integration and assimilation of republican values by the body politic.

Thus, the core reflection on the real nature of the Armenian problem regains its place, replacing the national and international analytic framework within a broader framework which is more sociological in nature. Framework equilibrium does not rest upon systematic stigmatization of the Other, who alone can account for all collective pathologies. In other words, Turkish negationism and Azeri racism (towards Armenians) cannot be the only explanation for our inability to resolve the Armenian Question. Rather, it is the Armenians themselves who are captive to the spirit of collective domination. It will be our objective to shed some light on this crucial question.

This introduction would not be complete without offering an overview of historiography as a boundary-marker of Armenian identity – the sixth and final element in attempting to understand the Armenian Question.

Armenian historiography has undergone several major transformations. The first took place between the fourth and fifth centuries with the Christianization of Armenia and the creation of the Armenian written language, which provided a solid foundation for biblical and teleological historiography. The second transformation is based on the relationship between history, religion and martyrology, thanks to work on the Battle of Avarayr in AD 451, which enabled Armenians to preserve their religious practices despite having been defeated militarily by the Persians. The third transformation relates to a model of historiography known as Khorenism (named after its founder, Movses Khorenatsi, the fifth-century Armenian historian regarded as the framer of the national historical narrative) which emerged, some would argue, in the eighth century. The fourth transformation occurred in the eighteenth century with Armenia's entry into modernity, a process which was never completed due to the political failure of social integration. The final and most recent stage in the transformation process was launched in 1991 with the end of the Cold War and the flourishing of globalization.

Part I

History and Memory: The Logics of Domination

Armenians have long experienced a condition of dominated people which structures them collectively and prevents any process of territorialization and empowerment of one field as regards the other. Therefore, Armenian monism is based on an undifferentiated sum of religious, political, cultural, social and economic elements which forms a unified and homogeneous whole controlled by national elites who hold most of the capital. Understanding the Armenian experience of domination, whether in the case of sovereignty or not requires the use of holistic rather than individualistic approaches. Indeed, from antiquity to the present day, the individual has, in the essentially traditional Armenian model, systematically disappeared behind the collective, with the possible exception of rare examples from Armenian diasporas implanted in Western societies based on democracy and human rights. This community–individual relationship is fundamental to understanding the Armenian issue because it refers to the question of modernity and individualism in political development.

Three types of domination have been exerted on the Armenians from the origins to the present day. There is no political power without land mediation. The first type of domination is therefore international: on the one hand, because as a human group, Armenians have never really been able to apprehend their territory as an instrument for defining and delimiting their political community; on the other hand, because from an early stage Armenia, as a territorial entity, emerged in an intense geopolitical environment where rivalries between powers were sometimes beneficial, but often fatal; hence the idea of a buffer, elastic, Armenia evolved subject to the circumstances of its neighbouring powers and the strategies of their central authorities. Armenia is also under politico-religious domination. As religion and politics are two inseparable categories embodied by the Church and the system of dynasts, the two main national institutions, the formation of an autonomous space for politics is off to a bad start because, from the beginning, the concepts of State and City in the Greek sense have been foreign to Armenians. These fabrication defects naturally result in major socio-political pathologies which are still rampant today. Finally, Armenia is under socio-economic domination. The Armenians have long evolved under the burden of a traditional tripartite society and Russian and Ottoman imperial systems that have shaped their identity and slowed down the establishment of a modern society and an autonomous strategy for the players.

Collectively, the Armenians are aware of the weight of this three-way domination. In an effort to break away from it, the Armenians have structured their thinking around a dynamic of emancipation, referred to as Haitadism, a true paradigm of a national sociology pairing liberty and security. Based on a structural–functionalist approach, this integration system relies on its own values, norms, identities and players to find its place in the international system. Built on this constructivist logic, Haitadism incorporates the whole of the social sciences into its transformation process and its ideological corpus is based on the mobilizing ideologies of its time to free the Armenians from any form of domination. Haitadism involves territoriality and extra-territoriality and also the memory–history duo in its system. It draws, from external systems, the resources needed to develop or transform it according to its needs; in return, it supplies its products. This system relies on the rule of 'hayababanoum' which means preserving, unifying and consolidating the Armenian being, its territory, its nation. This is a fragile balance which must be constantly stabilized and is why it is defined, in theory, as the only political system capable of structuring the Armenians as a political community to bring them together around a common destiny. However, given the scattering of Armenians throughout the world and the sporadic sovereignties that characterize them, Haitadism, due to its anteriority to the State, is fragmented into several development models – an atomized system incapable of integrating itself fully into a unitary legal and political framework. This validates the idea that such a system creates severely dysfunctional, often acute, almost incurable phases, inasmuch as it constantly wavers between ethnic foundations and national aspirations, restraint and openness, emancipation and hegemony. Thus, built on regular layers and having suffered multiple failures, as well as contradictions and intrinsic deformities, what was initially regarded as a mode of structural regulation for the Armenians has finally been transformed into a logic of Armenian domination. A source of emancipation from international, political, religious and social domination in the beginning, Haitadism has organized, in its turn, into a system of domination.

1

International Domination

Armenia embraces the plateau that separates the Black Sea from Mesopotamia from north to south and from west to east, Asia Minor from the Lesser Caucasus. As a people, Armenians have lived through many major world crises and are one of the few ancient peoples to retain their original name. At the crossroads of world rivalries, Armenia has often assumed the role of buffer zone and has emerged as a space of neutrality, expected to prevent conflicts between hostile powers. Yet Armenia has not always held this position as an intermediate space in the regional balance of power and, more often than not, has had that status thrust upon it. A buffer state is the object of various intellectual constructions: a place in which to seek refuge, a corridor or springboard. But throughout its long history, the fate of the Armenian buffer state has been to remain unspoken and uncertain.

This uncertainty partly explains the plurality of the legal status of Armenia, a diversity that has made its political development unique. Following the 1648 Treaty of Westphalia, rivalries between the powers laid the foundations of an international system that brought to the fore a series of diplomatic issues known as the Eastern question. While Armenia was always part of that question, as the vicissitudes of the international system evolved since the Congress of Vienna in 1815, a specifically Armenian Question arose. In this sense, Armenia belongs to the family of nations whose emancipation marks the history of nineteenth-century Europe – nations such as Greece, Hungary, Bulgaria, Albania, Serbia, Montenegro, Macedonia, Cyprus and others. Armenia became, in essence, a multilateral issue, that is to say one whose resolution involves several powers at the same time and interests that are sometimes complementary and more often divergent. Since the rebirth of the Armenian state in 1991, the Armenian Question has retained this multilateral character, becoming an international subject following the whim of progress in globalization, the evolution of law in the field of prevention and repression of genocide and developments in the status of the Nagorno-Karabakh dispute.

Yet Armenia did not get off to a good start. Just as the international system was preparing to address the contemporary dimension of the Armenian Question following the Russo-Ottoman war of 1877–1878, European peace treaties signed after the First World War were poised to bury it with the 1923 Treaty of Lausanne. Thus, between 1915 and 1923 the Armenian people went through three major tests: a physical extermination and massacre of 1.5 million during the genocide of 1915; political extermination with the 1920 Bolshevik collectivization of the independent Republic of

Armenia, which ended any pretence of state sovereignty; and diplomatic extermination produced by the removal of any reference to Armenia or Armenians at the 1923 signing of the Treaty of Lausanne between the European powers and the young Turkish Republic of Mustafa Kemal.

Could Armenians have avoided this historical debacle? Were they in a position to modify the power contest, the basis of the international system? Must one necessarily impute responsibility to foreign powers, especially to Turks, Russians and, to a lesser extent, Europeans? Revisiting these events is a difficult but indispensable exercise to better master the socio-historical process. Among other things, it offers new insights into the strategic orientations of contemporary Armenian elites and the state of their political thinking.

In 1991, after seven decades of Soviet dictatorship, Armenia once again found its place on the international scene on an equal footing with other sovereign nations in a post-bipolar order. The fall of the Soviet Union provided the opportunity for emergence of several sovereign states, including Armenia. The Armenian Question has never been so studied and universalized as it has since the restoration of Armenian sovereignty. This does not mean that Armenians acted on a principle of universality or even that they freed themselves from the domination of the international system. On the contrary, the international system is increasingly integrated and continues to exert pressure on the Armenian state to obtain, if not the removal of the Armenian Question from the international agenda, at the very least its attenuation. In other words, if the international community is willing to welcome Armenia as a state, does it not also invite Armenia to leave the Armenian Question on the doorstep of the world order?

An 'internalized territory'

According to the French sociologist Bertrand Badie: 'A territory is not a statistic, it is a construct.' 'Its use as an instrument of political action corresponds to a history, a set of inventions; its social role does not derive from an imperative, but from a more conditional mode.'[1] Territory then, has meaning only within a framework of domination by a people who occupy it as a structured political community. As already stated, due to its geographical location Armenia has more often constituted a buffer zone between rival powers than a structured political community. In early antiquity, Urartu was dominated by the Sumerians and the Assyrians. In classical antiquity, Armenia separated Rome from Persia. Later, in medieval times, the Kingdom of Armenia served as a buffer between Byzantium and the Persians, then as a buffer for the Arabs and finally, for the Seljuk Turks. Even beyond historical Armenia, in the Kingdom of Cilicia, Armenians were caught between Byzantium and the Ottoman Turks. Finally, in the twentieth century, the Republic of Armenia emerged somewhere between the Turks

---

[1]   Bertrand Badie, *La fin des territoires*, Fayard, 1995, 2nd edn (Paris: CNRS Éditions, Biblis, 2013), p. 11.

and Russians towards the end of the First World War. Such consistent historical turmoil transformed the Armenian space into a permanent theatre of war. According to some theorists, Armenia was built up through armed conflict, either because the Armenian character was warlike or because the people had become inured to conflict. The buffer space itself becomes the frontier. Such populations must adapt themselves to survive as intermediary groups between rival powers. This geopolitical peculiarity not only makes it difficult for mediating peoples to think of their own long-term survival, but it also provokes a relative detachment from any institutional form of space, leading to challenges with the social integration process. Political relations thus become all the more biased as the state itself disappears from the scene. This happens to such an extent that the very notion of the state and therefore of politics, becomes inappropriate. Can one speak of a 'territory' when a space lacks social integration and visible institutions and is characterized by shifting contours? As a former French ambassador to Constantinople, Paul Cambon, wrote in 1894: 'Where does Armenia begin and where does it end?'[2] We should not forget that the term 'territory' represents a real political and legal institution attached to the concept of the state. In the case of Armenia, which before 1991 did not constitute a sovereign state, it is better to speak of 'land' or 'soil' or, as Armenians say, *yerkir* (meaning country as land or soil). Therefore, until recent years, the principle of territoriality and its corollary 'borders', had never been integrated into Armenian political history.

The interstate system, whose logic dominated this part of the world for centuries, deprives Armenia of a legal culture specific to international law. The name Armenia did not appear in any official document before the bilateral Treaty of Batum, signed on 4 June 1918 between the Ottoman Empire and the Republic of Armenia and not until two years later, with the multilateral Treaty of Sèvres (1920), did the word 'Armenia' take its place on the international stage. Here again, the advance was short lived, since the treaty was never ratified. It would be another 71 years before Armenia would fully join the international system, following the dissolution of the Soviet Union and the proclamation of independence in 1991.

There are, of course, other stateless peoples without experience of international law – the Kurds, for example. Thus, during the course of its history, Armenia has experienced 12 legal conditions, from the highest degree of sovereignty to the total absence of any mention of Armenia.

To understand why Armenians have such a strong attachment to their national identity one must go back to the Kingdom of Urartu. This has given 'Armenia much more than a geographical identity or a certain level of material culture: it made possible the internalization of a country and its landscapes, a mental appropriation of a soil and its past'.[3] The area known as the Armenian Plateau is distinguished by its isolation, thanks to the surrounding mountains with their high passes and rough interior terrain, factors that have made it difficult to centralize power and exercise effective administrative control. Very early on, Armenians were, if not dominated, at least captive

[2] Quoted in Vahakn Dadrian, *The History of the Armenian Genocide*, Berghahn Books, 1995, translated from *Histoire du genocide des Arméniens* (Stock, 1996) p. 107.
[3] Annie and Jean-Pierre Mahé, *Histoire de l'Arménie des origines à nos jours* (Perrin, 2012), p. 34.

to their inhospitable geography, perceived both as a refuge from danger and a handicap to regional integration. The works of the seventh-century mathematician and geographer Anania Shirakatsi, author of *Geography*, disclose the ambiguous relation between Armenians and their geography during the Urartu era as well as in later periods. The 15 provinces identified by geographers (Upper Armenia, Armenia IV, Aghdzenik, Moks, Korchayk, Parskahayk, Vaspurakan, Turuberan, Siunik, Artsakh, Paytakaran, Utik, Gugark, Tayk and Ayrarat) did not all exist at the same time. Such a slippery narrative leads to the obvious conclusion that as difficult as it is for Armenia to acquire independence, unification may be just as challenging. Unification and independence are interdependent processes and constitute the core of the dilemma of the Armenian Question: should one first address the need for independence and the creation of a sovereign state, or should one act first to unify a national territory?

Sovereign Armenia

First state

Armenia's greatest expression of sovereignty was achieved in the reign of Emperor Tigranes the Great, descended from the dynasty of the Artaxiads, in the first century BC. His empire, which lasted barely 15 years, spread from the Mediterranean to the Black and Caspian seas. The Armenian myths of unity and the three seas were born: this is fundamental for Armenians and, even today, Tigranes' empire occupies a special place in their hearts. Moreover, between January and June of the 1919 Paris Peace Conference, the Armenian delegates officially presented a map of Armenia within its ideal borders modelled on the delimitations of the Armenian Empire of Tigranes the Great. On the recommendation of the conservative leader Boghos Nubar Pasha, leader of the Armenian National Delegation of the Mother See of Holy Etchmiadzin, this map included Cilicia – against the more pragmatic opinion of the Republic of Armenia delegation led by Dashnak writer Avetis Aharonian. The French newspaper *Le Temps* was not mistaken when, on 11 August 1920, the day after the signing of the Treaty of Sèvres recognizing Armenia's vast territorial franchise, it ran a headline proclaiming the 'Birth of the Armenian Empire'.

The Great Armenia of Tigranes resulted from the withdrawal of Rome and Persia. Yet filling the void left by weakened neighbouring powers proved too much for the Armenian emperor; the population was not sufficiently large to ensure sovereign control. The same difficulty arose in November of 1917 when the Russian armies withdrew under orders from a Bolshevik leadership newly empowered by victory in the October Revolution.

According to Simon Vratsian, Secretary of the Armenian National Council during the Great War and, in 1920, the last prime minister of the Republic of Armenia, the Armenian political class (particularly members of the Armenian Revolutionary Federation, or Dashnaks) were unsure which battle line they should hold.[4] A die-hard

---

[4] Simon Vratsian, *Mémoires, faits, figures, souvenirs*, 6 vols (Beyrouth: Mchag Press, 1965), pp. 178–182.

individual such as Andranik, a military leader from Turkish Armenia, wanted to hold the Van-Bitlis-Muş-Erzincan-Trebizond arc line, while pragmatists, such as Dro, the future defence minister of the Republic of Armenia and a native of the Caucasus, preferred to scale it down to a smaller, Bayazet-Bassen axis. The former won the challenge, leading to near total losses in the field against the Turks. Thus, the vast extent of the Armenian space produced a feeling of impotence rather than power and anxiety about forging territorial unity. It was clear that power was not only a matter of space. From a geopolitical point of view, this turned out to be a central ambivalence in the Armenian Question: how does one go about unifying a vast territory with only limited population resources decimated by genocide and threatened by the predatory practices of demographically superior neighbours?

Second state

This constituted a sovereign Armenia in Cilicia (c. 1070–1375), beyond the Armenian homelands. Cilician Armenia was divided between its Byzantine orientation, embodied by the Hethumid dynasty, originating in the Caucasus and claiming affiliation with the Ardzruni and its Latin orientation, embodied by the Rubenid dynasty which claimed Bagratid origins. Under the influence of the Crusaders, Cilicia, led by the Rubenids, was structured as a centralized state inspired by the European feudal model. Following the death of Leo I, the Magnificent and the resulting crisis of succession, the Hethumids took power through marriages between the two dynasties. In a relatively stable environment lasting until the arrival of the Mamelukes, the Armenian sovereign presented himself as *takavor Hayotz* (the king of the Armenians). Cilician sovereignty offered the first example of a westernized Armenian state, with institutions and a socio-political organization. Sovereignty followed the same lines as the empire of Tigranes the Great. However, as it evolved beyond historical Armenian territory and according to a monarchical, non-imperial state model, it is important to differentiate its status. Cilician sovereignty represented an unprecedented experience of recomposing an Armenian political space beyond the ancestral homeland. In a way, Armenians of the Ottoman Empire, at first in Cilicia and then, following the 1915 genocide, in the Near East, were the heirs of Cilician Armenia in terms of culture, that is until the Arabization of Near Eastern societies in the twentieth century – and in terms of religion, as the religious seat of Cilicia was in Antelias, Lebanon.

Third state

The Republic of Armenia (1918–1920) in the Caucasus is a separate case for three reasons. First, because it was necessary to build a nation-state in an environment where the only state model was the empire model, whether Russian, Ottoman or Persian, a form of state organization that was on the verge of extinction by May 1918. Creating the foundations for a nation-state in a multi-ethnic space where a mosaic of different groups were accustomed to living under imperial domination would be a major challenge.

Second, because Armenian territorial sovereignty would be based on the traditional Caucasian territory, a region in which the revolutionary movement had not fully developed (action had been ongoing for only two years, from 1903 to 1905). Until that time, the Armenian revolutionary movement had focused on liberating Ottoman Armenia.

Finally, because Armenian leaders sought to build a state that would be the heir to an imperial past without the necessary administrative experience. There was no functioning institutional structure when, on 28 May 1918, independence was proclaimed: Imperial Russia had been overthrown and any semblance of administrative organization had been destroyed by the war. The Armenian government held its first ministerial councils in Tbilisi, not in the Armenian capital Yerevan which, at that time, was little more than a market town. Moreover, the Armenia that was called into existence was a state permanently at war with Turkey, Georgia and Azerbaijan in a Europe that was itself a battlefield. Parts of the 1918 political borders were historical administrative delimitations of uncertain origin, hence the wars with Georgia in 1918 and Azerbaijan between 1918 and 1920. At the time, the Armenian population consisted mainly of Armenian refugees with a strong Turkic and Azeri component with whom relations, inflamed by nationalist sentiments, proved more a matter of overcrowding than a desire to live together in a shared space.

The elites of the 1918 Republic were divided between defenders of the state and opponents of the Dashnak regime. Beyond the war, however, Armenia did not really choose independence. Rather, it was virtually imposed under duress, as Hratch Dasnabedian, a Dashnak leader in the late twentieth century and author of *History of the ARF Dashnaktsutiun* explains.[5] The majority Dashnak leadership in Yerevan opted for national sovereignty on 28 May only following proclamations of independence in Georgia (26 May) and Azerbaijan (27 May) and three decisive battles between 21 and 28 May (Bash Abaran, Karakilisse and Sardarabad). The process was neither consensual nor linear: the independentists, led by Hovannes Katchaznouni, Alexander Khatissian and Simon Vratsian, called for an Armenian proclamation of independence following the collapse of the short-lived Transcaucasian Democratic Federative Republic which united Armenia, Georgia and Azerbaijan between 1917 and 1918. For the countries of the South Caucasus, it was independence or collapse. For the unionists, such as Avetis Aharonian, Ardaches Balayan and Roupen Ter-Minassian, as long as the territories were not free of the Turkish yoke, a proclamation of independence would be awkward and premature and a strategy that would lead to a split with Russia – a risky proposition given that the First World War was far from over.

The former prevailed but, in the Declaration of Independence of 28 May, the words 'independence' and 'Republic' did not appear, in contrast to the official proclamations of Georgia and Azerbaijan. It was only after the Treaty of Batum that the term 'Republic of Armenia' was used and then at the cost of great internal dissensus. Andranik did not recognize it for two reasons. He considered that the Turks were behind the push for sovereignty, as they would prefer a weak state as neighbour rather than a strong Russia. He criticized the power of his former Dashnak comrades who had proclaimed an independent republic without liberating or integrating the territories of Turkish

---

[5] Hratch Dasnabedian, *Histoire de la Fédération révolutionnaire arménienne Dashnaktsutiun, 1890–1924* (Milan: Oemme Edizioni, 1988), pp. 120–126.

Armenia; a dual argument that Dashnak opponents would use from this time up to 1991 to criticize the results of this 'Araratian Republic'.

Fourth state

The Republic of Armenia, born in 1991 amid the ruins of the Soviet Union, is a paradox. It restored a national sovereignty recognized by the international community in an increasingly globalized and interdependent world. The similarities and differences with the Republic of 1918 are many. Conceived during the First World War as a First Republic, today's Armenia is different from that of 1918 in that it is heir to a Soviet state apparatus, with its institutions, administration and rudimentary land use planning. As in 1918, partisans of the 'Republic of Eastern Armenia' – a way of affirming that there is another Armenia, an Armenia under Turkish domination which remains to be liberated – were opposed by supporters of 'the Republic of Armenia' and the latter won.

As with the First Republic, Armenia in 1991 was the focus of intense disagreement between supporters of independence (the Armenian National Movement led by Levon Ter-Petrosyan) and supporters of reunification with Nagorno-Karabakh (the ARF led by Hraïr Maroukhian). Indeed, the process of restoring sovereignty was carried out in the midst of the crisis of the Karabakh movement with its dual objectives: independence for Yerevan against Soviet domination and a movement in favour of reunification with Stepanakert against Soviet-Azerbaijani domination. Some felt obliged to support the movement in Yerevan and become an engine for independence within the Soviet Union, following the example of the Baltic countries. For others, it was vital to pursue economic sovereignty without political independence. For yet another group, following the example of the Islamic republics of Central Asia, nothing should be done against Moscow, given that sooner or later the Soviet Union would collapse and the various republics would gain their freedom and enjoy the fruits of independence without the slightest effort. Finally, a fourth group advanced the cause of the Stepanakert movement, aiming to reunite Armenia with Nagorno-Karabakh and avoid both the Baltic and Central Asian models of sovereignty.

Nearly 30 years after the declaration of independence, Armenia is a republic which, despite its difficulties, has never in history been as strong as it is today. Even though it is dependent on Russia for energy and military power, Yerevan plays the card of multilateralism and integration. For some, its independence has been questioned since the decision of President Serzh Sargsyan on 3 September 2013 to join the framework of a Eurasian customs union that includes Russia, Belarus and Kazakhstan. But, as others contend, what does it really mean to be independent in a globalized, interdependent and interconnected world?

Armenia under domination

With this development, the typology of Armenia's status broke new ground, moving from a country dominated by a foreign power to a country denuded of national sovereignty as defined by international law. Armenia, if it exists administratively, is no longer the subject of its own history, but the object of hegemonic powers which, in accordance with the policies of their central authorities, favour the manipulation of Armenian autonomy up to the point of 'de-Armenization' of the political space.

Fifth state

Next we consider Armenia under foreign rule but governed by an Armenian prince. This is essentially a pattern in the period of Persian domination, or 'Persarmenia', which followed the Urartian period and the first Armenian dynasties – Orontid and Artaxiad – up to the Arab conquest in 640, the entire period before and after the reign of Tigranes the Great. It also applies to the era of Georgian domination and the Bagratid kings in the twelfth and thirteenth centuries. The idea of existence as a state frequently takes root following the withdrawal of neighbouring powers.

Before the reign of Tigranes the Great, the kingdom of Urartu took advantage of the fall of Nineveh in 612, then of the Medes around 605–585 BC, before disappearing in its turn. The process of liberation of Armenia continued with the fall of the Achaemenid Empire in the fourth century BC, defeated by Alexander the Great, then with the decline of the Seleucids, the heirs to the Greco-Macedonian king. Shortly after the battle of Magnesia, lost by Antiochus III in 189 BC, the two Armenian Orontid satraps, Artaxias and Zariadris, proclaimed themselves independent. Of the two sovereigns it was Artaxias who, with approval from Rome, expanded to the east without, however, reunifying Armenian territory. Sophene, which is located in present-day south-eastern Turkey, remained outside the assembled territories at the death of Zariadris. Nevertheless, the Armenia of Artaxias, founder of the Artaxiad dynasty, came under the control of the Parthians.

After the reign of Tigranes the Great, Armenia, divided between Rome and the Parthian Arsacids, came mainly under Iranian influence, as evidenced by its institutions, social organization and decentralized nature – though the latter was also a legacy of its Urartian heritage. Armenia was largely Christianized under Persian domination, suggesting that the territory enjoyed a measure of autonomy under the Persians, who saw in this Armenian religious peculiarity a means for slowing down the expansion of Byzantium. Armenia was administered by governors drawn from an Armenian nobility designated by a foreign power. Following the disappearance around AD 220 of the Parthian Arsacids, the Sassanids established themselves at the head of the Persian Empire. In view of Armenians' strengthening spiritual beliefs in the region, the Parthians attempted to impose Zoroastrianism, leading in 451 to a revolt in Avarayr. At the time, Persarmenia and its capital city, Dvin, underwent a profound religious and political crisis. With the disappearance of the Sassanids in 639, under pressure from the expanding Arab Empire, the Armenian kings consolidated the emancipation of Armenia.

With respect to Georgian domination of Armenia under the Bagratids, Zakarid princes were assigned to lead parts of Caucasian Armenia against the Seljuk Turks. The Zakarid dynasty would later take advantage of the Crusades to re-centre Armenian institutions on their Armenian heritage and renew the Armenian religious heritage which had been destroyed in Ani and Dvin. The thirteenth-century Mongol invasions put an end to Armenian autonomy under Georgian suzerainty. The binational experience of the Bagratid dynasty, with both a Georgian and an Armenian branch, is recalled to this day in the speeches by Georgian and Armenian authorities as proof that, when united under a single dynasty, these countries can share a common destiny.

Can we speak of sovereignty in these two medieval cases? Even with a form of autonomous management, Armenia was not independent. The most convincing evidence is that Armenia lacked recognition as a player in the international exchanges of the day and did not mint its own coins. The first coins to bear a likeness of an Armenian sovereign go back to Tigranes the Great, but the inscriptions are in Greek. Neither the Orontids, nor their successors and much less the Bagratids concerned themselves with minting coinage. The first truly independent Armenian state to mint coins in the Armenian language was the Kingdom of Cilicia in the High Middle Ages.

Sixth state

This related to the division of Armenia between two empires, those of Rome and Persia (52 BC and AD 428). After the fall of Tigranes the Great, Armenia once again became a strategic point of contest between foreign powers and found itself dominated by Rome and the Parthians. Armenia Minor was ruled as a Roman governorate while Armenia Major or Greater Armenia came under Persian administration, except that the 'King of Armenia' received the royal crown from the Roman Emperor. The Persian Arsacids thus installed one of their own at the head of Greater Armenia, while recognizing a Roman protectorate. Here too, it is impossible to speak of independence, the choice of the sovereign being the object of an agreement between foreign powers (Treaty of Rhandeia, signed in AD 63). Thus, while Lesser Armenia remained a province of the Roman Empire, Greater Armenia lived under a complex regime. After the slightest upheaval, its status could change and its future became uncertain. Thus, during the Germanic invasions, Rome was obliged to reconsider the agreement with the Persians and sacrifice some of its suzerainty in Armenia for the benefit of the Sassanids. This was the first partition of Armenia. The second partition arose in 428 between Byzantium and the Persians, ending 'the Armenian state'.

Seventh state

In the period of Arab domination (AD 640–884) Armenia was initially autonomous, then became governed directly by the Arab Umayyad dynasty (661–750). Following the sack of Dvin by the Prophet's army in 640, Armenians and Arabs signed treaties of submission (650 and 661) under which the former remained a tributary state administered by an Armenian prince. Armenians enjoyed freedom of worship, religion and broad autonomy. At the turn of the eighth century, however, things changed. Disturbances outside the Caliphate – notably in the northern Caucasus following incursions by the Khazars – revolts within the Armenian province and Umayyad expansion into Central Asia diminished the strategic value of the Armenian territory to the point where the Caliphs decided to place it directly under Arab rule. Beside Armenia, the province of Arminiya included eastern Georgia and Aghouania, administered by an Arab governor, the Ostikan. After a period of Islamicization of

Armenian society, Armenia under the Bagratids and the Ardzrunis showed itself more conciliatory towards the Arabs than the Mamikonians and the Rshtunis, eventually regaining the confidence of the Abbasid dynasty (750–1258). Little by little, Armenia regained a degree of autonomy as well as a number of institutional and fiscal functions. The process of empowerment nurtured by the weakening of the Abbasids, who were faced with problems of succession, an economic crisis, Byzantine power and the revolt of Muslim vassals in Azerbaijan, continued until the establishment of the Kingdom of the Bagratids at the end of the ninth century. This final phase of Arab domination was marked by strong repression that contrasted with the first decades of Islamic hegemony. The Bagratids, who remained loyal to the Arab Ostikan, were rewarded for their fidelity with grants of titles and power, leading, at the end of the ninth century, to the formation of the eponymous Bagratid kingdom.

Eighth state

The Kingdom of the Bagratids (from the close of the ninth century to the end of the eleventh century) and the surrounding Armenian principalities were not sovereign states but vassal states of the Arab Caliphate. In this sense, it would be misleading to consider the rise of Ashot Bagratuni at the end of the ninth century as representing the restoration of Armenian sovereignty.[6]

When granting Ashot the Great the title 'Prince of Princes' in 862 and recognizing him as 'King of Armenia and Georgia' in 884–885, the Caliphate ceased sending Arab governors to support Armenians in their conflict with Byzantium. Stuck between the Byzantines and the Arabs, Armenia played an intermediary role. The Arabs wanted to contain Byzantine expansionism and historical Christian unity. Since neither Byzantines nor Arabs had the military means to overcome the other, they favoured Armenian neutrality. Armenia did not have a legal status. It did not mint coins, it was required to pledge allegiance to the Caliphs and for a while it paid a tribute tax to the governor of Azerbaijan, charged by the Caliphate to manage their Armenian province. Only during the reign of Ashot II, known as 'Yerkat', the 'Iron' king (914–929), could Armenia have been described as autonomous or as having limited sovereignty, a time when, free of the Caliphate's dominance, Armenia reclaimed the identity it had given up with the pact of submission and briefly exploited tensions between the Caliph and Yusuf, the governor of Azerbaijan. It was only during the reign of Ashot III, known as Ashot the Merciful (952–977) that the Muslim hold was reduced – though not broken. Founded on part of the historical Armenian territory, Ashot Yergat's Armenia went through a period of national unity that is remembered historically as a period of renewed sovereignty in the context of a decadent Caliphate and a Byzantine Empire in a phase of reformation. The process of emancipation for Bagratid Armenia was not recognized either by the Arabs or the Byzantines. The Arabs favoured Armenian autonomy for strategic reasons, while Byzantium never recognized the title 'King' of Armenian leaders or the autocephalous character of the Armenian Church. Beside the adversity of the Byzantines and Arab domination, Armenians were confronted with

---

[6]   Interview with Jean-Pierre Mahé, Paris, 3 June 2013.

the Seljuk Turk invasions from the East. Together, the Byzantines and Turks put an end to the Bagratid Kingdom and the intermediary role of the Armenian territory.

Ninth state

In its ninth 'state', Armenia was a province governed by a foreigner designated by the central authorities of a conquering power. These included the Achaemenid Empire, the Seljuk Turks (eleventh–thirteenth centuries) and the Mongol domination (thirteenth–fourteenth centuries). In these three examples, historical Armenia evolved according to the interests of the dominant power. In order to exercise control, the authorities often divided Armenia into administrative districts. The Achaemenid Empire split Armenia into two satrapies based on ethnic groupings. At the head of the groups, the Persian Emperor placed a family member. Thus, Artaxerxes I (d. 424 BC) appointed his son-in-law, Orontes, as the ruler of one of the two Armenian provinces, who in turn founded the first Armenian dynasty, the Orontids in the fifth century BC.

During the Middle Ages, Armenia was also affected by the fortunes of the hegemonic Seljuk and Mongol powers. Historical Armenia passed into the hands of the Seljuks before being divided into emirates. North-eastern Armenia was attached to Arran and Azerbaijan in a unit administered by the Gandzak emirs. The Kurdish Chaddadid dynasty, established in Dvin since 1022, administered the Shirak province, including the former Bagratid capital of Ani. The Seljuks of Asia Minor controlled parts of Western Armenia (Erzurum) and Southern Armenia (Manazkert, Kharpert). The northern part of Armenia's Vaspurakan was entrusted to the dynasty of the Shah Armens of Khlat, while the southern part was annexed by the Turkish dynasty of the Ortokids. The Mongol conquest in the thirteenth century was greatly facilitated by the fragmentation of historical Armenia, organizing its territorial domination into several *vilayets* or administrative regions, including the Greater Armenia *vilayet* (south and west of Armenia) and the Georgia *vilayet* (including Eastern Georgia and the Zakarid principalities). Northeast Armenia, governed by the Zakarids, was divided into three *tuman* (military administrative units). In the middle of the thirteenth century, the Mongol Empire applied an administrative concept of khanate. Armenia, Azerbaijan and the kingdom of eastern Georgia were under the direct authority of Hulagu Khan (r 1256–1265), the founder of the Ilkhanate dynasty. This territorial organization laid the foundations for the three provinces of the South Caucasus, of which the three current republics are the successors.

The second wave of the Mongol invasion, led by Tamerlane at the turn of the fifteenth century, resulted in incessant fighting against the Ottoman Turks and foreclosed the buffering strategy that had, until then, allowed Armenia some measure of autonomy. When Tamerlane died in 1405, his Timurid Empire was divided into several units. Armenia, conquered by Timurid troops, saw its eastern provinces pass under the successive domination of two Turkish tribal federations, the Kara-Koyunlu ('Black Sheep') established in Tabriz (Iran) and the Ak Koyunlu ('White Sheep') based in Diyarbakir. The Black Sheep dynasty fought the Timurid troops several times in Armenia, while a few Armenian feudal lords were able to administer the regions of Siunik, Vayots Dzor, Artsakh and Gugark.

Having taken the Timurid capital, Herat, in 1458, Jahan Shah, the leader of the Kara-Koyunlu, had to fight the Turkmen clan of the Ak-Koyunlu Turkmen dynasty, who came from Mesopotamia and were close allies of Tamerlane. It was in Armenia, near Van, in 1467, that the Kara-Koyunlu clan suffered a heavy defeat at the hands of the Ak Koyunlu, who then took possession of Armenia, Northern Mesopotamia and Azerbaijan. In 1499, the Ak-Koyunlu state was itself divided, with Armenia and Azerbaijan remaining with Alwand and northern Mesopotamia and Iraq going to his brother Muhammad. The Black Sheep and White Sheep dynasties operated in Armenia as a mediating power, ensuring a buffer zone between the Ottoman Turks in the west, the Timurids in the east and the Mamelukes in the south. In the fifteenth century, dominated by these competing Muslim interests, Armenia became a battlefield between two imperial powers, the Ottoman and Persian Empires.

Tenth state

The Armenian space was thus divided between the Ottoman and Persian Empires and subsequently between the Ottoman and Russian Empires. This was a very significant paradigm shift. In the seventeenth century, empire became the dominant model of government in the Near East; the era of principalities and monarchies was no more. Armenia, the theatre of incessant fighting between Ottomans and Persians, had to wait until 1639 to be protected by a durable but as yet unstabilized border. Most of historical Armenia found itself on the Ottoman side of the divide, with Iran retaining Caucasian Armenia. This is where the divide between Western Armenia (*Aredmedahayastan*) and Eastern Armenia (*Arevelahayastan*) began.

Historically, in the Ottoman Empire, Armenia was administered as a *pashalik*, a large district governed by a pasha. Known as 'Ermenistan', Armenia included Erzerum, Bayazet, Kars, Akhaltskha, Van and Diyarbakir. A second *pashalik*, namely Cilician Armenia, extended to Adana and Marash. In 1864, during the Tanzimat, the Sublime Porte launched its administrative reforms inspired by the centralization and standardization of French Jacobinism. Ermenistan was divided into six *vilayets* (Erzerum, Van, Kharpert, Sebaste, Bitlis and Diyarbakir), thus countering any national longings for a unified space. These six *vilayets* found themselves, in the last quarter of the nineteenth century, at the root of the Armenian Question, when the powers signatory to the Treaty of Berlin demanded that Constantinople undertake reforms to improve the living conditions of Armenians living in these provinces.

In the Persian Empire, Caucasian Armenia was divided into *khanates* (Yerevan, Nakhchivan, Karabakh and Gandzak to a different extent). Russian irruption into the Transcaucasus in the nineteenth century, in particular following the Russo-Persian treaties of Gulistan (1813) and Turkmentchay (1829) allowed Saint Petersburg progressively to take control of these khanates. The conquest of the Persian khanates was completed in 1877–1878 with the annexation of the Kars and Ardahan regions. Having fought each other 13 times, the Russian and Ottoman Empires shared Armenia until the aftermath of the First World War, which brought an end to the Ottoman Empire. None of the empires recognized the Armenian community as having a territorial identity. Rather, Armenians, especially in the late Ottoman period, were considered extra-territorial.

Eleventh state

The Armenian Soviet Socialist Republic (Armenian SSR) (1920–1991), successor to the 1918 Republic of Armenia, held most of the attributes of a state (territory, administration and institutions) without sovereignty. It was a province of Bolshevik Russia and one of the Soviet Union's 15 federated republics. Unlike Armenia at the time of the Bagratids, the Armenian SSR was a province fully integrated into a centralized system serving no purpose as an intermediate space. Finally – and unlike the Kingdom of the Bagratids – the Armenian SSR had no armed force or foreign policy – even though it did briefly, at the turn of the 1980s, have a foreign minister, John Guiragossian. For many years, the power in this federated republic was shared by three people: the first secretary of the Communist Party of the Soviet Union (CPSU), the first secretary of the Communist Party of Armenia and the number two of SSR, a non-Armenian. The legitimate tools of sovereignty, the use of violence and the power to regulate fiscal affairs were in the hands of Moscow, not Yerevan, which followed the objectives of central Soviet planning and did not mint coins. Like other federated republics, Armenia enjoyed a degree of autonomy in the post-Stalin period (1953–1956), but this was very limited.

However, as soon as Yerevan learned of the negotiations between the CPSU and the Armenian Revolutionary Federation (ARF) in the late 1950s, the Armenian SSR authorities upped their anti-Dashnak campaigns on the pretext that the Dashnaks were undermining Armenian SSR 'sovereignty'. It is not known whether Moscow instigated these anti-Dashnak diatribes to test ARF goodwill and receptivity to building bridges of co-operation. In any case, Soviet domination gave Armenia a security of sorts, under the 'protection' of the Red Army and the Warsaw Pact and Yerevan was transformed into an administrative centre. Soviet domination also impacted on the organization of social life and helped to develop the economic and cultural fabric of the republic. While this period sustained the Armenian dream of liberating Western Armenia under Turkish administration and NATO protection, Soviet domination mostly resulted in dividing Armenians between pro-Soviet legitimists and pro-Dashnak independentists, creating a climate of civil war between 1920 and 1939 and of Cold War between 1947 and 1991.

Twelfth state: Armenia no longer has any status within the Republic of Turkey

Historical Armenia at this stage no longer existed, split into a multitude of administrative units that made no reference to the Armenian past. Following the birth of the Turkish Kemalist state in 1923, the names of Armenian cities and regions were Turkified. Vestiges of Armenian identity were erased or destroyed, geographical sites renamed – Mount Ararat was renamed 'Ağrı Dağı', for example. And yet words such as 'Sason', 'Shaddakh', 'Vaspurakan', all historic Armenian regions, have remained strongly etched in the imagination of Armenians who, at the end of the 1960s, recalled the memory of a Turkish Armenia which for some had to be free, independent and reunited with Caucasian Armenia.

Thanks largely to its historical geography, Armenia has found it difficult to rise to the level of political expression. Difficulties in stabilizing its borders and institutionalizing its 'territory' have weakened it and caused it to lag behind other civilizations which have attained statehood. Thus, when the Eastern Question presented its Armenian chapter in 1878, Armenian elites found themselves in a paradoxical situation, with resources inversely proportional to the multilateral diplomacy they preached. This was expressed by one observer at the 1878 Berlin congress, who described the huge gap between the national delegations who had come to the congress equipped with an 'iron spoon' while the Armenian delegation was equipped with a 'wooden spoon'.

The Armenian Question, a multilateral issue

The Armenian Question has never been linear. In fact, it has a dual definition. The first is restrictive and evolves according to political circumstance. From the late nineteenth to the early twentieth century, the Armenian Question essentially dealt with reform in the eastern provinces of the Ottoman Empire, reforms that were approved on three occasions but which were never enacted: the first in 1878 with the Treaty of Berlin, then with the 11 May 1895 agreement between the European Powers and the Sublime Porte and finally, with the 8 February 1914 agreement between the European powers and the Ottoman government. In 1919, the Versailles Peace Conference examined the Armenian Question and the Great Powers (France, Britain, Austria-Hungary, Germany, Russia) awarded the Republic of Armenia sovereignty over the former Ottoman provinces, following the arbitration of American President, Woodrow Wilson. Nearly half a century later, the Armenian Question was again raised in international circles, this time in the early 1970s, when the UN Sub-Commission on the Prevention of Discrimination and Protection of Minorities (after 1999 known as the Sub-Commission on the Promotion and Protection of Human Rights) discussed the genocide. Then, towards the end of the Cold War, the matter resurfaced, first through Armenia's independence process and, secondly, through the handling of the settlement of the Nagorno-Karabakh case by the Organization for Security Co-operation in Europe (OSCE), in accordance with the four resolutions of the UN Security Council adopted in 1993 during the war between Armenians and Azerbaijanis.

For Armenians, the Armenian Question is not just a diplomatic issue: rather, since the development of the revolutionary movement, it is spoken of in terms of a popular dynamic, or Haitadism. This less judicial, less institutional expression has an ethical and moral significance with quasi-religious connotations. Outside academic and diplomatic circles the vast majority of Armenians do not speak of an 'Armenian Question' as a matter of international law or research, but instead use the expression 'Armenian cause'. In other words, the Armenian Question is understood as a matter of law while Haitadism is a matter of fairness. In this way, Haitadism refers to the struggle for dignity in the political, social and cultural dimension of collective integration. Politically, it is first and foremost a matter of the right to national sovereignty, as for any other people and second a matter of promoting the reunification of Armenians within a single territory to secure a future of peace and development. This is the meaning of the ARF slogan 'a free, independent, reunited Armenia'. The next step on the Haitadist agenda is to secure recognition of the genocide by the international community and

Turkey and with it, territorial, political, economic, cultural and symbolic reparations. The third and final step is to grant independence to the Republic of Nagorno-Karabakh without any concessions to Azerbaijan. On the social level, it is a question of defending the rights of the Armenian people under whatever regime. Under the empires, there was talk of improving living conditions, of protecting Armenians from the exactions of imperial bureaucracies. But it has also always been about guaranteeing an equitable land reform favourable to the peasants and in support of the redistribution of wealth. Finally, the social aspect refers to the struggle against Armenian emigration, a major issue under the empires but also since independence in 1991. From a cultural point of view, it is about organizing the Armenian communities established in the diaspora, safeguarding national identity and promoting the development of the Armenian language.

In contemporary history, the Great Powers have approached the Armenian Question or Haitadism in three different ways. The first has been through instrumentalization because, on the one hand, Armenia is not assigned to any cultural area in terms of its region (Arabic, Turkish, Iraqi) and, on the other hand, given their status as national minorities in the Ottoman and Russian Empires, Armenians have often served as pawns in the games of larger powers. More often as object rather than as subject of their history, they have sought to internationalize their problems, from the Russian conquest of Transcaucasia or to the eastward expansion of Napoleon's armies, to free themselves from the Ottoman yoke – to follow the Byzantine example. From the Russian–Ottoman war of 1877–1878, inspired by Bulgarian emancipation, this hope of internationalization has become concrete, first with the Treaty of San Stefano, then with the Treaty of Berlin. From this to the present day, the Armenian Question remains a lever in the hands of the powers who act in their own interests and often in connivance. This instrumentalization is based on national interests but also on clientelism towards the strong Armenian diaspora communities fully integrated into host communities.

The second way to address the Armenian Question is through multilateralism. From the beginning, the issue has been multilateral. Russia, Great Britain, France, Austria-Hungary, Italy and Germany, by collectively signing the Treaties of San Stefano and Berlin, expressed their interest in a problem which had, until then, been an internal issue in the Ottoman Empire. This multilateral approach undermines the false idea circulating among Armenians that they are isolated.

The third and final way is through realpolitik. While the Armenian Question is an instrument in the hands of the powers and a multilateral issue, it does not hold a privileged position on the world agenda. The question is often marginalized, treated as low priority, or, for economic reasons, linked to the pressures of Turkey. It has never become an international concern on the same footing as the Palestinian and Cypriot issues.

The international community has varying views of the Armenian Question. Their approach oscillates between denial and defence. There are states such as Kemalist Turkey who refuse to recognize the legitimacy of the issue, insisting it is merely an artificial Russian construct. There are other states such as Iran that, whatever the regime in Tehran, see in Haitadism a guarantee of their regional security against the influence of Turkey. These interpretations are shaped by geopolitical, strategic, political, economic, religious and social (humanitarian and educational) factors and reflect the three forms that Haitadism can take in the international system: Haitadism in motion, Haitadism in slow motion and Haitadism blocked.

Haitadism in motion

While both Russia and the United States consider that Armenia is geographically of major strategic importance and that geopolitical control of the country would strengthen their respective interests, their approaches are divergent. For Russia, Armenia remains a strategic priority and should not present a challenge to Russian hegemony. In an ideal scenario, Armenia and Russia would exist in symbiosis, with Armenia dependent upon Russia as a satellite of Russian authority. The United States, on the other hand, believes that Armenia should cultivate its independence and political authority. A strong and independent Transcaucasia with assertive republics along Russia's southern border would create a buffer between the South Caucasus and Russia, opening the possibility for growing American control at this critical international crossroads. At the end of the First World War, Britain, then present in the three Republics of the South Caucasus, implemented this geopolitical approach as a defence of local independence, at the same time forming a *cordon sanitaire* to guard against Russian – at the time Bolshevik – encroachment. Today, it is the United States that plays that role in the Western camp, with support from the EU and other states.

Russia

For Russia, the policy of penetrating into the Armenian world is part of its expansionist strategy. Formerly, as protector of Christians in the Ottoman Empire, Russia often relied on the Armenian element to advance its pawn in the Caucasus and Eastern Anatolia. Russia has always been distrustful of Georgia and Azerbaijan but knows that Armenia favours Russian presence in the region because of the Armenian–Turkish quarrel. Regardless of the regime in place in Moscow, Armenia is Russia's only ally in the region. The Armenian mountains allow Russia a vantage point from which to survey the surroundings, all the while providing a direct link with the Middle East. In this, Russian interests tend to present Armenia as a continuation of Russia in the region – 'a Russian outpost', as Boris Gryzlov, the president of the Duma declared in 2005.[7] With a view to strengthening Russian interests in the Middle East, especially since the outbreak of civil war in Syria, Moscow has worked to consolidate its defence system in Armenia, fearing that Transcaucasia would become a new front in the event Bashar al-Assad's regime in Damascus should fail. This is the same logic that was at work when, in September 2013, Russia strongly urged Armenia to enter into its customs union with a view to joining the Eurasian Union at a time when Armenian president, Serzh Sargsyan, within the framework of the Eastern Partnership between the European Union and six former

---

[7]   Gaïdz Minassian, *Géopolitique de l'Arménie* (Paris: Ellipses, 2005), p. 54.

Soviet republics, was leaning towards signing an association agreement with Brussels at the Vilnius Summit in November 2013. Even though Yerevan does not have a direct border with Russia, the Russians see this 'insular' Armenia as a southern Kaliningrad.

The expansion of Russia to the south also serves a military purpose: to consolidate a north–south corridor against the establishment of a horizontal Turkey–Georgia–Azerbaijan axis. The hypothesis of a pan-Turkish threat on the ex-Soviet southern border is integrated into Russian military doctrine, which interprets these movements as evidence of a Turkish-American alliance for the destabilization of the Russian strategic space and for the enlargement of NATO in the former Soviet Union. Therefore, Russia proposes three complementary possibilities for a counterattack. Initially, it renewed its military agreements for military bases in the newly independent republics (with Russian bases in Armenia up to 2044), invented a new rationale for collective defence, the CSTO, the armed wing of the CIS, urging the 'states' (South Ossetia, Abkhazia) to sign bilateral military agreements. In a second step, Russia pursued a policy of destabilizing the pro-Turk regimes in the region, attempting to impose a network of leaders loyal to Russian interests. Finally, Moscow encouraged pro-Russian movements to rise up against those republics hostile to Russia, including Abkhazia, South Ossetia and Nagorno-Karabakh.

The United States

In the history of the United States, Armenia has often received special attention from federal administrations. Neutral during the First World War, the United States gave decisive support to the young Republic of 1918, to the point of considering an American security mandate for Greater Armenia. Drafted by President Woodrow Wilson, the mandate was finally rejected by Congress, who could not envisage extending it to all territories of the former Ottoman Empire. As a result, the American government abandoned the plan. Washington was also slow to recognize the Soviet Union, foreshadowing American aspirations for freedom for the many nationalities trapped within the communist framework. In the twentieth century, America's policy for integrating the Armenian world resembled British policies of the previous century, namely the implementation of a containment strategy to check Russian expansion on the high seas. With the Cold War in full escalation and consistent with its traditional policy of isolating Russia, the United States adopted the Truman doctrine which reinforced a policy of a *cordon sanitaire* around the Soviet Union. The strategy for 'containing' communism was accompanied by one of destabilization in Moscow, a policy that required the co-operation of the peoples incorporated into the Soviet bloc, whom the United States imagined as future partners when the Soviet Union collapsed. Washington backed the Russian-dominated ethnic nationalities and, from the 1960s, reintroduced the Armenian Question in Congress and marked the commemoration of the 50th anniversary of the dissolution of the Ottoman Empire (Treaty of Sèvres), despite the fact that relations with Turkey had cooled as a result of the Cyprus crisis (1963–1974).

Since the collapse of the Soviet Union, the United States has encouraged the former Soviet neighbours to disassociate themselves from their previous relationships, inviting them to modernize their states, integrate into the world economy and join NATO. By pushing them to embrace liberal capitalism, the United States no doubt hoped to control these transitional markets and capture the new energy and trade routes through the former communist bloc. In 1994, by offering the post-Soviet states membership in the NATO Partnership for Peace, the United States also intended to monitor their military potential, weaken Russian geopolitical capabilities and strengthen their own strategic framework in Central and Eastern Europe. Unlike the other former Soviet republics, Armenia represented a particular case, as continuing Armenian–Turkish conflict slowed down American penetration in Armenia. The American strategy was to launch a process for the normalization of relations between Turkey and Armenia and in this way realign the South Caucasus with American interests. To this end, Washington ratcheted up its goodwill gestures towards Armenia, on the one hand, increasing financial support for local development in Yerevan – in the 1990s, Armenia was the state that received the most US credits per capita after Israel – and, on the other hand, by defending a pipeline project that would cross Armenia from east to west or from north to south, the east–west route being the most economical because of shorter distances. These projects would have had the advantage of imposing a regional *pax americana* between Turkey, Armenia and Azerbaijan. The south–north route, of course, would avoid Russian territory but would leverage the normalization of relations between the international community and Iran. The signing of the transitional agreement between P5 + 1 (the five permanent members of the UN Security Council plus Germany) and Iran in November 2013 was a first step towards the opening up of Iran, making Armenia and Georgia transit lands for the transportation of Iranian oil and gas to European markets.

Iran

For Iran, Armenia has always represented an alternative route to Europe, one that bypasses an unstable Middle East and offers a security guarantee against Turkish–Azerbaijani threats on its northern border. Whatever the regime in Tehran, Iran is committed to good relations with Armenia. During the Nagorno-Karabakh war in 1993, Iran did not oppose Armenian military operations intended to control south-western Azerbaijan, which allowed Armenia to advance its borders by 30 km into neighbouring Azerbaijan. The only non-Soviet state to have a direct border with the 'Nagorno-Karabakh Republic', Iran even offered to mediate the conflict, despite Tehran's wariness about the OSCE and especially, given the risk of deployment in its own backyard of an international observation force including NATO member states, despite the encirclement felt as a result of US presence in Afghanistan and Iraq.

Here again we find the analytic framework of a strategic cross with its two axes: the north–south axis, Moscow–Yerevan–Tehran and the east–west axis, Ankara–Tbilisi–Baku. As for Iran, on two occasions, in 1909 and in 1946, the Russians invaded the land to the north, while the south was occupied by Britain. To avoid a new strategic vacuum in the north, Iran sees in a strong Armenia a guarantee for Iranian national integrity and a buffer from any Russian threat. Furthermore, in Iranian logic, the more Azerbaijan suffers from military failures in Nagorno-Karabakh, the greater the chance of avoiding ethnic Azerbaijani tensions in northern Iran. As Armenia expands and consolidates its sovereignty, Turkish progress in Transcaucasia regresses, leaving Iran with considerable latitude for independent action. A symbol of this deep bilateral friendship was the inauguration in 2006 of the gas pipeline linking Iran and Armenia; Tehran thus supports Yerevan's opening up to the world, with its own identity markers, suggesting further reintegration into the international arena.

China

China's interest in the South Caucasus and particularly in Armenia dates to the early 1960s when the Uyghurs, a Turkic language-speaking population from Xinjiang or Eastern Turkestan, rose up in 1962 against the Chinese central government. During the Sino-Soviet schism, China expressed an interest in the Armenian Question in response to this growing Pan-Turkism and also to thwart Moscow's interests. Indeed, according to Beijing, the roots of the Xinjiang uprising were not only Central Asian, with a strong Soviet influence, but Turkish. Geographically speaking, China is located at the eastern end of the Turkic language channel and, as the Soviet Union's influence in Central Asia lessened, the conflict in Xinjiang re-emerged with violent overtones, as evidenced by the clashes in the winter of 1996 between the Chinese army and the Uyghur liberation movement. During the 1970s, Beijing established relations with Armenian forces fighting Pan-Turkism but dissipated when the Soviet Union took a stand for Greece and against Turkey in the Cyprus affair. In the early 1990s, China again became interested in Armenia. According to the Chinese authorities, who were among the first in the world to recognize the independence of the Republic of Armenia and to open an embassy there, eastern Turkey hosted training camps for the Uyghur rebels. It was therefore to reinforce its checks against the risk of disintegration of its Western territories that the Chinese government increased acts of economic and military co-operation with Armenia.

The Arab world

The Arab world has long been aware of the Armenians. Yet their interest in the Armenian Question is linked to the will of the Arab states to weaken Turkey. Syria, Iraq, Lebanon and Egypt became increasingly interested in Haitadism when Turkey became a strategic ally of Israel and Ankara acceded to NATO. During the Nagorno-Karabakh war, Syria and Lebanon delivered large quantities of weapons to Stepanakert's forces as well as many tonnes of cereals to the Armenian population. For the Arabs, the evolution of the Armenian Question depends on the Israeli–Palestinian conflict. Arab support is all the more important for Armenians as they want to emphasize that the Armenian Question does not feed religious animosity between Christians versus Muslims and so avoid Arab states' ill will and protect Armenian communities in the Middle East. When the AKP came to power in Turkey in 2002, the Arab states' interest in Armenia lessened, on the assumption that the Turkish government would distance itself from Israel. The Arab Spring changed things. The more strained the relations between AKP's Turkey and Arab regimes over the treatment of the Muslim Brotherhood in Egypt and support for the Islamist rebels in the civil war in Syria, the more statements issued by Cairo and Damascus favoured recognition of the 1915 genocide.

Georgia

For Georgia, which shares parts of its history with Armenia, the Armenian Question is a priority because it contributes to weakening Russia's hold on the South Caucasus and consolidating the emancipation of the three republics in the region. After the Georgian–Armenian war of December 1918, bilateral ties between the two states were reinforced as they implemented a common policy towards a Russia that was plagued by civil war and whose Bolshevik government aroused if not hostility at least mistrust. Since the collapse of the Soviet Union, tensions (relations with Russia and the fate of the Samtskhe-Javakhetia Armenian minority in Georgia) have alternated with normalization phases, as the two states wished to avoid the creation of a 'third Abkhazia' south of Tbilisi or a 'second Nagorno-Karabakh' north of Yerevan.

The Balkans

Bulgaria and Macedonia, once on the fringes of the Ottoman Empire, share an important historical date with Armenians. The 1878 Treaty of Berlin gave Bulgaria its independence and gave birth to the Macedonian question. The Treaty also placed Cyprus under British rule in exchange for a revision of the Treaty of San Stefano, in line with a Turkish–English agreement. The common experience of Turkish domination shared by Armenia, Bulgaria, Serbia, Romania, Montenegro, Greece and by extension Cyprus, has left a mark in the collective unconscious of these peoples. A form of natural, often religious alliance has built up between them against the Turkish power. During the Cold War between Bulgaria and Turkey and during the Cypriot crisis between Greeks and Turks under the umbrella of NATO, the people of the Balkans defended the Armenian Question out of Christian and anti-Turkish solidarity.

France

France holds a special place in the galaxy of states favouring the Armenian Question. For historical and political reasons, France is the Western state that has been most involved in Armenian national life over the past century. France pioneered recognition of the genocide from the 1980s onwards and has a long Armenophile tradition whose origins date back to the nineteenth century when the Armenian Chair was created at Inalco (National institute of oriental languages and civilizations). It is also reflected in the founding of the newspaper *Pro Armenia* led by Anatole France, Georges Clemenceau, Jean Jaurès, Pierre Quillard, Francis de Pressensé and Victor Bérard, who were outraged by European passivity in the face of the Armenian massacres of 1894–1896. France co-chaired the OSCE Minsk Group with Russia and the United States and encouraged several of its big companies to invest in the young state (Orange, Alcatel, Areva). More recently, France broke ties with Turkey by passing a law that penalized denial of the 1915 genocide – the bill was passed by parliament in 2011–2012 and subsequently rejected by the Constitutional Council.

Haitadism in slow motion

States that are receptive to this variant of Haitadism only have a limited political interest and eventually an economic interest in Armenia. Several nations see such dynamics as an instrument of economic domination to establish their presence in the region. Turkey, Azerbaijan, Georgia, Russia and Iran consider that Haitadism must be rid of its political substance and subordinated to economic processes that are much more important than its political development. In short, these states oscillate between tolerance and mistrust: tolerance, because they note a certain advantage when it takes on an extra-political dimension; mistrust as they keep a close watch on the strategy of the Armenian organizations likely to re-evaluate their initial plans.

Turkey

Turkey's stance on the Armenian Question is that it prefers the proximity of a small weak state to that of the Soviet or Russian power. Thus, the Young Turk regime called upon Ottoman Armenians to rise up against the Tsar shortly before the beginning of the First World War. In May 1918, the Ottoman Empire precipitated the fall of the Transcaucasian Federation (Armenia, Azerbaijan, Georgia), created in February 1918 and made every effort to create three independent republics on its doorstep. Istanbul quickly recognized the independence of Armenia and almost helped the Armenian insurgents after the revolt of 18 February 1921 against the Bolshevik power in Yerevan. In the midst of the Cold War and until 1959, the Turks and Dashnaks, under US mediation, even tried to co-operate against communism in the Middle East. Moreover, in 1991, Turkey welcomed the independence of the three South Caucasian Republics and imposed no conditions on Yerevan when its sovereignty was recognized. Turkey thus wishes to display its total lack of animosity towards Armenians, a convoluted way of asserting that it is time to turn the page on the 'events' of the First World War and look exclusively to the future. Since the arrival of the AKP in Ankara, a measured rapprochement with Armenia has been part of Turkey's de-Kemalization strategy. For the Islamist government, Armenia will eventually be an economic area dependent on Turkey. They did not oppose Armenia's accession to the Organization of the Black Sea Economic Zone, which is based in Istanbul, though the two countries have no diplomatic relations. It is also in this spirit that in Zurich on 10 October 2009, Turkey signed protocols to normalize relations with Armenia, in the name of its 'zero problems at its borders' strategy. Drawn up under the auspices of Switzerland, Russia, the United States and France, these documents have not been ratified by the two states. Under pressure from Azerbaijan, Turkey has added to its commitments additional conditions deemed 'unacceptable' for Armenia – to withdraw from the territories under its control around Nagorno-Karabakh in exchange for the opening of the border. Even if Turkey has not officially engaged in a process of remembrance, the term 'genocide' is no longer taboo in Turkish society.

Azerbaijan

As can be imagined, Armenian–Turkish rapprochement is not to the liking of Azerbaijan. To denounce this relationship – deemed 'against nature' – Baku has strengthened its ties with Russia and attempted to taint Armenian–Russian relations. For Azerbaijan, a sound definition of Haitadism is the belief that Azeri social mediation offers a basis for friendship among the peoples of the Caucasus against pan-Slavism. Several examples of Armenian–Azerbaijani collaboration come to mind. In 1905, after a merciless war, Armenians and Tatars (the former name of the Azerbaijanis in the Caucasus) signed a peace agreement without mediation from St Petersburg which was accused by both sides of having fanned the flames of interethnic hatred. In 1917–1918, Armenians and Azerbaijanis were in the same government of the Federation of Transcaucasia. In 1989, images were circulated of Armenian negotiators of the Pan-National Armenian Movement and Azerbaijani negotiators of the Azerbaijani Popular Front Party gathered in Riga, Estonia, to try to find a solution to the Nagorno-Karabakh conflict without the involvement of the Soviet central power.

Like Turkey, Azerbaijan would like to use its economic power to stifle Armenia, which has suffered a Turkish–Azerbaijani blockade since 1993. The only prospect of possible co-operation between Armenia and Azerbaijan is through cultural and social exchange. For this purpose, the Azerbaijani people use the following syllogism: the Caucasus is full of fossil fuels, which belong to Azerbaijan, the Caucasus is under the influence of Azerbaijan, whose economy accounts for more than three-quarters of that of the South Caucasus. Since the Nagorno-Karabakh ceasefire in May 1994, Azerbaijan has pointed to energy as the only reason for the international community's interest in the Caucasus. Baku does not see any problem with Armenians benefiting in turn from the dividends derived from the oil and gas adventure, provided, however, that they abandon their claim to the independence of the 'Nagorno-Karabakh Republic', a prerequisite that Haitadism is not ready to accept.

Georgia

The geographical location of Georgia gives it a privileged status in the establishment of peace in the Caucasus. As a major hub in the area, Tbilisi is in a position to implement a development plan for the region. Close to Armenia in terms of religion (Christianity) and history (the Bagratid dynasty), it is also associated with Azerbaijan over political (the problem of separatism) and strategic issues (mistrust of Russia). Georgia has all it takes to play a key role in building a hypothetical future Caucasian homeland. Of the three Republics of the South Caucasus, Georgia is the one that has always sought to preserve peace with its two neighbours. In 1918, it was Georgia that initiated creation of the Federal Republic of Transcaucasia, centred in Tbilisi. Much later, in the 1990s, Georgia took the initiative of organizing quadrilateral meetings between the heads of state of the region (the three South Caucasian and the Russian presidents). Georgia thus fosters regional peace within the borders bequeathed by the Soviet Union. Tbilisi recognizes the territorial integrity of its neighbours and thus rejects Haitadism as a threat to its sovereignty, since Armenians of the Samtskhe-Javakheti region claim autonomy within the framework of a federal Georgia. Under the presidency of Mikheil Saakashvili (2004–2013) following the 'Rose Revolution', Georgia maintained strong pressure on this border region with Armenia, to the point of condemning Georgian nationals of Armenian origin for espionage for a foreign power. Since the defeats of the Saakashvili camp in 2012 and 2013, Tbilisi has considerably reduced its pressure on the Samtskhe-Javakheti region and pardoned the Armenian prisoners, who had always protested their innocence.

Russia

For Russia, Haitadism is an unpredictable ideology that does not tolerate the process of bringing Russians closer to states hostile to Armenia. Moscow, whether imperial, Soviet or federal, has often worked at normalizing its relations with Turkey in the form of trade and economic partnerships. When Russia and Turkey meet, they may incidentally discuss the issue of Armenian irredentism between themselves. In the name of their mutual friendship dating back to the tsars and sultans and renewed by Lenin and Ataturk, the Soviets and Turks have often asserted that there is no territorial problem between the two countries – a way of saying that the Armenian Question casts no shadow on Russian–Turkish ties. This logic of Russian–Turkish economic co-operation was tested by Tsar Alexander III, but also by the Soviets whose policy in the Caucasus always favoured Turkey, from Lenin to the Second World War. It was in this phase of bilateral rapprochement that the Armenian territories of the Russian Caucasus were separated from Armenia in 1921 to the benefit of Azerbaijan and Georgia, for it was necessary to break Armenian nationalism. Hence a certain tension within the Armenian political class, divided between the supporters of this economic approach (the Armenian Communists) and the partisans hostile to this Russo-Turkish diktat (the Dashnaks). Since the beginning of the 2000s, the rapprochement between Putin's Russia and Erdoğan's Turkey is a reflection of this Russian–Turkish tradition and to some extent a source of concern for Armenians.

Iran

Iran has refrained from playing a Haitadist card and causing trouble as the Turkish–Russian rapprochement emerged for fear that it should become isolated on the regional scene. When Armenia turned away from Iran, Tehran chose to take an interest in Azerbaijan and sign economic agreements in exchange for non-intervention in Baku's internal affairs. Thus, when Armenia strengthened its cooperation with the United States and NATO, Tehran was concerned about the risk of a turnaround by Yerevan in favour of the West. This is why the Iranians are wary of the collaboration between Armenia and NATO, even though Yerevan has provided guarantees on its refusal to join the Atlantic Alliance.

Britain

The leading Western power until the turn of the twentieth century, Britain was no longer driven, as it was in the nineteenth century, by its intent to bar Russia's access to the warm seas. London had even tried to take advantage of the Armenian revolutionary movement – to the point of using it to house the headquarters of clandestine organizations at the beginning of the twentieth century – to weaken St Petersburg. But as Russian–Ottoman relations deteriorated rapidly, Britain chose to support the Sublime Porte, therefore against Armenian interests. It was not until the fall of the Russian Empire in 1917 that the British got hold of the South Caucasus and protected the route to India. Between 1918 and 1920, they supported the three independent republics and relied on them to prevent the expansion of the Bolshevik Revolution in the Middle East. London favoured the idea of a Caucasian confederation between the three main national components, as a factor of regional peace but also as a prerequisite for the exploitation of Caspian oil and gas. It was essentially for this reason that it appropriated Baku in 1918 to prevent the Germans from taking possession of it to feed their war machine. Indeed, this manna prompted London to work for regional stability and the maintenance of existing borders. Hence, its reservations about Haitadism meant, among other things, the reannexation of Nagorno-Karabakh to Armenia. Indeed, contrary to common belief, the first to speak out in favour of maintaining Nagorno-Karabakh within Azerbaijan was not the Bolsheviks but the British. Stalin merely endorsed the British decision in 1923 when he gave Nagorno-Karabakh the status of autonomous region. In the mid-1990s, after long negotiations, Baku signed an agreement with several Western companies, including BP, in a consortium of 'contracts of the century' aimed at facilitating access to Caspian oil and gas through Georgia. In respect of 1915 genocide, London never recognized the crime as genocide, in spite of overwhelming evidence against Turkey contained in the archives. Guided by reason of state – Turkey has been a reliable ally for Britain at least since the Treaty of Lausanne – London has always paid special attention to Turkish interests, even though in recent years things seem to be gradually changing.

France

There is another definition of Haitadism in slow motion: that of considering the Armenian Question only as a secondary, symbolic cause that is particularly sympathetic, an expression somewhat tinged with condescension, even a colonial stance. Such was France's position when its interests required that it draw away from Armenians, as it did in 1921 when the French troops withdrew from Cilicia. To the extent that Franco-Turkish relations offered attractive prospects for the French economy, the Armenian Question did not justify French sacrifice on behalf of a moral position. Today, Turkey is France's leading trading partner in the region. For many years, despite tokens of sympathy for Armenians, French foreign ministers have been cautious to avoid the word 'genocide' when questioned by colleagues in the National Assembly. Today, such circumspection is still occasionally expressed, even though France passed a law in 2001 recognizing the genocide. Above all, France's balanced position on the Nagorno-Karabakh issue within the Minsk Group which it co-chairs, is a source of frustration for French citizens of Armenian origin.

The United States

In an effort to accommodate its Turkish partner, which threatens to reconsider its alliance in the event America should formally recognize the genocide, the United States has emptied Haitadism of all political content and relegated the question to academia. American institutions fund Armenian chairs in universities but have no intention of bringing the Armenian Question into the political arena. In the guise of the First Amendment (freedom of speech), negationism is thus propagated within American universities – a discourse that voices Ankara's official position verbatim, even if it results in corruption scandals.

A blocked Haitadism

In addition to the first two interpretations outlined above which, if not favourable, are at least encouraging and considering that the issue of Haitadism does not yet qualify as an international question, there is a third definition that is much more problematic for stakeholders, namely the denial of Haitadism as a political force on the grounds that it is merely an instrument in the hands of the Great Powers, mainly Russia.

Turkey

For Kemalist Turkey, the Armenian Question does not exist and Haitadism is a biased, anti-Turkish ideology. For nearly 90 years, Turkey's attitude has remained one of defiance or indifference, arguing that this issue belongs to the past. Yet the Turks continue to see the Treaty of Sèvres as a threat to the territorial integrity of their country. Shortly after the fiftieth anniversary of the genocide, Turkish diplomacy objected to what it referred to as 'Armenian allegations' when, in 1967, the genocide file showed up on the agenda of the UN Subcommittee on Human Rights. Until the fall of the Kemalist regime in Ankara, the official line in Turkey had not evolved to the point of organizing anti-Haitadism in the world. With the rise to power of the AKP Islamists in 2002, the Armenian Question became focused on sensitive domestic issues, such as the Kurdish and Cyprus questions within a context of European Union/Turkey accession discussions. While the views of Turkish civil society now begin to acknowledge historical truths, the state apparatus remains inflexible even though the government no longer gets involved when Turkish journalists, researchers or writers point to the reality of the 1915 genocide, even on Turkish soil. The Armenian taboo has therefore been broken, but the assassination of the Turkish–Armenian journalist Hrant Dink in Istanbul in January 2007 cast doubt over the state's willingness to be flexible. Today, as a result of the space opened by Dink, a Turkish citizen from Malatya, an Armenian protestant and editor-in-chief of the bilingual newspaper *Agos* (the influence of which goes beyond Armenian circles), a new aspect to Haitadism is emerging in Turkey thanks to the pressure exerted by Europe on Ankara to begin its memory work, the process of normalization between Ankara and Yerevan and the liberalization of a Turkish society that longs to appropriate its own history in the context of globalization. This is unprecedented since the creation of the Republic in 1923. Armenian organizations guessed right: the first meetings or joint demonstrations involving Turks and Armenians living in Turkey and Armenians of the diaspora have been scheduled around 24 April, a time of year when commemorations are increasingly taking place in the major cities of the republic.

Azerbaijan

In Azerbaijan, the image of Haitadism is as negative as in Turkey and even more so due to the conflict situation in Nagorno-Karabakh. It is seen as a direct threat to Azerbaijan as a state and the Azerbaijani people as a nation; hence the emergence of Azerbaijani nationalism in reaction against Armenia and a declaration of war on Haitadism, which is deemed to weaken the formation of an Azerbaijani national identity. This antagonistic climate was heightened during the Soviet Union dissolution process, when Baku, in a play for sympathy from the Muslim world, characterized the Karabakh movement as terrorist and an incarnation of the spirit of the Crusades. In response to an Armenian ideology it considered racist, Baku used strong-arm tactics including exactions, massacre and war. Anti-Armenian organizations were openly active in the capital of Azerbaijan. Armenian elements became the exclusive target of attacks by the government, with then president Ilham Aliyev going so far as to assert that all Armenians are the enemies of Azerbaijan.

The only perspective the Azerbaijanis may be willing to contemplate in terms of neighbourly relations with Armenia is that Armenia should join them in building defences against Russian power. The more Armenia faces down problems with Russia and moves away from Russian tutelage, the more Azerbaijan consolidates its independence by taking advantage of these tensions. The less Armenia frees itself from Russian domination, the more Azerbaijan is confronted with the influence of Russia and Baku's sovereignty deteriorates.

Germany

For many years, Germany considered the Armenian Question a key element in the Russian plan to destabilize the Ottoman Empire. To preserve their interests with Constantinople and to prevent the Tsar's armies from spreading into Central Europe and the Middle East, the Germans had to crush Haitadism after encouraging it under the German–Russian agreement of 1887. Germany, however, quickly rescinded on the agreement and supported the Turks during the Armenian massacres of 1894–1896 and again in 1914 when it actually participated in the killings.[8] In the aftermath of the war, Germany did not break with its Turkish ally, instead helping to bury the question, until the Second World War when the Third Reich offered to liberate those under Soviet domination in exchange for support in the Axis war effort.

Until the shift in German approaches to the Soviet Union initiated by Chancellor Willy Brandt in the 1960s, Haitadism was of no interest to the West German authorities. As German–Soviet relations developed, the Germans denied the legitimacy of Armenian claims and positioned themselves as guardians of the territorial integrity not only of the Soviet Union but also of Turkey, by then a fully-fledged member of NATO. It was only with the opening of accession talks with the EU that Berlin, hostile towards Ankara's integration into Europe, modified its position regarding Armenians, calling

---

[8] Vahakn Dadrian revealed Germany's direct implication in the organization of the massacres in his 1966 book, *History of the Armenian Genocide*.

upon the Turks to reopen their border with Armenia and to acknowledge the crimes of 1915. In July 2005, the Bundestag passed a resolution blocking Turkish aspirations to join the EU, without so much as pronouncing the word 'genocide'. The Germans have thus seized on the Armenian Question as a foil to Turkey's accession to the EU.

The Armenian Question therefore suffers from a double deficit: a deficit of legitimacy, on the one hand, because its conception of peace is uncertain, its foundations are fragile and its actors scattered all over the world. There is also a deficit of legitimation because its unity as a cause is precarious, its conception of politics unfinished and its strategy confused. Its capacity for improvement depends essentially on its utility as an instrument for leveraging international processes of particular interest, so much so that Haitadism may be understood as a succession of opening gambits followed by expectations, of hopes followed by procrastination, disappointment and resentment. All of this is spread over a globalized Haitadist space, in such a way that, beyond its living, multifaceted representation, it is regarded as a unity sufficiently homogeneous to consolidate the Armenian collective consciousness and sufficiently heterogeneous due to being based on a fragmented political field, which accentuates its complexity. Hence the idea that its stakeholders' strategy still faces indifference, ignorance, incomprehension and obstacles from both states and from public opinion.

The three ordeals of Haitadism, 1915–1923

In eight years, between 1915 and 1923, Armenians went from joy – reforms and Greater Armenia – to violent or slow death in a world undergoing radical change. Who is responsible for such a change in fortunes? At the hands of the sultan or the Committee of Union and Progress (CUP), the Ottoman Empire was the main culprit; the Unionists' trials that took place after the war in Constantinople proved this beyond doubt. The main leaders of the CUP were condemned to death in absentia for engaging Turkey in the First World War and for the mass crimes committed against Armenians. The Young Turk regime that came to power after the 1908 revolution was at the heart of the programme, including its leader Mehmet Talaat Pasha, the interior minister and future grand vizier (prime minister) and the other personalities at the core of Ottoman rule. This regime conceived and executed the plan of extermination. But it was its successor, the Kemalist regime, that truly buried the Armenian Question.

What is sometimes referred to as the Vienna System or the Concert of Europe – a system of dispute resolution adopted in the early nineteenth century by the major Europe powers (France, Britain, Austria-Hungary, Germany, Russia) to avoid war and bolster their own authority – is also accountable to history, for its indifference to massacres and the handling of conflicts in the Ottoman Empire. Three European powers were particularly at fault: Imperial Russia for its passivity during the genocide, which the Soviet Union followed in 1920 by smothering Armenian sovereignty; Britain, for its duplicity towards Armenians generally and its intermittent support for Constantinople, which depended upon good relations with St Petersburg; finally, Germany – and to a lesser extent Austria-Hungary – for endorsing the massacres of 1894–1896 and the 1915 genocide in the name of its alliance with Constantinople.

Armenians themselves, however, were not blameless. While the responsibility of the genocide cannot be attributed to the Armenian revolutionary or conservative circles, is it possible that these two currents engaged in foolhardy actions during this period without really considering the consequences? Again, to avoid misunderstandings, we must insist that no Armenian political force can in any way be associated with this unprecedented burst of violence. As Archag Tchobanian, a conservative publicist, wrote in 1926 'no Armenian political force has joined the ranks of the genocide leaders of 1915'.[9]

One could argue that since Caucasian Armenia became communist in 1920, Armenian civilization was preserved and its heritage protected. Such a claim overlooks that Armenia was then subjected to the history of a foreign power, in this case the Russo-Soviet power, written by leaders unconcerned about the memories of the nationalities they administered in a climate of terror. Soviet totalitarianism introduced a rupture, as if 1917 was the first year of a new era, when all proletarians united under the banner of communism marched forward to a new history. To understand the causes of this decade of dread (1915–1923), the next part of this study will be structured around three sequences (1915, 1920 and 1923) in addition to three dynamics: the international context, the evolution of Haitadism and inter-Armenian relations.

1915: physical extinction: The European concert

The degradation of relations between the Ottoman state and its constituent nationalities and in our case, Armenians, resulted from a long historical process with roots in the 1648 Treaty of Westphalia, itself the product of nearly three centuries of conflict over principles of sovereignty, territorial integrity and the organization of European secular power. It was in the name of sovereignty and according to a process of transformation of the Ottoman Empire into a homogeneous Turkish state that the Ottoman authorities embarked upon the extermination of the Armenian people. This amounts to what Raymond Kévorkian called in his book *Le Génocide des Armeniens* 'destruction for the sake of reconstruction'.[10] The unprecedented violence reached a peak of atrocities in 1915 but the first elements emerged with the decline of the Sublime Porte among its European and Black Sea territories in the eighteenth century. Despite ideological differences between the Hamidian period and that of the Young Turks, the tragedy of 1915 was the only logical outcome of a declining power obsessed to the point of paranoia with the seemingly endless process of dismemberment.

Inclusion of the Ottoman Empire in the Concert of Europe by virtue of its European possessions proved to be a serious mistake. The Concert orchestrated Western statecraft and was, by definition, a system of exclusivity. It included Constantinople when it was in the interests of the major powers to do so and excluded the Ottomans when it was not. At the time, there were indeed many people at the bedside of 'the sick man of Europe'. The Ottoman Empire was caught up in the machinations of the Great Powers, believing that by so doing it was promoting its own territorial integrity. However, in

[9]   Archag Tchobanian, *La nation arménienne n'est pas fautive* (Paris: H Boghossian Press, 1926), p. 5.
[10]   Raymond Kévorkian, *Le génocide des arméniens* (Odile Jacob, 2006), p. 9.

choosing one or another camp – often but not systematically against its sworn enemy, Russia – the Sublime Porte, exploited by the Europeans, found itself exploiting its own national minorities as a means of begging foreign interference in its internal affairs. For Armenia, such instrumentalization was part of an international system which, for centuries, had produced inequalities and massacres.

The Ottoman Empire enjoyed a special position: any change in its status and its borders required the assent of the Great Powers. In short, these five nations competed for control of the international arena. Alone, they could do nothing. Together, they could act, but none dared to jump into the fray unilaterally. They counted on this rule to ensure the complicity of certain impoverished pawns, particularly the national minorities. From the beginning, the international order guaranteed by the Concert of Europe ensured the process of minority destruction and then this system degenerated at the expense of Armenians. Inhabiting a space that lacked political and economic integration, removed from any modernizing tendencies and socially categorized as *dhimmis* (non-Muslims living in a Muslim country but enjoying certain protections) they constituted relatively easy prey.

On 3 March 1878, at San Stefano, Turkey and Russia signed a peace treaty very favourable to the victor, the Tsar, but untenable for Austria-Hungary and Britain. According to Article 16 of the Treaty, Russia agreed to evacuate the conquered territories once 'the High Porte has committed to carrying out without delay the administrative reforms necessary to guaranty Armenian autonomy and security against the Circassians and the Kurds'. London saw in this Russian land grab a threat to its interests in India and a violation of existing treaties. Vienna, for its part, considered that the disruptions in the Balkans resulting from the Treaty of San Stefano were contrary to its plans for the region. As a result, the Austrians and especially the English did everything possible to force a revision of the treaty, enlisting the help of German Chancellor Bismarck, who saw in these negotiations an opportunity to reposition Germany at the centre of the European game, convening a conference in June which ended with the signature on 13 July 1878 of the Treaty of Berlin.

In the Balkans, several territories gained independence, including Serbia, Romania, Montenegro and, to some degree, Bulgaria. However, the Macedonian question arose between the rival Eastern powers, the Hapsburgs, the Ottomans and Tsarist Russia. Russia ceded to European pressure and withdrew from most of the conquered territories. Thus, Article 16, promising security for Armenia, was transformed into Article 61 of the Treaty of Berlin, according to which the Sublime Porte 'undertakes without further delay the improvements and reforms required by local needs in the provinces inhabited by Armenians and to guarantee their security against the Circassians and the Kurds'. There was no longer any mention of autonomy for Armenia. The application of the reforms was left to the goodwill of Constantinople, which is to say, postponed indefinitely. In Berlin, contrary to Armenian belief, the Armenian delegation was not included in the workgroups, but rather heard as a witness of the situation in the provinces. Judging from the results, it cannot be said the Armenian delegation was particularly effective. And for good reason: while Armenians were making representations, Britain secretly obtained control of Cyprus in exchange for concessions on reforms in eastern Anatolia. This was the beginning of a marathon of related causes: the Armenian, the Macedonian and the Armenian–Cypriot–Macedonian common destiny.

In the eastern provinces of the Ottoman Empire, the situation continued to deteriorate. By suspending the Ottoman Constitution in 1881, Abdul Hamid II halted application of the principle of equality, undermining the political map laid out by the Berlin agreement and encouraging Kurdish and Circassian exactions against Armenians. For Constantinople, the provinces of Eastern Anatolia represented the heart of the Empire. The Ottoman core might tolerate the loss of European or Middle Eastern provinces, but the slightest weakening of their positions in eastern Anatolia would cut them off from their memory and their ancestors who had arrived in the Middle Ages along this invasion route. Eastern Anatolia also represented the point of equilibrium for the distribution of power in the Ottoman Empire. If Russia were to advance its pawns, the others would have to react quickly. The Germans understood this. Having confirmed a general policy of reassurance vis-à-vis Russian concerns, they repositioned themselves at the heart of the European game. Bismarck sought to remove tensions towards the European periphery, where Germany could avoid direct involvement. He therefore used the Russo-Turkish war to entice the English away from the European theatre and to prevent a Franco-Russian alliance against the Kaiser. For this reason and with Machiavellian singleness of purpose, he signed the Reinsurance Treaty with Russia on 18 June 1887, which contained an additional protocol with secret clauses: in the event of Russia advancing on Constantinople, the Bosphorus and the Black Sea, Germany would remain neutral, a stratagem that it was hoped would dissuade Britain from moving against Russia.[11] Was there a link between the secret agreements of the Russo-German treaty and the revolutionary agitation that shook Armenia at the time and led to the creation of the Armenian Revolutionary Federation (ARF) in 1890? It is difficult to say, but the possibility that the Russian high command transmitted this 'Anatolian' dossier to its field commanders should not be discounted and would account for the sudden agitation. Such discretion, if it occurred, certainly paid off. The Armenian revolutionary movement was launched and Okhrana (the Tsar's political police) was powerless to stop it, despite Bismarck's resignation, the end of the Russo-German alliance in March 1890 and the installation of Chancellor Leo Von Caprivi – all of which signalled a return to the traditionally tough diplomacy towards Russia.

Neither the massacre of 250,000 Armenians between 1894 and 1896, nor the agreement of 1895 nor the actions of Armenian organizations supporting foreign intervention put an end to the passivity of the European powers faced with rescuing the minorities of the Ottoman Empire. On the contrary, there were allegations of complicity between Abdul Hamid II's anti-Armenian strategies and European passivity in pursuing the Ottomans for crimes that were widely reported. Russia was co-operating with the Turkish imperial police to dismantle Armenian revolutionary networks. Germany and the Hapsburgs could see no objection in allowing the sultan to

---

[11] Christian Baechler, *L'Aigle et l'Ours, la politique russe de l'Allemagne de Bismarck à Hitler* (Brussels: Peter Lang, 2001).

massacre Christians. Britain itself indirectly assisted with the annihilation of nearly 1,000 Armenian revolutionaries who in early June 1896 had negotiated a cessation of hostilities in Van in exchange for their expulsion to Persia under Turkish escort. The British vice-consul of Van did nothing to rescue them, although he had given his guarantee of protection at the time of surrender.

The greater the confusion on the ground, the greater the silence of the European powers and the greater the radicalization of the Armenian revolutionaries. Conflicts between Armenian communities escalated while agrarian reform, the central issue for the Armenian Question, still failed to make it onto the public agenda. Unpunished Kurdish raids on Armenian villages intensified. Armenians held off opposition at Zeytun, the centre of Armenian resistance and in Sassun, the theatre for two separate uprisings, one in 1894 the second in 1904. Such resistance, however, changed nothing. At the same time Armenians attempted to challenge European governments and their opinions by occupying the Ottoman Bank on 26 August 1896.[12] The first hostage-taking in the history of modern terrorism was to call attention to and stop the massacres then unfolding in eastern Anatolia. The operation claimed by the ARF ended with the expulsion of the hostage-takers to Europe, but also in retaliation with the state-endorsed massacre of 7,000 Armenians in Constantinople. Was it necessary then to mount this spectacular operation? Many Armenians pointed to the ARF as having provoked the tragedy. First, one should look to the despotism of Abdul Hamid II in assigning responsibility for this crime. If the reforms had been made as promised, the revolutionaries would not have resorted to a terrorist coup. By denouncing the ARF, the community effectively ostracized the movement, asserting a religious character for Armenian resistance while discrediting violence as a legitimate political means to an end. Finally, it should be noted that this audacious act did, in fact, put an end to the massacres in the East, whereas no other approach was effective.

The Young Turk Revolution of 24 July 1908 restored hope. Under the banner 'Freedom, Equality, Fraternity' inspired by the French Revolution, the crisis of July 1908 opened a new page in the history of the Ottoman Empire. Various Ottoman nationalities rallied around the idea of 'Ottoman-ism and equality'. Armenians and Turks congratulated themselves. The sultan's power was curtailed. Even if Abdul Hamid II was not deposed, the sultanate was made to bear responsibility for the crimes of the past. The new executive power would restore the Constitution of 1876 and work to unite all layers of Ottoman society. The immediate cause for the Revolution of 1908 – namely, halting the dismemberment of the Ottoman Empire – was not achieved by the Young Turks. In October 1908, three months after the Young Turks came to power, Bulgaria unilaterally proclaimed its independence. The next day, Bosnia and Herzegovina was annexed by Austria-Hungary and Crete seceded to join Greece. In 1911, the Ottomans lost Tripolitania at the end of a new war against Italy. Each time, the European powers acceded to and even encouraged their allies in making the changes.

Domestically, the groups that remained loyal to the sultan launched a counter-revolution in 1909 that failed but resulted in the massacres of 20,000–30,000 Armenians in Cilicia. At no point did the Europeans demand accountability from the Ottoman

[12] Armen Garo, *Jours vécus* (Beyrouth: Editions Vosguetar, 1986).

authorities. This tragedy was considered to be an internal affair of the empire and the powers chose not to interfere. They certainly followed events, taking note of the deposition of Abdul Hamid II and of his replacement by his brother, Mehmet V. They did not intervene, however, even when it was shown that the Young Turks' party, the Committee of Union and Progress (CUP), were responsible for these massacres. The European powers preferred to attribute the excesses to *ancien régime* reactionary elements. So, once again, the law reflected by default the principle of rationalizing impunity, Turkey was, at last, a constitutional monarchy and the Young Turks needed time to take the reins of power and develop its institutional pedagogy. In reality, there was an intense behind the scenes struggle between the French and the British on the one hand and the Germans on the other. Each camp counted on its contacts within the CUP to defend its interests, but it would be the grand vizier who determined which power would be favoured.

The Balkan wars in 1912 and 1913 accelerated the political crisis in Constantinople. The coalition of Christian states in the Balkans imposed a stinging defeat on the Ottoman Empire, which caused it to lose most of its European territories, including Thessaloniki, the stronghold of the young Turkish officers who instigated the 1908 Revolution. The European powers, beginning with Russia and Britain, judging that the Ottomans could no longer hold their European possessions, preserve the peace or ensure the security of their European subjects, encouraged their Balkan allies to declare independence. In the confusion between two Balkan wars, growing nationalist sentiment and the influx of émigré Balkan Muslims into Eastern Anatolia, the Russians revived the questions raised by the Treaty of San Stefano, which concerned living conditions and agricultural reform among the populations of Eastern Anatolia. It was the Russian government that first raised the Armenian Question and it was the Governor General of the Caucasus Viceroyalty, Vorontsov-Dashkov, who urged the Armenian Catholicos of Constantinople, Kevork V to raise the issue in a meeting with Tsar Nicholas II in St Petersburg. In Russia, the time for repressing Armenians of the Caucasus had passed. For more than ten years, the Tsar's authorities had persecuted Armenian organizations in the empire. Once again, Armenians would become a source of leverage serving to justify Russian armed intervention in the Ottoman Empire. This led to the Russo–Turkish agreement on the reforms in eastern Anatolia signed in February 1914.

A new act instrumentalizing the Armenian community, pushing the Armenian Question onto the international stage, quickly found itself at the centre of two European alliances: the Triple Alliance (Germany, Austria-Hungary, Italy) and the Triple Entente (Britain, France, Russia) both of which concerned themselves with advancing their respective interests in the Ottoman Empire. When war began to loom in Europe in June 1914, Britain urged the Ottoman Empire to remain neutral in the event of a conflict. The CUP, at the time working very closely with Germany to modernize the Ottoman military and state transport infrastructure and tending towards support for Germany, ultimately launched a surprise attack on Russian installations in the Black Sea, effectively entering the First World War on the side of the Triple Alliance. The two inspectors appointed to supervise the February 1914 agreement for land reform in Eastern Anatolia, Major Nicolai Hoff (Norway) and the diplomat Louis-Constant Westenenk (the Netherlands) were thus asked to leave Ottoman territory.

The time for diplomacy and reform had ended. Contrary to what Turkish and some Armenian historians argue, it was not the ARF that called for the creation of Armenian battalions in the vanguard of Russian mobilization but Vorontsov-Dashkov, Governor General of the Caucasus Viceroyalty and the Armenian Catholicos Kevork V. Both men worked to mobilize Armenian anti-Turkish sentiment in the war effort, Russian cynicism even going so far as to deploy 250,000 Armenian conscripts to fight the Germans on the Western front. The imperial calculation was simple, however: what was being promoted were the interests of Russia, not those of Armenians.

The ARF and the CUP

With respect to the central issue of the December 1907 agreement between the ARF and the Young Turks, we should remember that this was not the first time the ARF had contacted the Turkish leadership. In 1896, following the ARF assault on the Ottoman Bank, Sultan Abdul Hamid dispatched a delegation under Haroutioun Pasha Dadian to ARF's Genevan headquarters to mediate the resumption of reforms in Armenian Eastern Anatolia in exchange for a cessation of revolutionary hostilities. After four rounds of negotiations between 1896 and 1898, no agreement was reached and party leadership decided that it was up to the sultan to take the first step and that the decision to suspend armed operations was incumbent upon militants in the field, not the political leadership who were, after all, far removed from realities on the ground. Dashnak party members among the remote provinces of the empire also considered that the decision should be left to the second congress of the ARF, planned for 1898. Finally, the second congress voted to pursue revolutionary action, including preparations for an attack on Sultan Abdul Hamid II.

After this failure, the ARF was approached by the Young Turks, notably Ahmed Riza, to collaborate in overthrowing the sultan and restoring the Constitution of 1876. A 1902 Paris meeting of the sultan's opponents proved unproductive because the participants were not sufficiently prepared to act. Christapor Mikaelian categorically rejected any alliance, going so far as to publish this decision in an October 1900 article, 'Union with the Turks', in the party organ, *Droshak* (Standard).[13] Mikaelian wrote: 'So long as the Turkish opponents have not proved their revolutionary conviction on the ground by concrete political acts against the sultan, a union, any union is impossible.' He further intended to negotiate with the Young Turks on an equal footing and firmly opposed any pact with the nationalist branch of Ahmed Riza who, in his opinion, defended options against the Armenian Question and the Armenian people more firmly than against the sultan himself.[14] Knowing the reputation of Abdul Hamid II, the words of Mikaelian suggest the strong reservations one of the main leaders of the Young Turks movement inspired in him. He was even cautious about the idea of fighting alongside the Turks for the reestablishment of the 1876 Constitution. As he

---

[13] *Droshak*, October 1900.
[14] *Lettres de Christapor Mikaelian*, Publication of the ARF Dachnaktsoutioun (Edition Hamaskaïne, 1993), pp. 110–114.

was suspicious of Turkish nationalism, he wrote to his comrades in Paris on 24 January 1900 that he perceived in this instrument of fundamental law the means by which to strangle the Armenian Question and to remove it from the international arena. Everything seems to indicate that the ARF was a long way from signing a strategic alliance with Turkish opponents to the sultan.[15]

At the end of the second congress of the opposition parties to the sultan, which took place in Paris in December 1907, the ARF signed an agreement with Ahmed Riza's CUP and endorsed the reestablishment of the 1876 Constitution. The ARF ceased all political violence in the Ottoman Empire, ended its illegal activities and suspended the publication in Paris of its journal, *Pro Armenia*. How, then, can one explain the ARF's about-face? First, the death of Christapor Mikaelian in Bulgaria on 5 March 1905, while handling a bomb intended for Sultan Abdul Hamid II, left the ARF without leadership. The main obstacle to signing having been accidentally dismissed, the way of the alliance might be considered in another light. There were other reasons for this shift. The ARF was emerging from a revolutionary phase that had been particularly challenging. The Sasun insurrection planned for 1905 had been defeated by a pre-emptive attack by the Ottoman army in 1904. Several *fedayi* leaders had been killed – Hraïr Tejork, Achot Yergat, Kaïl Vahan, Vahan Manouelian and Torkom in 1904, Mrav in 1905 and Kevork Tchavouch in 1907 – and the party's military apparatus was in disarray.[16] In the Caucasus, the 1905 agreement signed with the Tatars following a year of conflict and bloody exactions on both sides, showed that peace between Christians and Muslims was achievable. Dashnak leaders had shown they were capable of achieving a union with lay Turkish and Persian Muslims when, in 1906/1907, the ARF aligned themselves with the Iranian revolutionaries for the proclamation of a first constitution for the Persian Empire.

If the Dashnak networks in the Russian Caucasus were methodically dismantled and ARF leaders arrested and thrown into prison, the party leadership judged that an alliance with the Young Turks' CUP would vastly improve prospects for success in Ottoman territories and create a base for withdrawal and a refuge for ARF leadership in the Caucasus. Some European socialists, such as Jean Jaurès and Pierre Quillard, editor-in-chief of *Pro Armenia*, urged Armenians to seal a partnership with the Young Turks against the sultan – an option that would confirm the Dashnak candidacy put forward at the Second International in 1905 and voted at the 1907 Stuttgart Congress. Finally, in the spring of 1907 at the fourth congress of the ARF, held in Vienna at Austrian socialist headquarters, the scene was set for the fraternizing between the ARF and the CUP. The congress advocated federalism in both empires and endorsed the decision to merge the two causes (Ottoman and Caucasian Armenia), as if a boundary between the Russian and Ottoman Empires no longer existed. This reversal counteracted all rational geopolitical representations and formed the cornerstone of the ARF's strategic model for the Dashnak doctrine. A complete surprise to the international

---

[15] Ibid.

[16] 'Fedayi' is a term borrowed from the Arabic *fedayeen* – he who would 'endure martyrdom for a cause', a devotee or warrior.

system organized around state borders, the fourth congress of the ARF merged the two-state proposal into one for a single Armenian state, a purely imaginary political reality given the situation on the ground. The fundamental error of the ARF was to adopt a system of representation that takes a direction completely at odds with the various European imperial strategies, resulting in total incomprehension by Concert of Europe. The congress adopted an asymmetrical strategy in favour of Turkish Armenia, even though it was the architect for the cause of liberating Caucasian Armenia. But this promotion never meant equality or fusion of the two fronts.

It was therefore a beleaguered ARF who signed the 1907 agreement with the CUP. An agreement challenged from within by Antranik, Roupen and Ichkhran de Van, for whom the July 1908 crisis was in no way a revolution, but a *coup d'état* fomented by the military whose ambition was to save the empire and to maintain dominance over the other nationalities making up the state. Dashnak leadership, composed essentially of Caucasus Armenians, pursued its course of extolling the progressive spirit of the country's new leaders. The ARF participated in the 1908 legislative elections on an electoral list related to the CUP and won four out of 14 parliamentary seats from the Armenian millet and a total 288 parliamentary seats. The ARF thus became the legitimate interlocutor of state power, so that it was necessary to remove opponents of the agreement with the Young Turks.[17] Soon, however, tensions resurfaced following the Adana massacres. Antranik and Roupen Ter-Minassian hoped for a break in relations with the Ottoman power. even as the Party leadership prepared its fifth congress in Bulgaria (September 1909). At the initiative of their parliamentary deputies and only a few days before the the meeting opened, the Constantinople Dashnaks signed a new agreement with the CUP. Mikael Varandian, the ARF theorist and editor-in-chief of *Droshak*, pushed his cynicism so far as to publicly denounce those Armenians of Cilicia who, shortly before the Adana massacres, brandished 'emblems, national flags, effigies of Armenian kings and other chauvinistic acts'.[18] This led to total incomprehension among party minorities, including among the Hunchakian democrats (the Social Democrat Hunchakian Party). But the alliance resumed its course, with the ARF introducing socialist theories into Ottoman public discourse, while fully supporting the constitution, constitutional governance and the principles of equality among Ottoman subjects. For the party, acting as a guarantor of constitutional legality led to the mistaken idea that it could contain the excesses of the CUP when the latter broke with Ottomanism in 1909, to embrace social Darwinism and pan-Turkish nationalism driving the homogeneity of the Turkish race. The Dashnak leadership were not fooled. For them, too, the crisis of Adana was, from the beginning, an internal transformation characterized as 'saving face'. Publicly, the ARF behaved as a loyal partner of the CUP, supporting the CUP leadership wherever possible and denouncing Italian aggression in Tripolitania. Internally, it mobilized its military arm from 1910

---

[17] Gaïdz Minassian, 'Les relations entre la ARF et le CUP', *Revue d'Histoire arménienne contemporaine*, I, 1995, pp. 45–99.

[18] Mikael Varandian, *La patrie renaissante et notre rôle*, in 2 volumes (Geneva: Publication ARF, 1910), p. 135. This subject is repeated in *Droshak* nos 7, 8 and 9 (June, July and August 1909), in a long article in three parts, 'The Situation and our Responsibilities'.

and began to stockpile weapons to cover all eventualities. In 1909, Roupen Ter-Minassian had attempted, unsuccessfully, to free himself from the Ottoman Empire by creating a revolutionary front composed of all nationalities and changing the ARF's name to the 'Revolutionary Federation'.

Following several imperial crises, the Italian–Turkish War of 1911, the *coup d'état* against the CUP in 1912 and a social crisis that pitted the CUP against the ARF, democratic illusion gave way to disenchantment. The conditions for a political break had been created and the ARF acted. At the conclusion of the 1911 sixth congress of the *Dashnaktsutyun*, the ARF voted to break with the Young Turks. However, the ARF leadership did not want to make the announcement in the middle of the Italian–Turkish War and waited until 18 July 1912, having made every attempt to bring the CUP back on board. For the Dashnaks, the decline of the state, the failure of public authority in the countryside, the anachronistic nature of Ottoman society and the CUP's renunciation of democratic reform were the reasons given for this fateful decision. The ARF gradually returned to their underground existence, transferring its decision-making processes back to *Yerkir*, the rural areas where they had strong support.

The Balkan wars further focused tensions within the ARF. The party's Bulgarian branch entered the war on the side of the coalition of Christian states. Armenian volunteer battalions were mustered under the leadership of Antranik and Karekin Nejteh. The ARF formally condemned the Balkan states for their aggressive posture but no longer had the means to maintain its troops in Bulgaria. Many Turkish historians use this Dashnak support for the Balkan revolt to justify their thesis of Armenian betrayal as early as 1912, while forgetting that these Armenians were, in fact, Bulgarian citizens, beginning with Antranik and Karekin Nejteh, both of whom were performing their national military service in Sofia.

The ARF held its landmark eighth congress in Erzerum in 1914, just as the war broke out in Western Europe. At the congress, four trends emerged with respect to an eventual Armenian orientation vis-à-vis the European conflict.[19] The pro-Turkish line represented a very small minority view: Ruben Ter-Minassian even proposed to muster an Armenian force to fight alongside the Ottoman army against Russia. The pro-European current, embodied by Roupen Zartarian and Agnouni, was also in the minority. Hamazasp proposed that an Armenian force be constituted to go along with the Russian Army, a proposal that was rejected by the congress. Ultimately, the loyalist current that would prevail: Armenians must fulfil their civic duties in their own native communities. The congress then urged Turkey to proclaim its neutrality. Dispatched by the CUP on a last-ditch mission to include the ARF in a governing coalition, Dr Behaeddin Chakir was informed of the position of the ARF and responded: 'This is a conspiracy! At such a critical moment, you would support the Russians and refuse to defend the government.'[20] Just how does one construe a proclamation of respect for loyalty to two states as a 'conspiracy' or even, as 'support for Russia'? What deniers have maintained for decades, namely that the ARF had decided to fight alongside the

[19] Vratsian (n. 4) vol II, p. 228.
[20] *Armenia*, no 29, 16 February 1916.

Russians, is an historical error. The eighth congress did not decide this but left the question for Dashnaks in the Caucasus to settle. Within party circles, tempers flared. In Constantinople, Armen Garo urged his comrades in the Caucasus to create battalions under Russian command, while deputies Vartkes Serungulian and Krikor Zohrab (independent) supported the creation of battalions freed from all tutelage. In fact, the first steps were taken by Russian political and Armenian religious authorities. Dashnak military leaders had already mobilized and the Social Democrat Hunchakian Party (SDHP) in the Caucasus and throughout the Ottoman Empire favoured the creation of special Armenian units to serve under Russian command. Here, without a doubt, was the single greatest error of this party.

In Tbilisi, Simon Vratsian requested that fellow Dashnak, Armen Garo, return to Ottoman territory, fearing that any agitation to create an Armenian force in the Russian Caucasus would endanger the safety of Armenians in Turkey. A former representative from Erzerum to the Ottoman parliament – Talaat Pasha had done everything to prevent him from re-election – Garo's action is often cited by contemporary Turkish historians as evidence of Armenian betrayal in justifying the genocide. Negationists, however, cite the Armenian revolt in Van (April 1915) as justification for the repression and deportations, while forgetting three fundamental facts: first, that Dashnak leadership in Van, notably Aram Manoukian and Hovannes Katchaznouni, firmly opposed the creation of pro-Russian battalions. Second, on 16 and 17 April 1915, several Dashnak leaders, including Ichkhran and MP Archag Vramian were assassinated by Turks on CUP orders. Under such circumstances, the Dashnak leadership in Van, fearing reprizals, called on Armenian youth to reject the mobilization order. Finally, Armenian persecution in the region of Van had already begun. In order to avoid reprizals, local Armenians were obliged to call upon Dashnak leadership to organize their own defence. How can one denounce the April revolt in Van when the massacres began in Erzerum and Cilicia in January and February 1915, against the backdrop of Turkish defeat at Sarikamich in January of the same year?

'Bloodletting'

With respect to Armenian unity, the problem was twofold: Could the parties unite? Could progressives and conservatives, lay and religious look in the same direction? Between 1890 and 1908 several attempts were made to create unity. All failed. From its inception, the founders of the ARF insisted on forming a single organization to federate Armenian interests. The SDHP exited the Federation soon after it was founded, considering it insufficiently 'socialist'. The alliance was never actually consummated because the two main leaders, Christapor Mikaelian (ARF) and Avedis Nazarbekian (SDHP) could not agree. Following the massacres at Van in 1896, internal differences within the SDHP led to further divisions and disagreements regarding centralized functions and the place of socialism within the party. The majority and factions supportive of a centralized party system, aligned themselves and remained loyal to Nazarbekian. A minority group broke away and reformed itself as the party of the Hunchakian Refounders. The ARF attempted an alliance with the Refounders but, distrusting their leader, the writer Arpiar Arpiarian, whom the ARF accused of sharing intelligence with the sultan's secret services, suspended all contact with the Refounders. The party leader, Arpiarian, was assassinated in Cairo on 12 February 1908 by terrorists working for the SDHP.[21]

The question for all became what position should be taken apropos Ottoman power. Until the Revolution of 1908, the break between the religious and the revolutionary was clear. The Armenian Patriarchate in Constantinople was recognized as the official interlocutor of the Sublime Porte and led the fight against the revolutionary pressures that threatened the public order and the integrity of the Armenian millet. For the revolutionary parties, it was precisely the inaction of the religious hierarchy which exacerbated Armenian insecurity, especially in the provinces. Beginning in 1908, the divide came to be less about the revolutionary or religious orientation of the Armenian struggle as it was about the role of parliament and the struggle between constitutionalists and anti-constitutionalists.

In 1908, the SDHP rejected any collaboration with the CUP while the Hunchakian Refounders and Armenian conservatives close to the Patriarchate of Constantinople joined the ARF alongside the new Ottoman power. Contrary to what some Armenian historians argue, it was not just the ARF who collaborated with the CUP, but the majority of Armenian political forces. This became even clearer on the evening of the failure of the April 1909 counter-revolution when, in the Armenian National Chamber – a legislative body attached to the Patriarchate – voices rose to proclaim 'Long live the Constitution, long live the CUP and long live the Ottoman Empire'. One cannot suspect that this Chamber was in the hands of the ARF, even if the Federation's status as a privileged interlocutor of state power gave it a certain base within this body. The ARF, however, remained a minority. Similarly, the matter raised in 1912 concerning whether the Armenian Question should be submitted for international review by the Great Powers, was not a matter for the ARF but for religious authorities, including the Patriarchate and its National Chamber, which decided on 21 December 1912 to defer the question of Armenian reform to the European powers. For the ARF, reviving the spectacle of the Treaty of Berlin, Article 61 did not seem like a good idea; if Armenians wished to serve as an instrument in the hands of the European chancelleries, the Ottomans knew only too well how to deflect and manipulate the resulting pressures. It was not until 1913, following the *coup d'état*, that the ARF gradually acquiesced to the internationalization of the Armenian Question, all the while opposing the Russian–Turkish project of February 1914, because it was contrary to the principle of a unified Armenian territory.

When the Ottoman Empire entered the war in November 1914, the Imperial Special Organization was already in place. It was supervised by Dr Behaeddin Chakir and charged with the dirty work of the massacres. Armenian conscripts of the Ottoman army were disarmed and reformed as the first battalions of soldier-labourers, the famous *amele tabouri*, officially assigned to 'works of public utility'. The decision to exterminate Armenians was made between 20 and 25 March 1915 after several meetings of the Committee on Union and Progress, gathered in Constantinople

---

[21] Stéphan Chahbaz, *Arpiar Arpiarian*, Altapress, Beyrouth, 1988.

following the return from Erzerum of Chakir. On the night of 23–24 April 1915, when the Allies attempted a landing in the Straits of the Dardanelles, the Turkish authorities rounded up nearly 250 Armenian notables in Constantinople and ten times that number (2,342 persons) throughout the empire.

The genocide that followed was the single worst civil disaster of the First World War. The lives of 1.5 million men, women and children were either disrupted by exile and deportation, or simply ended on the spot. The liberation of Van on 19 May 1915 by the troops of Dro, commander of the 2nd Armenian Volunteer Battalion in the vanguard of the Russian army offered a glimmer of hope in the face of 55,000 deaths in the vicinity of the citadel city. The Turkish thesis, supported by historians such as Robert Mantran, recalls that the Turks also suffered at the hands of the Russians and vengeful Armenians.[22] The advance of the Russian armies on the Caucasian front was claimed as reprisals and war crimes against Turkish civilians left to themselves by the retreating Turks. Near Van (May 1915) but also in Erzerum (February 1916), Trebizond (April 1916) and Erzindjan (July 1916), where the Russian army advanced into Ottoman territory, there were numerous reprisals against Muslim populations unable to anticipate troop movements. Responsibility for these abuses is blurred. Some Russian sources cite the active involvement of Armenian soldiers. Armenian sources describe Armenian battalion leaders acting on orders from the Russian General Staff. Is it fair, though, to compare the meticulously planned and executed mass extermination and the reprisals that the Turks describe as war crimes? A planned genocide perpetrated across the greater part of Ottoman territory could only have been the prerogative of a state whose intention must have been to 'eliminate the Armenian nation', wrote the US Ambassador to Constantinople, Henry Morgenthau.[23] Common sense requires that pro-Turkish sources at least recognize that genocide is a separate case in a hierarchy of crimes against humanity. This same falsely comparative approach was taken again following the Second World War, with Holocaust deniers describing the intentional fire-bombing of Dresden between 13 and 15 February 1945, in which many tens of thousands of German civilians were killed, as a crime against humanity equivalent to the Jewish Holocaust. Following the destruction of 1915–1917, nothing was left of the ancient civilization of Eastern Anatolia. The survivors found themselves in camps in the Syrian desert. Only the Armenians of Constantinople and Smyrna were spared. Everywhere else they were massacred, in Ottoman Europe, Asia Minor and the Caucasus.

To summarize, the defects of the international system, a European diplomacy of complicity, the metamorphoses of Ottomanism into Turkish nationalism and confusion over the crisis of July 1908 – was it a revolution or a *coup d'état*? – went a long way to explaining how the Ottoman state went from unpunished massacres in 1894–1896 to the genocide of 1915. In one of his conversations with Morgenthau, Talaat Pasha said of the Armenians: 'We have put an end to the Armenian Question, we have eliminated the Armenians because they wanted to extricate themselves from our domination.'[24] In

---

[22] Robert Mantran, *Histoire de l'Empire Ottoman* (Fayard, 1992), p. 624.
[23] Henry Morganthau, *Ambassador Morganthau's Story* (New York, 1918), chapter XXIV.
[24] Cited by Gérard Chaliand and Yves Ternon, *Le génocide des Arméniens* (Brussels: Editions Complexe, 1984), p. 112.

1919, at the Versailles peace conference, Lloyd George, British Prime Minister, declared: 'Armenia was sacrificed on the triumphal altar that we erected',[25] referring, of course, to the negotiations concerning reforms in eastern Anatolia. From the Armenian perspective, two lessons were to be learnt from this extinction. First, the Armenian parties did not achieve in the 1908 revolution the political objectives for which they had been created. One might ask whether, in fact, the objectives were ever achievable. This question leads to the second lesson: was it reasonable for a party like the ARF with its many weaknesses (loose governance structures, a history of clandestine behaviour, lack of electoral experience, an insufficient popular base among the Anatolian peasantry and limited military experience) to stake for itself such a strong symbolic position? The Armenian parties' legal standing as players in opposition to the declining Ottoman power and a resurgent popular movement (the CUP) required considerable resources and an organizational capacity that the Armenian community simply did not possess.

1920, political extinction: The double challenge

By 1920, Armenians had been totally caught up in the genocide whirlwind. As the world watched helplessly – Russia, France and Great Britain delivered a missive addressed to the Sublime Porte dated 24 May 1915, which accused the Ottoman government of crimes against humanity and summoned the empire to give account of its actions when the conflict was over –Armenians stumbled through two other major events: the Bolshevik Revolution of October 1917 and the 1918 Turkish liberation struggle led by Mustafa Kemal against the allied powers seeking to enforce the Treaty of Sèvres. Armenia was caught in a pincer by these indissociable events, whose different stages led first to the birth of an independent Republic of Armenia and just as quickly to its death.

The world was watching what some historians such Georges-Henri Soutou have called 'the beginnings of the Cold War'.[26] The end of the 1914–1918 war confirmed the deaths of the Central and East European empires, creating dozens of nation states, often cobbled together from random administrative and ethnic boundaries. In Russia, a civil war raged between white and red Russians, even though political power was held by the Bolsheviks. Lenin seized upon the overthrow of the Romanoff dynasty to disengage Russia from the conflict and conclude a separate peace with Germany, signing the Treaty of Brest-Litovsk in February 1918. In accordance with the treaty, Russian armies withdrew from conquered territories, abandoning eastern Anatolia to itself and dashing Armenian hopes for retaking their ancestral territories. Here, then, was the revival of an autonomous Armenia, even if it had been emptied of its Armenian population. In Turkey, the war of liberation loomed on the horizon as an uprising of officers led by Mustafa Kemal against the sultan – the figurehead of an empire that no

---

[25] Cited by Dadrian (n. 2) p. 134.
[26] Interview with Georges-Henri Soutou, in *Le Monde*, special edition, February–April 1914, p. 8.

longer existed. The prospects for peace in Europe and the risk that the Allies would decide the fate of the Ottoman Empire to the detriment of Turkish power represented the worst fears of the Turkish insurgents. They condemned the cowardice of the Constantinople authorities, who seemed ready for any compromise if it would secure continuity and bureaucratic power. The prospect of dismantling the Osmanli Empire provoked great anguish among the insurgents, whose nationalist ideas for a Turkey which would be free of British, Italian, Greek, French and Armenian influence had become very popular.

Second, the victorious allies were wary of Bolshevik Russia and of its first attempts to cultivate proletarian revolution in Germany. To guard against this, the Allies attempted to isolate the Bolsheviks by supporting both politically and militarily the white Russians as well as those states struggling with the communist threat. In the final months of the war, the British took control of the three states of the South Caucasus to prevent the Germans from getting their hands on Baku's oil. At the end of the war, London reinforced its presence in the Caucasus as a means of protecting its Indian holdings as well as to containing the communist push southward. Regarding Turkey, the Allies preferred the cooperation of authorities in Constantinople while remaining distrustful and even dismissive of the Kemalist movement. The priority was to monitor communism and prevent the Bolsheviks from getting their hands on the riches of the Middle East, whether under British or French mandate.

Finally, the presence of Western forces in an ethnic Russian or Turkish region served to draw Kemalist and Bolshevik antagonists who, from 1919 overpowered their respective rivals and found common cause in excluding outside interference. Armenia thus found itself between Turkey and the Bolsheviks. Another form of bilateral connivance, the Lenin-Kemal duo, served to reinforce the Bolshevik perception of Armenia as a 'Bourgeois Republic', whose existence was based only upon the Allies' willingness to cultivate support in the region for weakening their sworn enemies. As for the Kemalists, their opposition to Armenia is not only historical but political and strategic: to fight against Armenia amounted to rejection of the Sèvres plan, namely a vision of a Turkish Republic reduced to its Cappadocian perimeter. The independence of Greater Armenia was therefore an aberration for Russo-Turkish shared interests. For the Bolsheviks, Armenia required effective Soviet domination and protection from the Turkish threat. For Kemalist Turkey, the key was an independent Armenia occupying its own Caucasian space and without any trace of its Eastern Anatolia remnants and free of any foreign presence. Faced with this Kemalist–Bolshevik alliance, the European commitment to colonial administration, their limited expeditionary forces and the lack of appetite to relive the carnage and butchery of 1914–1918 seemed insignificant indeed. Nobody wanted to fight for the Caucasus and certainly not for Armenia, a country that had been an ally during the war but also one that could be sacrificed as a matter of reorganizing the two former empires, despite promises and treaties to the contrary. Armenia became all the more dispensable as the Allies came to see in Kemalist Turkey an independent and stable bulwark to fight against the spread of communism. From an initial Kemalist–Bolshevik collusion against Armenia, the new international order would henceforth favour Turkish–European combinations, with Britain and France at the forefront.

An independent state, but for how long?

In the international game, the Armenian government had to overcome three challenges. The first was to restore an independent state and establish it for the long term. Composed mainly of former refugees and without a political centre – the first ministers' councils of the Armenian government of Hovannes Katchaznouni met in Tbilisi and not in Yerevan – possessing neither an economy nor social organization, Armenia struggled to recover from the ordeals of war and genocide. One of the peculiarities of this new sovereignty was its genesis. At first, the October Revolution prompted the three main Caucasian administrative entities to assemble in a Transcaucasian Federal Republic to ensure continuity and stability, to pool reconstruction efforts and jointly address the harshness of war in the Caucasus. But the powers decided otherwise. What was initially an original and supranational idea, favourable to peace and federalism and proposed as a rampart against nationalism and the risks of inter-ethnic conflicts, was destroyed by the Germans and the Turks. The former targeted Georgia to control the flow of oil from Baku. The Ottoman Empire, still in the hands of the Young Turks, co-opted Azerbaijan, playing the pan-Turkism card. Armenia remained stuck in the middle, without any prospects if not to take control of its own destiny and face political modernity. Upon declaring its sovereignty, the Republic of Armenia had an area of 11,000 square kilometres. Its territory, however, was destined to evolve according to various clauses and treaties engaged to end the war. Here again, even if the elites of the three Transcaucasian nations shared responsibility for the collapse of the Transcaucasian Republic, the neighbouring powers favoured the defence of their national interests. From the moment Armenia became independent, the question of borders was raised, crystallizing local passions, especially on the former Tsarist, multi-ethnic administrative districts. Such was the case in the Gandja district upon which Karabakh depended, the scene of armed conflict and ethnic killings of Armenians, but also of the Nakhichevan district, which had also been transformed into a war zone with attendant massacres. The tensions were such that, during its 30 months of independence, Armenia was at war with all its neighbours except Iran. In the eyes of many observers, the Republic of Armenia was an example of a republic in permanent conflict, headed by hawkish governments.

Restoring an independent state required from its authorities the assumption of an entirely new diplomatic role. As a first exercise in foreign policy, Yerevan's sovereignty over its territory required international recognition among the community of nations, allowing Armenia to erect a multilateral framework of existence and responsibility in matters of peace and security. The Peace Conference refused to invite as permanent members the former enemy powers or the young states under construction, whatever their position during the First World War: whether pro-Triple Entente or pro-Triple Alliance. This proved to be a cold shower for Armenia, an ally to the Entente on both fronts. Despite calls from some politicians, the Gang of Four (Clemenceau, Wilson, Lloyd George and Orlando) remained firm in its position: Armenian sovereignty would only be recognized by a decision of the Council of the League of Nations, meeting in session between 19 and 27 January 1920, almost two years after the proclamation of independence of the First Republic of Armenia. The government did its best to open diplomatic representations to ensure state security and visibility among the community of nations, going so far as to open an Armenian legation in Japan, where Armenia was represented by Diana Abkar (real name Aghabekian) (1854–1937). Some would suggest that this extension to Tokyo was pointless. That said, Japan participated actively in the peace negotiations and was among the signatories of the Treaty of Sèvres on 10 August 1920. Thus, the establishment of diplomatic relations with Japan could not really be presented as shocking.

The restoration of the state also meant securing its borders and, if possible, revising them given that the Ottoman Empire was on the losing side in the war. In 1918, Armenia had been reduced to 11,000 square kilometres; by the summer of 1919, following the Treaty of Moudros signed between the Allies and the Ottoman Empire on 30 October 1918, it had been expanded to 46,000 km². In accordance with the terms of the treaty, the Ottoman Empire was to return to its pre-war borders and surrender the provinces of Alexandropol and Kars to the Republic of Armenia. This provoked Turkish anger; they were upset about returning confiscated territories to Armenians. Thanks to British intervention, Yerevan prevailed in its case for repossession of the province of Kars. Armenia also expanded southward with the integration of Nakhchivan, a province of mixed ethnic composition and to the north, gaining control of Lori province and obtaining a co-management agreement for control of the Akhalkalaki province with the Georgians. In the East, the Karabakh territory raised heated controversy but, despite its ethnic Armenian majority, it was awarded by English arbitration to Azerbaijan. Western Armenia itself became the object of intense competition between the Turks and Armenians on the one hand and the Russians and Allies on the other. Just as they had in April 1917, the Provisional Russian Government, emanating from the February Revolution, granted autonomous status to Turkish Armenia. In January 1918, Lenin and Stalin, the Nationalities Commissioner, signed the decree authorizing Armenian self-determination. Such an overview of the evolution of Armenian borders resonates strongly with Armenia in the twenty-first century. All the issues on the Yerevan agenda in 2015 had been subject to special examination a century earlier.

Finally, restoration of the nation state required the integration of populations established within the borders. However, the difficulty for the authorities turned out to be how to ensure harmonious cohabitation between Armenian refugees from Turkish Armenia with Tatar-Turkish (Azerbaijani) populations, a nearly impossible combination as the inter-ethnic relations were strained and the two groups were at loggerheads. As long as the Federative Republic of Transcaucasia existed, the illusion of civil order prevailed, but reciprocal hatreds are stubborn and it took only a spark to set off the powder keg. Furthermore, no sooner had they been constituted, than the three nation-states exchanged the spirit of national solidarity and neighbourliness for nationalist bickering. In Armenia, reconstruction of the national community required that the state provide security and social stability.

The Armenian government, however, failed to manage as it should have the integration of Muslims living in the territory of the republic, especially as Muslim refugees continued to flock towards centres of opportunity consistent with the completely random system of border protection. Between 1914 and 1923, the Caucasus and Eastern Anatolia were the scene of massacres, forced displacement and other abuses. Armenians very often found themselves on the wrong side of the balance of power, subject to massacres in their homelands. Driven out of Baku, Tbilisi and other ethnically mixed regions, Armenians turned out to be the big historical losers. In this context of survival, among the arrangements made in Yerevan and unbeknownst to the government, Roupen Ter-Minassian, then minister of defence, launched 'the fierce plan' in the summer of 1920.[27] Developed with former Armenian fedayi (militia) chiefs, this called for the forcible expulsion of Muslims from the lower Araxe valley. At that time, there were 600,000–700,000 Muslims in Armenia. In 1926, the first census under the communists, Soviet Armenia numbered 881,000 inhabitants, 84.4 per cent of whom were Armenians, 10.1 per cent Azerbaijanis and 0.3 per cent Kurds.[28] Where did the Muslims go? According to Anahide Ter-Minassian, these statistics make it possible 'to get a better idea of the events of the summer of 1920'. Indeed, this demographic question was also raised for the Armenians of Baku, Karabakh and Nakhichevan, who, if not massacred, had at the very least been driven from their homes. Most Muslims were expelled and, as one might expect, suffered hardships. In these population movements, abuses were certainly committed by the troops of Ter-Minassian. It is impossible to give an exact number of deaths, but at that time, whether by Ter-Minassian or the by Armenian authorities, there was no intention of exterminating Muslims as such. However, Anahide Ter-Minassian and other post-independence historians refer to these tragic events as an 'Armenization' policy, while the thesis of ethnic cleansing cannot be ruled out.[29] The works in the Armenian language that mention these facts openly use the words 'pureratsum' and 'makrakordzum', which mean respectively 'purification' and 'cleaning'. Armenia and its neighbours were embarking upon the formation of a nation state, centralized and with a tendency towards integrating populations, including the most refractory. These violent acts were instigated by a minister of defence who was worried about the threat of pan-Turkism and Azerbaijani nationalism, whose maps all but denied Armenian existence in the Caucasus.

Finally, at that time, Armenia seemed locked in deadlock. Georgia was supported by the British. Azerbaijan was supported by the Turks and the British. Armenia could only turn towards Russia, but Russia was too far away and itself torn by civil war. By September 1920, with the state in turmoil and most government officials unaware of the abuses, Simon Vratsian, the last prime minister of independent Armenia, went so far as to publicly reprove Roupen Ter-Minassian, 'You are an Ittihadist!',[30] using the name of the Young Turk party, the authors of the 1915 genocide. At no time, however, did Roupen Ter-Minassian, either in his memoirs or in other writings, express any regrets about this policy. Rather, he gave a cold reading of these events and continues to enjoy, among certain Armenian historians, great respect for 'Armenizing' the state.

[27] See also Annie and Jean-Pierre Mahé, (n. 3) p. 522; Roupen Ter-Minassian, *Mémoire d'un révolutionnaire arménien*, 7 vols, 2nd edn (Beyrouth: Hamaskaïne, 1972), Anahide Ter-Minassian, *La République d'Arménie* (Bruxelles: Editions Complexe, 1989), p. 216.
[28] Ibid, Anahide Ter-Minassian, p. 217.
[29] Anahide Ter-Minassian, 'The Role of the Individual: The Case of Rouben Ter-Minassian' (1993) 46(1–4) *Armenian Review* 181–184; Achot Nercisyan, *Edit Print* (Erevan, 2007), p. 281.
[30] Vratsian (n. 4) tome IV, p. 190.

What alliance for what protection?

The second challenge for Armenia concerns the need for strategic alliances. Should Armenia align with the West or with Bolshevik Russia? The question was posed in all the newly independent states of Central and Eastern Europe, those who were born after the fall of the empires and found themselves torn between the freedom ideal peculiar to Western Europe and the pragmatism imposed by their direct proximity with Communist Russia. Armenia was faced with manoeuvring between two types of domination, one respectful of its sovereignty, the other willing to integrate the communist mould: nothing new for a state whose history was a permanent back and forth between East and West. Indeed, the Republic of Armenia, with its narrow margin for manoeuvre, was faced with choosing between two types of peace, two modes of development and two civilizations. Under such circumstances, the Armenian authorities, preferring discretion in their choice, opted for a methodology that called for the accompaniment of historical events without anticipation, such that by riding the wave of power they negotiated with all powers. As early as 1918, Yerevan, among Triple Entente Allies, enjoyed the benefits that were provided by the First World War. The defeat of the Ottoman Empire ensured an enlargement of its borders, while British trusteeship of the South Caucasus states offered a privileged link with the victorious western Europeans – especially as Russia drifted off into civil war, so that by the end of the First World War no one could predict the outcome of the Russian contest for dominance in St Petersburg. At the same time, the Armenian government played the cautious card, exiting from the war while forging relations with both the white Russians and with the Bolsheviks, the country's relatively weak geopolitical position mitigating against open alignment with one or the other camp. Based on Woodrow Wilson's Fourteen Points and direct US intervention in the region, Armenia saw a way out. Since the Ottoman Empire had lost the war and would be held accountable to the Peace Conference for its responsibility in the conflict and as the victim of crimes against humanity perpetrated by the Ottomans, the Republic of Armenia had a direct interest in collaborating with the Western victors. It was all the more interesting given that prospects were favourable for creating a Greater Armenia, as proposed by the 1920 Treaty of Sèvres. The linkage of Armenia to Western Europe could have been rendered definitive had the United States accepted the Armenian mandate, as President Woodrow Wilson wished. But the US Senate rejected this proposal in June 1920, on the grounds that the mandate was to be exercised throughout the South Caucasus and not simply for one of the states allied during the war. It was between the spring and summer of 1920 that things got complicated for Yerevan. While negotiations between Kemalists and Bolsheviks accelerated both with respect to the bourgeois republics of the Caucasus but also in terms of overturning the Treaty of Sèvres, the Armenian government refused to give up the Western parts of the map, considering that the Allies would never grant territorial gains to Armenia if it were to pass under Soviet tutelage. It was for this reason that, on 1 May 1920, the Armenian government violently suppressed a communist insurrection against the pro-Western Dashnak regime hostile to Bolshevik Russia. The revolt was put down by former Armenian fedayi leader Sebouh acting on orders from Roupen Ter-Minassian. The damage was done and the Bolshevik response fell squarely on Yerevan. If, on 10 August 1920, Armenia, the Western Allies and the Ottoman Empire signed the Treaty of Sèvres, on 24 August Moscow responded without equivocation, signing, at Turkey's request, a preliminary treaty without mention of territorial sovereignty, in which Russia undertook not to sign or recognize any international treaty not ratified by the Turkish Grand National Assembly, an exclusively Kemalist institution and to provide arms and gold to the troops of Mustafa Kemal, determined to put an end to Allied occupation of territories created by the Treaty of Sèvres. At the same time, the Dashnaks and Bolsheviks agreed in Tbilisi to stop the fighting between Armenian and communist partisans in Karabakh, Zanguezur and Nakhichevan. Armenia was thus embattled, with pressure of Turkey on one side and the appetite of Bolshevik Russia on the other. The realism of the Kemalist–Bolshevik pact superseded the idealism of an alliance with Westerners.

Had Armenians become over-reliant on the promise of Western solidarity? Without a doubt, but they had no choice. The fact remained, however, that when Armenia was attacked by the Turks in 1920, no Western power intervened in its favour. The mountains of Armenia were too far for an expeditionary force of Allied troops exhausted by 1914–1918. In the same way, when Armenia came under Soviet rule on 2 December 1920, putting an end to its independence, no Western state gave it any support.

The Turkish neighbourhood

In 1918, following the Treaty of Brest-Litovsk, the Ottoman Empire took advantage of the withdrawal of Russian troops to resume its offensive against Armenia. Every advance of Turkish troops resulted in new massacres of Armenians. In May 1918, the Armenian resistance blocked Turkish advances. Contrary to the Armenian version of the story, the spirit of Armenian resistance alone could not have stopped the Turkish offensive and produced three military victories upon which to found a nascent republic. The Ottoman Empire had bet that a South Caucasus neighbourhood, with a subdued and much diminished Armenia free of Russian tutelage, was to be preferred to a triumphant Russia poised on the Turkish border. On the Armenian side, pragmatism prevailed over the spirit of revenge. Indeed, it took courage for Foreign Minister Alexander Khatissian, at the head of an Armenian delegation, to travel to Constantinople between June and September 1918 to negotiate the future of Turkish–Armenian relations.[31] Pragmatism was all the more necessary considering that the Armenian delegation was to negotiate with the young Turks government represented by Talaat Pasha and others responsible for the 1915 genocide. Armenian refugees were still in the Syrian desert outside Deir ez-Zor and civil society was decaying while Yerevan amounted to little more than a refugee camp for the hungry and the destitute. Through all of this and despite the difficulties and pressing national interests, where did these men find the strength to negotiate with Turkey? As recounted in Khatissian's memoirs:

---

[31]   Alexandre Khatissian, *Eclosion et développement de la République d'Arménie*, Publication of the ARF *Dashnak*soutioun (Athens, 1989), pp. 107–122.

'As can well be imagined, the interview with Talaat was for us a torture.'[32] Two years later, Levon Chanth would refuse to negotiate with the Kemalists in the name of morality; we can only wonder how Khatissian and his fellow delegates, Avédis Aharonian and Mikaël Papadjanian, managed to stay composed. It is a challenge to understand a government that authorized its representatives to negotiate with the executioners while condoning the emotional reaction of a delegate who refused contact in the name of ethics. No doubt the issue was no longer one of consistency but the survival of what remained of national sovereignty. Be that as it may, Turkish-Soviet connivance put an end to Armenia's political independence on 2 December 1920, with the transfer of power to the communists.

Which national unity for which political project?

National unity had always been lacking, both with respect to the nature of the state and with respect to the question of Turkish Armenia. Since Haitadism pre-dates the nation state, the question of the relationship between ideology and state is paramount. Is Haitadism soluble in the state? Two schools clashed during this period. On the one hand, there was the democratic school that promoted the rule of law and institutional development, led by Alexander Khatissian, Simon Vratsian and Hovannes Katchaznouni for whom Armenia had become a sovereign state, requiring authorities to keep their commitments and put in place institutions respectful of fundamental freedoms, with a separation of power and a clear distinction between the affairs of the state and those of the party. While the ARF held an overwhelming majority of seats in the Parliament of 1919 (72 out of 80), in the eyes of these thinkers the ARF had to remain independent and resist the temptation to transform Armenia into a single-party state. It was for this reason that these men sought a government of national unity, neither of the right nor of the left, neither Dashnak nor Hunchak. On the other hand, the authoritarian school led by Aram Manoukian, Roupen Ter-Minassian and Hamo Ohandjanian considered that Armenia was an embattled state and that the first duty of a state at war was to secure national borders and the ensure public order. For these men, it was early to speak of reform, of separation of powers and other institutional modernizations. The ARF represented the overwhelming majority of voters and it was only fair that the powers of state should revert to the party. This would ensure popular integration, facilitate government action and accelerate the application of emergency measures. For them, national salvation lay in creating a revolutionary state governed by a 'World Bureau' of the ARF, a small government exclusively composed of Dashnak leaders. A state of law versus a revolutionary state; democrats versus republicans; the state versus the party. These were the choices that confronted the 1919 ARF congress (the ninth congress), meeting for the first time in an independent republic and ending with a compromise: the World Bureau would propose to parliament a list of members likely to form the government, including the name of the prime minister. In exchange, the

---

[32] Ibid, p. 110.

Dashnak party would refrain from direct intervention in the affairs of the executive. The compromise proved insufficient, however, since, from the first Bolshevik agitations in the spring of 1920, the World Bureau interfered directly in government affairs to restore order in the republic. In so doing, it overthrew the government of Khatissian to install a directorate headed by Ohandjanian.

The nature of the state is a determining factor for the nationalist expression that elites wish to promote. The integration of Turkish Armenians required that the state integrate their history and their aspirations. Not to do so and thereby to reject their hopes would be tantamount to declaring exclusion for this population. For more than a year, this question stirred public debate between supporters of full nationalism and those of republican nationalism. Armenians from Turkey, mostly refugees supported by fedayi chiefs, starting with the best known among them, Antranik, called for the restoration of a Greater Armenia and the appointment of some individuals to key institutional positions within the country. After a year of reflection, the government decided in favour of incorporating Western Armenians into the Civil Service, a decision symbolized by the Act for a Free, Independent and reunified Armenia, proclaimed on 28 May 1919, a year after independence. By this act, the Republic of Armenia expressed its claim of rights over the Western Armenian territories, its desire to integrate homeless Armenian populations and to incorporate their history. The Republic of Armenia sought, above all, recognition from the peace conference that ended only a few days after the Armenian parliament had completed its work on the Act. Paradoxically, this Act would have unfortunate consequences for Armenian unity. The other parties in the governing coalition, largely from the Caucasus, decided to leave the coalition in protest against a measure taken unilaterally or in a spirit of 'adventurism' peculiar to the Dashnak mentality. Boghos Noubar Pasha, president of the Armenian National Delegation and supporter of West Armenian inclusion, adopted contradictory attitudes. First, he envisaged the formation of a single, indivisible nation. Then he decided that the Republic of Armenia should not speak on behalf of Western Armenians and denounced the coup.

We find this same immaturity on the diplomatic level. A small country fragmented into small pieces, Armenia had the luxury of being represented at the peace conference by two opposing delegations. The first, heir to the Holy See of Etchmiadzin at the time of the 1912 reform movement, would speak primarily on behalf of Anatolian Armenians, while the second represented the newly created Armenian state. After a few months, the two delegations, one of whose legitimacy derived from religious authority, the other from secular, political authority, agreed to present a united front for the negotiations. Reconciliation had not been easy to achieve, especially regarding the question of borders. Contrary to the customary accounts given in the Armenian press, partisans of a Greater Armenia or, an Armenia-of-the-three-seas (Black, Mediterranean and Caspian or *Dzov é Dzov Haifastan*), were not the Dashnaks but Boghos Noubar Pacha. For the Republic of Armenia, it would be unreasonable to persist in claiming Cilicia, a maximalist position which the Allies would not have accepted but would have guaranteed a territorial equivalent to Armenia at its zenith under Tigranes the Great in the second century BC. For Boghos Nubar Pasha, however, an Armenian project which promoted reunification of Turkish and Caucasian Armenians without Cilicia would have been treasonous. In the interest of unity, the delegation presented the maximalist project, which was rejected as inadmissible because of Cilicia.

In fact, this belated unity, which shattered following the peace conference, reflects two things. On the one hand, those who recognized in the Republic of Armenia a pre-eminence to represent all Armenians and those who disputed the 'Dashnak Republic's' legitimacy in speaking for all Armenians. Hence the exacerbation of the division between Dashnak and anti-Dashnak. At the same time, there was the split between religious and political authorities. Would secular law voted by the republic have the ascendant over divine law recognized by the Armenian Church?

The Western powers' acquiescence in accepting Kemalist–Bolshevik conditions and their relative inability to help the small states combined to disappoint the legitimate aspirations of the Armenian people who desired freedom. Victims of their own ideals, these young states came up against the hard facts of history, geography and realpolitik. Historical circumstances and their respective geographies placed them in a situation in which Russia and Turkey were the only direct and inevitable neighbours, not Europe, much less the United States. The fact remains to this day, despite globalization and increasing global interdependence. Historical and geographical facts have always proved mightier than fine speeches and diplomacy that is not supported by action.

For Armenians in particular, many lessons were to be learned from this political extinction. First, independence was imposed by circumstances rather than desired by the community itself, the goal of self-determination had not been widely shared by the elites; sovereignty as an ideal will always yield priority to physical security. For the majority of Armenians, such fatalism is not a matter of weakness but of common sense. A second lesson is that party divisions can be fatal, as they were for Armenians. Finally, when neighbouring powers share a geostrategic perspective, they are likely to guard jealously against foreign intervention. In Armenia, geopolitical pragmatism was far more effective than idealism. Even if aspects of the Treaty of Sèvres still beat in the hearts of Armenians, the treaty was a thing of the past, buried by the Kemalists and Bolsheviks one evening in the autumn of 1920, during the Sovietization of Armenia.

1923, diplomatic extinction: The Armenian Question overtaken

Exterminated in Turkey, dominated in Russia, Armenians were in trouble, but all was not lost. A final test awaited them: to rescue the Armenian Question from oblivion. This would prove a diplomatic challenge beyond any they had so far encountered, as the demand was not based on a physical reality of occupied territory nor on the legality of the sovereign state and much less because of consensual understanding of the question. In the end, Armenians would emerge deeply divided from the Sovietization of the Caucasus.

Europe was slowly recovering from the First World War. Pacifism had become so widespread in Western societies that European governments hastened to negotiate peace with Mustafa Kemal not only to contain Bolshevik Russia, but also to prevent Turkey from pursuing strategic targets and oil fields in Iraq. With time, the Turks accomplished their objective of undermining Sèvres. Western Europeans, with the

British in the lead, accompanied the movement and unravelled the canvas of Sèvres, first with the London conference in February 1921, then with the Franco-Turkish agreement on the withdrawal of French troops from Cilicia in October 1921 and finally, with the 1923 Treaty of Lausanne which buried the Armenian Question once and for all. As proof, it should be noted that an Armenian delegation did not participate in the proceedings of the Lausanne Conference, Turkey having used its veto to refuse them a seat. In addition, the Turkish delegation made arrangements with the others to withhold publication of a treaty annex which granted a general amnesty to Turkish leaders who might have been charged for war crimes committed between 1914 and 1922. In reality, the 1923 balance of power favoured a triumphant Turkey, victorious over the Ottomans and in league with the Soviets. The clauses of the treaty referred only to 'non-Muslim minorities', the name 'Armenia' having entirely disappeared from the official documents. If the idea of a homeland for Turkish Armenians had been rejected initially by Armenian diplomats, the Armenian National Delegation finally agreed, while the Republic of Armenia delegation rejected the idea categorically. Ironically, it was the maximalists, led by Boghos Nubar Pasha who were satisfied with the most modest proposition, that of an Armenian homeland, an idea that, in the end, was rejected by Turkey.

Kemalist Turkey had manoeuvred so well that it managed to sign several treaties with Bolshevik Russia on behalf of the formerly independent Republics of Transcaucasia, thus blocking prospects for Georgians, Armenians and Azerbaijanis. The Armenian Question was thus emptied of its substance. In the East, Soviets and Turks smothered it with the provisions of the treaties of Moscow (16 March 1921) and Kars (13 October 1921). Neither Moscow nor Ankara wished to hear anything further about the Treaty of Sèvres. Soviet diplomats ironically offered the suggestion that if Armenians needed space, they could always settle in the Kuban region (southern Russia between the Black Sea and the Volga Delta). In the West, Turkey had freed itself of European humiliation, abolished the system of capitulations and rejected outside interference.

The Armenian Question did not vanish completely in the early 1920s. In the Caucasus, it experienced ups and downs, especially during the Bolshevik repression that swept Armenian society with Sovietization. Armenian communists tracked down Dashnaks, liquidating Armenian officers to avoid any risk of military retaliation. The repression was so strong, in fact, that on 18 February 1921, ten days before the insurrection of Kronstadt, the Armenians revolted and drove the Soviets out of Armenia. Soviet power returned to Yerevan in April, this time definitively.

Dashnaks and Bolsheviks

While the exiled communities settled as best they could into their adopted countries, far from massacres and revolution, the Armenian parties found themselves strongly divided between independents and legalists. The former, ranging themselves under the banner of an ARF and calling for peaceful and unarmed resistance, expected the Soviet regime to collapse quickly, especially since the rebellious spirit of 18 February 1921 was not shared by all Dashnak leaders.

The Legalists yoked themselves to a team of conservatives from the Ramgavar Party with pro-Soviet progressives of the SDHP, who saw in Soviet Armenia a guarantee of existence and security. In fact, the game was subtler than the rough attacks by each on the other might indicate. The Bolsheviks attempted to exploit dissension and sought to undermine the ARF not only in exile but also in Soviet Armenia. Unlike the other national parties of the formerly independent Republics, Soviet Armenian maintained a Dashnak presence in Yerevan, which, while clandestine, was tolerated to the extent that it organized four regional congresses up until 1933 and sent a delegation to the tenth congress of the ARF which was held in Paris in 1924. Shortly before this meeting, the communist regime ordered several waves of Dashnak arrests, organized the public trial of the ARF and called a special meeting for a vote on dissolution of the party in Soviet Armenia, a ridiculous move aimed at co-opting the Dashnak rank and file in favour of the Communist Party and undermining the work of party headquarters in Paris. The very real tensions between the Dashnaks and Bolsheviks did not prevent the existence of some channels for dialogue. For example, Moscow authorized Yerevan to issue a call for Armenian intellectuals, including Dashnaks, to return to the motherland.

Among Bolshevik attempts to destabilize the Dashnaks, the most elaborate was that of Hovannes Katchaznouni, former prime minister of the Republic of Armenia. In the spring of 1923, on the occasion of the party conference in Vienna, Austria, Katchaznouni, then working out of Bucharest, Romania, submitted a report on a party's action plan for the coming years. This report, 'There is nothing left for the ARF to do',[33] had a huge effect among the Dashnak ranks. Considering that it was more of a pamphlet than a considered policy document, the speakers decided not to invite him to defend his proposals. These consisted of saying that the communists had taken over government functions from the ARF and that it was incumbent upon the ARF to remove itself from the public sphere to allow the Communist Party to pursue the reconstruction of the country. As a result of his comrades' decision, on 15 August 1923 Katchaznouni resigned from the Dashnak. Having taken the initiative, he asked the Soviet-Armenian authorities to help him publish his report and distribute it in Armenia, a godsend that the communists hastened to support, just when a special congress had been called for the dissolution of Dashnak and only a few months before the tenth congress of the ARF. On 15 May 1924, Katchaznouni directly addressed the Soviet authorities with 'a request to return to Armenia to pay his debt to the Armenian people and serve his country'.[34] The Soviet authorities allowed him to return to Yerevan to pursue his career as an architect. His return proved unsatisfactory and he died in 1938, a victim of Stalinist purges.

Moscow and Yerevan published Katchaznouni's 1923 report in various languages. It is a text marked by the spirit of defeat and a desire for revenge and an attack on the ARF during the Hamidian Era at the end of independence. Katchaznouni attacks the ARF's revolutionary acts, the strategy of the party whom he faulted for certain abuses. He

---

[33] John Roy Carlson (Arthur Derounian), *The Armenian Revolutionary Federation Dashnagtzoutioun has Nothing to Do Any More: The Manifesto of Hovhannes Katchaznouni* (New York: Armenian Information Service, 1955).

[34] Hovannes Katchaznouni, *Post-mortem* (Beyrouth: Mchag Press, 1965), pp. 12–13.

condemns the party for its authoritarianism within the Republic of Armenia and for the tendency to address problem solving exclusively through war. He further denounces the record of Armenian governments of the First Republic. This report became bedside anti-Dashnak reading in the Soviet Union and among the diaspora and a major point of reference for 1915 genocide deniers. Here again was proof of danger of falsifying theories in history. To begin with, the Russian, English and French versions of the report were incomplete. The Turks and Soviets expunged the pro-Dashnak passages as well as any that may have spoken ill of Ankara and Moscow. In his correspondence with Simon Vratsian shortly before his departure for Yerevan, Katchaznouni wrote: 'You call my book a pamphlet against the ARF. That is wrong. To say that "the ARF has nothing left to do" does not mean to be against the ARF, but it does mean to oppose those Dashnaks, who do not want to understand that they failed and who, while possessing the symbols of the movement are incapable of acting.'[35] Undoubtedly, the agents of the NKVD (People's Commissariat for Internal Affairs) manipulated the former prime minister who, although known for his arrogance, his eccentricity and his contradictions, was receptive to Soviet proposals and found himself caught up in Dashnak–Bolshevik tensions. Taking advantage of the Dashnak leader's desire to return home, the Bolsheviks would have asked him to 'prove himself' by publicly disavowing the ARF.

The cycle thus came full circle: following physical extinction, the Armenian Question completed its political interment through diplomatic collapse. It was crushed by Soviets and the Turks in the name of the struggle against the bourgeoisie and Western interference – concepts embodied in the Treaty of Sèvres. Europeans and Americans sacrificed it to realpolitik and the fight against the communist menace. From the Armenian perspective, the time for settling scores outweighed the struggle for national rights: the settling of old scores between the pro-independence and the pro-Soviet legalists, but also within the parties themselves. Under Soviet domination, Armenia engaged in a separate history. Under the domination of states in the Middle East, Europe and the Americas, the colonies of Armenian exiles were being rebuilt in a climate of general indifference.

[35] Ibid, p. 249.

2

Political-Religious Domination

No assessment of Armenia's history and place in the world would be complete without a detailed examination of its religious development and the complex relationship between its religious structures with the nation's political life.

If Armenians have succeeded in reconstituting themselves to confront the successive trials in their long history, this is essentially because of a vital cultural institution: social organization according to dynasties. Despite the work of scholars such as Nicolas Adontz, Hagop Manandian, Gérard Garitte, Cyril Toumanoff and Nina Garsoïan, this system of Armenian socio-political organization does not yet enjoy the same recognition as the Armenian Church in the national consciousness. Yet the system of dynasts is one of the most characteristic components of the historical life of Armenians and a factor of major importance, insists Nicolas Adontz in the preface of his book *Armenia in the Period of Justinian: The Political Conditions Based on the Naxarar System*.[1] What were the origins of this model of power? How has it been shaped and developed over more than 1,500 years and across changing socio-political realities? How did the system collapse and what remains?

Traditional Armenian law is based on a tripartite model of society and its corollary, the patriarchal family. Any analysis of power must account for this tripartite division of society (princes, lesser nobility, peasants), for which the dynastic model is an important element of stability. The patriarchal family is the backbone of traditional society, regardless of the rank of the group in question. Contrary to what some Soviet-Armenian historians argue, this system of dynasts cannot be likened to the feudalism of Western Europe; it is, in fact, the reverse of the European medieval model. In feudalism, the king, as suzerain, is theoretically at the top of the feudal pyramid; he is lord among lords. In dynasticism, there is no vassalage. The dynasts are princes, independent of each other, who decide to entertain relations of equality among themselves, with customary regulations necessary for collective defence. The system lasted until the Ottoman conquest in the fifteenth century, while dynastic organization persisted notably in Karabakh in the eighteenth century and paradoxically, in an original formulation, in the revolutionary model of the nineteenth century, then under the Soviets and in post-Soviet Armenia.

---

[1] Nicolas Adontz, *Armenia in the Period of Justinian: The Political Conditions Based on the Naxarar System* (Lisbon: Gulbenkian, 1970).

The system's contemporary avatars

Despite five centuries of domination, the system of dynasts has survived as the socio-political reality. During the eighteenth century, pockets of resistance among Armenians of the Karabakh region were able to perpetuate this secular system through the four Melikdoms of the Artsakh, which alone constituted quantitatively and geographically reduced versions of the old dynasticism, impervious to Frankish Western influence. Recent research can help to confirm the Armenians' missed encounter with modernity and also complete the link between medieval dynasticism and contemporary Armenian political life, from the revolutionary movement of the end of the nineteenth century to the republic through the Soviet period.

In founding the ARF in 1890, Christapor Mikaelian favoured the federal principle as a mode of functioning. His choice was based not only on the methods used by the European anarchists of the day, but also on an historical sense of what was essential to the smooth running of his enterprize: the rugged geography familiar to his Armenian countrymen, bearing in mind the history of the confederacy of the 60 kings of Nairi who battled the Assyrians. No one could imagine dominating the Armenian space without taking into account the *gawars* created by the fragmented topography of Greater Armenia. To Mikaelian, it would also have seemed prudent to build unity for the movement around the notion of a 'federation', thus including both those who saw federation as a strategy for territorial co-operation and those concerned with the association of ideas and men. Finally, the idea of federation was in vogue at the time, as turn-of-the-century revolutionaries widely believed that the next step for the multinational empires would be their transformation into federal states. This shift was popularized in Russia by the Revolutionary Socialists but also in the Balkans and the Caucasus, where the revolutionary parties planned, on the one hand, for a Balkan confederation and, on the other, for a Transcaucasian confederation. But the originality of the ARF founders, alongside their links to antiquity, was the principle of defensive solidarity inherent in the dynasty system. Simon Zavarian was one of the intellectuals of the Dashnak who had best studied the ancient history of Europe and Asia.[2] At one of his conferences in Constantinople in 1909, he drew a parallel between the cantons of Greater Armenia and the ancient Greek city states, which were independent of each other in times of peace but gathered in a spirit of fraternal solidarity when threatened by war. The founders of the ARF saw in this system, practised in both Greece and Urartu, a basis for their own model of defence and political development in the eastern provinces of the Ottoman Empire. Starting from this postulate of security, the Dashnak system formed a defensive grid where centre and periphery would be interdependent in times of war and autonomous in peacetime.

If, in the system of dynasts, the territorial domain constituted the basis upon which families understood sovereignty and upon which they based their authority, until they

---

[2] Simon Zavarian, Publication of the University of Erevan, 1991. Conference presentation by Simon Zavarian, 24 August 1908 on centralization, Constantinople, pp. 22–73.

became confused by certain geographical names, the organization of the Dashnak network reproduced this model of interpenetration and equilibrium until they adopted a revolutionary vocabulary inspired by ancient dynastic names: Sassun, Vaspourakan, Rechdounik, Mokk, Taron, Shadakh and Tayk. The quasi-mystical link between people and the land they hailed from extended to the revolutionary period: Roupen of Tarone, Aram of Van, Ichkhan of Van, Akhber of Moks, Keri of Dersim. Just as the kings of the medieval period bore nicknames accorded by custom, the revolutionary movement resumed the tradition – going so far, at times, as to baptize their leaders with the names of historical figures: the Bagratrids had a king by the name 'Achot Yergat' (Achot the Iron). The revolutionary movement counted among its leadership an 'Achot Yergat' (Armenag Levonian), an 'Aghpur Serop' (Serop the Wellspring) (Serop Vartanian), 'Hraïr Tejoghk' (Hraïr from Hell) (Armenag Ghazarian). The similarities are striking and in the same way that the *ichkhan* were masters in their field and did not accept any competition, in the organization of the ARF each *gawar* or *cheurtchan* (grouping) was directed by a central committee presided over by a chief whose authority was indisputable. Thus, in the Sassun, Hraïr Tejoghk ruled as absolute master and could not accept the dissent of Antranik, who had to leave the region or adopt a low profile. In the Vaspourakan, Van Ichkhan demanded the resignation of Roupen Ter-Minassian for incompatibility and threat to his authority. In Tabriz, Prince Hovsep Aghoutian had a falling out with the young Nikol Douman, who was subsequently forced out of the province to avoid the worst.

Just as dynasticism was anchored in decentralization as a strategy to avoid the personification of power by a powerful king, the ARF had, from the beginning, advocated decentralization as a mode of functioning. At the origin of this movement, Simon Zavarian obtained from his peers the establishment of a system in which the *gawars*, who were more in tune with reality on the ground, formed the backbone of revolutionary progress. In keeping with the custom of decentralized power, Zavarian deprived Mikaelian, who favoured centralized authority, from enjoying power. Just as the *primus inter pares* was forced to cohabit with the other great names of the Armenian aristocracy, Mikaelian, prince-designate, had to deal with the other tendencies of the ARF, which it should be remembered was known between 1890 and 1892 as the 'Federation of Armenian Revolutionaries'. Just as medieval central power did not fundamentally assume its supremacy in the dynastic order, the ARF's *kendron* (centre) never embodied a strong authority. At the end of the second congress in 1898 in Tbilisi, the ARF decided to create two governing bodies, the Western Bureau (Europe, America and Constantinople) and the Eastern Bureau (Caucasus, Iran and Eastern Anatolia). The parallel between dynasticism and Dashnakism is obvious here in terms of the rejection of a central power and the refusal to personify that power.

Clannish behaviour was another sign of rapprochement between the two models. In the order of the great families, the spirit of family solidarity made it possible to ensure the stability of the domain, the interests of the clan and the transmission of power. In Dashnakism, in addition to family networks that allowed the appointment of parents to key positions, the system for reproduction and stability was based in part on ethnic solidarity. Mikaelian himself relied extensively on his family network originating from his home village of Akoulis, in the *gawar* of Korten, in Nakhichevan, to subordinate party ranks to his authority. Dashnak networks of the Caucasus gained the upper hand in the 1920s over the Anatolian Dashnaks of Turkey and imposed an anti-Soviet line within the ARF. The Dashnak networks in Lebanon imposed an interventionist conception of the party in the 1960s to the detriment of the European and American branches of the ARF. Finally, the combined networks of Armenians in Iran and within Armenia itself managed to stifle the dissonant voices in the ARF regarding the policy of President Robert Kocharyan.

If traditional Armenian society is tripartite (lords, soldiers, peasants), the social model advocated by the ARF rests on three social classes: intellectuals hold political power (the pen), fighters hold coercive power (the sword) and the peasants work the earth (the shovel). The models complement each other if in the dynastic system the *nakharars* hold political power, while in the Dashnak model the executive officer acts as lord. If in the dynastic system the *azat* are soldiers and the cornerstone of the system, the ARF military corps (*mardagan khokhourt*) is the mainstay of the Dashnak system. If in the system of the dynasts the *ramik* and the *chinakan* owe allegiance to the other two orders, the Dashnak militants owe obedience, discipline and modesty.

Under the Soviets, conflicts between Soviet law and family law were frequent in the sense that communism never quite succeeded in penetrating the foundations of family unity. As in the period that followed Stalin, the Armenian communist regime found in the system of families articulated around the triptych *khenami, dzanot, paregam* (in-laws, friends, relatives) the basis for social cohesion and to strengthen stability in the country, post-Soviet Armenia regenerated the foundations of a neo-patrimonial state. Armenia's post-communist system reproduced the outlines of the traditional tripartite society but with two new aspects. A new social group found its way into society – the oligarchs – while Armenia formed a military force to deal with the Nagorno-Karabakh war. Thus, the Armenian neo-patrimonial model is structured around three orders: the ruling elites and homogeneous community of political leaders (party men), the ecclesiastical (high representatives of the Church, led by the Catholicos) and the economic (oligarchs). Clan leaders frequently agree to organize inter-family marriages: the son of a leader with the daughter of a minister. Clan chiefs also ensure that relatives are placed in key positions: Mikayel Minasyan, son-in-law of the President of the Republic, Serzh Sargsyan, was appointed ambassador to the Vatican; Armen Sargsyan, brother of Prime Minister Dicran Sargsyan, served for a long time as Ambassador to China. The list of examples of nepotism in Yerevan would be too long to provide but confirms the thesis that some 50 large families rule Armenia. The second order, the national army or 'Askaïn Panag', is an essential institution for the republic at war and is a cornerstone of the garrison state. Finally, the general population and civil society must obey the third order to find their place or must leave in search of a better life. This social organization represented the legal face of the Republic of Armenia; there was also an underground world of organized crime, one which the communist model had more or less contained. The collapse of the Soviet Union accelerated the perversion of the patriarchal system through the rise to power of a mafia system whose clan ramifications sometimes extend across continents (Europe and the Americas), facilitating the development of illicit structures among the world's legal states.

The impossible separation of the throne and the altar

Owing to its position at the crossroads of empires and its rugged topography, Armenia has struggled to move from geographical to political expression. It is impossible to grasp the nature of the Armenian problem if one tries to distinguish religion from politics. These categories have been combined and recombined throughout history, much more than in the West. Politics has had religious undertones since its pagan origins and the religious community itself has been profoundly politicized since the Christianization of Armenia in the fourth century. Evaluating the interdependence of the now and the hereafter allows us to better understand the pervasive natures of politics and religion in Armenian society and why, among Armenians, the politics and religion of ancient and medieval Armenian thought are an open manifestation of politics as autonomous space. Hence the notion of an establishment church,[3] dear to the historian and orientalist Jean-Pierre Mahé. When the Church replaces a state that cannot be found or otherwise has abrogated its responsibilities, one may reasonably conclude from familiarity with Armenian history that religion has replaced politics in the formation of the Armenian nation. Just as the Church covered the state as an institution, religion covered politics as the secular field of the nation. This continued until the twentieth century. In the nineteenth century, the poet and doctor Nahapet Rusinian (1819–1879) was heir to this strand of traditional thought. Although he was a contributor to the 'Armenian Millet's Rules of Procedure of the Ottoman Empire in 1863' and was inspired by the ideas of the Enlightenment, he proposed to delete the word 'political' from the Armenian language, 'to assure', posits Gérard Libaridian, 'a proper interpretation of national objectives'.[4] Thus, there would be no autonomous space for politics, just one sprawling religion that would spread through all national institutions and permeate the national social body.

With the disappearance of dynasticism in the fifteenth century, the Armenian Apostolic Church became the only living institution. How did we get there? Why did we have to wait until the twentieth century to record the beginnings of political autonomy among Armenians, whereas in most European countries the nation-state model has been fully accepted? Were attempts made to emancipate politics in ancient and medieval times? What are the theocratic references to the Armenian socio-political model? What is the nature of the relationship between Christianity and Dashnakism, the two pillars of Armenian political thought?

Neither fundamentalism nor secularism

Political and religious power were essentially interwoven during the Christianization of Armenia in the fourth century. Before this decisive turn, religion was not overtly influential over monarchs. Paganism never influenced the state as Christianity would

---

[3] Annie and Jean-Pierre Mahé, *Histoire de l'Arménie des origines à nos jours* (Perrin, 2012).
[4] Gérard Libaridian, *L'Arménie moderne, Histoire des hommes et de la nation* (Paris: Karthala, 2008), p. 63.

later do, even if during the Urartian period a cult of Khaldi, the god of war, served as the established state religion. According to Greco-Latin sources, there existed, at the time of Tigranes the Great, an Armenian pantheon similar to that of Greece. Pagan temples are sufficiently numerous in Armenia to attest to the popularity of local cults, among them Anahid (the immaculate, a goddess of Iranian origin) who was widely admired in Armenian society. Under the Artaxiads (189 BC–AD 12), religion was an important, but not incontrovertible, institution in Armenian society. Under the Arsacids, the rather syncretic religion of Zoroastrianism was adopted by the Armenian elites. Then, under the Sassanids, a harsher and more intransigent variant of this form of monotheism was imposed, of which one peculiarity was a lack of distinction between the temporal and the spiritual, as proposed by Armenian religious doctrine. Is it for this reason that the vast majority of classical Armenian historiography has been focused on a narrow religious reading as a way of explaining a turning point for the history of the Christianization of Armenia and the creation of the Armenian alphabet? Undoubtedly, the political dimension of this paradigm shift is just as, if not more, important than its spiritual dimension. It was only in the third century that the process of evangelization developed in Armenia. In AD 240, at the court of King Tiridates II (217–250), competing evangelists, one Manichaean and the other Christian, staged a public debate with the intention of converting the monarch. They failed. The strategy of King Tiridates IV (298–330) consisted of freeing himself from Roman and Persian tutelage and to reestablish Arsacid political and religious legitimacy by restoring the role of the Armenian king as the Anointed of God, as Tigranes the Great had been in 66 BC. As 'king of kings', the sovereign would be recognized as having a direct link to the deities. Since the sovereign's fall from grace, he derived his power from the emperor or Roman consul. The sovereign was therefore a king who no longer enjoyed divine access to God, a sub-king.

The second reason was that the sovereign had to deal with the *nakharars*, who had largely turned to Iran and Zoroastrianism whether by conviction or interest; to be well regarded by the Iranian monarch was always advantageous. On the sidelines of the Zoroastrianism of the elites, the Armenian campaigns were dominated by a traditional paganism; the king had to find consensus and then impose his legitimacy. By choosing a minority religion and favouring a Greek current, whose figurehead was Gregory, over the Syriac current, the sovereign tried to receive the power of the God of the Christians. According to legend, Gregory was of Parthian origin, but nothing is less certain. Originally from Caesarea, Cappadocia, Gregory, whose father was killed by Anak, the father of King Tiridates IV, was of noble ancestry. This amounts to saying that he was assimilated into the royal family or that this affiliation was added to legitimate his fundamental role, since by becoming patriarch – at the time one did not yet speak of the Catholicos – Gregory replaced the leader of Zoroastrianism in Armenia. Since this religion is monotheistic, the transition to Christianity came about quite naturally. In this capacity, he inherited one of the most prestigious offices of the kingdom. The fact that Gregory was a noble of Parthian origin presented certain advantages. He was consecrated and his legitimacy confirmed by appointment. Ironically, the Christianization of Armenia was not completed by an Armenian protagonist. Tiridates IV was an Armenian of Parthian descent, while Gregory was himself a Parthian prince. Hripsimé and Gayane, the two virgins who were converted to Christ, were Roman.

From the beginning of the fourth century, the monarchy made every effort to establish the new religion, both as an institution and in society. Dealing with the nobility, the king found it difficult to convince the *nakharars* who nevertheless shared his political destiny. He clashed with his princes, especially those of the Siunik, who were subordinate to Persia and who understood the real intentions of the sovereign. They did not convert to Christianity but rejected the dominion of a Christian king, instead aligning themselves with the Persian 'king of kings' who professed respect for their territorial autonomy. Among the populace, attached as they were to their traditions, the new religion was slow to find favour. It was, after all, a foreign faith practised in a foreign language. Religious leaders read in Greek and Syriac and then translated the Word of God into Armenian. But the graft did not take.

Henceforth, the ambition of the monk Mesrop Machdots, in creating the Armenian alphabet, would not be to nationalize an Armenian identity but to evangelize the Armenian people. It took a century for Armenian political and religious elites to impose the message of Christ. For Christianity to really penetrate the popular strata, the clergy had to preach in the vernacular. As a result, the creation of the alphabet served primarily to proselytize. The same applied to the written canon that appeared with Christianity. Canon law is itself alien to the local context and the written canon only emerged in the fifth century, with the creation of the alphabet. Under cover of religious education, the king and clergy mobilized literacy to end paganism and its orality. It is clear, then, that the monarch used religion and religious education for political reasons, as an instrument of domination.

There was another reason for the development of writing at the beginning of the fifth century. Beyond the need to translate the Bible, King Vramchabouh (392–414) had become aware of the decline of the Armenian state, weakened by pressure from the Byzantines and the Persians. The monarch and the patriarch Izaac of Armenia (Sahak the Parthian) entrusted Mesrop Machdotz, translator of Greek to the royal chancellery, to codify an Armenian alphabet, because, without such a record, Armenian culture would be lost. The translation of the Gospels, however, could not be reduced to a single pedagogical dimension as it contained a national mission of survival. From the fifth century onwards, Christianity became the socio-political reality and cement of the Armenian nation.

This symbiosis between the spiritual and the temporal, the religious faith and the national ideal constituted, as of the fifth century, the basis of Armenian religious doctrine. We know that in the Christological polemics of the fourth and fifth centuries, namely the debates on the divine and/or human nature of Jesus, which shook the different patriarchal seats (Antioch, Alexandria, Jerusalem and Constantinople), Armenians recognized the conclusions of the first three councils – Nicaea in 325, Constantinople in 381 and Ephesus in 431. At the Council of Nicaea, Christians condemned the Arianism that came from Alexandria, acknowledged the divinity of Christ and affirmed that the Father and the Son were consubstantial. In Constantinople, Christians pushed by the powerful Byzantine Christian Empire recognized the divinity of the Holy Spirit as equal to the other two figures of the Holy Trinity and Byzantium as the centre of the Christian world. In Ephesus, Christians condemned dyophysitism (the belief wherein the humanity and divinity of Christ are separate natures), which was defended by the bishop of Constantinople, Nestorius. The Armenians' religious creed rests on the conclusions of the Council of Ephesus: that the human and the divine are united, that the divine is superior but that it co-exists with the human – that is, miaphysitism. Such was the dogma of Ephesus and St Cyril of Alexandria which, while it consecrated the unique nature of the incarnate Word, remains distinct from monophysitism, which proclaims Christ to have only one divine nature.

Throughout its history, the Armenian Church has clung to this intermediate line, despite the difficulties and trials that neighbouring powers and different religions have tried to impose. In 451, in Chalcedon (today Kadikoy, on the Asian shore of Istanbul), several hundred bishops who were gathered in council condemned the monophysitism of Eutyches.[5] They proclaimed the double nature of Christ and increased the authority of Constantinople over the Christian world. Armenians rejected these conclusions in 553 at the Dvin Synod on the grounds that they contradicted those of the first three Ecumenical Councils and they rehabilitated the Nestorian theses. For Armenians, how could Nestorianism, previously considered a heresy, become the doctrinal norm for Christians? Indeed, if Armenia challenged Chalcedonism, it was as much for the sake of independence and preservation of an autonomous national identity as it was out of theological conviction concerning the nature of Christ. Faced with the Byzantine ogre who sought to dominate and assimilate other local Christian rites, Armenians supported non-Chalcedonism. Faced with the other Eastern Christian denominations who opted for extreme monophysitism, Armenians held the line on miaphysitism. In addition to these interdenominational tensions, an additional source of concern arose between Armenian Christianity and Persian Mazdeism at first and then between Christian Armenia and Islamic Arabia. Thus, from the fifth to the seventh century, Armenians were forced into a defensive posture based on three rejections: the refusal of Byzantine Chalcedonism; the refusal of the Persian Mazdeism at Avarai in 451 and, finally, the rejection of Islam.

Despite the creed of Ephesus, medieval Armenia was far from being a model of religious homogeneity. Armenian leadership included arabophilic or mazdeophilic or byzantophilic *nakharars*. In the eyes of the Christian world, Armenians were considered heretics, while in the eyes of Muslims, they were infidels. How, then, in this matrix of tensions, was the clergy able to safeguard the particularism of its faith between the rival monotheisms? Basically, because of two political factors.

The first was strategic and of foreign origin: it was a calculation by the Persian king Khosrow Aparvez (591–628) who seized Byzantine anti-Armenian policy as an opportunity to push Armenians towards anti-Chalcedonian Christianity. In 591, following an agreement signed with Persians, the Byzantine Emperor Maurice attempted to reimpose Chalcedonism in Armenia, going so far as to favour the election of a Chalcedonian Catholicos, Yovhanes Bagarantsi. The reaction of Catholicos Movses II Eghivardetsi (574–604) was so strong that it caused a schism shortly after his death. By seeking to create a parallel hierarchy and an alternative doctrine, Byzantium committed the irreparable in the eyes of Armenians, who were by then traumatized by the Byzantine effort of domination and indoctrination. This schism lasted until 610/611, shortly after

---

5   Tradition holds there were 630 bishops.

the assassination of Byzantine emperor Maurice in 602, following which the Persian king retook Persian Armenia and suppressed this parallel religious authority. It was in this sense, as an anti-Chalcedonian, that King Khosrow Aparvez presented himself as the defender of Armenia. On the one hand, he called for support from Armenian *Marzpan*, Sembat Bagratouni, a Sasanid ally, while at the same time organizing an ecumenical council at Ctesiphon in the presence of the Armenian Catholicos, Komitas Aghtsetsi (611–628), with the hope of encouraging extremist monophysitic theses in Armenia and creating a buffer doctrine between Byzantium and Persia. The council of Ctesiphon was a success: the monophysitic doctrine was adopted, putting Armenians under pressure. The Persian king had known since 451 that Armenians would never again worship Ahura Mazda, so his focus had been on encouraging them to adopt monophysitic extremism (julianism), a minority in Armenia defended by Yovhannes Mayragometsi (c 575 to c 650/660), a talented theologian and a Sasanid protégé.

Hence the second conscious and dogmatic factor. Komitas I decided to call to his side the Julianist doctor to coach him. Mayragometsi, however, had important support in Persia and aspired to succeed Komitas I. As in Zoroastrianism, religion subsumed politics – which was not without the Persian king's displeasure – such that the non-Chalcedonian Armenian party drew a parallel between Zoroastrianism and Julianism, including in the political and legal fields. By an extraordinary combination of circumstances, the situation of the non-Chalcedonian party became clearer: in 627, the *marzpan* Sembat Bagratouni died; in 628, the Catholicos Komitas died and the king of the Persians was assassinated two years before the arrival of the Arabs in Iran. Having at once understood the danger, the Armenian clergy and princes acted to remove Yovhannes Mayragometsi from power. The threat of Julianism was thus reduced, without there being any certainty that the Julianist references had, in fact, been removed. Mayragometsi's legal and theocratic work was of the utmost importance for Armenian canon law. Indeed, it was thanks to his tireless efforts that the Armenian canonical legislation enacted at the Synod of Sahapivan in 444 was enlarged by theological considerations inserted into the *Book of Letters*, an official compilation of the Armenian Catholicos from the fifth to the eighth century. His ultra-monophysitic theses went much further than Gregorian reform or Western papacy, which never thought of suppressing secular, imperial or royal law for the benefit of canon law alone. As the principal author of the canons, Mayragometsi proposed eliminating the secular and customary law in favour of 'monachization' (the process of becoming monastic orders) of the Church and the clergy by means of an intensive ecclesiastical tax policy. If his projects had been realized, Armenia would probably have tipped into fundamentalism, in that the clergy would have become concerned with political law while canonical law would have diluted the customary law as an exclusive Julianist doctrine.

The arrival of the Arabs in Iran and Armenia preserved Armenians from the latest Byzantine attempts to destroy their miaphysitic doctrines. The concordat concluded between the Catholicos Sahak III Dzoraporetsi (677–703) and the Umayyad caliphate guaranteed Armenians their doctrinal independence from the Chalcedonians and allowed the Arabs to obtain military and fiscal commitments from these Christians in exchange for physical protection. However, this agreement contradicted religious policy. At the Synod of Manazkert (726), convened by one of the most important

Catholicos of all time, Yohvannes Awdznetsi (650–728), the Armenian clergy remedied the situation. Thanks to the mediation of Catholicos Awdznetsi, taxes were reduced and a moratorium was placed on doctrinal plurality within the Church. Awdznetsi convened the Synod of Dvin in 719, during which the Church adopted liturgical unification. Through his writings, Awdznetsi promulgated *The Book of Armenian Canon*, which unified canon law. Thanks to the process of legal normalization, the Armenian Church was able to base itself on a miaphysitic creed derived from the theses of Ephesus, even though, by the tenth century, Chalcedonism had regained some interest in Armenia. And yet, says Aram Mardirossian, if Chalcedonism largely failed, traces of the Julianist doctrine in Armenian theology remain largely visible. The Church, however, did what it could to erase the unavowable past, falsifying names or inserting fakes as necessary. Still, Mayragometsi's legacy cannot be camouflaged. One has only to consult *Le Sceau de la foi*, the theological work attributed to the Catholicos Komitas published in the seventh century, to detect the marks of this outstanding doctor.

The creed of Ephesus allowed Armenians to respect the balance between canon law and customary law, between church and dynasticism, between religion and politics. This point of equilibrium is a guarantee of assurance in which the human and the divine are inseparable and where reality and faith are one.

Yet, Armenian history has included several episodes in which politics enjoyed pre-eminence, notably under the kings Tigranes the Great, Arsace II (350–368), Pap (370–374), Leon II (1199–1219) and Hethum I (1226–1270). Like other kings, these monarchs confronted forces opposed to the success of the royal project, which consisted in creating the basis for a centralized state. Despite the difficulties and desperate struggles and against all odds, these kings, especially the Arsacids, persisted and achieved their ends. The special geographical conditions of Armenia have often been mentioned as a handicap to the efforts of an Armenian monarch to consolidate his authority. In the time of the Artaxiads, Tigranes the Great adopted plans to build new roads to project his authority. It is also commonly known that the regional princes did everything in their power to prevent the emergence of a centralized state. What is less well known is the negative role that the Church played in the consolidation of state authority. Monotheism allowed the clergy to occupy one of the first dynastic places with the family of Gregory, the Gregorids (Pahlavouni). The dynasty of the Arsacids was forced to contend with the rise of this new faith and King Tiridates probably did not weigh up all the consequences that stemmed from the universal and monotheistic character of Christianity. On the request of the family of Patriarch Saint Gregory, Tiridates multiplied his donations of land, including from his own domain and from those of *nakharars* whom he had managed to dominate. This immense heritage allowed the father of the Armenian Church to increase his political power by surrounding himself with a clientele.

Traditionalism and messianism

Christianity and Haitadism revitalized the relationship between religion and politics in the eighteenth and nineteenth centuries by introducing the notion of place into the construction of Armenian identity. Before this, the Church had relied exclusively on an extra-territorial approach to politics. As the guardian of identity and as the only institution recognized by the imperial powers, the Church enjoyed considerable prerogatives among the Osmanlis and the Romanovs, by virtue of which it directed its religious community and according to which it could be assimilated as a 'state within the state'. From the moment the idea of territorial identity spread among Europeans, Armenians did not hesitate to follow it, adopting a national identity associated with a geographical space. The new conception was based on the memory of a medieval Armenia that was sovereign according to the principle of territoriality developed by Karabakh princes David Bek, Hovsep Emin, Shamir Shahamirian and Israel Ori, working in the seventeenth and eighteenth centuries for the liberation of Armenian territories in Eastern Turkey. Each time it was done under the impulse or with the consultation of the clergy. The involvement of the Church in this process of territorial identification reconnected with the Armenian political–religious tradition following three centuries of subjugation. It took on an even greater dimension in the nineteenth century thanks to the efforts of Father Khrimian Haïrik, who became Catholicos of Etchmiadzine in 1892.

But this new impetus was not shared by all the dignitaries, notably the Patriarchate of Constantinople, who continued to see the territorialization of politics, namely the Revolution, as a source of potential disaster for Armenians. For Khrimian Haïrik, it became important for the Church to move from an extra-territorial tradition peculiar to the Armenian millet of the Ottoman Empire to territorial identity or traditionalism, which consisted in accompanying the *Zartong* (Revival) of the nineteenth century. Because the Revolution risked pushing Armenians towards a dynamic of social emancipation, that is outside the religious sphere, it became a necessity that the Church-nation renew its links with its territory. Religious factions did not want to abandon the political terrain to the secularized parties at the end of the nineteenth century and felt it was legitimate to return to the historical function of the Church. Furthermore, when the parties emerged between 1885 and 1890, the Holy See of Etchmiadzin either followed them with lively interest or oversaw them directly, especially the *Armenagan* party, which had sworn to support religion. The relationship with the Church of the other two parties, the SDHP and the ARF – the secular movements – was less fluid, especially for the Marxist and anti-clerical SDHP.

With the ARF positioned midway between the Armenagan and the SDHP, relations with the Church were of another dimension and of more significant interest to our study. Indeed, as a synthesis between the traditional and the modern, the ARF allowed itself to be won over to the idea of a revolutionary traditionalism, presenting itself in the guise of secular messianism which transcended the Church. In other words, the three main founders of the ARF, Christapor Mikaelian, Simon Zavarian and Stepan Zoryan (alias 'Rostom'), each defended a different approach to religion. Rostom, a Marxist socialist, proposed that Armenians should tear themselves away from religion and find an alternative way to progress because salvation is outside religious faith, God having abandoned his creation. Simon Zavarian, formerly a follower of the anarchist Mikhail Bakunin, opted for a fundamental approach to religion. 'There is no man, no nation without religion. All men and all nations are believers'. In Constantinople in 1909 he told his comrades: 'the ARF is already a kind of religion because it has its martyrs'.[6] Dashnakism was therefore a moral order based on Christian values and, in the name of national unity, the religious and the political were inseparable. 'These grow in cohesiveness and give birth to traditionalism', wrote Simon Zavarian, the 'secular saint' elected in 1906 to the presidency of the General Assembly of the Holy See of Etchmiadzin, which for the socialist and revolutionary leadership of the day was surprising – surprising, that is, for all but the ARF. As for Christapor Mikaelian, whose education in a religious setting led him to opt for a middle-way approach to the revolution, proceeded from an instrumental approach to religion. Inspired by the thinking of Emile Durkheim, he believed that society can only remain cohesive if there is a commensurate sacralization of collective feeling.

Faithful to the link to be maintained with the past, the ARF was deeply influenced by a current of thought for which Dashnakism constituted either the strong arm of the Church or a form of political religion. For the first, like Jean Loris-Melicof, a founder of the ARF and nephew of a Tsarist minister and Mardiros Markarian alias 'Safo', one of the people responsible for the attack on Sultan Abdul Hamid II on 21 July 1905, the party should put itself at the service of the Church. This clerical approach was based on the idea of national unity and the lessons learned from the confiscation of the property of the Armenian Church ordered by Tsar Nicholas II in 1903. The Church and the ARF thus found grounds for co-operation and overcame their former rivalry. Party leaders even proposed to institutionalize this co-operation at the ARF's third congress in Sofia in 1904. The proposal was rejected, however, not because the secular Dashnaks were in the majority – in fact the laity were always a minority – but because to pursue the goal of co-operation the ARF would have had to put itself at the service of the Church and not at the centre of the political game.

Hence the second trend, embodied by Roupen Ter-Minassian or Nigol Aghbalian, according to which the masses were to receive the new ideology: Dashnakism as a faith. Here we find elements of Antonio Gramsci's thought regarding the link between politics and religion. But unlike the Marxist theorist, the Dashnaks added a dose of Messianism: Dashnakism would be messianic and fundamentalism a necessary principle for the foundation of the nation. The ARF thus became a new 'political church'. A party unlike the others, it was the organization of the Armenian people with all its components united around the revolutionary ideal, like a new dynastic order regulated by statutes, which were called *ganonakir* or 'the book of canon' in Armenian. For this fundamentalist current, the ARF programme represented a sacred instrument, equivalent to 'the Torah, the Koran and the Bible all together'.[7] Contrary to the Church, however, Roupen Ter-Minassian stated:'There is no dogma in Dashnakism because congresses – or conclaves in which delegates act as secular cardinals – were planned to avoid enclosure within narrow, proscribed thought.'[8] This precaution clearly did not take into account the place occupied by the struggle for national liberation in the ideological corpus of the party. This struggle indeed constituted the dogmatic basis,

---

[6]   Roupen Ter-Minassian, *Mémoire d'un révolutionnaire arménien*, 7 vols, 2nd edn (Beyrouth: Hamaskaïne, 1972) p. 369.
[7]   Roupen Ter-Minassian, *L'organisation de la FRA* (Yerevan, 1991), p. 11.
[8]   Ibid.

just as the class struggle did for the communists. In the communist utopia, the class struggle and prospect of a clear victory on a universal scale and the emergence of a classless society constituted the fulfilment of history conceived as progress. In the Dashnak utopia, the struggle for national liberation and the prospect of a society of nations at peace constituted the end of history conceived as a necessity. For the communists, the Dashnaks were heretics and vice versa.

Christianity and Dashnakism testify, each in their own way, to a redeeming belief in the Messiah. Dashnakism is a mixture of science and mysticism, of the real and the spiritual, of reason and religion, of modernity and respect for the patriarchal family model. The three founders were presented as the Holy Trinity, with the father (Christapor), the son (Rostom) and the Holy Spirit (Zavarian). Together, these constitute a single person (given name, alias and surname) as Dashnak memory immortalized them: 'Long live Christapor "Rostom" Zavarian'. There is only one God, the Revolution and Christapor is his prophet.

Apart from during the First Republic of 1918–1920, the links between Christianity and Dashnakism were never broken. In 1918, the ARF, with an overwhelming majority in parliament, intended to separate the Church from the state and, from its first efforts at drafting a constitution, where religion was presented as a matter of private conscience, Armenia could not become a religious state, much less a theocracy. During the Cold War, while in exile and in the midst of rivalries between pro- and anti-Bolsheviks, the ARF recovered control of the dioceses under the authority of the Holy See of Antelias (successor of the Holy See of Cilicia), provoking a kind of 'schism' with Etchmiadzin in 1956 upon the election of Zareh I as the head of Antelias against the advice of the Catholicos in Soviet Armenia, Vasken I. Until the Second World War, communism vigorously fought the clergy in Armenia and throughout the Soviet Union. In the name of revolutionary atheism, Moscow closed places of worship, confiscated church patrimony and debunked religious authorities. In Soviet Armenia, for example, Catholicos Khoren I was assassinated in April 1938.

The repression of the clergy was so severe in Yerevan that, by 1945, there were only four monks left to participate in the congress to elect a new Catholicos.

Until de-Stalinization in 1956, religion survived based on the model of patriarchal family loyalty to Armenian theology. From 1953 to 1956, the Church gradually regained its place as an exclusively Armenian bastion within the national social organization of the country, even if the 'cold war' with 'Antelias the Dashnak' was not over. Among the diaspora community, the Armenian Church had slipped into thinking of Haitadism as a politico-religious actor, notably through the World Council of Churches, whose position in favour of recognition of the 1915 genocide found new impetus under the leadership of Nechan Sarkissian, as a member of the Council executive and future Catholicos of Antelias (1983–1995) and Etchmiadzin (1995–1999).

Since Armenian independence in 1991, the state has gradually rebuilt itself according to the political and religious foundations of Armenian tradition. The Church strengthened its place in society until it attempted, at the instigation of Armenian President Levon Ter-Petrosyan, a process of unification for the dioceses of Etchmiadzin and Antelias, electing Karekin I of Antelias as the head of the Holy See of Etchmiadzin in 1995. In the Republic of Armenia, there is no formal separation between Church and state, religion having established itself as a common thread both within and without national institutions. At the time of his inauguration as head of state, the president of the republic swore an oath on the Bible and the state placed at the disposal of the Church all security instruments necessary to fight against sects. The Republican Party in Yerevan has been in power since 1995. The basis for its power is an alliance between economic liberalism and social conservatism, a mixture of structural reforms and the defence of Christian values. Today, the Republic of Armenia is a model of political and religious syncretism in which the Catholicos Karekin II occupies one of the most important positions in the hierarchy, like the Catholicos within the system of dynasts.

No political system

The notion of a centralized state is very recent. Until the fall of the Soviet Union it was not possible to evoke the notion of a modern state in Armenia, for there was no political centre redistributing power and acting as a source of integration. If the centrality of power is a foreign notion to Armenians, it is necessary to go back to the origins of the system of the dynasts to explain why. The great families prevented the king from creating the conditions of a political centre because they feared a concentration of authority. Secluded in their bastions, they stood against the monarch who needed to structure his power from a nerve centre. Hence the absence of the city-state, prior to the emergence of Yerevan, first under the Dashnaks and then under the Bolsheviks.[9] Indeed, until 1918, Armenian political life had no centre. At the time of the revolutionary movement, the only urban units that had any capacity to impose their authority were Tbilisi and Baku, two non-Armenian cities, while Yerevan was a village. Western Armenia lacked any semblance of an urban centre: Kars? Van? Erzerum? These cities have never played the role of political centre, even if, strategically, Erzerum enjoyed a special place in Dashnak geopolitical representations.[10] The former Armenian capital Garine (Erzerum) was the centre of gravity for the Dashnak system. Just as there is no centralized state, the notion of a *res publica* peculiar to Western civilization had no meaning in Armenia. The Armenian social body dismissed any responsibility for public affairs. The Greco-Roman references – Plato, Aristotle and Cicero – did not find fertile ground among Armenians. The Arsacid dynasty attempted to import the model of the Roman state; it saw in this universal state an effective instrument of domination. But it never took hold. Thus, Armenians have no tradition of public space because the popular classes never counted. The field has never been prepared as the public and private spheres are indistinguishable.

Under such conditions, the notion of political integration and social contract are illusory. Relations between the public authority and the general population cannot be

[9]   K Kuzalian, *Le développement de la pensée politique arménienne et la FRA* (Paris: ARF Press, 1927). K Kuzalian, *Problèmes historiques* (Beirut: Société d'éditions 'Araz', 1937). See also Taline Ter-Minassian, *Erevan: la construction d'une capitale à l'époque soviétique* (Rennes: Rennes University Press, 2007).

[10] Roupen Ter-Minassian, *Arménie* (Beirut, 1948; reprinted in Tehran, 1991), p 43.

brought into harmony because Armenians as a group have experienced only unequal societies (ancient, medieval, imperial, Soviet), where the peasantry were disenfranchized and the concept of the individual was non-existent. How, then, were conditions of trust to be developed between the elites and the people in a model that lacked any sense of hierarchical empowerment within the social group and among political actors? This was impossible and resulted in the popular distrust of the elites, the nobility and the parties. The whole enterprise of the revolutionary movement had been to rectify these defects of integration in order to create the conditions for a new ethics based on trust and the idea of a social contract between the elites and the 'people' – a mythified people identified based on a territorialized identity. Now, where Christapor Mikaelian might see a new era based on the progress and rights of individuals and the nation, the religious might see the spectre of an approaching catastrophe. In the eyes of the religious, the revolution was the cause of trials that have proven fatal for Armenians, so the best way to avoid these problems is to ban the cause: politics. There is, moreover, an important fringe of Armenians who share a deep distrust of politics and yet another who strongly identify with the Church as the sole representative and bearer of cultural heritage. Hence the profound break with the revolutionary movement, whose vocation is precisely to propose a secular and modern Armenian identity. Here, again, the exercise ended badly. When Armenians speak of a lack of unity, they defend a quasi-illusory fundamentalist conception of the one and indivisible nation. Their dispersal and their inability to integrate power and society to propose new modes of regulation are obstacles to any process of unification. The nobility disappears. The parties do not integrate. The media are restricted in terms of audience and the free press does not exist; their status as intermediaries is, therefore, non-existent. In short, citizenship is a concept foreign to historical reality. Armenians have shifted from the Ottoman millet and Caucasian religious community to Soviet totalitarianism or exile in democratic states (the West, Greece, Uruguay, Argentina) or authoritarian states (Near East). How then can we talk about citizenship and the rights of individuals under such conditions?

Unbeknownst to himself, Christapor, a supporter of a new Armenian ethic, could only see evidence of the weight of tradition in the Armenian social order. He came up against the ambivalent nature of politics in the Armenian mentality; the weight of the family system and the similarities between his partisan system and the dynasty system. Dashnakism, as an essential vector of Haitadism, has not been able to complete the transformation of political power to modernity, as the parties have failed to project Armenians into a political identity independent of their religious identity. This secularist characteristic of every modern state has been defeated by the very nature of the Armenian revolution, the hybrid form that mixes politics and religion, tradition and progress, state and federation, nationalism and socialism. Haitadism, as a whole, did not succeed in reducing the multiple ties of personal dependence from which the dynasty system, embodied by the Church from the fifteenth century onwards and by parties from the end of the nineteenth century, drew their substance. The assertion of power by the parties was also compromised by the inability to assemble the nation around legitimate and consensual figures. Finally, Haitadism failed in its ambition to diversify the political institutions recognized by all so that, when faced with this incapacity, instead of creating a mechanism of adhesion, Haitadism presented itself under the guise of a proto-system of domination and constraint. Although Haitadism advocated defending the rights of Armenians both as a national group and as individuals, it has certainly tried to value the rights of the subjects of the two empires, notably in constitutional Turkey, but it has not succeeded in creating a climate of trust with the population because of lack of means, lack of social contract and the coercive power of the two empires. In their fullest expression, both Haitadism, the restrictive and Dashnakism, the modernizing impulses, have finally been translated as the emergence of another proto-system of domination in which intended modernism, whether political, national or secular, has, in fact, developed as simply another mechanism of coercion and dependence. This is an inevitable process, for any formation of a state implies a system of domination, but an unfinished one, because this phenomenon of the institutionalization of inter-Armenian relations has failed – because of wars and massacres – to become an ideological corpus, an instrument for controlling mentalities and a bureaucratic apparatus.

Another socio-political pathology, the Armenian proto-system, whether anterior to Haitadism in the absence of normative unity, is a source of tension and rivalries. By definition, the system of dynasts is a pattern of permanent tensions, insecurity and infidelities. Joseph François Laurent, writes: 'One always finds an Armenian ready to go and fight another Armenian.'[11] The system of the dynasts has institutionalized treason – since the prince is not the vassal of the king, but the owner of his domain, he can betray the king by allying himself with a neighbouring power. It is a right. In this way, the system of the dynasty favoured the instrumentalization of Armenian princes as neighbouring powers sought to place the monarch at a disadvantage. Everyone profited from this system of insecurity. The neighbouring powers exploited one family against another. Princes allied themselves in pursuit of their own interests, often against the king's interests. Even the Church, instead of supporting the union and marking the end of quarrels among the great families of Christendom, did the opposite. It was, in fact, in the interests of the Church that the great families should remain divided, a situation that would weaken the king and hence the temporal and political power in the territory.

Finally, as further signs of the unbroken link with the past, the roots of Armenian political vocabulary refer to royalty. 'President' is translated as *Nakhakah* or 'first crown'. The concept of 'minister' is translated as *Nakharar* and refers to 'lord' or 'dynasty'. Even today, Armenia uses the term *sparapet* to designate the head of the armed forces, incarnated in the view of Armenians by none other than Vazgen Sargsyan, hero of the Nagorno-Karabakh war, minister of defence and and former prime minister, who was killed on 27 October 1999 during the terrorist attack on the Armenian parliament. In fact, constitutionally speaking, the president of the republic is the leader of the armed forces, which suggests another link between fidelity to tradition on the one hand and, on the other hand, political modernity.

---

[11] Joseph François Laurent, *L'Arménie entre Byzance et l'Islam, depuis la conquête arabe jusqu'en 886* (Gulbenkian Foundation, 1980).

Politics in the diaspora

Is it possible to dissociate politics from territory and power? Today, as a result of globalization and telecommunications and the diasporization of national identities, much has been written about what might be called the 'end of territoriality' and the transformation of political identity outside the institutionalized territory. Armenians have long experience in this field; projecting themselves into extra-territorial politics is not new. To understand the background of this phenomenon, we must return to the eleventh century and the first appearance of political anchoring outside the territory of origin. Byzantium, during the period of the 'Macedonian' dynasty (867–1056), exerted strong religious and political influence on Armenia, giving Armenians an early familiarity with extra-territorial politics. Macedonian dynasts kept an eye on Armenia, while managing the affairs of the Empire from Byzantium. This aspect of political culture was accentuated over the course of massacres and migratory waves as the link between territory and diaspora became diluted in the historical record. Should we employ the term 'diaspora' here, as its definition is neither clear nor unanimous; in any event, it is used more often to describe a phenomenon than a concept. Whether understood in its biblical or modern conception, the word, which derives from the Greek for 'dispersion', has a singular significance for Armenians. It did not appear with the great tragedy of 1915, but during the fall of the Bagratrids in the eleventh century. If usage dates from the Middle Ages, the word 'diaspora' (*spiurk* in Armenian) acquired special meaning for Armenians only following the end of the First World War. Until that time, Armenians more often spoke of 'colonies', 'communities', 'refugees' and 'exiles'.

The connection of the diaspora to politics raises two points. The first is based on the idea that a diaspora originates with civil societies and that their influence refers to the impact of a diaspora on international affairs of the motherland. Before the advent of 'modern' society in Europe in the eighteenth century, Armenian families who had been disrupted or broken up had little or no direct bearing on the current affairs of the *Yerkir*. The greater the emancipation of civil society in democratizing states, the more disrupted family relations weighed on the decision-making processes there.

The second point concerns not only the *Yerkir* but also the symbolic power and political-religious particularism independent of territorial identity. When the first emigrants reestablished themselves in Armenian identity enclaves abroad, they did not break with their country of origin nor position themselves as an outpost of the 'mother community', such that there was no clear difference from the common thinking of the group left behind. In both cases – on the spot but without sovereignty for the one and expatriated and powerless for the other – the relationship to the territory is virtually identical. In both cases, the power was symbolic, based on a sense of ephemeral politics. In other words, the first groups of emigrants became an extra-territorial extension of Armenian identity. It was not until the eighteenth century and especially in the nineteenth century that the sensation of living in the diaspora changed under the influence of modernity and the rise of national feeling with or without territory. Nation and territory provide those who remain behind with a sense of belonging to a land whose purpose is to serve as a platform for cultural aggrandizement and political sovereignty. For those living abroad, the same ideas produce a mythification and abstraction of the ancestral territory as the source of cultural difference and a desire to preserve a specific identity.

Among Armenians, the revival of politics took place far away from their ancestral territories. It was, therefore, a reconstruction of the policy on the basis of elements that are necessarily foreign to the majority of the group who were left behind and out of step with the new ideas. In the East, the revival of politics took place in the eighteenth century in Madras, India, where young intellectuals who came from trading circles – Hovsep Emin, Movses Baghramian, Shahamir Shahamirian and Haoutioun Shemavonian – published texts that considered a particular form of national liberation and constitutionalized identity. Under the influence of the ideas of the Enlightenment (Montesquieu and Locke above all), this movement in Madras defended a rational and economic view of politics, in terms of interests that Europe could derive from a sovereign Armenian power.

In the West, the revival of politics took place in Venice, where young clergymen from the Catholic world – Mekhitar de Sébaste, Mikaël Tchamtchian and Ghoukas Intchitchian – orchestrated the Armenian cultural revival based on humanism. Concerned about ecumenism, the Venice movement defended a cultural and religious vision of politics, namely the participation of Armenians in the spread of European civilization considered superior to other world civilizations.

Other centres of rebirth emerged, in Constantinople and Tbilisi and, among pockets of Armenian resistance in the eighteenth and nineteenth centuries, in Zeitun or Karabakh for example. None, however, had as profound an effect on Armenian political development as the two complementary movements of Madras and Venice.

It was from these two poles of political revival that there emerged a process of secularization of expatriate Armenians, despite not having had much of an impact on the majority of the group. The reasons for the lack of impact were that these two groups operated from abroad. They may have been in contact with Armenian religious authorities, but they did not act directly on Armenians of the two empires. The two groups did not share a vision of politics, which could have fostered the empowerment of those within the imperial institutions. Finally, these two movements contained a certain number of paradoxes. Venice, in the heart of Europe and modernity, conveyed an essentially religious message, while the current of the times was essentially redolent of the philosophers and lay thinkers of the Enlightenment. Since the Mekhtaris message was essentially Catholic, the majority religion in Western Europe at the time, the people did not see in this 'progressive' order anything more than an extension of the traditional Vatican discourse. It was a Catholic message, whereas Armenians were mostly affiliated with the Armenian Apostolic Church.

Meanwhile, Madras, at the heart of Asia, was mistakenly considered hostile to progress but developed a message that was modern and influenced by British thinkers. It was à priori favourable to secularization but inspired by the *Book of the Canon of the Armenian Church*.

So, the process of secularization of Armenian identity – or, more appropriately, of proto-secularization – was launched, but two remarks are nevertheless necessary. On the one hand, this twofold movement was based on national awareness and on a metaphysics of collective identity. Both Madras and Venice brought a fundamental sociological dimension to the perception of politics, but because of geographical distance the two movements were quickly assimilated to an idealistic perspective of national renewal. It was this that constituted the basis of politics in the diaspora. Whether one was religiously inspired in Venice or economically inspired in Madras, politics was nourished by elements of a spiritual nature: one sublimated what resembled national consciousness on both sides of historical Armenia and found oneself arguing policy without a territorial basis within the territory of origin. The territorial basis existed but did not go beyond mythification. From a political point of view, this resulted in a clear break with reality. Among Armenians, from the Middle Ages to the present age, politics thus passed from deterritorialized political and religious particularism to an idealistic conception, which was itself deterritorialized. Hence, the recurring idea of deterritorialization was exacerbated by the distance from the territory, or the reality. It was only in the nineteenth century that the revolutionary movement proposed the first elements of realism in the conception of politics. But here again, messianism gained the upper hand over pragmatism.

Although the expatriate centres in Venice and in Madras experienced difficulties introducing themselves into the socio-political reality of historical Armenia, they participated in the nineteenth-century process of Europeanization of the empires of the Orient, building on the ideas of the Enlightenment. From such European colonization was born the first revolutionary groups of the second half of the nineteenth century, but also the first Armenian Protestant centres in Constantinople – the source of new identities.

In the course of migration to Europe and the rest of the world, centres of diasporic activity found themselves confronted with a plurality of references to the country to which they had been attached. These multiple references did not promote the unity of a collective consciousness focused on a central fact. Among the Jews, nothing can replace Jerusalem as a single political–religious centrepoint. But, in the Armenian diaspora, the focal points of Armenian identity are less clear – especially since there is not one Armenian diaspora but many, originating from various states and cultures. In Lebanon and Syria most Armenians are from Cilicia, which is reflected in geographical references specific to this province that is currently a part of Turkey. In France, the French of Armenian origin come from different Ottoman provinces, as well from Cappadocia and historical Armenia. Therefore, points of reference are necessarily diverse.

3

Socio-Economic Domination

Armenians' long history of foreign domination has conditioned their mindset and prepared them for economic and social dependency. The people have long paid tribute and taxes and have contributed to the fiscal policies of their conquerors and the Church.

Since the end of the Middle Ages, socio-economic domination has taken three forms. First, the integration of Armenians into the Persian, Ottoman and Russian Empires split them into several economic models that were governed by the arbitrary bureaucratic policies then in place: tax levies, notably those of the Osmanlis and the Romanovs, transformed the social bases of the Armenian family model, locking them into economic systems that were by nature unequal and in which they were the greatest losers.

Second, socio-economic domination, which resulted in the modernization of the Ottoman and Russian Empires in the nineteenth century, also changed the relationship between individuals and their communities. The process of Westernization and the rationalization of policies that were inaugurated in the nineteenth century by enlightened rulers in faraway Constantinople and St Petersburg disrupted the Armenian community. Torn between the newly expressed need for personal emancipation and the necessary respect for ancestral traditions, Armenians and their institutions struggled to adapt. The new attitudes included individual empowerment and loyalty to the home community, the rise of nationalism, an awareness of working-class conditions and disparities between the Armenians of Russia and Turkey, as well as those between the cities and the provinces, the weight of religion and progress towards secularization and rivalry between the apostolic Church and the rising Catholic and Protestant orders. To these many transformations that were driven by the outside world, we must add internal factors: the social and economic transformation of the Armenians, who were affected by massacres, emigration and the resulting demographic changes, which led to an Islamicization and Turkification of the Ottoman territory.

Third, despite socio-economic dependence, Armenians resisted modernity and found refuge once again in a particularly lively sociology of religion that was deeply rooted in local attitudes. They owed this to their fidelity to the message of the Church and to the place occupied in their daily lives by the work of the eleventh-century mystical monk Gregory of Narek.[1] This aspect of religion was so prevalent that it survived genocide and Soviet totalitarianism. Neither the Ittihadism of the Young

---

[1] Gregory of Narek, *Paroles à Dieu*, Introduction, translation and notes by Annie and Jean-Pierre Mahé, (Peeters, 2007).

Turks nor the Stalinism of the Bolsheviks succeeded in separating Armenians from their unshakable attachment to the *Nareg*, a bulwark of familiar sayings that rejected all assimilation. This work succeeded in reinforcing Armenian identity but did little to encourage Armenian resistance to domination.

Subject to systems of inequality

Between integration into empire and the end of the First World War, Armenian patriarchal society suffered two socio-cultural shocks. On the one hand, there was the absorption of the traditional Armenian model by imperial societies. On the other hand, there was the meeting between the Armenian community order and the Westernization of Ottoman and Russian societies. In the aftermath of the war, while there was hardly anything left of Armenian patriarchal society in the new Turkey, the family system adapted itself to communism as remnants of this model were recreated in the Armenian colonies overseas. From the fifteenth century onwards, Armenian social history followed a pattern of successive hardships for families who were, in fact, heirs to a rich heritage. With the exception of democratic Western host societies, it is clear that the Armenian patriarchal model is more at ease with economic systems that promote inequality.

The social organization that was in place among Armenian religious communities in the rival empires changed from within but did not completely change the order of things. The process of Armenian modernization was not taken to its logical conclusion: namely, the development of a new social group. A bourgeoisie was created to ensure continuity with the past and to encourage modernity. As a pre-bourgeois group, Armenian merchants were occasionally successful in passing for old nobility. For the most part, however, they failed to assume the political and social role that could reasonably have been expected of a bourgeois class connecting both aspects of the Armenian world. An examination of Armenian social history going back to the eighteenth and nineteenth centuries reveals that a proper Armenian bourgeoisie never developed past the stage of embryonic social groups in non-Armenian urban centres, such as Tbilisi, Baku, Constantinople and Smyrna (Izmir). These never arose in Armenia proper. This is hardly surprising since, as we have seen, historically Armenia did not cultivate urban centres or trading activities connected to the outside world – an additional factor that distanced Armenians from modernity. This is the principal lesson to be learned from observing the social organization of Armenian communities when confronted with empires in transformation.

At the beginning of the nineteenth century, there were over 3 million Armenians, most of whom were settled in the Ottoman and Russian Empires, with a scattering in Persia, India, the Balkans and Western Europe. Nearly two-thirds of Armenians were settled in the eastern *vilayets* of Turkey and in its capital, Constantinople. (The census of 1831 counted a total population of 160,000. In the 1860/1880 census, Armenians living in Constantinople numbered between 250,000 and 300,000.) In the early twentieth century (c. 1910), just across the Araxe River from the Persian Empire, Armenians accounted for approximately 1.8 million Tsarist subjects. If they shared a religion, a system of writing, a spoken language (with Western and Eastern dialects) and common historical references, the worlds in which they lived were very different: The Ottoman Empire was both a Muslim state, protector of Islam's holy places and a caliphate led by the sultan, defender of the faith and Islamic high authority in the world. The Russian Empire, however, was an Orthodox theocracy. If in the nineteenth century Russia was a conquering empire in full expansion, the Ottoman Empire was on the defensive following the loss of many territories in Europe and around the Mediterranean. Socially, this difference was fundamental and makes it possible to better understand how Armenians of the Caucasus, galvanized by the Russian spirit of conquest, felt for their brothers who were 'prisoners' in Turkey; a protective instinct that the Russians manipulated with great deftness when they proclaimed themselves protectors of the Empire's Christian and Orthodox populations. Regardless, in both empires, Armenians were a dominated people.

Physical insecurity in the Ottoman Empire

It is difficult to understand Armenian social reality in the Ottoman Empire if, from the outset, there is no distinction between the Armenians of Constantinople or *Bolis* and the Armenians of the eastern provinces, the *vilayets* of historical Armenia: foreign worlds under a shared political roof. These worlds depended on different political systems. The first existed in the capital, with its centres of power, its institutions, its veneer of order and legality, its openness to Europe. The second was the world of the *vilayet* or, the provinces, where insecurities (tribal raids, food shortages and arbitrary authorities) and social injustices were the norm. If the language, religion, ethnicity and status as *dhimmi* were common to both rural and city dwellers, the living conditions of the people and their environment were different and varied according to whether one lived in the city or in the countryside. The Church linked these two faces of the Armenian community and assumed the role of community mediator, as specifically intended by a grant of privilege from the Sublime Porte in 1764. Under its aegis, the Armenian millet constituted an example of loyalty and integration within the framework of the Ottoman political balancing of extra-territorial nationalities, such as other non-Muslims, Christian Armenians and Jewish *dhimmi* (ie 'protected' citizens but nonetheless outside the law). The Armenian was a *raya*, a second-class citizen, subject to higher tax burdens than the Muslim populations. Armenians were not allowed to ride horses or carry weapons and were prohibited from wearing certain colours. They did not have a right to lodge a complaint against a Muslim. Nor could an Armenian hold public office.

In the Ottoman countryside, life was very much as it would have been in medieval times, particularly in its lawlessness, a circumstance that contrasted directly with urban life, where Armenian circumstances were different especially if one were a member of the *Amiras* or emir class. Since the sixteenth century, the sultan had relied on this Armenian social group, made up of bankers and financial intermediaries, servants of the state whose rise to power in the eighteenth century revealed the rapid development of capitalism in the Ottoman Empire. Indispensable for the collection of taxes, especially in times of war, at the turn of the nineteenth century the *Amiras* formed a financial oligarchy of about 100 families (eg Balian, Ayvazian, Yeramian and Dadian) whose positions allowed them to exist as hereditary dynasties at the heart of the Ottoman system. If they adopted the behaviour of traditional Armenian aristocracy, the comparison ended there. Armenian *Amiras* did not constitute a dynastic, therefore, political system, with its balance of functions within their caste and particular roles as was the *primus inter pares* in the medieval model. The Amiras had no drive to govern, no *orinapar* or *ichkhanapar*. They led the Church, however, dominating the assembly of clerics and laity that elected the patriarch. Upon investiture, the patriarch received the imperial *firman* in exchange for a large payment which only the *Amiras* were able to provide. The latter also controlled all activities related to the Patriarchate, including administrative law, charitable contributions, education, publishing, the justice system and culture.

The Tanzimat disrupted this traditional order. The decline of the *Amiras* benefited the rise of another social group, the *Esnaf* – merchant guilds and corporations of artizans and shopkeepers, hitherto excluded from community affairs but in direct contact with the Armenians of the Eastern vilayets and with Armenian merchants on the road in India, Europe, Iran and Russia. After more than four decades of struggle between *Amiras* and *Esnafs*, equivalent to the upper and lower middle classes, between 1820 and 1863, the latter managed to progressively occupy key positions within the community. The democratization of the millet benefited from these exchanges between city and countryside. The adoption in 1863 of community by-laws – dubbed Internal Regulations of the Armenian community – which Armenians treated as a national constitution, summarized the victory of the *Esnafs* over the *Amiras*. Democratization also coincided with the Armenian cultural awakening, which, because of a lack of secular theorists, treated political subjects in such a way as to make a mockery of Armenian conservatism and the luxury of the Church. This cultural profusion wreaked havoc with traditional ideas and with authors such as Dzerents (1822–1888) and Mamourian (1820–1901) and coincided with new demands, such as the defence of women's rights by Serpouhi Dussap (1841–1901). The literature of the period led Constantinople's Armenians to rediscover the virtues of the countryside, the *Yerkir*, in direct contrast with the opulence and hypocrisy of the city. Poets such as Meguerditch Bechiktachlian (1828–1868) and Tovmas Terzian (1840–1909) attacked religion and extolled national momentum, freedom, nature and love, themes also found in theatre, the works of Hagop Baronian (1843–1891) and, above all, those of Yervant Odian (1869–1926), the father of Armenian satire. This period of cultural flourishing corresponded with a flowering of culture and the dispatch of young people to France and Switzerland to complete their university studies and also with the development of Armenian schools in the capital as well as in the provinces, where students were taught vernacular Armenian, foreign languages and new disciplines. The Church had no choice but to follow the movement, especially since its monopoly on Catholic doctrine was challenged by the sultan's authorization of Catholic and Protestant millets among the Armenians – two orders receptive to European modernity and popular with provincial Armenians.

Paradoxically, the Tanzimat transformation of Ottoman society did not give rise to the results expected by its promoters in the Armenian countryside. The Armenian peasant world emerged from the Tanzimat reforms even more disorientated than it was when Abdul Hamid II ascended the Ottoman throne. If the Tanzimat produced in Constantinople a blossoming of the arts, a flourishing press and daring new writers overthrowing old ideas, in rural Armenia inequalities were exacerbated. Even within the Armenian millet, the 1863 reform failed to promote equality or better representation for rural Armenians in the Patriarchate. Rural Armenians were still under-represented in church assemblies, even though they made up a significant majority of the Ottoman Armenian population and remained so even after the 1908 restoration of the constitution. The opening of the empire aggravated the social disparities in the provinces and allowed correspondents of the foreign press to see for themselves the misery and insecurity of Armenian peasants, who were living sedentary lives and were confronted by a difficult co-existence with nomadic Kurdish tribes and the resettlement of Balkan Muslim refugees among the *vilayets* of the Black Sea and the Caucasus. The abduction of women (for forced marriages or harems) and children (for enlistment as Janissaries or as labourers when the authorities offered to teach them a trade) was common practice, with abuses numbering in the thousands. The traditional Armenian family entered the nineteenth century in disorder and in total uncertainty. The Armenian community was not prepared for the promised rural reforms, which would only have exacerbated their complete isolation from any modernizing impulse. The Ottoman tradition destabilized Armenian culture to its foundations and Tanzimat modernization ended all hope of a better life. There remained the inevitable salvation through revolt. The first Armenian secret societies appeared in the years 1870–1880. In the beginning, these were formed by teenagers without schools and landless peasants and brigands without families, all converted into activists with a desperate cause, mobilized against injustice.

Risks of assimilation into the Russian Empire

Just across the Araxe River, in the Russian Empire, the Armenians of the Caucasus offered a distinct but parallel approach. It was distinct because the nationalities of the Empire were treated in more or less the same way by the central Russian power. Armenians, however, were integrated into society and did not live in a climate of isolated insecurity like their Turkish cousins. Otherwise, the socio-economic picture in the Caucasus was similar to that of the Armenians of Cilicia. A large majority of Caucasian Armenians were peasants. Etchmiadzin was the only institution recognized by the central authorities, especially since Peter the Great had recognized the Armenian Apostolic Church under the *Pologenia* (regulation) promulgated on 11 March 1836. The Tsar designated the Catholicos and, in exchange for political domination, *Pologenia* granted religious and cultural autonomy to Armenians. Less fragmented geographically than the Armenians of Turkey, those of the Caucasus evolved mainly in five governorates: Tbilisi, Yerevan, Kars, Elizabetpol and Baku. After several administrative divisions that were more or less faithful to patterns of ethnic settlement, Armenians found themselves to be the majority in Yerevan (60%) and nearly a third of the population of the former khanates of Tbilisi (28%), Elizabetpol (33%) and Kars (30%). There were Armenian pockets in other parts of Great Russia, especially around the

Black Sea and in the North Caucasus but also in Moscow and St Petersburg, not to mention the 100,000 Armenians in Iran, a group that was culturally close to the Caucasian Armenians.

While serfdom prevailed throughout Russia, it hardly existed in Armenia and Azerbaijan. By a decree of 1846, the imperial power recognized the nobility of *moulk* and *tioul*, essentially Muslim and the hereditary nature of the land. A special regime was established in the governorate of Yerevan, where 80 per cent of Armenian villagers were state peasants while the remaining 20 per cent were owner peasants. The fate of peasants established on the estates belonging to the Armenian Church was no better. Rates, taxes and other forms of servitude overwhelmed them. The Armenian peasantry was therefore poor, dependent upon landlords and exploited at will. This dependence pushed them to leave the arid lands of the South Caucasus to swell the population of the two main cities, Tbilisi and Baku, where they excelled in crafts, trade and exploitation of oil and gas. The Mantachev, Khougassov, Mirzoev and Liazanov families made their fortune in oil in Baku.

Armenian peasants did not really benefit from the Russian reforms of the nineteenth century. Encouraged by their church, Armenians welcomed the Russians as liberators, fought for them during the expansion in the eighteenth and nineteenth centuries, but were not rewarded for their loyalty. Russia had a policy of assimilation for ethnic nationalities, which gained in physical security but lost their autonomy.

At the end of the nineteenth century, Armenians represented about 4 million people spread over three empires. Their journey through the modernization of the Ottoman and Russian empires took place between exacerbated anxiety and lost hope. In Turkey, their physical safety was even more threatened than it had been before the Tanzimat period. In Russia, assimilation in the name of Christian solidarity ruptured the community between those who lived totally in the Russian frame, without any political sense and those who superimposed their dreams of liberation from Turkish Armenia onto Russian expansionism. But this was an abortive vision, because, in both empires, those who had the capacity to carry the idea of emancipation, the bourgeoisie, were largely absent. The Armenian bourgeoisie seems to have been too closely integrated into the workings of the state to judge whether it would be useful to reorientate state activities in favour of a national group. Perhaps it simply did not believe in its own Armenian politics. What is certain, though, is that without the participation of the bourgeoisie in revolutionary dynamics, there could be no fertile encounter with political modernity and much less the idea of a nation-state. Without the participation of a national bourgeoisie, which was isolated geographically and socially from rural living conditions, the revolution passed into the hands of the peasantry. Disconnected from the mainstream of ideas and defended by teachers without a natural leader, or a consensual project for the community, this group was also not up to the task.

Sociology and religion

As a unifying vector of the Armenian nation, religion is a form of bond, a thread of identity. The Church, however, is not exempt from responsibility for maintaining the mentality of domination that characterized Armenians. Why would they accept such injustices? This is a question that crosses one's mind when reading their story. 'They could not do otherwise' writes the historian and orientalist Jean-Pierre Mahé, 'it is we who imposed the behavior'.[2] As we have already seen, religion can be a source of dispute, but the recourse to violence was invoked by rural priests, not by the patriarchs of Constantinople or Etchmiadzin, eager for power and hostile to any insubordination. In Constantinople, the patriarchs were terrified that by thwarting the sultan they risked destabilizing the *Amiras* upon whom so many real and imagined privileges depended.

On the eve of conversion to Christianity, Armenia had a divided religious profile. Rural areas had been stamped with a properly Armenian paganism, alongside Zoroastrianism from the Arsacid period to which the nobility adhered for reasons that were more political than religious. In only a short century, Christianity managed to instil religious unity while preserving the pagan past both in practice and in the Zoroastrian monotheistic mentalities useful for the organization of the clergy. From this point, Armenia would become the crucible of pagan cultural thought, supervised by a functioning Zoroastrian clergy. Paganism and Christianity merged to create something very specific, such that the chronicler Goriun called upon Armenians to rid themselves of the 'rust of useless cults', referring to pagan rites, a reality that would never actually disappear. Armenian Christianity was superimposed on paganism to become what is perhaps the most pagan of Christian rites. Theologically speaking, Christianity absorbed paganism without suppressing it. Thus, many Christian ceremonies still celebrated today have their roots in pagan cults, such as the Madagh (bread and boiled mutton) festival and the Vartavar festival (dedicated to water deities).

According to one observer, the process of rationalization or secularization changed the situation in the West. As a result of religious disputations, European Catholicism gradually became more of a faith than a dogma, especially following the reformation. As Benjamin Braude stated: 'Faith is a religion that has gone through the process of secularization.' Enlightenment ideas completed this process in Europe. In Armenia, however, the process of enlightenment ended in Venice with the Mekhitarists, under the influence of Europeans and for the Armenian merchants in India, under the influence of the British. If the Armenians of the Caucasus and the Middle East remained faithful to religion as a customary practice, those settled in the West seemed more receptive to the practice of a secularized and more modern faith. The Armenian Church has therefore remained a religion of observance, namely observance of customary practices. It is also a religion of precise gesture and is very demanding in terms of knowledge of rites and services.

[2] Interview with Jean-Pierre Mahé, Paris, 3 June 2013.

Part II

Attempts to Change the Course of History

It is neither fate nor curse. History is not written by dipping a pen of enslavement in the inkwell of memory. It must be free from all domination, unburdened from the weight of the past without denying it, yet one must take a necessary step back to be able to understand the real world around us, without judging the responsibilities of yesteryear but objectively learning lessons from the suffering endured. Face the world as it is, not as your forefathers would like it to be, such is the motto of the defenders of realism and modernity. This break in history, which marks a new era in the collective future, is destined to embrace the themes of its time, their guidelines and their power struggles, their illusions and their realities, their archaism and their progress borne by older or younger actors. Giving up the absolute, stifling memory, frozen and monopolized by the guardians of the politico-religious temple of Armenian identity, is resuming the course of one's life, taking one's destiny in hand and planning one's own path, without determinism or contingencies. It means opening new horizons and trying new social relationships. It is communicating like everyone else, with a common language, representations shared by the greatest number and it is most of all (re)learning the meaning of universal values to better anchor those of one's specificity in history.

This surge of historicity was set in motion three times by the Armenians in our contemporary period. The first time was the revolutionary movement, proud of its new conception of identity and politics, its bases and instruments, its messages and messengers. The second time was during the Soviet episode when, in the name of realism, Armenians who were then prisoners of communist totalitarianism or dispersed throughout the world struggled to rebuild an identity and heal the deep wounds of the past. Finally, the third attempt at breaking from the course of history occurred during the revival of the Armenian state in 1991, at the time of the fall of the USSR and the end of the cold war, a qualitative leap that propelled the entire nation and humanity in a twenty-first century that had not yet begun. Each time, men and women attempted to write new chapters of their nation's history with instruments and ideas within their reach which they considered essential for the construction of a better life. After all, they thought, do Armenians not have the right to write a future as rich as their past?

4

The Revolutionary Movement, 1878–1914

The revolutionary movement aimed to free itself from the domination discussed in Part I of this book. Exogenously, it emerged as the logical consequence of the European inability to enforce the Berlin Treaty across the Ottoman Empire. Faced with this failure, the Armenian revolutionaries came to the conclusion that they had to take control in one of two ways: either insist on European mediation for the implementation of reform or go beyond the framework of diplomacy that restrained liberation and resort to direct action. Endogenously, the revolutionary movement fed on the injustice meted out to Ottoman Armenians, whose servitude only ended when fair and lasting agrarian reform was put in place in the Osmanlis Empire. The revolutionary movement, therefore, decided to focus initially on the cause of Armenians in Turkey and then on the liberation of all Armenians from both empires. First, the movement hesitated between respect for international law and treaties. Second, it was torn between the liberation of all Armenia and solely its western side, Turkish Armenia. Third, it was torn between chauvinism and internationalism. Fourth, it found itself at the crossroads of various ideologies: traditionalism (rural areas) and liberalism (urban areas) originating from the Ottoman Empire and populism (rural areas) and Marxism (urban areas) specific to the Russian Empire. Moreover, as it was divided across several empires, the revolutionary movement was unclear about its purpose. State or federation? Independence or federalization? It remained unclear about its strategy: should it prioritize the liberation of the nation or the reunification of territories? Finally, the division between nationalism and socialism was the finishing touch to the architecture of a revolutionary movement that lacked unity and cohesion. Yet, this national liberation movement's common denominator was the need to create an autonomous space for politics, the (re)construction of the nation and the fight against injustice.

One person epitomized all the contradictions of the revolutionary movement: Christapor Mikaelian (1859–1905). He alone embodied a social construction of politics and encompassed all these inconsistencies and similarities. As he moved forward, the whole Armenian national revival took shape and found its pace in cities and rural areas, in the empires and abroad. Aware of the discrepancies of the revolutionary times before anyone else, he took on all these paradoxes, divergences and incompatibilities to better regulate them, find areas of convergence and also to dissipate any uncertainty among the revolutionaries about the legitimacy of their fight. Mikaelian was more than the founder of a party or the prophet of the revolution: he embodied authority; he was an incubator for ideas and principles. Hence, when he created the ARF in 1890, the foundations of Christaporism were already laid.

Christaporism was a sociological method of union and an instrument of liberation in line with the realities of its time. On the methodological level, Christaporism was a break from memory and was based essentially on action in the positivist tradition of Auguste Comte (1798–1857). It held the idea that to regenerate and become healthy, society must focus on the duties of individuals – as stated in the ARF's Rules: 'there are no rights but only duties'.[1] It relied on the people as a social actor and built its analysis around social fact. It structured the modern birth of politics and strove, in the name of perpetual peace, to construct in the pure Kantian style of a world federation of free national unities. In terms of resources, Christaporism was based on the two main ideas of the late nineteenth century and early twentieth century, nationalism and socialism, as well as all that social science, beginning with sociology, history and geography, could provide as founding elements.

Christaporism, the embodiment of politics

Mikaelian was born on 18 October 1859 in the village of Upper Agulis, located in the Goght'an district, in the Nakhchivan province, at the southern edge of the Russian Empire and on the border of the Persian Empire, close to the Ottoman Empire. At the heart of the three empires, the town of Agulis had traditionally been known in Armenian history as a leading commercial and cultural centre in the region. Located at the crossroads of trade routes, Agulis was able to prosper from the seventeenth century through economic exchanges and the local Armenian merchants' spirit of openness, with some of them, such as Zacharia, developing early relations with European trading centres, such as Livorno, Amsterdam, Madrid and Lisbon. The residents have kept this spirit of openness and solidarity between peoples and it is likely that Mikaelian, himself a member of a family of merchants, was raised in that tradition of respect for others, of knowledge and relations with the outside world. He grew up in a family of seven children but was soon confronted with death: first his mother, then two brothers and later his grief-stricken father. He was a reserved child, close to his four sisters with whom he maintained a steady correspondence throughout his life. He was a serious student, educated in religious schools and part of a generation of children who benefited from the development of the school network in Russian Armenia. Because of its commercial tradition, Agulis, where Armenians, Tatars and other minorities lived either in separate or mixed neighbourhoods (Christapor himself lived in an Armenian–Turkish district), promoted foreign language teaching in schools and especially French, which Christapor was comfortable with. After the death of his father, he was raised by his uncle, with whom he was occasionally in conflict and his older sister, who watched over him like a second mother. Having attracted the attention of the teaching staff, Christapor was invited to continue his studies in Tbilisi where he spent six years

---

[1] This narrative-inspired quote was also cited by Ziya Gökalp, the theorist of the Party of Union and Progress of the Young Turks and Pan-Turkism.

(1874–1880). It was during his training in Tsarist Georgia that the young Armenian, shocked by the working conditions of the peasants and workers, became acquainted with political ideas, especially those circulated by the Narodnalia y Volia movement – a secret society which gave birth to the first political party in Russia promoting populism and terrorism. A sympathizer and later a member of this clandestine group, he devoured subversive literature but did not allow himself to become locked into a dogma. He was there to learn and defined himself as a citizen of the world, of Russian education – at this time he still went by the name of Christapor Mikaelov – and was open to anything that may have anything to do with the revolutionary idea. Impervious to the problem of nationalities, Christapor joined a circle with internationalist values and sympathy for the cause of Russian moujiks freed from serfdom since 1861. After his clandestine activities were revealed to the school's management, he was expelled. He returned to his village, where he taught social sciences in his former school.

Christapor and the 'Bergsonian synthesis'

We do not know the direct causes that reorientated Mikaelian's thinking towards the national question but, from 1878, the Armenian theme seems to have been increasingly central to his activities. No historian has studied this central episode of Mikaelian's biography and we cannot dismiss the idea that he had sincere conviction combined with an excessive ambition to leave his mark upon his time, with every opportunity being taken to assert his authority. His transition from internationalism to national concerns occurred gradually, but as a series of sudden developments took place: the Russo–Turkish war of 1877–1878, the decline of Narodnalia y Volia after 1881, the reactionary turn of Alexander III and the closing of Armenian schools by decree of the Tsar in 1885.

The early 1880s were decisive years for Armenian political development. At that time a few small and underground groups were supporting the Armenian cause, but none of them operated beyond the perimeter of their respective leaders' villages and they did not have the necessary means to carry out a large-scale action capable of persuading the Armenians to engage in a national trajectory away from Russian political life. For the first time, Armenian political development made a move away from the Russian course of history and began advocating autonomy, as did other nationalities fuelled by the same impulse for emancipation. But the rift never really happened. For many Armenians in the Caucasus, political affairs, though they may have existed in principle, were an extension of Russia and not a break from the Slav world. Politics as a structuring phenomenon was Russian or was not. This anchoring in the future of Russia was at the core of the dysfunction of Haitadism. Either it was detached from Russian nationalism, in the name of freedom following its own course, with the independence of Armenia as a goal, or Haitadism was an autonomous but inseparable subsection of Russia because, in the name of national security, the ultimate goal could only be the reunification of territories, beginning with the liberation of Ottoman Armenia with the purpose of federating with Russia. Mikaelian was well aware of the scope and differences in this split between independence and federalism. For him, overcoming such contradictions required a great knowledge of political theory.

In the mid-1880s, Mikaelian left Tbilisi to continue his training in Moscow. He immersed himself in revolutionary literature and read everything he could lay his hands on: Alexander Herzen, Nikolai Chernyshevsky, Petr Lavrov, Nicolai Mikhailovsky, Robert Owen, Georg Wilhelm Friedrich Hegel, Herbert Spencer, Immanuel Kant, Auguste Comte, Emile Durkheim, Henri Bergson and Karl Marx, whose materialist dialectic gradually infiltrated Russian student circles. Raised as a Christian and familiar with national populism, Mikaelian reorientated his position to fit into a vague pre-Marxist socialism while immersing himself in Kant's ideas. By 1887 he had run out of money and left Moscow to return to Tbilisi. This time, his mature mind, universalist ethics and solid ideological corpus convinced his peers to follow the paths of revolution. In Moscow, he had become close to Simon Zavarian, a serious agricultural engineer and a disciple of Bakunin. In Tbilisi, where he worked as a subeditor for a Russian newspaper, *Novoye Opozrenie*, he befriended the voluble Stepan Zorian, alias Rostom, a Marxist adept with explosives and a brilliant organizer of subversion. Other students followed him in his revolutionary mission to liberate Turkish Armenia from the Ottoman yoke. In the second city of the empire, Mikaelian's private life became complicated. He resisted the temptation to deceive his friend, Lavroussevich – he had fallen in love with his wife Ekinia. She was a young Russo-Polish Jewish revolutionary, the daughter of a Russian general. Mikaelian left Tbilisi in a hurry for Agulis in 1889 after creating a Young Armenia organization. He reappeared in the city in July 1890 to answer the incessant calls of Ekinia with whom he had been exchanging letters. She announced that she was divorcing her husband, so Ekinia and Christapor no longer had to hide. They were married and had a son named Roupen.

Other less personal reasons were behind Mikaelian's precipitous return to Tbilisi. By the end of August, he had launched the ARF. All the revolutionaries living in Armenia gathered in Tbilisi in the summer of 1890. There were Armenagans determined to play the federation game without being absorbed because, unlike other movements, in their stronghold of Van they would be first in line in the event of Turkish aggression. There were Hunchakian Social Democrats, such as Roupen Khan Azad and Hagop Meghavorian, determined to take the lead in the revolution because their programme was the most successful and they had political connections in Europe and Russia, including Plekhanov. There were also bourgeoisie led by Constantine Khadissian and Levon Sarkissian, who were determined to raise the flag of nationalism to avoid socialist contagion and the scattering of forces. There were also liberals such as Jean Loris-Melicof, a nephew of the Tsar's minister and Agnouni, who were keen on the Westernization of the movement. Finally, there were relatives of Mikaelian himself, such as Abraham Dastakian, who were known for their flexibility and political experience. How could all these contradictory currents be integrated into a single organization? Mikaelian was not satisfied with the nature of the first two Armenian parties. He regarded the Armenagan Party as too regionalist, too chauvinistic and too close to the Church. To him, the SDHP seemed too internationalist, too far removed from the social realities of the Armenian peasant in Anatolia and its socialist programme too unrealistic. He was not satisfied with liberals who lacked the stamina for action. Finally, he could not join the bourgeois nationalists as a left winger with a proletarian background.

Until his death in 1905, Mikaelian spent his time perfecting and refining his federation, moving from one city and country to another and making the necessary adjustments. He was fully aware of its fragile structure. He knew that Armenians were divided on all levels and that only the will of men living in the real world could consolidate the foundations of his federation.

Despite the hardships experienced by the ARF throughout its history, it is surprising to note that its balance between socialism and nationalism managed to survive. Haitadism and its main actor, Dashnakism, existed before the formation of the Armenian state. The ARF was thus able to maintain its unity thanks to a political programme that satisfied both socialists and nationalists. To understand this uniqueness, let us recall that the ARF was a multipurpose organization whose recruitment capabilities appeared in its very name. Mikaelian chose the term 'revolutionary' without specifying its content: was it a national revolution (*Zavarianism*), a democratic revolution (*Varandianism*), a social revolution (*Rostomism*) or a territorial revolution (*Doumanism*)? It does not really matter, because Dashnakism was neither right wing nor left wing, neither progressive nor conservative, neither pro-European nor pro-Eastern. As a left-wing movement, it could be Marxist, anti-Marxist or part of national socialism. As a right-wing movement, its identity was reflected in its liberalism, radical or traditional nationalism or even in the context of a struggle for national liberation at the service of a mythical socialism. Indeed, whether socialist or nationalist, the word Dashnak often served as a catch-all for a single aim: settling the Armenian Question.

Hopes and disillusionment

Dashnakism had its own codes, images, truths and hopes. It also had its own tones and rhythms. A new world unfolded with each of its representations. It offered a new reading of the past and present and anticipated the future. Time had no secret for true believers, who revisited all sectors of social activity to better dominate it and impart its destiny. This new ethics was also weighed down by uncertainties and disillusions. To choose Dashnakism was thus to be reincarnated in an Armenian society, to organize and reify it. It was also to create or reproduce an identity without really taking a stance on national conservatism or universal progress. In other words, Mikaelian's federation followed an ideology of instinct, where the urge to destroy was hidden behind the noble intention of gathering people around the project of a new Armenia.

A spontaneous and organized movement

Between hopes and disenchantment, what did the federation actually give birth to? Let us first recall the circumstances of its creation. As the historian Anahide Ter-Minassian points out, 'the ARF was founded in 1890 but it was not really created at that time'.[2]

---

[2] Anahide Ter-Minassian, *La question arménienne (The Armenian Question)*, (Marseille: Edition Parenthèses, 1983) p. 67.

Hratch Dasnabedian's statement is even clearer: 'The General Congress meeting in Tbilisi in the autumn of 1892 was, in fact, the founding Congress of a new party, this time unified and solid.'[3] More recently, Kevork Khutinyan, a post-Soviet historian, wrote on the occasion of the centenary of the first congress of 1892 that it was then that the ARF actually took shape, not at the 1890 congress.[4] What really happened in 1892? By changing its title from the Armenian Revolutionaries Federation to the Armenian Revolutionary Federation, Mikaelian aspired to make the movement into a sort of conglomerate of different political sensitivities fuelled by the sole purpose of action. Designed around this unity of action, the ARF could not be anything other, because it was clear that if the Dashnak movement had renounced the federation label to take on that of a party, it would have been unable to rally the Armenian nation around this new ethics. The ARF's opponents had perfectly understood the dilemma and had been successful in their efforts to prevent a merger between the federation and Haitadism by quickly giving the ARF the label of political party – on an equal footing with their own formations that were loyal to Haitadism. The idea that one could be a Haitadist without being a Dashnak had made its way into the Armenian nation. Not only did the Dashnaks' adversaries dissociate the ARF from Haitadism, while sometimes reappropriating its ideas and at other times its practices, but they also managed to reduce the Dashnaks' role to that of an actor – certainly the most imposing in the construction process of the Haitadist system, but far from Mikaelian's initial aspirations. Indeed, no formation had a monopoly on politics and Haitadism, even if their heirs claimed the contrary.

The ARF's opponents were not the only ones responsible for the dissociation between the federation and Haitadism. The Dashnaks themselves were divided on the question of different points of view in the system. Some sought to surround themselves with adverse forces in the name of democratizing the system. Others tried to embody the system by bringing about relay parties. How did the Dashnaks break away from Mikaelian's original idea? He did not invent the philosophy of contemporary history. Based on the metaphysical vision of his predecessors, he conceived the revolutionary period as an historical and scientific process that owed its existence to a spontaneous reaction of the masses, removed from the political scene, rather than to a specific decision. Mikaelian's whole philosophy relied on the idea of preserving this spontaneity. According to his plans, the Federation and Haitadism were going to form the new expression of an overall dynamic. This movement was named the Armenian Revolutionaries Federation (*Hai Heraporakaneri Dashnaktsutyun*), with the plural form particularly significant in that it reflected the necessary convergence of different revolutionary ambitions that were already in existence. As early as 1892, when the federation was renamed the Armenian Revolutionary Federation (*Hai Heraporakan Dashnaktsutyun*), the Dashnaks deviated from Mikaelian's concepts. While he continued to use the terms 'federation', 'movement' and 'Droshakists' to describe activists, other leaders spoke of 'party', 'organization' and 'partisans'. Gradually, therefore, Mikaelian was dispossessed from his federation.

---

[3] Hratch Dasnabedian, *Histoire de la Fédération révolutionnaire arménienne Dashnaktsutiun, 1890–1924* (Milan: Oemme Edizioni, 1988), pp. 120–126.
[4] Kevork Khutinyan, *La naissance de la Fédération Révolutionnaire Arménienne (The Birth of the Armenian Revolutionary Federation)* (Yerevan: Ardakers, 2000).

Was Dashnakism a form of totalitarianism in disguise? By grouping all relations between actors and systems into a single structure, the Dashnak movement was, as J-L Talmon stated 'a kind of democratic Messianism announcing a bright future that required a rapid upheaval of the world to become reality'.[5] The totalitarian face of Dashnakism embraced all social strata, encompassed a vast movement of individuals. The Dashnaks' Armenia was thus inclined to absorb all Armenian society. Indeed, it penetrated the entire social body, encroaching on all aspects of human life and controlling them. In other words, the Dashnaks set out to conquer the individual.

Owing to its protean nature, the Federation was an interface between utopia and reality. As an organization that intended to redistribute values and symbols, the ARF endeavoured to occupy a key position in Armenian political life. The middle ground status it aspired to gave it a partisan identity with multiple labels that justified its commitment on all fronts. The non-institutionalization of trends was then a means of effective mobilization throughout the world (Russia, Turkey, Iran, Europe, the United States until 1920). It allowed the ARF to benefit from important financial reserves when the Dashnak machine was in difficulty. It used social and national integration as part of its project of constructivist socialism. As a whole, it was a syncretic system, indisputably associated with Mikaelian's strong personality. His political thought was shaped by his experiences, hence the ambivalent character of his doctrine, which expressed flexibility in the face of life experiences and external phenomena. Yet what his doctrine lost in theoretical rigour, it gained in persuasive power and authenticity. Mikaelian thus displayed no particular affiliation with the political currents that proliferated in the nineteenth century. He was a practical man who, more than any other Armenian leader, instrumentalized modernity and tradition to serve the revolution and a new ethics of politics. Not only did he have a touch of genius, despite all the difficulties in gathering around him individuals who had nothing in common, but he also managed to turn his federation into a lasting phenomenon.

What were the different trends within the ARF? *Christaporism* was the result of a triple synthesis. The first aspect referred to the diversity of ideas inherited from the fathers of the revolution: Khatchadour Abovian and new identity; Mikael Nalbandian and the people's revolution; Khrimian Hayrig and national order; Krikor Ardzrouni and modernity and individuality; and, finally, Raffi and the sacredness of the territory. The second element comprised Kantian liberalism, Armenian Christianity, Russian populism and European Marxism.

The third element of Christaporism came in the form of Zavarianism (Khrimian Hayrig and a combination of liberalism and Christianity), Varandianism (Krikor Ardzrouni and a combination of liberalism and Marxism), Rostomism (Mikael Nalbandian and a combination of Marxism and populism) and Doumanism (Raffi and a combination of Christianity and populism). Such was Mikaelian's organization, powered by eight currents with the founder of the Federation at the centre:

---

[5]   Jacob L Talmon, *Les origines de la démocratie totalitaire* (*The Origins of Totalitarian Democracy*) (Paris: Calmann-Levy, 1970).

1. The *traditionalists* (half-Zavarianist, half-Doumanist), originating from Ottoman rural areas, were often made up of fedayis, stamped with anti-Turkism and Russophilia, attached to the land and ancestral values, consequently hostile to modernity and supporters of communitarianism and a patrimonial state.

2. The *military* (Doumanist), originating from both empires, these were true political missionaries, ingrained in rural areas, the territory and its liberation, a key principle of national salvation. They were hostile to modernity, both anti-Russian and anti-Turkish and advocates of a mythical socialism and a revolutionary state.

3. The *philosophers* (half-Doumanist, half-Rostomist), heirs to Russian populism and the myths of territory, federalist and pro-Russian and anti-Turkish, they remained faithful to a primitive socialism of the Narodnolia y Volia type, in favour of a federation between the two Armenias.

4. The *technicians* (Rostomist), mostly from Russia, supporters of the federation and the social revolution, advocated revolutionary socialism, in line with the Russian SRs.

5. The *economists* (half-Varandianist, half-Rostomist), originating from the Caucasus, artizans of a Marxist socialism, in favour of a Transcaucasian federation (therefore suspicious of the Russians) and the liberation of Turkish Armenia. They were open to modernity and the democratization of society.

6. The *diplomats* (Varandianist), originating from both empires, were Western-orientated, evolutionist and reformist. They practised democratic socialism and intended to progress gradually.

7. The *literary* (half-Varandianist, half-Zavarianist), originating from the great cities of the Ottoman Empire, supporters of a cultural revolution based on the education of the masses, oriented towards the rule of law and the modern state – a community of citizens.

8. The *moralists* (Zavarianist), originating from Turkey or totally inculcated with the psychology of the Armenians of Turkey, in favour of national or humanist socialism and of the nation-state and the national revolution, without class struggle or division between the religious and the secular.

At the end of the ninth congress in Yerevan in 1919, the ARF established its final objective, unchanged to this day: the creation of a free, independent, reunified, democratic and socialist Armenia. Free: in the sense of individual freedom as advocated by the Rostomists. Independent: a nation-state, as favoured by the Zavarianists. Reunited: the union of all territories, as prioritized by the Doumanists. Democratic: a democratic and evolutionist society in line with the Varandianists. Socialist: as in Mikaelian's schema, which covered the whole Dashnak system: national socialism, mythical socialism, revolutionary socialism and democratic socialism. Thus, it was not until 1918–1920, when Armenia became independent, that the ARF put an end to a period of disillusionment marked by abrupt political changes and medium-term objectives. Yet, rather than a unanimous position, this revealed deep internal disagreements, as much about the mode of legitimation of the state as about the political regime to be put in place. In order to maintain unity in the liberation movement, the Dashnaks opted for compromise. Thus, the formation of Armenia brought together all trends around the idea of a cultural revolution, based on the rescue of the Armenians and on the principle of colonization of the Armenian lands. They justified the creation of their Armenia along the principles of the revolution's voluntarism, national self-determination, the benefits of international law and, finally, the historical rights linking the Armenian people to their land. As a result, the differences between Mikael Varandian and Nigol Douman, Simon Zavarian and Rostom seemed less significant than their rhetoric might have led the observer to believe.

Even so, it would be a mistake to assume that such compromise was sufficient to create unity. In reality, the ARF never ceased, throughout its development, to be the locus of tension between schools of universalist and particularist thought, mainly interested in the need for identification with the ARF, the embodiment of Dashnak socialism's ethics. The name 'Armenia' symbolizes this partisan unity. But when it comes to legitimizing space, disagreements emerge again. Indeed, which 'Armenia' is it? Ottoman Armenia? Russian Armenia? Reunified Armenia? What is more, the name Armenia gives no indication of the country's legal framework or its regime. Is it a nation state or a national unit attached to a free world confederation? Is it a republican or a communitarian regime? The leaders never came to a decision because Mikaelian had never decided himself and they preferred to envisage a true, mythical Armenia in which some saw a modern, final achievement and others a traditional, spiritual entity. From its conception, Dashnakism has thus positioned itself halfway between modernity and tradition, between democracy and ethnicity, between secularization and religion – in other words, amid all that participates in the concept of Armenian identity.

As such, is the ARF a party or an organization? For Rostomists and Varandianists, it is a party of social transformation. For Zavarianists and Doumanists, it is a popular national organization. In fact, Mikaelian laid the foundations for an Armenian International. Just as Marx had created the First International in 1889, ancestor of the Second Socialist International, Mikaelian founded a similar phenomenon that spread around the world, beginning in Turkey, Russia, Europe and America, now rooted in more than 40 countries scattered across five continents. Within this Armenian International, everything is subject to discussion and interpretation. Not surprisingly, the Dashnak liberation movement was built on these dualities of identity. As a democratic movement, the ARF considers that the people, not religion, are the engine of history. They enjoy political rights superior to religious duties. For those who join this democratic school, the ARF represents one of the actors of Haitadism among all other political movements inspired by the same desire to solve the national problem. As an identity movement, the ARF embodies the guardian of Armenian spiritual tradition and memory, with land, religion and language as a means of defence. But it is no longer Haitadism; it is pan-Dashnakism. Internal struggles, beyond raising the legitimate issue of exercise of power, also reflect an identity quarrel where the partisans of a democratic, modern and secular Haitadism oppose the partisans of a totalitarian, ethnic and religious pan-Dashnakism. In short, the ARF has not yet begun, for fear of discord, the break between politics and religion or history and memory, in order to exist and develop, despite pressures, for as long as rationalism, individualism, traditionalism and mysticism co-exist in Haitadism.

5

Grounding the History of a Fragmented Identity, 1920–1988

Deprived of politics either by exile or by integration into the Soviet Union, it was by means of culture that Armenians finally came to terms with their own history. Re-examining Armenian architecture or literature, one is easily convinced of their influence on the collective consciousness. As a complement to politics in matters of sovereignty or as a substitute for politics in the case of domination, the cultural realm has experienced several periods of expansion, ultimately concluding with the new golden age of literature at the turn of the twentieth century, which was led by a generation of writers unrivalled in importance since the thirteenth century. Following the 1915 genocide and the Sovietization of Armenia, what remained of the national elite was particularly anxious to show, sometimes in unconscious forms, that cultural creation was not buried among the ruins of the massacres. In order to grasp the significance of the messages from the writers and cultural actors of the Armenian arts following the First World War, an examination of the legacy of the previous generation of writers, proposed by the magazine *Mehian* (Pagan Temple), reveals some important aspects. Indeed, one cannot properly evaluate the literary production of the years 1920–1930 without referring to this circle of writers who favour the 'sovereignty of a unified Armenian literature'.[1]

This crucial role of culture applies both in the diaspora and Soviet Armenia. The shared millennial cultural heritage proved a useful link between Armenians on both sides of the Iron Curtain. At first sight, literature seems to have fulfilled the mission of joining parts of the national story, like a jigsaw puzzle that combined representations of the past with elements from the future, made up of drama but also of hope, of hardship but also of life, of displacement but also of difference. Culture also functions as a tool for safeguarding the Armenian language.

Reconstructing history through literature

A republic without power, a state without sovereignty, a people without society, refugee colonies without a homeland; it is against this dark backdrop that, for better or worse,

---

[1] *Mehian*, No 1, 1 January 1914.

Armenian literature resurfaced in the early 1920s and was substituted for politics in an attempt to reconnect with history. Too heavily invested in partisan affairs, Dashnaks, communists and crypto-communists (the SDHP) and conservatives were tearing each other apart, whether for control of the diasporas or over the more central question of the legitimacy of the Soviet Republic of Armenia. They did not, however, succeed in tangibly affecting the subjects that concerned their compatriots scattered around the globe. But literature succeeded in filling this void with breathtaking realism, from the Caucasus to the United States via the Middle East and Europe and particularly France, where a community of Armenian writers distinguished itself from similar communities in Beirut, Boston or Yerevan. The Armenian exiles in Paris were dominated by a group who were profoundly marked by the nightmares of the First World War and the genocide. Krikor Beledian, professor of Armenian literature, remarks that there reigned in Paris a unique atmosphere derived from an experience unprecedented in Armenian memory, that of confrontation with the foreigner, the Other. This is not only an asset in the sense that it provokes openness and imagination, projection and identification, but also because 'it is where the confrontation with the surrounding world has been the strongest, the most dangerous and the most altered, this is where literature seems to have been most fruitful'.[2]

The Birth of National Communism

The reintroduction of Armenian identity into history can be considered in two ways. In the Soviet Union, reconstruction was collective; the history of identity was inscribed in the various stages of the construction of communism: five-year plans, collectivization, struggles within the CPSU and concerning Soviet power, Russification of the Armenian language, witch hunts and Stalinist purges. The Soviet Republic of Armenia was little more than a subdivision. As a territorial unit, it was fully integrated with the central government's orientations, with imposed agendas, politics and historical viewpoints. It had no room for manoeuvre and the power of Yerevan was symbolic at best. Even in its extra-territoriality, it was felt that society operated on the basis of 'foreign' Russian domination and was a cultural base under close surveillance. Armenian identity struggled to find expression through politics for the obvious reasons concerning deprivation of sovereignty, the Sovietization of minds and Stalinist totalitarianism. The cultural thus became a refuge for both society and local authorities, as well as the Yerevan government. The Soviet Republic of Armenia was a 'cultural republic, disenfranchised from its territory and destabilized' by the central power that decided everything. It was not until the death of Stalin in 1953 and during the de-Stalinization that followed in 1956 that, like the other Soviet Socialist Republics, this 'depoliticized republic' entered a process of collective redress for identity, starting with the rehabilitation of national elements, reinvesting with meaning historical landmarks that broke with Marxism but continued to be permeated by the dynamics of the central

---

[2] Krikor Beledian, *Cinquante ans de littérature arménienne en France* (Paris: CNRS Editions, 2001), p. 436.

government. The process of nationalization of the collective identity affected the whole of society, to the point where there was a reinstatement of the politico-religious and commensurate instrumentalization of the Church, an important refuge for Armenian identity. Major Armenian cultural figures such as Khatchadour Abovian, Raffi and Yeghiché Charents were rehabilitated. Dissident writers such as Gourguen Mahari and N Armen were released from prison. The statues of Stalin were dismantled in favour of a new symbolic policy: the Motherland Monument, followed by the elevation of the victims of the 1915 genocide and heroes of the 1918 Sardarabad victory. Armenians from the Nagorno-Karabakh autonomous region were allowed to fulfil their aspirations to join Yerevan. A whole series of military heroes were reintegrated into national history, while care was taken not to mention their Dashnak membership. New talent thus emerged from the shackles of Soviet realism: Hrant Matevosyan, Z Khalapyan, Berdj Zeytountsyan, Ag Ayvazyan and Sylva Kapoutikyan. Finally, in the context of the Cold War, Moscow authorized Yerevan to incite speeches against Turkey, a member of NATO. In short, the authorities encouraged new forms of thought, loosening the grip of Soviet Socialism without solving any problems; national rehabilitation had its limits. Thus, between 1953 and 1988, the Soviet Socialist Republic of Armenia 'nationalized', focusing on Yerevan as a centre of national identity and the creation of new social associations and connections with the diaspora. This was a national communism.

The central and unifying element for rehabilitating the national story remains the genocide memorial in Tsitsernakaberd, Yerevan, which began with a public demonstration by hundreds of thousands of Armenians on 24 April 1965, the fiftieth anniversary of the events commemorated. The memorial represents an unprecedented strategic, political, cultural and identity accomplishment in the history of the Soviet Republic. Despite pressure from the central government, which tolerated the commemoration without giving it all the weight it deserved, the new generation of Armenian activists seized upon the event to connect with history. Contrary to what one might believe, this act was not intended to safeguard a memory but to express a sense of symbolic sovereignty detached from any form of domination, including Soviet. With the slogan 'Our lands, our lands', for its protesters – those who two decades later, in 1988, would be found at the head of the Karabakh movement in Yerevan – it was a way to appropriate their own rights, their collective and also their individual identity and a way to free themselves from the wounds of the past and the present. It also broke with the image of an immobile Soviet-Armenian society and stereotyped totalitarian behaviours. It was necessary to bring down the wall between the Soviet 'power' and a society that was exhausted by an official discourse at odds with national aspirations. Through this process of decompartmentalization, Armenians celebrated their own 'May 1968', finding at the same time a way to depict the future with the hope of democratization and with a consciousness free of collective thought and aligned with individual rights. Inspired by Khrushchev's Soviet Union liberalization policy, the Yerevan movement was not without risk. It took place nine years after Warsaw Pact troops intervened in Budapest (1956) and only three years before the collapse in 1968 of the Prague Spring. Despite arrests, Armenians had their 'Yerevan Spring', and made a decisive turn in the political history of Armenia, in its relations with the world and with its own diaspora. Indeed, in the post-Stalinist period Armenian political thought was allowed to be associated with social issues related to the Cold War, with the appearance in Yerevan of dissent personified by the National United Party (NUP), which favoured the independence of Soviet Armenia and the struggle for human rights. Arrests, internments and executions continued throughout the Brezhnev era: Armenian filmmaker Sergei Parajanov was imprisoned for his cinematographic creations and labelled subversive; NUP leader Parouïr Haïrikyan was arrested in 1969 and suffered nearly 18 years in a Soviet gulag; and other separatists, including the future prime minister of the Republic of Armenia Antranik Markaryan, were also arrested. In 1979, Stepan Zadikyan, Hagop Stepanyan and Zaven Baghdassaryan, three separatists and alleged perpetrators of the Moscow metro bombing of 8 January 1977, were executed after a show trial in the Russian capital. In 1977, with the support of Andrei Sakharov, dissidents in Yerevan set up an Armenian Committee, known as the Helsinki Committee, to monitor the implementation of the Helsinki Accords. Despite repression, *zamisdat* (self-published literature) and other clandestine publications spread throughout the Soviet space and beyond, thanks to networks within the Armenian diaspora.

Ending of illusions in the diaspora

For the Armenian communities of the diaspora, this was a time for host society integration. Naturalizations accelerated after the Second World War. Second-generation sons and daughters of genocide survivors took their places in urbanized societies across Europe and the United States. These new French, American or other citizens excelled in crafts, commerce and other professions that gave them the freedom to pursue their aspirations while keeping an eye on a first generation that still had only partial use of its host country's language. It was also a time for mixed marriages and the development of new mores in keeping with host society practices. As a result of such transitions, a triple divergence grew in the Armenian world: a geographical gap between the motherland and the diaspora; a cultural gap between Western and Middle Eastern diasporas; and a social gap between the first and second generations of Armenian immigrants. Immersed in host country societies, the new generation became aware of the individual right to live at the tempo of progress in a new homeland. Members of the second generation circulated freely, occupied positions of responsibility, pursued graduate studies, entered the civil service or the private sector, developed businesses and founded medical bureaus or consultancies. They lived in the host culture and became largely disassociated from the traditional community sphere, based on the triptych of church–party–association. The process of acculturation took place naturally in these communities in exile. In literature and the press, bilingualism took precedence over the use of the Armenian language and Culture (with a capital C) took precedence over the vague and somewhat politicized concept of a diaspora. The churches were empty and political parties clashed over Soviet-style socialism. The first fraternal-type associations (Association of Residents of Kharpert, of Van, etc) disappeared, relinquishing their place to arrangements infused with an ambiguous host-country/Armenian culture of integration without the possibility of return. The damage inflicted following the Neghkart of 1947 (deceptions, arrests and confiscations) ended any temptations that might have remained concerning repatriation to the mother country. The present was to be found in the host country and the future was written in the ink of individualism.

Faced with rampant assimilation and community resettlement, some people took up the challenge of extricating Armenians from their memories, to break with the past in terms of history and Armenian awareness. This was done by leveraging knowledge as an element of community awareness. Thus, in 1958, Georges and Diran Khayiguian, Jacques Nazarian, Robert Donikian and former students of the Mekhitarist college, Samuel Moorat college of Sèvres, with Kegham Kevonian, Manoug Atamian, Vartkes Solakian, Manoug Pamoukdjian and Jacques Donabedian met under the banner of the Center for Armenian Studies (CAS) and endorsed a historicizing, modern and pedagogical approach to the Armenian Question. This approach was republican, respectful of individuals, aware of the reality of Soviet Armenia without endorsing the regime – and it broke with the traditional Armenian parties. The aim of the CAS was to propose a new, didactic, realistic and unifying platform. One particular innovation stands out: the language used for communication was no longer Armenian, but French. As for didactics, the organization's very name suggests that it could only be through the production and diffusion of historical knowledge that the Armenian Question could be rescued from oblivion. Realistically, it was not a question of messianic advocacy for a return to the country, but part of a bicultural approach that took into account the local conditions for integration. Finally, with respect to unification, the only thing that could rationally unite French–Armenian citizens and make sense was not Soviet Armenia – the logic of the Cold War had been well established in Armenian mentalities well before the break in 1947 – but recognition of the genocide and the fight against the Turkish enemy.

Inspired by the memory of the Shoah, these young Armenian intellectuals pledged to mark 24 April differently, offering various commemorative propositions: street demonstrations, closing shop as a sign of mourning and the publication of brochures on such subjects as, for example, 'Armenian National Mourning'. For such individuals, it was essential to resurrect the Armenian Question and to take to the streets. The effect was immediate: the new generation subscribed to both the underlying substance and the form of this initiative, which stood out against the conformity of churches and parties. This new approach reinforced Armenians in recognition of their individuality, with the means of communication appropriate to social realism (use of French and English in publications and speeches as an outward sign of an emancipated Armenian identity). This was not to the liking of the Armenian political parties, especially the ARF who intensified provocations in the press and provoked clashes with the CAS. The old guard understood that the modernizing alternative would divert community attention and resources from party needs, weaken Dashnakism and deprive the parties of what little political influence remained among the diaspora communities, fragmenting their authority and opening the gate to political competition. Political party resistance did not, by itself, explain the difficulties encountered by the CAS. The other reason arose from internal tensions, between those who drifted to the far right in the name of anti-Turkish sentiment, bringing with it the period of terrorism between 1975 and 1985 and those who were determined to maintain the initial course, republican and pedagogical. The drift towards fascism would prove fatal for the CAS, which progressively lost its following and resources. Undoubtedly, the creation of the

CAS marked a break in the conception of identity and the strategy to follow to make sense of history. The attempt to introduce the Armenian Question into history using realism and recourse to education by speaking directly to individuals follows in the footsteps of the Armenian literary circles from before the Second World War. Its extinction in the 1980s was the result of intense political pressure as well as a pronounced inability to expand its audience and overcome internal differences

6

Rebirth of the Sovereign State, 1988–1998

In 1988, in the midst of an historical upheaval caused by the attempted transformation of the Soviet Union led by first secretary Mikhail Gorbachev, appointed in March 1985 following Brezhnev's long reign and the Andropov and Chernenko interregna, Armenians returned to politics and ideas of state and nation. On both sides of the Iron Curtain, the profound feeling that emergence onto the stage of history was timely, called forth a national feeling which was shared with a world that was discovering for itself the state of decay of a rundown Soviet system. The entry of the Armenians into the twentieth century had not been pleasant. Would their exit from the century of totalitarianism, war and genocide be more auspicious? It was said that the time of Russian and Soviet empires destroying national histories was over, that the time of Russo–Ottoman or Bolshevik–Kemalist collusion had passed, that the era of international community indifference to the problems of emerging nations was gone. Henceforth, the way was clear for globalization, national unity and national self-realization. It would be possible to envisage an individual and collective future by shaking loose from the past, while not denying it. It would also be possible to sit at the global table of nations alongside other powerful and not so powerful states. Furthermore, it would be possible to put Armenian identity on a normal footing and give it the means for development. Finally, by gaining closure on the Soviet period, it would be possible to reconnect with national history. The real questions, those frozen by Bolshevik socialism, could now be tackled. History had resumed its normal course and the Armenians would once again be masters of their own destiny.

The historical break in 1988 against the background of *perestroika* (restructuring) and *glasnost* (transparency) took place with the aim of preserving world peace, especially on the Old Continent. This breakthrough revived the idea of a Greater Europe from the Atlantic to the Urals and a common European home. Armenia was part of this historic moment and its return to the world stage became a movement that carried new hope for a peaceful and reunified Europe: the Karabakh movement, whose aim was to reattach the autonomous region of Nagorno-Karabakh, a predominantly Armenian province that had been administered by Azerbaijan since 1921 following a Stalinist decree. Such popular momentum, accompanied as it was by unprecedented events in the Soviet Union, formed a basis for the latest turmoil in the Cold War and a vast emancipation movement for Soviet nationalities, from the Baltic countries to Central Asia. Did these nationalist movements accelerate the fall of the Soviet Union? Today, more than a quarter of a century later, Soviet scholars agree that even if they were not the central factor in the Soviet Union's dissolution, they were a severe blow to Soviet integration, exposing a lack of resilience to the national forces across Soviet territory, including in Russia itself. The Karabakh movement, deep-seated in Armenian society, was at first a test for Gorbachev's perestroika, for his sincerity and historical responsibility and for his determination to transform the ossified Soviet model into a new hope for administered populations. The test was a fiasco for Moscow and for its policies towards ethnic minority groups. We will not concern ourselves with the origins of the movement, whether it was spontaneous or organized, even though the role of the KGB and the GRU (Red Army Intelligence Service) have been dominant in popular thought. Indeed, in a totalitarian system where civil society with its stereotypical behaviours is not recognized as an autonomous actor, it is impossible to imagine a movement of such magnitude – more than a million people on the streets of Yerevan and tens of thousands of Armenians in Stepanakert, the capital of the Nagorno-Karabakh Autonomous Region – without the consent and authorization of the Soviet central authorities. In other words, the Armenian claim was based on popular demand for redress of an injustice that was presented by a central authority which never questioned its own legitimacy. We are not concerned here with retelling the story of an emancipation movement. The archives are not yet open and there are already many books that discuss the different phases in the Karabakh cause and the war that ensued. Rather, we are concerned with assessing how this historic moment constituted a revival of politics before it switched focus to economic issues and effected two qualitative leaps, two changes of scale and two successive forms for validation of national identity, with the restoration of Armenian sovereignty being the key ingredient.

The decisive moment for Karabakh encapsulates all aspects of the Armenian Question and its ambivalences. Freedom or security? National or individual dignity? Reunification or independence? The republican model or the national model (Armenia–diaspora)? Examination of these dilemmas can be considered in two stages. The question of Nagorno-Karabakh arises from two movements often complementary in substance if strategically contradictory. Should we first reunite Nagorno-Karabakh with Soviet Armenia and so avoid antagonizing Moscow, or pursue independence for the Republic of Armenia and relegate the question of territorial attachment to a secondary issue? In other words, the alternatives were based on a major dilemma: to promote reunification would be to express confidence in Soviet Union permanence. To favour independence would be to admit doubts about the Soviet Union and thus to venture into a new paradigm and its intrinsic challenges: independence and the responsibilities of national sovereignty.

The Karabakh movements

When it exploded in 1988, the Karabakh movement crystallized everything that Armenian identity embodied around the world. All of a sudden, Armenia and Armenians made their entrance onto the world stage through the front door, the door to freedom and hope for the future. Memory and expectation clashed in unification messages from Nagorno-Karabakh to Armenia. The diaspora and the motherland had only two messages: *Miatsum* (Unification) and *Karabakh mernè* (Karabakh belongs to us). The international press took an interest and Armenians found themselves on the front pages of the major Western dailies. National pride overcame humiliation and affliction: Armenians made history. During the collapse of the Soviet Union, the world speculated about the awakening of national movements in the communist bloc and looked on with curiosity and astonishment at the huge demonstrations in February 1988 in Stepanakert and Yerevan that were organized to address injustice and history. Western countries followed with interest the developments in the Caucasus and saw there an opportunity to test Gorbachev's openness to change in the Soviet Union and reparations for Stalin's excesses. But if all eyes were focused on the centre of power and the ability of the Kremlin leadership to emerge from totalitarianism, the US and Europe were mainly concerned with preserving peace and security. If ethnic minorities were to open a new chapter in Soviet history, perhaps the last chapter of the Empire of Lenin, for the US and its European allies it was inconceivable that this could be shot through with violence. The preservation of peace depended upon the stability of the Soviet regime, which would, according to Gorbachev's pledges, support change from within, avoiding any escalation of tensions and thus any dangerous Western interference in Soviet affairs.

In other words, if humanity were to move from a stable but unjust world to an unstable but just world, this reversal must not be achieved at the expense of peace. The Karabakh movement directly reflected these concerns on peace and security. It signalled the return of East European nations to the historical narrative, bringing to mind the Treaty of Versailles which failed to focus on the problem of Eastern borders considered dependent on Bolshevik Russia, who was absent from the 1919 peace conference. By the end of the 1980s, the people had awakened and, with them, their narrative return to reality. By the final decade of the twentieth century, it was not the end of history that unfolded but a historical revenge of the small nations. From the Balkans to Central Asia, European peoples loosened the shackles of an oppressive narrative that was not of their making and a burden that concealed ethnic identity, in the name of a communist utopia which had been devastating but was now on its way out.

The rebirth of nations

This reaffirmation of history took place as nations returned to the course of politics and truth. The Karabakh movement embodied the dignity of those who were overcoming the ideology that communism could hold sway over national identities and impact socio-historical processes. Baltic peoples, Ukrainians and Caucasians aspired to resume the course of their own history. For Armenians, the Karabakh movement was little more than an extension of the Yerevan 'Spring of 1965', with young protesters of the Khrushchev years becoming Karabakh movement leaders in 1988. National dignity had to prevail over Soviet conformism. If, at first sight, the Karabakh movement was part of this logic of building a reunited republic within the framework of the Soviet Union, it contained two parallel rationales: Yerevan and Stepanakert. On both sides there was a desire for reunification and the restoration of an Armenian state, a desire to write history and, in so doing, take into account the lessons of the past. There was a commitment to maintain a strong mobilization of the popular movement, whatever the cost. But the two rationales were at odds over the essence of the Armenian Question.

Stepanakert was supported by the traditional elements of the diaspora, including the three parties (ARF, SDHP and the Armenian Democratic Liberal Party), churches and conservative organizations. The conflict was seen as post-colonial in nature; the enemy was not Moscow but Baku. The Armenians had to free themselves from Azerbaijani domination, whose 'nationalist' policies had expelled all Armenians from neighbouring Nakhichevan. Prior to the Sovietization of the Nakhichevan in 1921, the population of the autonomous republic attached to Azerbaijan was 54 per cent Armenian; in 1988, it was 2 per cent. For Armenians, one man was responsible for the policy of intimidation and ethnic cleansing: Heïdar Aliyev, a native of Nakhitchevan and a member of the KGB since 1944. Throughout his career, he made every effort to enforce pro-Azerbaijani policies in the enclave. Further promotions only encouraged his efforts, initially as first secretary of the Republic of Azerbaijan in 1969 and then as member of the CPSU Politburo in 1976, a position he held until the arrival of Gorbachev in 1985. In Nagorno-Karabakh, where Armenians represented 94 per cent of the population in 1921, as opposed to 79 per cent in 1989, the example of Nakhitchevan is universally known. It was therefore out of the question that Armenians should suffer in the 1980s what their compatriots had endured for three decades (1950–1980). The demonstrations initiated this process of decolonization. The Stepanakert movement did not oppose Moscow; on the contrary, it needed Moscow to accelerate the process of 'de-Azerbaijanization'. For the leaders of the Krounk Committee – intellectuals, academics, Communist Party members, KGB agents and ordinary Soviet citizens – the priority was to be free of Baku's tutelage without conceding final arbitration to Moscow. The intention was to achieve if not the annexation of this autonomous region to the Soviet Republic of Armenia at least an attachment to Moscow. To this end, the Krounk Committee stepped up its diplomatic efforts in Moscow and organized local referenda on the reunification of the two Armenian territories.

In Yerevan, supported as it was by pro-Western circles of the diaspora, especially in France and the United States, the situation was different. The conflict was secessionist and democratic in nature, similar to movements in the Baltic countries, Georgia and Ukraine. The common opponent was Moscow, which did not hesitate to deploy institutional instruments and the resources of Mother Russia to divide the Federated Republics. If for a time – from the initial awakening to the general strikes of autumn 1988 – the Yerevan movement aligned itself with the position in Stepanakert, the democratic variant began with the arrest of the leaders of the Karabakh Committee of scholars, academics and former dissidents formed in the aftermath of the 7 December 1988 earthquake that ravaged the north of Armenia. For the Karabakh Committee, Moscow's cynicism as Gorbachev procrastinated over a review of the Nagorno-Karabakh issue aggravated the situation and was perceived as a return to the policy of allowing it to fester, thereby preventing resolution. While the Karabakh Committee appreciated the steps taken by the central authority to democratize the Soviet system, it kept in mind that the periphery could also force normative changes within the framework of Soviet law. Faced with the immobility of Moscow and the onset of repression in Yerevan, where the first deaths were recorded in June 1988, the Committee radicalized its position and called for a general strike in August of the same year. The aim of the strike was to paralyse the entire Soviet economy which was already damaged, based as it was on a system of interdependence.

Two events strengthened the position of the two branches of the movement. First, in February and November 1988, the massacre of Armenians in Sumgait and Kirovabad, Azerbaijan, reopened the wounds of the genocide. These were the first massacres in Europe since the Cypriot crisis of 1974. In Stepanakert, but also to a degree in Yerevan and throughout the diaspora, calls for international solidarity appeared and grew in volume. The European Parliament cautiously voted resolutions in March 1988 that brought Member States' attention to the disturbing situation in the Caucasus. On the ground, calls for self-defence were made with increasing frequency. The memories of the Armenian warriors re-surfaced and the first self-defence brigades were created, modelling themselves on the fighters of the nineteenth-century revolutionary movement – going as far as to reproduce the outfits of the time and the military rituals (photos, bandoliers, beards and moustaches). The militarization of the movement and society as a whole was inescapable, but the Karabakh Committee refused to yield to the logic of war and saw in the event the hand of Moscow and a policy of intimidation from Gorbachev. This opinion was not shared by the three traditional Armenian parties, who on 12 October 1988 signed a joint call for the lifting of the general strike in Soviet Armenia, a measure that they considered to be dangerous, counter-productive and useless. For them, it was necessary to end the strike and focus on the real enemy, Pan-Turkism and the threat to Armenian security of a Turkish–Azerbaijani alliance, solely responsible for the woes of the Armenians. In Yerevan, the Karabakh Committee poured cold water on this, denouncing the 'betrayal' by the Armenian parties, including the ARF, who were accused of negotiating a return to Soviet Armenia against guarantees of respect for Soviet legality. For the Armenian parties and their political allies in the Caucasus, the fight against pan-Turkism was not a mere diversion or a fantasy but a reality. Only rapprochement with Moscow could ameliorate the geopolitical consequences and there was no alternative to a balanced and responsible policy towards the Russian capital.

Second, the Spitak-Leninakan earthquake of 7 December 1988 (25,000 dead, 15,000 wounded and 530,000 homeless) opened the borders of the Soviet Union to international aid. The Armenian diaspora united in solidarity with their injured brethren. The earthquake marked the beginning of a new era between the two facets of the Armenian nation that had been immortalized by the slogan *Meg Jorovourth, Meg Haïrenik* ('One People, One Fatherland'). For the first time since the end of the Second World War, Western police forces, civil security personnel and press, mainly from NATO countries, found themselves in Soviet territory. The world was stunned to discover the obsolescence of a Soviet system that was incapable of providing the most basic social services, including housing and first aid for the wounded and poor. Gorbachev and his entourage were faced with this evidence. This natural disaster completed what the Chernobyl nuclear disaster of 1986 had begun: awareness that the Soviet Union was moribund.

Different trends

The split between the two branches of the movement indicated there was no possibility of reconciliation. From the liberation of the Karabakh Committee in May 1989 to the Moscow coup of August 1991, the culmination of the fall of the Soviet Union, the Karabakh movement found itself divided around ideas of sovereignty and guerrilla warfare, aspects that reflected an essential question: within the rationale for national reconstruction where did power lie, in Yerevan or Stepanakert? Was the political movement an extension of changes operating within the Soviet system or should it take its own autonomous direction and propose an alternative? Neither of the branches was able to answer this fundamental question concerning which steps should be taken. Instead, both sides concerned themselves with which strategy to adopt to loosen the grip of the Soviet Union and open up new perspectives.

There were four strands of thinking about the appropriate response. First, there were those who supported a Central Asian scenario in which nothing would be done and the process of decomposition of the Soviet Union should be allowed to follow its course, in which case sovereignty would be restored naturally to the capitals of the Soviet Republics. This was the position of the most conservative Armenian circles. They were a minority who would eventually prove nostalgic for the Soviet Union. It served no purpose to awaken the political demons and, in any case, everything was and would continue to be decided in Moscow because Armenians were not capable of taking their destiny into their own hands.

Then there were those who backed an economic scenario, feeling that it was important to revive the economy of the republic. Political sovereignty would flow from national recovery. This policy of adaptation to the realities of the market (agrarian reform, gradual privatization, creation of cooperatives) would allow Armenia to prepare a war economy in case of escalation against Azerbaijan, to play the hand of economic sovereignty without offending Moscow's sensibilities and prepare the country to enter world markets. This economic option, advocated by Vasken Manukyan, a member of the Karabakh Committee and several engineers and technocrats represented a real innovation in Armenian political thought.

The armed resistance option considered that by taking up arms the Armenians would finally succeed in reunifying the two territories. Already in 1989, the first signs of this tragic scenario could be seen. Everything suggested that the further the Soviet system broke down, the more the warmongers would be heard. This armed option avoided an anti-Russian strategy, striking mainly at Pan-Turkism and Baku and reawakening the patriotic fervour against feelings of defeatism. In Nagorno-Karabakh, in Armenia and among the diaspora, supporters of the military option were called by some the 'party of war' and 'the party of Karabakh'. In Armenia, an Armenian National Army was created, but after the death of an Armenian deputy in Yerevan in August 1990, it was dissolved and replaced by the Yergrabah movement (defenders of the land), led by Vazgen Sargsyan, future minister of defence of the Republic of Armenia. Among the diaspora, the ARF defended this bellicose approach, using it to prepare its return to Armenia.

Finally, there was the Baltic scenario – an option advocated by the Karabakh Committee, which became the Pan-Armenian National Movement (PANM), led by

Levon Ter-Petrosyan, future President of the Republic of Armenia. Its view was that the Armenians had to cooperate and build with other national movements and advocate independence through solidarity between the republics against the central Soviet power. On 23 August 1990, the PANM moved into action: the Supreme Soviet of the Soviet Republic of Armenia, led by Ter-Petrosyan, proclaimed the sovereignty of the Republic of Armenia. In common with the Baltic states, this new authority announced that Armenia would not participate in the review of the draft treaty of the Union of Soviet Republics (USR) concocted by Gorbachev to save the Union. Aware of the benevolence of the United States, which was increasingly determined to play the national card against a moribund centre in the hands of conservatives, the new national elites helped each other without recourse to Moscow. In Riga, Latvian separatists supported negotiations between the Armenians of the PANM and the Azerbaijanis of the Azerbaijani Popular Front. In Vilnius, in 1990–1991, Ter-Petrosyan acted as a mediator in negotiating a compromise between Lithuania and Moscow. In both cases, however, these efforts proved to be a failure.

The Moscow putsch of August 1991 brought the four strategic tendencies into focus. Following the defeat of the putschists and the victory of Boris Yeltsin, the symbol of a nationalist and independent Russia, Ter-Petrosyan coined a catchphrase that was taken up by the media. 'The centre is dead' was a way of saying that the republics no longer depended upon central authority. The Soviet Union was over. In Nagorno-Karabakh, Armenians continued to suffer on all fronts, while the Red Army/Azerbaijani Special Police Forces launched Operation Ring to stifle local resistance. This sought to strangle Armenian claims by gradually tightening the vice. The failure of the coup, brought this operation to an end but not without a significant impact for Yerevan and Stepanakert: a dozen Armenian villages were lost north of Chahoumian and the entire district was threatened.

The two main tendencies, the separatist PANM and the Unionist ARF, rejected responsibility for this military setback, each seeking to be the incarnation of political renewal. For the PANM, the military strategy served to reinforce Moscow's anti-Armenian policy. For the ARF, the independence strategy had pushed Moscow into the arms of Baku. They were both right and wrong. It is difficult to understand how the leaders of the PANM, legitimized by the Karabakh movement and heirs of the Karabakh Committee, could have abandoned the defence of the Armenian province to this extent without measuring the potential consequences of their anti-Soviet policies in the field of battle. Similarly, it is also difficult to understand how the ARF, a symbol of independence and, to a certain extent, of anti-Sovietism, had come so late to the table of independence that it appeared in the eyes of many Armenians, including among its own supporters, to be a hostile force for Armenian sovereignty and supporters of the USR treaty, which would never see the light of day. Without any doubt, the ARF continued to believe that the Soviet system was sustainable. Thus, just as it did in 1920, the ARF advocated principled opposition to Moscow, convinced that the Soviet Union's collapse was imminent. In 1991, the ARF adopted a moderate position towards Moscow, believing that the Soviet Union would continue. In both cases, the ARF was wrong. In fact – and to come to the ARF's defence – humanity was witnessing the end of the bipolar world that had characterized the twentieth century and the geopolitical upheavals that brought about the historical break. As for the PANM and the ARF, both depended upon the ambiguity of Haitadism. With the twenty-first century we turn a page in history, to examine the political struggle for independence and reconstruction of a nation state at war.

A paradigm shift

Europe was ablaze from the Balkans to the Caucasus, the fate of the continent and its peoples in the balance. With the violent eruptions that engulfed parts of former Eastern Europe, it was the question of borders that came to the fore. How could administrative boundaries be transformed into political boundaries? Should they be recognized in their current state or be modified? In the name of peace and security, the international community could not risk redrawing borders – perceived as a factor of stability in the international system – but it could not ignore the growing national movements in the 'other' Europe. One by one, the Soviet Republics proclaimed their independence. Even the 'Republic of Nagorno-Karabakh' did so in September 1991, affirming that if it had been a part of the Soviet Republic of Azerbaijan, it by no means felt compelled to be part of the newly independent Republic of Azerbaijan. The resurgence of these states, heirs of the republics of 1918–1920, raised all the issues of transition to democracy, Which democracy for which state? What power for which society? What form of state, republic or nation?

In common with other peoples freed from Soviet repression, the Armenians lived through a bona fide paradigm shift and would henceforth face real challenges. The 1991 break was universal; it was geopolitical, strategic, military, political, diplomatic, economic, national, cultural, ecological, identity and social. It would be geopolitical because Armenia would open itself to the outside world, to find its place in the new world order proclaimed by George Bush, without renouncing relations with Russia.

It would be strategic because Armenia would very quickly join the Commonwealth of Independent States (CIS), the successor to the Soviet Union and its security organization, the Tashkent Treaty, a collective security agreement managed by the Russians.

The break would be military in that Armenia was inspired by Charles Tilly's idea that war made the state and the state waged war, taken with Carl Schmitt's theoretical conception of the state as being constructed by apposition to a clearly identified and structured enmity, which, in the Armenian case, meant the Turks and a Pan-Turk alliance between Turkey and Azerbaijan.

The break would be political in that society would have to transform itself from a totalitarian state to a state of law based on democratic principles. A state has institutions that require vigilance and renewal with provision for the transfer of power. Armenia regained some attributes of sovereignty by enlarging its institutions and organizing state functions into ministries, including defence and foreign affairs.

The change would be diplomatic in that Armenia, with its large diaspora and numerous expatriate communities, would need to implement a realistic foreign policy to account for its condition of being at war, its national interests and the nation's state-building priorities. Should Armenia adopt an idealistic outlook, promoting multilateralism and human rights, especially given the legacy of the 1915 genocide? Or should the nation orientate itself towards a transnationalist approach, based on the civil society networks of the diaspora? Should Armenia seek to innovate, considering that it was a state of two territories and should it promote the integration of new values, norms and rules into the international system? Beginning in 1991, Armenia opted for the classical theory of international relations, realism in line with the Hobbesian model.

Changes would certainly be economic in that the country would have to transition from a managed economy to a market economy via the intermediate step of a war economy. This would require considerable effort for a small home market of 3 million people with little business experience and only limited technical expertise. Could Armenia muster the ability to overcome geographic isolation in the midst of countries at war (Georgia), in internal crisis (Turkish dealings with the Kurds) or involved in an international crisis (the Iranian contest with the West)? Such adaptations would undoubtedly be even more difficult if the economy was being bled dry and devoured by a mafia system and corruption.

The national break launched by the 1991 assertion of independent sovereignty concerned whether Armenia should adopt a republican approach that excluded Armenians from the diaspora in its development or, in the name of a national model of reconciliation, should attempt to integrate expatriate communities and incorporate their collective history and the memory of the genocide. Since the earthquake, diaspora communities had been providing regular, consistent and indispensable assistance to Armenian society. How would Armenia show gratitude?

The break was cultural in that the fall of the Soviet system accompanied a collapse in artistic expression. Publishing houses failed and readerships evaporated. Living conditions became so difficult in post-Soviet society, with its weak currency, lack of external trade and non-existent public services, that public spaces for cultural entertainment were reduced to a bare minimum.

Ecological change was brought about by the need to repair and restore ecosystems and nature ravaged by communism. Despite the country being situated at over 900 metres altitude, it suffered from rampant pollution, falling water levels in Lake Sevan, an aging energy infrastructure dependent upon a nuclear power plant (Medzamor) of the same design as Chernobyl and a complete lack of health, safety and hygiene regulations. The situation was dire and national infrastructure required major investment.

Armenian identity would also have to be transformed, freed from the habits of domination and a form of identity alienation. The revival of Armenia would have to be extended beyond identity-based issues into modernity and competitive business practices. All sectors of the country would have to be administered and managed by a new generation of better-trained leaders.

Finally, social change would have to be anticipated and integrated into Armenian cultural practices. As the Soviet system collapsed, unemployment soared, precipitating unexpected career choices. Engineers became street sellers, academics became taxi drivers and teachers without classrooms or students enlisted in the Nagorno-Karabakh volunteer battalions.

Armenian society was in the throes of radical change. Empowerment is a condition of success for a society in transition and for a society looking for a social contract as a way of structuring relations with a state apparatus. It is difficult, however, to imagine the creation of a bond of trust between elites who lack political experience and segments of society who lack the basic instruments of integration and social regulation. The social mechanics of communism had been corrupted and no longer functioned. New approaches were needed to modernize society and to adapt it to the universal values of a consumer world. In this generalized chaos, the population was left with no choice. They either went to war as militiamen or they fled the country for a better life. Military engagement and emigration became the two new social realities. Each village mustered a self-defence brigade for the front while carefully cultivating its list of emigrant families en route to Europe, Russia or the United States. The situation was all the more catastrophic because the first generation of Armenian administrators lacked any real administrative experience and were focused on war and foreign policy. They had no idea what it meant to be accountable and barely understood the nature of political gamesmanship or parliamentary politics. Democratic accountability was still underdeveloped in these post-Soviet states.

Victory of Haitadism over communism

Hope springs eternal. In common with the other independent republics, Armenia was walking both alongside and in the same direction as history and nothing seemed able to stop it, not even the four challenges that Yerevan faced when leaving the Soviet Union. The first of these, the challenge of independence, confirmed the victory of Haitadism over communism. But could Haitadism be taken up in the state when it pre-dated even Armenian sovereignty and was backed by two antagonistic formations, the PANM and the ARF? If so, could it be completely integrated? From 1991 to 1993, a division of roles seemed to emerge from negotiations between the ruling PANM in Yerevan and the ruling ARF in Stepanakert, especially after the first parliamentary elections in December 1991 and January 1992. A process of reconciliation was under way. Armenian military victories at Khodjalou airport in February 1992 and the capture of Shushi in May 1992, the last Azerbaijani stronghold in Nagorno-Karabakh province, opened the way for territorial reunification by annexation. The Nagorno-Karabakh Republic was now finally united with the Republic of Armenia. The two Armenian leaders, Levon Ter-Petrosyan and Hrair Maroukian, sealed the sacred union, symbolized by the creation in March 1992 of the Armenian Fund, a para-state and pan-national organization charged with raising funds in support of the reconstruction of Armenia in all spheres. The Khodjalou operation ended with the massacre of civilians fleeing the fighting through a humanitarian corridor. Baku accused the Armenians of deliberately organizing the massacre. Yerevan and Stepanakert both declared that the action was a conspiracy by the Azerbaijan Popular Front and the Aliyev clan, who persuaded the civilians, Meshkets Turks, to remain on the spot and thus bear the brunt of Armenian reprisals, leading to the downfall of Baku. The President of Azerbaijan, Aliaz Moutalibov, who was overthrown shortly after the defeat in February–March 1992, concurred with this version of events. Images of slain civilians, however, impelled the international community to put pressure on the Armenians, who were perceived as the cause of the massacre. Yerevan, however, refused to take responsibility for the events, crediting instead numerous testimonies – not only from survivors, but also from Azerbaijani officials and foreign journalists – which contradicted the Azerbaijani viewpoint. Where the truth lies, between a massacre driven by Armenians or an Azerbaijani plot hostile to the Mutalibov regime, is not known. What is clear, though, is that most Armenians, historically accustomed to the role of the victim, were incapable of imagining such a role as alleged 'slaughterer'. It was as if their sense of victimization prevented any assumption of responsibility for such vengeful acts. The Azerbaijanis described the events at Khodjalou as a 'genocide'. They sought to put the international community on alert and make Armenia appear as an aggressor to cover up the massacre of Armenians committed by Baku between 1988 and 1992. These include the little-known massacre in Maragha in April 1992 and the better-known Baku massacre of January 1990. This marked the beginning of the war on national memories.

Reconciliation between the PANM and the ARF would be short lived. In April 1992, the Dashnak speaker of the Nagorno-Karabakh parliament, Arthur Mkertchian, died in unexplained circumstances. In the summer of 1991, Armenia had suffered a series of military defeats in the regions of Chahoumian and Mardakert. In June 1992, General Secretary Hraïr Maroukhian was expelled from Armenia by a decree issued by President Ter-Petrosyan for an alleged coup attempt on the eve of its 25th world congress, the first in Armenia since 1919. These events served to crystallize bipartisan tensions. Ter-Petrosyan would have the last word and Maroukhian was marginalized within the ARF and a collaboration with the new regime was instigated. In reality, there was insufficient room at the highest levels for these two strong personalities. The former embodied globalization, the post-bipolar world system and wanted to represent the future; the latter symbolized third-world status and détente during the Cold War, reiterating the past. In December 1994, six months after Maroukhian's hospitalization in Athens following a brain haemorrhage which happened in questionable circumstances, the Armenian President suspended the ARF and its affiliates from any activity in the republic for undermining the security of the state. This radical step came after a series of assassinations that were attributed to the Dashnaks, who in their turn claimed a conspiracy plot and followed the installation of an authoritarian regime in Armenia six months before the parliamentary elections of 1995. Despite these tensions, negotiations between the two parties never stopped. The PANM, however, had managed to wrestle power from the ARF; state power had triumphed over revolutionary power.

Second or Third Republic? Third or Fourth Republic?

The second challenge concerned the Soviet-era heritage. One thing is certain: following the constitutional referendum of 6 December 2015, Armenia changed its constitution and laid the groundwork for a new republic, with the election in 2018 of a new president. But which republic was it to be? The Third Republic (1991 to 2018) – after that of 1918, or the Fourth Republic following the Soviet Republic of Armenia and the post-Soviet Republic (1991–2018)? The parties, both those in power and those in opposition, as well as Armenian society in general, opted for the Third Republic, considering that the achievements of communism were part of their history, that they offered positive evidence in different fields (education, research, health) and that it was pointless to do away with those advances, even if the new regime attributed all of Armenia's problems to the failures of the Soviet system – as if Yerevan were responsible for nothing, not even the mistakes and crimes of the Armenian SSR. To speak of the Third Republic is therefore to endorse the heritage of the Armenian SSR, the treaties signed in the early 1920s by Yerevan as well as those signed by the Soviet Union in the name of Armenia. Unlike the new Republic of Georgia, which came into being in 1991 and almost immediately cancelled the treaties signed by Tbilisi since 1920, the young Republic of Armenia did not question the terms of its treaties. This means that the Republic of Armenia recognizes its current borders and the amnesty measures contained within the treaties of Kars and Moscow, which apply to those responsible for the massacres and abuses committed during the First World War. In reality, if we follow Haitadist logic, the Republic of Armenia born in 1991 out of the ruins of the Soviet Union was a historic breakthrough and should be seen as the Second Republic on the grounds that the Soviet Republic of Armenia was neither a subject of international law nor ever a sovereign power. If the Armenian elites retain the Third but not the Second, it would be in recognition of a Soviet heritage and Russian patronage; it is a legal and political aberration because it leaves Armenia in a post-Soviet bind. The controversy around the label of Second or Third Republic brings to the fore notions of successor state versus an inheriting state. As we know, as a general rule a successor state is not bound by the treaties signed by the predecessor state which apply to the territory. This is the case in present-day Georgia. However, this specialist in international law points out that the 1978 Convention (Vienna) contains a special rule with regard to territorial treaties, particularly those establishing borders. These treaties apply to the successor state without it having to give express consent, nor is the successor state able to reject them, except on grounds of invalidity. The International Law Commission considers this rule to be lawful following jurisprudence and international practice. This is the crux of the question of the border between Turkey and Armenia, which we will discuss later.

To leave the war

The third challenge was how to end the war. Azerbaijan had a new president, Abulfaz Eltchibey, a former Nakhchivan dissident from the Azerbaijan Popular Front. He had a mission to take his country into pan-Turkism, which was seen as a path to salvation and development. Armenia sought to take advantage of this miscalculation. Solidarity with Turkey was not to the liking of Russia, Iran, Europe or the United States. Moscow would have liked to see Azerbaijan and Georgia return to the fold of the CIS, but these two former republics refused to join the new multilateral organization. At the same time, the Russians supported the Armenians and the separatist Abkhaz and South Ossetian forces. Between March/April and September 1993, the Armenians launched a victorious offensive: Kelbadjar, Aghdam, Fizuli, Ghoubatli, Djebraïl, Zanguelan fell into their hands. Close to defeat, Aboulfaz Eltchibey was removed from power and replaced by Heidar Aliyev, who was hailed as a saviour. After signing a first ceasefire with the Nagorno-Karabakh Republic authorities in September 1993, Azerbaijan announced its accession to the CIS. At the same time, Georgia, defeated in Abkhazia and South Ossetia, did the same. Russia won. The Security Council adopted four resolutions between April and November 1993 to secure a lasting ceasefire in Nagorno-Karabakh and to open prospects for peace, to be overseen by the OSCE.

This was not the last of Heïdar Aliyev, though: he signed lucrative contracts with Western oil companies to open up his country and construct new energy pipelines on the East–West corridor. He reorganized his defence forces in preparation for the launch of an offensive, but this concluded with an uninspiring failure. The Armenian victory was total. The international press wrote about the 'Armenian steamroller', which nothing seemed to be able to stop. The Armenians imagined they would take the Kura river and simply walk into Baku. On 12 May 1994, a new ceasefire was signed in Bishkek between Armenia, Azerbaijan and the Nagorno-Karabakh Republic. Azerbaijan was in disarray and was faced with an Armenia which, although weakened, had never seen military success as clearly as in 1993. Militarily, the Armenian soldiers were feared by Chechens and Afghans who had come to the rescue of their Azerbaijani brothers. Diplomatically, Armenia took advantage of these harsh defeats for Baku. Security Council resolutions did not condemn Armenia, which was cited only once – with the international community soliciting it to use its influence with the Armenian forces in Nagorno-Karabakh to facilitate the ceasefire. Politically, the construction of the nation-state was firmly established on the foundations of military success, a bit like wars of conquest in previous centuries. At home, Armenians took their revenge on history. Any feelings of defeat had disappeared and even though there was no triumphalism in the official discourse, the psychological trauma gradually faded in people's minds. With the slogan 'Never again', which is to say, 'no more Armenian massacres', the military succeeded in capturing the hearts of Armenians. 'Fedais' yesterday, 'azadamardig' (freedom fighters) today in Karabakh, the Armenian soldier thus became a professional fighter in a national army under construction. Armenian society sang the praises of the national army, which resumed its rightful place in the organization of the state and the corridors of Armenian power. The spirit of the *Azat* class was reborn. The military successes thus put an end to the long demise of Armenians that had been taking place since the first century BC. At first sight it might seem unlikely, but it is difficult to grasp the extent of this feeling of dignity, justice and reparation, which Armenians have been exploiting since the end of this war without taking into account the feelings of defeat and chaos that had previously trickled through society and into their consciousness.

Anticipating the shock of globalization

Finally, the fourth challenge: the return to nation-state status took place at a time when the world was shifting to a globalized view. How could Armenia at the same time lay foundations of the nation-state, promote the national ideal and find its rightful place on the world map, as the international community invited these newly independent states to venture into the twenty-first century? Since 1994, the latter question has been the priority. The idea of reconstructing an Armenian identity specific to the twenty-first century has been raised. Why 1994? This was the year of the ceasefire in Nagorno-Karabakh and the introduction of the first structural reforms promoted by the International Monetary Fund (IMF) and the World Bank. It was also the year in which the ARF was suspended by presidential decree, a party that the PANM considered a threat to government plans because it embraced traditional legitimacy as the best defence of political pre-eminence over all other categories of Armenian identity. The PANM, however, in its desire to bring Armenia into the twenty-first century, split Haitadism and politics in the interest of promoting economics. Tomorrow's Armenian identity had to shed its thick skin of ideologies – communism, Haitadism and its main component Dashnakism – to flourish in a new combination of religious, cultural and economic factors. In other words, the Armenian, in his new clothes, had to recover his ancestral values concerning the one who prays, the one who writes and the one who trades. All were essential to a restored, independent and depoliticized state and conducted themselves politically in ways other than those based on territoriality and ideology. There was no place for politics in the traditional sense of the word, so the ARF and all organizations with a strong political identity were barred from finding their place in the future Armenian ark. The 1994 break, which followed the paradigm shift of 1991, definitively removed Armenia from the influence of Haitadism, plunging Armenia into the post-modernist movement and its triumph over rationality, resonating with this popular world (and especially European) trend.

Reinventing identity

Historical identity

This post-modern process for reinventing identity has five key components. The first is based on the historical identity crisis in 1991. Henceforth, the Armenian people would have to be self-reliant, generate their own resources and take full responsibility for their state recovery plan. The priority would be to normalize Armenian identity in keeping with universal standards and avoiding idiosyncrasies. From that moment, history would no longer be a vector of identification, but 'a false discipline', to quote Levon Ter-Petrosyan, himself a historian, because this field has weighed negatively on the shoulders of the people for far too long. In the PANM reference volume, *The Norms of the Present Time and Armenian Political Thought*, published in 1997, the ideologist Kdritch Sardaryan theorized about new perspectives for Armenian identity in the twenty-first century from the vantage of a break with the past. One of the most striking symbols of this break is the change in the words of the national anthem, *Mer Haïrenik* (*Our Motherland*). The new first stanza runs:

Our homeland, free and independent,
Who lived from century to century,

Her children today call her
Armenia free and independent.

This replaces the original version's

Our homeland, miserable and abandoned,
trampled by her enemies,
has summoned her sons now
to be revenged with anger and bitterness.

Giving up the memory of genocide

The second component, which flows from the first, is the construction of an identity completely separate from the memory of the genocide. 'Recognition of the Armenian genocide is not a priority for Armenia's diplomacy', says former Dashnak Gerard Libaridian, special adviser to the head of state and then vice-minister of Armenian foreign affairs.[1] Its teaching, moreover, is banned from school programmes. Through this fundamental break with the existing Armenian identity, the authorities do not seek to deny the reality of genocide, but wish to build a collective post-modern iconography based on normality: genocide belongs to the past, to history and to the forbidden twentieth century, a terrible world for the people but one that is now gone. One cannot build a new Armenia and fresh identity based on such historical drama. To teach the genocide to schoolchildren is incompatible with the idea of the new republic and the determination of the younger generations to live their lives to the full. Any politicization of this theme is counter-productive and the intention of the new government is to limit discussion to a moral and ethical vision of the tragedy.

A new look at the Turkish question

Naturally – and this is the third component – to turn aside from the recognition of genocide obviously tilts Armenia towards Turkey. According to the Armenian authorities, new relationships must be formed. The government's ambition here is twofold. On the one hand, it means talking with Turkey on an equal footing, unreservedly, without any posture of revenge. This means that the genocide must not be brought up in talks and instead left to historians to assist integration in the region in the name of a policy based on being good neighbours. Armenians must look to the future. The first contacts with Turkey were made in two ways. Bilaterally, Turkey recognized Armenia as early as 1991, although it did not open an embassy in Yerevan. Armenian President Levon Ter-Petrosyan attended the funeral of his Turkish counterpart Turgut Ozal in 1993 during the war in Nagorno-Karabakh, despite the blockade of Armenia imposed by Baku and Ankara. In the same year, Ter-Petrosyan met twice with Colonel Turkesh, the leader of the Turkish far right, close to the Grey Wolves, a fascist militia sympathetic to Pan-Turkism. In 1994, the Turkish Ministry of

---

[1] Interview with Gérard Libaridian, *Baykar*, April–May 1994. See also *Haïk*, organ of the MNA, 28 April 1995.

Foreign Affairs welcomed the Armenian government's decision to suspend the ARF from pursuing its activities in Armenia. Finally, in 1996 the two countries inaugurated the first direct air route between Istanbul and Yerevan. Multilaterally, Armenia and Turkey have both joined the Istanbul-based Black Sea Economic Co-operation Organization. Yerevan cooperates with Ankara for another reason, to dissociate Turkey from Azerbaijan. By currying favour with Turkey, Armenia seeks to reopen its common border – unilaterally closed by Ankara in 1993 in solidarity with Baku. Yerevan seeks to obstruct Azerbaijan in its strategy to isolate and instil an economic blockade. But the powers in Baku are not worried; Turkey has no intention of opening its border even though, in Ankara, the authorities have always tried to offer opportunities to Ter-Petrosyan, considering it better to collaborate with this moderate president rather than dealing with ARF radicals as neighbours.

Through this policy of openness towards Turkey, Armenia sought to rebuild the foundations of a new identity and a logic of peace. Above all, Armenia needed to reach a settlement of the conflict with Azerbaijan, enabling it to look to the future with less apprehension. The negotiations under the CSCE Minsk Group (a commission of the OSCE) reached a compromise between Armenians and Azerbaijanis. Yerevan and Baku agreed on extensive autonomy for Nagorno-Karabakh in Azerbaijan, the creation of a corridor to Lachin controlled by the Armenians, the evacuation of Armenian-controlled territories and a demilitarization of the whole area. For Yerevan, it was necessary to act quickly while Azerbaijan was weak and Russia, not yet returned to its former strength, remained incapable of applying its former Soviet spin. Baku needed to act quickly to launch pipeline construction projects. Both capitals shared a common goal, which was to launch a gas pipeline under the control of a Western, mostly Anglo-American, consortium linking Azerbaijan to Turkey via Armenia. This peace pipeline called for the establishment of a regional security system guaranteed by the United States. Washington, in turn, agreed to continue negotiations based on compromise. Thus, the PANM, whose legitimacy derives from its policy of reattachment of Nagorno-Karabakh to Armenia through armed struggle and civilian sacrifice, opted for the return of the province to Azerbaijan. 'The Republic of Nagorno-Karabakh' led by Robert Kocharyan did not approve the Armenian-Azerbaijani arrangement and notified Yerevan, Baku and Moscow.

Another conception of the homeland

If Armenia agreed to surrender the territories under its control and renounce the independence of Nagorno-Karabakh, it was because it endorsed a different conception of the homeland. This is the fifth component. For the PANM, in the wake of globalization, the territory had lost its political and strategic importance so that the strengthening of Armenia itself had become more important than its territorial expansion. The question was no longer a matter of political alignment but of economic interests. Armenia must uphold the concept of a market space before that of a territory, seen as an archaic concept and generator of wars. The Armenians had suffered too much in conflicts and wars which they had often lost. It was necessary, therefore, to rouse a sense of economic identity latent in every Armenian, while downplaying the political and territorialized aspects of national identity. 'We will make Armenia the most important business centre in the Caucasus', declared Armenian Prime Minister Hrand Bagratyan in May 1995.[2] Armenia would achieve peace through economic means, recovery and regional union within the context of globalization. A new vocabulary was emerging in Yerevan: reform, privatization, market economy, market activities and the banking sector. The Armenian sense of identity would be based on economic liberalism and social conservatism. On the one hand, authorities advocating individualism and new values for a society in transition were undermined by the meaning of these values. On the other hand, they advocated the development of traditional values and a renewal of the religious discourse through Karekin II, Catholicos of Cilicia, elected Catholicon of Etchmiadzin as Karekin I, on 5 April 1995. The state thus initiated a process of unification for the Armenian Church, seeking to repair the errors of the anti-clerical communist past while strengthening the role of the Armenian family. By doing so, however, ARF leadership, a majority in the Catholicosate of Cilicia, were placed in an uncomfortable position vis-à-vis its rank and file: either support the president's initiative for the benefit of national unity or condemn him in the name of party interests. The ARF supported the president's choice, even though this undermined relations between the membership and party leadership. This transformation of identity to one based on an interaction between the economic, the cultural and the religious also led to moves to dissociate the power of rationality to solve problems. The new identity thus took shape based on an economy subject to liberal reforms in a country devoid of capitalist experience, on the basis of religious mystery and the anticipated reunification of the Church and a presumption that reunification would restore and enhance the role of the Armenian family in society.

Divergence with the diaspora

Ultimately, the diaspora failed to understand why the construction of the state around an exclusively republican identity should be translated through the formalization of national fragmentation between Armenia and the diaspora. For the latter, the authorities should have profited from moves towards unification of the Church to reinvest the national sphere with the harmonization of Armenian identities both in the country and abroad. The name-change for the majority in parliament bore witness to this. The power of the Pan-National Armenian Movement passed to the republican bloc – or from the nation to the republic. Could Armenia be personified solely around the republic's identity, leaving the diaspora on the sidelines? The main elements of the Armenian diaspora did not understand this qualitative leap. They failed to grasp the consequences of regained sovereignty, or the importance of the rebirth of the state for international relations and did not understand this break within a break, which they took as a further estrangement from Armenia, or even as discrimination against itself. The diaspora expected that the theme of genocide would find new expression among Armenian institutions, which would then be addressed by the state at international

---

[2] *Haik*, 11 May 1995.

levels. The diaspora could not comprehend why the fight against this injustice was not a priority on the Yerevan diplomatic agenda, especially when, in 1994, the world discovered the horrors of the Rwandan genocide – which served to rekindle policy debates on genocide prevention and hence the status of 1915. The diaspora saw the benefits of independence and reunification with Nagorno-Karabakh as a pan-national ideal limited only by realism and considerations of statecraft for a state under reconstruction. To this contrasting analysis of identity, one might add a psychological dimension and confrontation between two collective torments: the social angst of Armenia, at war and lacking everything, contrasted with the psychological anguish of the diaspora expressed in terms of the genocide and from the point of view of the victim.

In other words, in the 1990s the Armenia–diaspora relationship was characterized as ambiguous between the 'have-nots' and the 'victims'. The balance of power between Caucasian Armenians and the Armenians who were formerly of the Ottoman Empire but who today found themselves amid the diaspora was inverted. Owing to a lack of resources, the 'destitute Caucasian' served as a model for a 'diasporic victim', to teach the latter about patriotism, the power of the land and Armenian particularities – to justify the difficulty of reform or to camouflage incompetence. Lacking hindsight, the 'victims living amid the diaspora' were transformed into givers of lessons to the 'Caucasian poor'; lessons of insight into world affairs and the sense of responsibility needed to realign the country, as if they had the experience of state governance and social management. In both cases, frustration prevailed over common sense and several worlds were exposed, both at the micro-social scale in the diaspora and within Armenian society in the Caucasus. The latter was paralysed by the war, the collapse of communism and the new challenges of independence. Armenian micro-societies in the diaspora were trapped in memory narratives, ignorant of the responsibilities and requirements of a sovereign state, of disorder and corruption and unaware of the growing cultural gap between them and the motherland. This mother country prohibited dual nationality and they felt that they were considered as spoiled children, cash cows and donors. In fact, with the communist model destroyed, the Armenians in the Caucasus were trying to hold onto what they had left – family tradition, faith, prominent positions in the state apparatus and traditional values and behaviour – while in the diaspora, the traditional community model was fragmenting; some elements were unable to adapt and others made progress as members of an individualistic culture.

The switch to a liberal utopia

As this new identity emerged, its authors made the first moves in an ambitious plan to turn Armenia and Armenians into a kind of liberal utopia, with a new system of beliefs, where the unpublished values were expected to live in harmony with the former extra-political traditions in the cultural–religious–economic triad. The initial years of the liberal transformation were mixed. On the one hand, the country had launched major structural reforms with varying degrees of success. The transitional society was lagging behind, unable to benefit from the changes brought about by the market system. The modernization of the Church was underway and Nagorno-Karabakh's reunification with Armenia was progressing, albeit slowly. On the other hand, the downside of the reforms was revealed through worrying trends, notably widespread unemployment and rampant emigration. Nearly 700,000 people left the country between 1991 and 1998, the foundations of a new Armenian diaspora in Europe, Russia and America. The economic reforms favoured the old communist nomenclature and created conditions for an alliance between the family system and the resurgence of mafia clans, out of which the oligarchy and its first oligarchs emerged. Nepotism and clanism constituted the heart of this neo-patrimonial state, similar to all post-Soviet states. Power passed from a communist clientelism to a proto-liberal clientelism, where personal relations always took precedence over institutional relations. Under the auspices of the PANM or the Republican Bloc, Ter-Petrosyan's Armenia laid the foundations for this system, where the old tripartite social model was gradually resurfacing: the Soviet-liberal nomenclature instead of the aristocracy, the national army instead of the upper classes or Azat and the people instead of the *ramik*. The neo-patrimonial state was liberal, but it was also a religious, and military or even a deep security state with a confederacy created between the army, the intelligence services (KGB), the police and the paramilitary militia *Yergrabahs* (Defenders of the Country).

Armenia continued to be a politico-religious system where political autonomy was diminished, given the recent transformations, the inexperience of the new elites and the direct relationship between Ter-Petrosyan's Armenia and Yeltsin's Russia. Until 1998, Armenia went through a major crisis every year because of the selfishness of the new elites and the megalomania of the ruling class. In 1995, the Armenians adopted a constitution by referendum and reappointed the majority government following legislative elections which, according to the reports of observation missions, were tainted by electoral fraud and were notable for the absence of the main opposition party, the ARF. Russia recognized the 1915 genocide – a decision celebrated by Armenian society and the diaspora. Although the Armenian government had kept a low profile on the subject, Russian recognition prompted a revival of efforts to gain international recognition of this tragedy. In September 1996, Ter-Petrosyan was declared president of the republic after a controversial presidential election, seeing off his rival, Vazgen Manukyan. Armenia then entered a political crisis. The Republican bloc proved unstable. Three months later, in Lisbon, at the summit of the OSCE, Russia, which was gradually emerging from the domination of the Yeltsin clan after their laborious re-election in June, abandoned Armenia over one of the points of the Nagorno-Karabakh negotiations. Yerevan was isolated diplomatically. Moscow thus made it clear to Ter-Petrosyan that times had changed and that it would also be necessary to prepare Armenian society for the post-Yeltsin period, a diplomatic way of saying that an identical process was underway in Armenia. In 1997, the new deal began with the appointment of the president of the Republic of Nagorno-Karabakh, Robert Kocharyan, as prime minister of the Republic of Armenia. Observers saw in this the start of karabakhization in Armenia. In the autumn, Ter-Petrosyan reported to the Armenian people on progress in negotiations and presented the basis of a peace plan for Nagorno-Karabakh, which antagonized ized part of his majority, the opposition and the authorities in Nagorno-Karabakh. Kotcharyan openly hinted at the existence of cohabitation within the Armenian executive. On 3 February 1998, after lengthy negotiations and disturbing circumstances regarding a change of control at the pinnacle of the state, Ter-Petrosyan announced his resignation as president of the Republic of Armenia. Deprived of its guide and mentor, the transition to a liberal utopia broke down and the construction of the new identity was interrupted. The new strongmen of the regime, Kocharyan and the *sparapet* ('supreme commander of the armed forces'), Minister of Defence Vazgen Sargsyan, took control. It was the question of Upper Karabakh and an arrangement between his own entourage, the opposition and Russia that brought about the downfall of the Ter-Petrosyan regime. The Armenian state thus settled into post-Sovietism and began to consolidate a more traditional identity, albeit one with fewer destabilizing aspects. As a sign of this gradual return to the past and history, the ARF was recognized and rehabilitated. Its most important leaders were released from prison and invited to find their role in the Armenia of Kocharyan and Sargsyan. Armenia thus turned the page of ultra-liberalism.

Several observations are possible here concerning the admission of Armenians into history. Each shares an identical desire to change the collective destiny and abandon the logic of domination, humiliation and chaos. In each case, the elites intended to normalize political thought, adapting it to the new realities of the day while opting for a course midway between tradition and modernity. This included the communist period, when the Soviet-Armenian leaders relied upon the family as a core value for the social organization of their federated republic. However, even if similar ambitions spanned the century, the approaches and methods were different. The revolutionary movement of the nineteenth century used politics as the price for admission to history, laying the foundations for an unprecedented territorial identity. During the Soviet period, communist elites and Armenian micro-elites in the diaspora used culture to find their way into history, focusing on reconstruction and the salvaging of a social identity. Finally, the restoration in 1991 of a sovereign Armenia emphasized the economy and a generalized market approach as the source of national renewal. In contrast to the pragmatism of these three trends, it was not realism that bound them in their quest for historical determination, but an ideal that consisted in achieving their ends – the ideal of building or shaping a new Armenia, as if historical grounding meant searching for a model in which everyone would find their place in accordance with the rules laid down by a comprehensive and inflexible formula for an unassailable utopia. Whether we consider the Dashnak utopia with Haitadism at its core, a communist utopia with its classless world or a liberal utopia with its commodification of the Armenian world, these three attempts at historical grounding all convey the idea of the new man. This principle, which we might summarize as *Homo dashnakus*, *Homo sovieticus* and *Homo liberalis*, is the product of a coercive and autocratic approach to power and methods arising from a lack of sovereign tradition or experience among the elites of a society that lacks any semblance of a social contract between the leaders and the people and affords no respect for this oft-fantasized entity – when it exists – in its rights – when they exist. Is this tantamount to saying that for Armenians to enter history it must be through a utopian prism, an extreme form of a dream that takes precedence over reality? This is difficult to answer, but what is obvious is that each of these three processes of historical grounding has failed in the face of memory flashbacks, as if the road to an exclusively Armenian history has contradicted the fundamental Armenian identity.

Part III

The Power of Memory

History and memory are powerful forces. Using different methods they have the capacity to question the established order and the dominant philosophy. If questioning facts and discovering new revelations which disturb the comfort of the gods is typical of history, memory is more often the crucible of anguish, or concern. Memory is tantamount to trying to stop the passage of time, to invalidate both the real yesterday and today and to respond with the sense of memory brandished as the standard bearer of a rejuvenation of a collective identity. As such, memory stifles individuality and the defence of one's rights, precludes objectivity and distorts the event and its meaning. But memory does not just rhyme with the arbitrary interpretation of the past, the malaise of the present or the fear of the future. It releases resources that reality either ignores or does not want to see. It implies the transmission of an inheritance to succeeding generations, a national purpose and re-education against decadent ideas or fear for extinction. Fear, transmission, design and reeducation, these four pillars of the realm of memory, see their basis strengthen during an identity crisis. Under these circumstances, it is better to build on the strengths of these roots rather than to venture out into the slippery terrain of the world as it is, especially when you have real, ephemeral or painful experience. Thus, if one lets oneself be separated from reality by the power of memory, one becomes better placed to find freedom later. But nobody can deny reality, because no one really wants to. Memory guarantees a status that is vital for the individual and the community. But nobody talks about it and everyone prefers to nestle in its womb. True to Paul Valéry's formula, 'memory is the future of the past'. Armenians use their past as a handrail to help them up the steps towards a supposedly bright future.

In the twentieth century, the power of memory was expressed in three ways. First, in the context of the Haïtadist Cultural Revolution at the turn of the 1970s. A return to the past, this cultural revolution aimed to regenerate the Haïtadist proto-system and offer new perspectives that went beyond Eastern traditionalism and Western individualism. Using a structuralist approach articulated around the promotion of the Armenian language and non-conformist use of a collective and globalized awareness breaking with the fatalism of the diaspora understood as an accident of history, this cultural revolution laid the foundations for a memory of identity, a memorial dialogue, memorial practices where the memory of the dead serves as a bond in a process of national homogenization for a diaspora spread over several continents. Such packaging for this new identity was intended for display of the Armenian Question as the standard-bearer of its renaissance on the international scene ultimately to be absorbed within the communities of the Armenian diaspora around the world.

The power of memory was voiced for a second time in Armenia when President Levon Ter-Petrosyan resigned in favour of Robert Kotcharyan in 1998. This 'transmission of power' can be seen as a decisive step in the manufacture of national identity. The Armenian state is perceived as heir to a long history and a 3,000-year civilization whose heritage permeates institutions, society and the nation as a whole, including the diaspora. This Haïtadist shift towards a transnational and protective approach guides the Armenian state from a 'liberal' calling to a memory vocation. This commemorative state ruled by Robert Kotcharyan (1998–2008) and then Serzh Sargsyan (since 2008) remains firmly anchored in post-Sovietism and is thus a patrimonial model.

This intransigence of the limitless power of memory is inseparable from a third and final source, but this time coming from outside: the genocide denial of Kemalist Islamist Turkey. In the name of the new Kemalist Republic, Turkish historiography is founded, among other beliefs, on the idea of what Alexandre Toumarkin calls 'settling on the Ottoman past'. It is a powerful mechanism whose explicit objective is to ignore the suffering of the Armenians and leave them incarcerated in their own distress. Kemalism sees things simply: as the Armenian genocide never took place and the Armenian Question is no longer on the agenda, it means that the Armenians themselves do not exist. Thus, we must prevent the genie of history escaping from the bottle. In this way, the Armenians remain in their position of victim. Since the AKP (Justice and Development Party) Islamists came to power in 2002, the theme of genocide – 'Soykirim' in Turkish – has entered the Turkish public consciousness and is part of the identity crisis into which post-Kemalist society and consequently Armenians around the world have sunk. To reach an understanding of this 'genocide denial industry', as Taner Akçam, a Turkish historian based in the United States, calls it, a detour to consider the fundamentals of Turkish historiography.

7

The Haitadist Cultural Revolution, 1972–1991

'To forget is to betray' ... It was to the sound of this commemorative and guilt-laden slogan launched on the occasion of the fiftieth anniversary of the genocide in 1965 that Armenian identity revival was conceived. At its height in 1972, this would transform itself into identitarianism. A radical break with the collective comfort that had prevailed among the Armenians of the diaspora was necessary. Moreover, it was necessary to find common ground with the memory of a lost world that had to be revived through the use of the West Armenian language. Although hugely damaged after the events of 1915, Western Armenian did not yet bear the stigma of a dead language such as ancient Greek or Latin, but it was an uncommon dialect and, although surviving, lacked roots in a homeland. In the 1960s–1970s, saving this language, especially in the Western world, signified a great battle for the new generation of Armenian leaders of the main community organizations, including the churches, the Armenian General Benevolent Union (AGBU), political parties and, in particular, the ARF and its affiliates. As Immanuel Wallerstein wrote, 'languages are not neutral, they carry a vision of the world'.[1] The preservation of the Armenian language was therefore the key element in the structuralist transformation that was the Haitadist Cultural Revolution. Inspired by this dominant sociological trend that reached its zenith in the 1960s, a new generation – the first born outside Armenia – found in the use of the Armenian language the locus for the construction of a new identity across the diaspora, one which was inevitably destined to break free from the chains of acculturation.

As with any phenomenon of severance, the Haitadist Cultural Revolution was based on a logic of exclusion disguised under a veneer of inclusion and integration. This non-inclusive return to the past based on language resurgence and identity implied a reliance on the use of the social sciences. The rediscovery of an ancient world, of an idealized and sublimated identity, of a glorified culture and a sanctified revolutionary movement – although omitting any historical perspective – relies upon the disciplines of anthropology, ethnography, history, geography and sociology. In reality, the use of the human sciences was piecemeal and approximate, essentially because, for these scientific methods, reason or objectivity are more disruptive than they are corroborative. In fact, the Haitadist Cultural Revolution focused as much on distancing itself from history as it did on searching for new representations of identity. What were the

---

[1]   Interview with Immanuel Wallerstein, in *Socio*, No 1, March 2013, p. 162.

fundamental elements of this crisis of values and how did they evolve before their collapse in 1991?

Foundations of a new identity in crisis

The Haitadist Cultural Revolution proved to be a process for shaping the identity of the Armenian diaspora. It revolved around four axes.

Rediscovering a lost world

The first mechanism was the rediscovery of a world that had been lost and dispersed. Ancestral customs, past beliefs, oral traditions, ancient Armenian *krapar*, liturgy, folklore, culinary arts, the great historical frescoes of David de Sassun or the exploits of the *fédaïs* (warriors) were immortalized in newly published editions of the memoirs of the leaders of the revolution. The authors whose literary careers were swept away by the events of 1915 were republished. When new stories and literature found their way to publication, such as those of Mouchegh Ichkhan from Lebanon, they were aligned with earlier twentieth-century authors. Publications by intellectuals were dusted off and the memoirs of former leaders were published in Armenian. Everyone was encouraged to immerse their consciousness in the complexities of the past. Nineteenth-century Armenian social life and the ancestral values and traditions were revived. This return to the past served to glorify the memory of Armenian villages, where the arduous lives of the Armenian peasantry were elevated to the level of example. It was through such re-education of conscience, with education and the family becoming the mortar that held everything together, that the foundations of a new Armenian habitus were laid. The family was ultimately the social structure around which the homogenized diaspora of tomorrow would be built. Whether the links were geographical or ethnic, the clan was to become the basis from which the bona fide and reconstructed family would invigorate the community model from within.

A second mechanism for reconstructing Armenian identity was the bilingual school, which from primary school through to high school was destined to become the norm in all communities. The Armenian school thus became a political space in which consciences were remodelled, where omnipresent symbols and ideological themes were used as weapons. From an early age, schoolchildren were accustomed to hearing tales with a dualistic flavour, the *good Armenian* against the *bad Turkish*. When they left this environment, students were naturally inclined to love the country, the land and the people that had populated their young minds in the same manner as ingrained grammatical laws. Through such methods of political education, schoolchildren standardized their actions and gestures: having achieved their goal, with the 're-educators' stating that this standardization was the binding element for future society. By the end of the 1960s, the ARF's educational policy was granting important resources to its 'Ministry of Culture', the Hamaskaine Association. Dashnak schools were structured around Haitadism, so that all disciplines would be Haitadist. Human sciences and biological theories such as Darwinism were widely taught. History was

Haitadist, literature was Haitadist. Anthologies of Armenian poetry and the stories of revolutionaries were staple features in the teaching of literature. In short, everything was done to avoid the slightest risk of personal contemplation and discovery.

In 1980, the ARF's Californian branch undertook research on a panel of 2,214 students from Dashnak schools. It showed the following results: 60 per cent of students were members of Haitadist organizations; 56 per cent were from Dashnak families; 73 per cent of students considered that the use of the Armenian language differentiated 'good Armenians from bad'; 90 per cent understood the meaning of Haitadism; 88 per cent of students defended the idea of a 'free, independent and reunited Armenia'; 90 per cent believed that Armenians in the diaspora acknowledged armed struggle as a political means of expression; 55 per cent of students thought that the Armenian community of Lebanon was the best place to address the Armenian problem; and finally, 76 per cent of students declared themselves ready to devote their available time to Haitadism.[2] Despite these disturbing results, the 're-educators' showed concern, concluding: 'We must strengthen the supervision and teaching of Haitadism in institutions. The Armenian pupil must be given special attention. Haitadism must be the main focus.'[3] This message seems to have evaporated. Ten years later, the historian Rubina Piroumian published *The Armenian Cause*, in which she wrote: 'Students must communicate in keeping with the rhythm of Haitadism in their daily activities.'[4] In most of the curriculum, students are not required to think or reason using anything other than a Dashnak schemata.

The exclusion of signs of foreignness is the golden rule. Even if the term 'ghetto' does not explicitly appear, it is in the minds of those behind this revolution. Its characteristics are largely endorsed by Armenian communities, in which a more restrictive form of communitarianism is increasingly the norm. The social structure is modelled on ethnicity, which is the key idea that accompanies the reclamation of memory. It is unavoidably imperfect but is nonetheless faithful to an unknown past, honestly recounted although transmitted by haphazard fragments and approximate illustrations. The intention is to make the diaspora appear as an accident of history. Diasporization means the inevitable assimilation and expansion of family ties; it entails a slow death, with the removal of the third generation while the genocide survivors disappear. Preventing and fighting against the course of history are at the heart of the Haitadist Cultural Revolution. However, a reintegration of identity through the sharing of a common memory of genocide is transmitted from generation to generation, to be safeguarded at all costs. Individuals are cut off from the realities of their new homelands, with the erstwhile figures of the revolutionary movement being present at the

---

[2] Study published in *Aztag-Drochak Hebdo* (*Dashnak*, Beirut), on 23 March 1980 and launched by the *Haïtadisme* work group of the 'Chanth' committee of the ARF, with three Armenian high schools of *Dashnak* obedience of Los Angeles, 'Ferahian', 'Mesrobian' (10th, 11th and 12th grade) and 'Rose and Alec Philibos' (10th and 11th grade). Studies on the knowledge of Haitadism. Of the 2,214 students, 279 answered the questions (ie 12.6 per cent). Several answers were allowed. This sometimes explains a total greater than 100 per cent.
[3] Ibid.
[4] Roubina Piroumian, *Cause Arménienne* (Los Angeles, Western Prelature of the Armenian Apostolic Church of the United States 1990) p. 10.

revolutionary dinners or banquets, their faces lining the walls of the houses. Safeguarding identity has become a policy, expressed as *hayababanoum* (preservation of Armenian identity), the basis of the term *hayoutiun* or Armenity, which takes its place in Armenian political, social and scientific vocabulary. But this Armenity, which proliferates from one community to another, presupposes a unique model of identity that will have to be redistributed on a global scale – across state borders – and be strengthened with measures based upon the recognition of genocide.

Requiring recognition

Having launched the roots of an integrated and memorial communitarianism, the message of the Haitadist Cultural Revolution for the world outside is a demand for recognitions. The use of the plural is appropriate because it is not only a request for recognition of the genocide but also of the collective and individual Armenian identities, political and cultural, community and civic, professional and family, ethnic and social, victim and subject. In other words, if the Haitadist Cultural Revolution reorders the cards of Armenian identity, its activists become multifaceted identity entrepreneurs. As Caillé wrote, 'the quest for recognition is a social phenomenon in its entirety'.[5] What is the meaning of this search for recognition? It is an obsessive desire to exist, the search for recognition of an existence both as individuals and as a human group in the world of the living, equal to the rest of humanity having abandoned collective humiliation. It is also a quest for dignity and self-esteem in the context of a world that is believed to be righteous, based as it is on civilization and therefore the defence of the human race. In the words of Haud Guéguen and Guillaume Malochet: 'to recognize is to identify, it is sometimes to admit that something has happened'.[6] But in the Haitadist Cultural Revolution, this recognition cannot be individual because the pain is collective and the wounds profound. It must therefore include the entire group. To recognize is to identify and to bestow justice on the victims and to help their descendants abandon humiliation. This makes no sense unless they complain and indicate their desire to obtain compensation for the harm suffered. In the Armenian approach to this issue, the logic of reparations is total, psychological, symbolic, cultural, political, economic and territorial; hence the will of the Haitadist Cultural Revolution to demand recognition of the genocide and its consequences in the public sphere and in the international arena. This is the raison d'être of the worldwide Committee for the Defense of the Armenian Cause (CDAC) created by the ARF in 1965. Third-party recognition of Armenian suffering relieves the weight of the trauma and alleviates the victims' humiliation. This psychological interpretation of the quest for recognition is part of a desire to be free from the domination of the drama, which consists of a pall of oppressive memories which prevent any real liberation. This is the fundamental difference between the individualist and rational approach adopted by the Center for

---

[5]   Alain Caillé (Editor), *La Quête de reconnaissance, Nouveau phénomène social total* (Paris: La Découverte, 2007).

[6]   Haud Guéguen and Guillaume Malochet, *Les théories de la reconnaissance* (Paris: Discovery, 2012).

Armenian Studies (CAE) and the ARF's collective and memorial approach. The former is an attempt to repair the damage using a liberating, pragmatic and functional logic. The latter is part of a domineering, ideological and structuralist approach in which the victims and descendants of victims are just parts of the sum, in view of the fact that the Haitadist Cultural Revolution is an all-embracing awareness of the exclusive, globalizing and moveable diasporic space.

A Third World approach to identity

At its heart, the Haitadist Cultural Revolution takes its inspiration from the Third World and the Middle East. It wants to be independent of the Cold War even if it is completely absorbed in it. To understand this, one needs only observe the relationship between the Haitadist Cultural Revolution and Soviet Armenia. At best, the revolution supports the latter. At worst, it recognizes the entity without supporting the communist regime. It does not oppose the Soviet Union, as the ARF did until 1963 before switching into the neutral camp, while remaining outside the club of non-aligned countries. It intends to overcome the East–West dilemma and adhere to the logic of the liberation movements in Vietnam, Palestine and Cuba. With memories of its revolutionary past, the ARF shows solidarity with these Third World movements that are fighting for their rights, declaring its admiration for the previous figures of the Armenian revolution. To make this connection with the past but also with its geopolitical environment, the ARF convened its twentieth congress in 1972 in Vienna, Austria, a neutral country but also host country for the famous fourth party congress of 1907. Whereas the congress of 1907 advocated a Greater Armenia, the 1972 congress advocated the idea of a borderless pan-Haitadism, that of an integrated diasporic space and a specific relationship with Soviet Armenia. Just as the congress of 1907 reaffirmed socialism as a doctrine of the party, hailed by the ARF's accession to the Second International the same year, the 1972 congress reintroduced the principle of socialism into the programme after several decades of anti-Sovietism and alignment with Washington. Finally, just as the 1907 congress embarked on Messianism as a substitution for politics, the 1972 congress called on Armenians to fulfil the sacred mission of serving the Armenian cause against Turkey, Soviet colonialism, American imperialism and Western decadence. This new extra-territorial Messianism emerged as an alternative to traditional anti-Sovietism, which no longer made sense when the relaxation of East–West relations and Ostpolitik in Germany were taken into account. This shift towards a Third World mentality has anti-Turkish elements. The simpler and more coherent message is critical for shaping the cultural revolution and influencing the kind of conflicts. This political creed plays on a consensual memory that is shared by all Armenian actors but exhibits an ethnic shift, in keeping with the formula of Lord Acton reported by Benedict Anderson in *The National Imaginary*: 'Exile is the nursery of nationalism.'[7] The Haitadist Cultural

---

[7]   Benedict Anderson, *L'imaginaire national, réflexions sur l'origine et l'essor du nationalisme* (Paris: La Découverte, 1996).

Revolution is transformed, becoming 'diaspora nationalism',[8] as Ernest Gellner puts it. This nationalism from the outside carries with it a responsibility for the reformulation of old national or religious hatreds and their re-exportation back to the country of origin. Mixing imagination with historical fundamentals, this Armenian 'diasporic nationalism' intensifies in the same way everywhere in the world, whatever the social model of the country of adoption. Third World attitudes, anti-Turkism and diasporic nationalism find themselves intermingled in a single independentist logic. But this time, it is not a mobilization announcing claims for the sovereignty of Soviet Armenia. The focus on the remembrance of 1915 proposes to celebrate a less destructive and therefore more consensual memory than the liberation of Soviet Armenia. For the ARF, the goal of a 'Free, Independent and Reunited Armenia' was maintained, while the strategy focus was shifting. The thrust of remembrance shifted the political message from a demand for Soviet Armenian sovereignty to that of the independence of Turkish Armenia, whose territories, once liberated, could be attached to the Armenian SSR and thus to the Soviet Union. In the official discourse, this rhetorical difference is not immediately obvious. The narrative is recomposed from within: independence, yes, but first the liberation of the territories of Turkish Armenia. Henceforth, Ankara would be the priority target for the Armenian struggle.

How should this strategic change be translated? Essentially, in three ways. First, by claiming recognition of the genocide of 1915, with the objective to obtain compensation and to place Turkey in a situation where it can offer concessions, including of territory. Thus, the fight for the recognition of the genocide is not an end in itself, but an instrument to advance the cause and to recover territories. Second, by the fidelity to revolutionary Messianism, answering those who criticize this irredentist attitude towards Turkey, considering that it is unrealistic to hope to obtain territorial reparations. The Haitadist Cultural Revolution retaliates by underlining that no one can predict the future and, just as the peoples of Latin America, Asia or Africa have liberated themselves from Western colonialism, even the slight possibility of one day seeing Armenia overcome Turkish guardianship is not to be overlooked. Everything rests on the consolatory expression 'One day, Armenia will be released'. To dedicate one's destiny to the power of time is to cultivate revolutionary messianism, but it is also to ensure peace of mind and allegiance to revolution. Under these conditions, the revolution prohibits any concession to Turkey and time can be an asset, but never a handicap: it dominates everything. And finally, by armed struggle, terrorism or political violence directed against Turkey.

Manifestations of the revolution

The Haitadist Cultural Revolution is complete in its value system but also in its manifestations, which can be categorized in four major groups.

---

[8]   Ernest Gellner, *Nations et Nationalisme* (Paris: Payot, 1989), pp. 146–156.

The Lebanization of Armenian identity

The first and undoubtedly the most visible is the process of Lebanization of the Armenian diasporic identity. This characteristic has affected everything. At this time, Lebanon was the state where the Armenian diaspora was the most homogeneous and structured and best incorporated into the host country. Geographically, its population was already strongly 'Armenized' and the national territory was structured around the Armenian presence. There were Armenian communities in East Beirut, in Bourj Hammoud in Jounieh and in Andjar on the plain of Bekaa. Furthermore, the Armenian religious community was organized around the Apostolic Church and Holy See of Antelias, along with its ministers and deputies, its parties and its educational, cultural, sports and social institutions. The multi-confessional nature of Lebanese society facilitated the implementation and development of the Armenian community. In Lebanon, one is first and foremost a member of the community into which one is born, even before one is Lebanese. At the time, the Armenian community in Lebanon amounted to more than 200,000 people, almost exclusively from Turkish Armenia (from the eastern vilayets and from Cilicia) and all had been subjected to deportations during the period of the genocide. These former refugees nurtured their ties to their homeland in their collective unconscious, a factor that would significantly impact the origins of the Haitadist Cultural Revolution. The earlier refugees had managed to create a successful network of schools – and it would be remiss not to mention the Nechan Palandjian or 'Djemaran' school created by the ARF-affiliated 'Hamaskaine' association, located in the majority Muslim area of West Beirut. At the outset, the community was led by the great political figures of the revolutionary movement and the First Republic of Armenia (Levon Chanth, Nigol Aghbalian, Simon Vratsian, then ARF World Bureau member Hratch Dasnabedian). Political and cultural life was thriving with universities, Armenian research institutes, libraries, bookshops, archive centres and a diverse, but party-dependent, media. It was in Lebanon that the Armenian dailies of the diaspora enjoyed their largest circulation, between 5,000 and 7,000 copies for *Aztag* ('The Postman', Dashnak editorial line) and *Zartong* ('The Awakening', Armenian Democratic Liberal editorial line) – and this was where the Armenian language had real foundations, allowing it to contribute to the development of social bonds in a more consistent way than elsewhere. Former ministers, men of letters and professors of Armenian literature met in Armenian Lebanon. Beirut, the hub of economic and financial activity throughout the Middle East, became the cultural capital of the diaspora, an extension of pre-war Constantinople or Paris after 1918.

The Haitadist Cultural Revolution exemplified a crisis of growth, whereby the Lebanese community model would finally export its know-how across the Armenian diaspora to better redistribute and subsequently dominate all activities. The Lebanese capital would assume the role of political centre, concentrating the leadership of the Armenian parties (ARF, PSDH, Armenian Democratic Liberals) and becoming indispensable for the defence of Soviet and American interests regarding the Armenian Question. As a financial centre, Beirut hosted a monetary fund set up by the ARF in the early 1960s, to which all national branches of the party contributed, in order to create the nerve centre of the Haitadist Cultural Revolution. The money raised – more than

$1 million – deprived other branches of the Dashnak of material resources, thus limiting their effectiveness. The Lebanization of the party was also demographic, as a result of the waves of Armenian migration from the Middle East to the West after the Lebanese Civil War (1975–1990), the Revolution in Iran in 1979 and the Iran–Iraq War (1980–1988). Once in America or Europe, the Haitadist Cultural Revolution found pockets of immigrants among the expatriate communities on whom it could rely to spread its message. Finally, the revolution was also a way to reconnect with political violence or terrorism. From 1973 to 1975 and from 1985 to 1986, Europe, the United States and Oceania would be the scene of several hundred attacks mainly claimed by two organizations: the Armenian Secret Army for the Liberation of Armenia (ASALA) and the Justice Commandos of the Armenian Genocide (JCAG). Created at around the same time (1972–1974) in the heat of the Lebanese crucible and inspired by the Palestinian, Vietnamese and Latin American liberation movements, ASALA and JCAG intended to shake Armenians out of their torpor and awaken international consciousness to the injustices inflicted upon the Armenian people. Through attacks mostly against Turkish official targets, the two organizations broke with conservative and peaceful party methods. ASALA broadened its strategy to strike non-Turkish interests in Europe and elsewhere, eventually provoking a split following the 1983 attack at Paris's Orly airport. Drawing on the Armenians' long experience of terrorism – beginning in the nineteenth century and following the Russian model of direct action – these two clandestine movements worked with a professionalism worthy of the US secret service. It was not until the turn of the 1980s that the world caught its first glimpse of the perpetrators, as leaders of the Haitadist Cultural Revolution fell into the hands of the police and were publicly displayed on network television screens: Max Hraïr Kilndjian (JCAG) was arrested in Marseille in February 1980;[9] Alec Yenikomechian and Suzy Mahserejian (ASALA) were apprehended in Geneva in October 1980;[10] Mardiros Jamgotchian (ASALA), was arrested in Geneva in June 1981;[11] Vasken Sislian, Kevork Guzelian, Aram Basmadjian and Agop Djoulfayan (ASALA), the four commandos of Operation Van, were arrested after taking staff of the Turkish Consulate in Paris hostage on 24 September 1981;[12] and finally, Hampartsoum Sassounian (JCAG) was caught in January 1982 in Los Angeles.[13] For ten years, the news of the attacks alternated with news of the Armenian Question and

[9]   Max Hraïr Kilndjian was sentenced in 1982 to two years in prison for complicity in the attempt to assassinate the Turkish ambassador in Berne, Switzerland.

[10] Alec Yenikomechian and Suzy Mahserejian were injured in handling the bomb intended to kill a Turkish diplomat. They were arrested on 3 October 1980 in Geneva. After a wave of ASALA attacks, Switzerland decided to release them and extradite them to Lebanon.

[11] Mardiros Jamgotchian murdered the first secretary of the Turkish embassy in Geneva on 9 June 1981. He was sentenced to 15 years in prison. After a wave of attacks by ASALA, he was extradited from Switzerland to Lebanon.

[12] Vasken Sislian, Kevork Guzelian, Aram Basmadjian and Agop Djoulfayan were sentenced to seven years in prison on 31 January 1984 during a trial in Paris, in which Meline Manouchian, wife of resistant Missak Manouchian, Henri Verneuil, pleaded in their favour.

[13] Hampartsoum Sassounian was arrested for the assassination of the Turkish Consul General on 28 January 1982. He was sentenced to life imprisonment. Since that date, 'Hampig', as he is known, has served his sentence in St Louis Obispo prison in California.

complementary actions carried out at the UN in Geneva or in other parliaments in seeking recognition of the genocide. Although the operations were terrorist operations, Armenians preferred to speak of 'resistance' and its leaders' intentions were of pursuing an armed struggle as if the people were at war. While most terrorists were of Lebanese or Middle Eastern origin (Syria and Iran), candidates for illegal action came from throughout the diaspora, particularly France, where ASALA could rely upon a political arm, the Armenian National Movement led by Ara Toranian.

The actions of both groups started at the same time and ended in 1985. This is unlikely to have been a coincidence, for three reasons. The first was that state security policies were becoming more effective and counter-terrorism measures were beginning to bear fruit. The second was that pressure from world powers, including Soviet and American, was getting stronger: in 1982, the head of JCAG, Apraham Achdjian was kidnapped in Israeli-occupied Beirut. In 1983, the Soviets and Syrians pressured ASALA to the point where it committed indiscriminate violence against Westerners at Orly airport in Paris, causing a split between the Hagopian 'El Moudjahed' clan, which maintained links with international terrorist networks and the Monte Melkonian clan, which headed the ASALA-Revolutionary Movement fringe faithful to the Armenian cause against Turkey. Finally, for internal reasons and as a result of misunderstandings that arose in the latest operations, the Haitadist Cultural Revolution reached the height of blindness with the bombing in Orly and the radical attack on the Turkish embassy in Lisbon in 1983, resulting in the deaths of the perpetrators who became known as the 'Lisbon Five' after their suicide mission. The latter was an act unprecedented in Europe in the twentieth century especially as it was never properly explained by its perpetrators. The Lisbon operation is commemorated each year by the Dashnaks and, with due respect for proportion, it was the first and last suicide action in the Western world before the attacks of 9/11.

Until the early 1980s, this Armenian attention-seeking terrorism enjoyed the sympathy of both the Americans and the Soviets who saw in these actions justice for Turkey's 1974 invasion of Cyprus and the September 1980 military coup in Ankara. The Armenian commandos rarely struck at Turkey on its own territory, nor ever really threatened Ankara and Turkey's territorial integrity. For a comprehensive assessment of Armenian terrorism, we cannot overlook the influence of the Cold War. World power competition has been overlooked for too long and underestimated by observers. It is impossible to understand the Armenian terrorism strategy without observing that Armenian geography corresponds exactly to East–West rivalries. In other words, when a Turkish ambassador or military attaché is shot by the Armenians, it is not only a representative of Turkey who is assassinated, but also an official belonging to a NATO Member State.

The similarities between these two armed groups end there. There was also rivalry among terrorist groups, including the settlement of scores and inter-Armenian assassinations. Although the JCAG was affiliated with the ARF, ASALA formally denounced Dashnak conservatism, seeing it as responsible for the disappearance of the Armenian Question until 1970. Where the JCAG was fully geared towards genocide recognition, ASALA openly advocated the liberation of the territories of Western Armenia. If the JCAG did not adopt a distinct ideology, ASALA became recognized for its Marxist view of resistance and class struggle, albeit at a distance and devoid of a social aspect. It is not clear what this vernacular Marxism refers to, if not solidarity between oppressed people. If the JCAG was an autonomous group operating with its own resources, ASALA relied on solidarity and collusion with Palestinian armed groups and also Greek, Kurdish and Irish groups. The JCAG prioritized political marketing by using an unpronounceable acronym and had a preference for communications somewhat akin to a branch of a state secret service. ASALA, in contrast, proposed overt dramatization of their actions using strong communication techniques and symbolism: hooded faces, training videos, logo design and direct rhetoric. But most of all, if memory with a cause completely permeated the JCAG organization, the world would have to wait until 1983 to see the group change its name to the Armenian Revolutionary Army – ASALA hesitated between memory and history. Memory, as shown by its fidelity to the Haitadist Cultural Revolution and to the liberation of territories. History, by its solidarity with the peoples of the Third World and the struggle of the oppressed against imperialism and colonialism.

The cultural clash between East and West

As already stated, the mass exodus of Armenians from Lebanon and the Middle East to Europe and the United States, mainly as a result of the political crises of the 1970s and 1980s, caused shock waves. in their thousands and against the official position of the political parties, they greatly increased the size of Armenian communities both in France and the United States. The movement was so significant that these migratory waves rejuvenated the associative and community fabric of some expatriate communities, such as in Canada, land of asylum for emigrants from the Levant. More often than not, there was little integration within the formerly established communities but simply a stacking of Armenian identities, with the first diaspora of the 1920s fully integrated and successive layers of less-assimilated Armenian-Lebanese emigrants. In France, this created a cultural upheaval, while in the United States the semi-communitarian model managed to absorb these newcomers for the most part, notwithstanding some very strong differences in identitiy. In addition to these migratory flows, the massive arrival of a new diaspora from Soviet Armenia, completely disconnected from the Haitadist Cultural Revolution, profoundly affected the balance of Western Armenian communities.

The cultural divide between the West and the East essentially concerned notions of citizenship and community. The communitarian shift resulting from a move towards a Third World approach to identity was not particularly well received among Armenians settled in Europe or the United States, who perceived themselves essentially as citizens, for the most part having acquired such status at the turn of the 1950s and wanted no part of a refugee ghetto community. The Lebanese-inspired principle that one is first Armenian before one is a citizen of one's host country found little favour in the West. Similarly, there were divergent approaches to the notion of human rights: in the East, human rights were seen as collective rights, whereas in the West, the term refers to individual rights. Similarly, there was no tolerance for political violence, this as a mark of respect for legality and for security, but also as a means of distancing such aggressive forms of identity affirmation at odds with all forms of humanism. The break between the individual, legalistic reaction and the collective and radical tendency is related to the notion of the 'self'. In the Western cultural space, the individualistic reaction signals the emergence or coming-of-age of 'me', whereas in the Eastern cultural space, the 'me' does not exist and is trampled by an all-pervading 'we'. To refuse the revolution was to affirm and defend one's sovereign 'I' against the domination of a collective identity.

Fostering a new organizational model

In the name of Dashnak memory, party leaders at the turn of the 1970s were determined to provide a messianic context for the metamorphosis of the Armenian identity. The new understanding was of revolutionary continuity with the first generations of activists and turned its back on the conservatism of the outgoing leadership, overly conspicuous in its conformity and rejection of the ideals of the armed struggle. Established in about 30 countries, organized around a political hub located in Beirut, the Dashnak looks more like an Armenian International than a political party as portrayed in the classical political science texts. The ARF sees itself exclusively as a political party in exile with a single programme, a simple message and a single way of working. To refer to the ARF as international would suggest acceptance of the dispersal across a diaspora, whereas by presenting itself as a party in exile the organization reserves for itself the possibility of a return to Armenia, even if this idea was defeated by the results of Stalin's repatriation plan in 1947 and Khrushchev's in 1961. More than 100,000 Armenians from the diaspora returned, only to depart again for their host countries, particularly to France. The leadership of the Dashnak party saw itself as pre-eminent, sweeping away the slightest opposition or dissidence and at the same time ruling out any organic plurality in the Dashnak movement.

Conversely, pluralism would become an inevitable reality, intrinsic to the Dashnaks, which we should recall means 'federal'. Etched into history, these currents experienced a revival in the 1970s under Sarkis Zeitlian, a Lebanese, heir to Zavarianism; Khajak Der Krikorian, an Iranian native and follower of Dumanism; Garo Mehian, a former prisoner of the Soviet gulag and resident of France who became a vector for the ideas of Mikael Varandian; and finally, Hraïr Maroukhian, an Iranian living in Beirut who subsequently moved to Athens, where he distinguished himself as a keeper of the ideas of Rostomism. We should not forget the pro-Arab traditionalist currents followed by Papken Papazian, originally from Iraq and living in Beirut, the populist and pro-Russian views of Edward Hovannessian, who was himself from the Soviet Union, the Social Democrat, Hraïr Khalatian, from Iran and the pro-Western liberal trend which was followed by Hratch Dasnabedian, who held dual French and Lebanese citizenship and lived in Beirut. Party unity is found through the restoration of socialism but is less noticeable for its internal unifying themes than it is in the rejection of external ideas. These include the *nejtheism* of Karekin Nejteh, banned in the 1970s by the ARF so as not to offend the Soviet Union but also to maintain a distance from this variant of fascism, bringing with it bad memories of Dashnakism in the 1930s and 1940s. With the shift to a Third World stance, Dashnakism embraced two socialist alternatives. One can be seen as a process of socialization and humanism in the Zavarian mode. Scientific socialism is only transitory and cannot be grafted onto social reality unless it can be considered progressive, rather as Baathism is among Arabs, a combination of pan-nationalism, progressivism and the revolutionary. The alternative is Marxism, which made a sensational breakthrough among the younger generation, especially when allied with Dumanism, which won out over Maoism in Iran and France. Such was the alternative, which envisioned utopian socialism as an attainable prospect. However, it was also backed by the Rostomists, who saw an inspirational variant in the self-managed socialism inspired by Tito. Such currents, however, were wary of dialectical materialism, so that Varandianists as well as Zavarianists were careful to preserve their own motivating forces. For the former, this was the democratic ideal as the main fuel for the revolutionary movement, while for the latter, nationalism was the driving cause. In reality, ARF socialism was vague and approximate, cut off from reality in the homeland and severed from the daily life of Armenian populations, who were affected more by the policies of their respective states than by the Dashnak agenda. Apart from solidarity with oppressed peoples, the façade of neutrality and the universalizing Dashnak newspeak, the Lebanization of the Armenian diaspora was overtaken by Baathization and eventually a Nasserization of the ARF across the globe, as if it were the only Armenian equivalent of pan-Arab progressivism. But how are Christapor, Rostom, Zavarian and Baathism related? Not at all.

The Lebanese–Iranian leadership that became established between 1963 and 1972 effectively broke with the ARF traditions and seized power over all the national branches, thus imposing a democratic centralization. Centripetal tendencies had already arisen in the history of the party, but never had they been imposed in the same way as at the turn of the 1970s. Here, the global party bureau imposed an *ichkhanapar* (authoritarian) power to the detriment of an *orinapar* (conformist) power. This considerable shift towards democratic centralism encountered opposition from defenders of decentralization in France and the United States, but these opponents would gradually be sidelined, then ized, before being excommunicated by the party. The Lebanization of the party operated as a system for exclusion, readjustment and redefinition of the national branches, some of which were dissolved, notably in Cyprus and France, before being reconstituted in the spirit of party discipline. It was also a system of youth indoctrination, a breeding ground made all the more fertile as the re-education took place with the backdrop of terrorism against Turkey.

Indeed, the anti-Turkish strategy also revealed differences with the revolutionary struggle against the Ottoman Empire. At the beginning of the revolution, the leaders never considered the Ottoman state and its people as enemies. The Hamidian regime was the only enemy. For Dashnak leaders, the priority was agrarian reform in the Ottoman Empire and religious and ethnic issues were to be found in the background. The triumvirate at the head of the party did not take action against the Kurds and the Turks. Mikaelian taught history to young Muslims in his village and Turkish students attended his funeral in March 1905. Simon Zavarian was nicknamed 'Defender of the Kurds and Turks' because he refused to allow the revolution to happen at the expense of populations who themselves had suffered at the hands of the central power.[14] Finally,

---

[14] Roupen Ter-Minassian, *Mémoire d'un révolutionnaire arménien*, 7 vols, 2nd edn (Beyrouth: Hamaskaïne, 1972.

even more explicitly, Rostom frequently repeated that the ARF was not a nationalist party but a party of class struggle and that the enemy was the Hamidian regime and not the Turkish and Kurdish peoples.[15] This open-mindedness, very often ignored by observers of the Armenian Question, contrasted with the narrow and sectarian spirit of the ideologues of the Haitadist Cultural Revolution, who did not hesitate to speak of the ARF as a 'nationalist party' in Lebanon or in the United States or as a 'socialist party' in France as a way to broaden its appeal and improve its image with the party of François Mitterrand.

This organizational governance led to two types of behaviour. Bureaucratization took control of all the resources until the apparatchiks turned into intellectuals, marginalizing as they went the few elements that remained to them of 'intelligentsia'. Bolstered by their party heritage and carried along by the Haitadist Cultural Revolution, Dashnak executives and militants saw in these achievements the starting point for hegemonic behaviour that was not without a sense of superiority towards ordinary Armenians. The sense of belonging to this new chivalrous order convinced them that their membership of the ARF was the culmination of a commitment, while any good Dashnak would recognize that, according to the tenets of Mikaelian, 'the struggle is permanent' (*Haradev gueriv*).[16] On the other hand, this process of ethnic self-selection resulted in some Armenians becoming obsessed with individual recognition and a search for standing within the community, not unlike what happened at the time of the Armenian millet under the Ottomans. By occupying such or such official function within the community – for instance association president – there arose a desire for public recognition, even if merely symbolic.

Revolutionary fortunes

Not everything was black and white during this paradigm shift from the 1960s to the 1970s. It was not simply about accumulating failures, excesses and indoctrination. There were four issues that arose from this structuralist turning point that to this day impact Armenian political reality. First, albeit messianic, the restructuring of the diasporic identity was an act of globalization before its time. The Haitadist Cultural Revolution was distinctive in that it created a space of ethnic homogeneity which bordered on the standardization of identity around the Lebanese model. Even if intergenerational relationships between the young and the old of the Armenian diaspora in the United States or France were stormy or chaotic, they provoked such a modernization that the existence of a real social life outside the homeland was brought into being, whereas assimilationist logic led these communities directly towards their long-term disappearance. One might retort that there may be other models to safeguard or develop an identity rather than this deterministic approach and that in any event it was not necessary to go through a culture shock between Armenians from the East and Armenians from the West. If the Haitadist Cultural Revolution foreshadowed an

---

[15] Speech by Rostom, at the fourth ARF congress, Vienna, 1907. *Matériaux pour l'histoire de la FRA*, vol 3 (undated), 69th session, 6 April 1907, pp. 184–185.
[16] Christapor Mikaelian, *Pensées révolutionnaires*, édition de la FRA, Athènes, 1931.

Armenian variant of today's globalization, this process happened on the basis of an approximate and exclusive repoliticization of attitudes.

Furthermore, the renewed interest in the Armenian Question, whether at the UN or in national or European parliaments, bore fruit. If the macabre prophecy of Talaat Pasha that 'there is no Armenian Question for the next fifty years' when executing his plan to exterminate Ottoman Armenians came true, the Armenian Question nevertheless returned to centre stage 50 years after the genocide.[17] The resurgence of interest, however, was accompanied by a misunderstanding of its causes, its nature and its perspectives, by many observers. Comments at the time and even today prove that it is far from being properly comprehended, even if its initial message is simple: recognize the injustice inflicted upon the Armenian people by an unpunished genocide carried out by a negationist Turkey.

The Haitadist Cultural Revolution also contributed to Armenian well-being during the Lebanese Civil War. While the other communities were tearing each other apart in Beirut in competition for a tract of land or a district, all tendencies of Lebanese Armenians adopted a position of 'positive neutrality', a bit of crypto-communist Arab rhetoric which proved especially useful in Lebanese chaos. Traditionally aligned with the Lebanese Christians, Armenians correctly gauged the Arabization of Lebanese society and played the card of taking the middle ground in this complicated confessional system. In the 1989 Taif accord, which ended the 15-year civil war, all parties recognized the positive, responsible and peaceful behaviour of the Armenian community in Lebanon. They praised the courage of its religious authorities as well as its political parties, starting with the ARF, the only organization on the ground able to protect the Armenian neighbourhoods of East Beirut by mustering a few thousand-strong militia. This militia, often little more than armed civilians, had to simultaneously fight Christian militias and Muslim armed groups. It is true that the Soviet Union guaranteed the protection of Lebanese Armenians and made this known to all the warring parties, which made it possible to dissuade this or that force from terminating this unique community. Certainly, the United States could count on the Armenians of Lebanon as very effective mediation networks. But it took all the composure of the leaders of the Haitadist Cultural Revolution to save their interests on the ground. Despite the Armenian predilection for terrorist action, which exposed them to retaliatory acts – these occurring on several occasions during 1981 and 1982 – the Lebanese Civil War seriously interfered with revolutionary plans. Lebanese Armenians and the ARF in particular, were to be commended for adopting the attitude of responsible Lebanese, whose engagement was for the preservation of peace and sovereignty. Forty years after the beginning of the civil war, if the warring did not prevent the waves of Lebanese emigration to the West, it is clear that Armenians today enjoy the respect of their Lebanese neighbours and full recognition among Lebanese institutions for the sacrifices their leaders have made to save this exclave of Armenia in the land of the East.

---

[17] Quoted by Gérard Chaliand and Yves Ternon in *Le génocide des Arméniens* (Brussels: Editions Complexe, 1984), p. 112.

Finally, the activism engendered by the revolution allowed Armenians in Europe and the United States to lay the foundations for a solicitation of national parliaments. From the 1970s, the activities of these groups among the American and French political parties, who were well aware of the importance of the Armenian electorate, made it possible to customize the Armenian Question and to open up their strategy to include secondary but morally just causes. In the United States, pro-Armenian lobby organizations engaged with representatives of the major states of the Union: California, Massachusetts, New York and Florida. If today 49 states of the Union have recognized the genocide, Armenian-Americans owe this to the pioneering work begun in the early 1970s. The professionalization of the Armenian lobby in the United States was so straightforward and effective that today it is considered the second strongest ethnic lobby on US soil after the pro-Israel lobby. Even if progress concerning the Armenian Question reflects a corresponding desire among American and French parties to expose themselves more fully to Third World causes in support of clientelist relationships within these communities, it is difficult not to make reference to the invisible and time consuming work undertaken by these people of good intentions among the Haitadist revolutionary network. Even if such lobbying resulted in an ethnic push in an integrationist federal United States or Republican and Jacobin France, the political and social ties created have allowed the Armenian memory to benefit from an array of symbolic and material rewards. For example, these have included the presence of high public officials at Armenian ethnic events, the creation of Armenian friendship societies, with broad support in the US Congress or the French Parliament and monetary grants awarded to Armenian cultural associations.

A negative global balance sheet?

What appeared as a memorial power – the renewal of identity – in fact hid systemic weakness: that of an unequal struggle against assimilation. Just as the revolutionary Armenian movement was stopped in 1908 by the Young Turk revolution, the Haitadist Cultural Revolution left a sentiment of unfinished business for two reasons. On the one hand, various crises in the Middle East undermined the dreams of the fathers of the revolution – the war in Lebanon (1975–1991), the Islamic revolution in Iran (1979), the Iran–Iraq War (1980–1988) – and provoked waves of Armenian emigration to Europe and America, which not only deprived the revolution of its power base but upset the equilibrium among Armenian micro-societies on these two continents. On the other hand, the logic of indoctrination was incompatible with Western democratic societies; it was inconsistent with the aspirations of second- and third-generation (post-genocide) Armenians who wanted above all to get on with their personal and professional lives. The Haitadist Cultural Revolution was out of step with the legal institutions of societies that resisted all forms of armed struggle, the nerve centre of the revolution. Had the Haitadist Cultural Revolution been limited to its Middle Eastern dimension, it would have gained coherence but lost all meaning for the good reason that the cultural revolution was conceived only in its fullest and most complete version as a means for controlling the entire diaspora and as a strategy to dominate remembrance and identity construction.

More than 40 years after its beginnings, the balance sheet for the revolution was mostly negative. It had succeeded in transforming the identity of the Armenian diaspora as sectarian, depriving itself of cognitive resources essential to understanding the world while preferring to limit itself to narrow sectarian views. The revolution promoted a traditional community model, ossifying the stereotypical behaviour of these creators and creatures. And so, by defining the diaspora as an accident of history, it was totally mistaken. Among Armenians, the diaspora is a historical tradition dating back to the tenth century. It is not a historical exception. Built on false foundations and false calculations, the Haitadist Cultural Revolution did not anticipate the paradigm shift resulting from the restoration of the Armenian state. It abandoned the sense of history when the independence of Armenia for which it was conceived was made for it. On the other hand, it has undeniably scored social and political points. It has regenerated social bonds among Armenians organized in networks, a foretaste of a form of ethnic globalization. It has also made various national parliaments aware of the Armenian Question and taken up arms to break the wall of silence, thus supporting the idea that the use of arms is not necessarily a zero-sum strategy, provided that a revolutionary movement can retain its coherence and legitimacy while remaining in alignment with clearly defined movement policies. In principle, the Haitadist Cultural Revolution emerged as a way to fight the crisis of meaning that affected Armenians of the diaspora. In reality, it has resulted in a crisis of identity among the recipients, as if the latter had been faced with a difficult choice: to make the structuralist shift and relive from the inside a feeling of Armenity while at the same time accepting the loss of 'personal freedom' to accept domination by a collective 'we'. Alternatively, to refuse this structuralist shift is to take one's destiny into one's own hands while remaining on the margins of the Armenian micro-societies, the holders of traditional Armenian legitimacy. In fact, this unfinished revolution never left its crisis state because it was muddled by a conflict of values. Should Armenians be satisfied with the resources of the past to exist collectively, going so far as to legitimize violence, give up modernity, stifle the truth under the cushion of remembrance, in short, prevent history from emerging out of one's memories?

8

Turkey or the Unique Case of State Denial

It is impossible to evaluate the influence of Turkey's negationism without considering from the outset that research is subject to state historiography. State negationism and historiography form an inseparable partnership. The French historian Pierre Vidal-Naquet perhaps offers the clearest explanation of this relationship. In his seminal book *The Assassins of Memory*, published in 1987, he writes:

> Of all historiographies, the worst is of course state historiography and states rarely admit to having been criminals. Perhaps the most painful case in this field is the case of the Turkish historiography of the 1915 Armenian genocide. Let the Turks insist on the state of war, on express Armenian wishes for the Russian offensive, on localized conflicts between Armenians and their neighbors, during which the former did not always behave storied lambs. What could be more natural? But that was not the Turks' position; Instead, they offered the perfect example of a historiography of denial. Let us put ourselves in the shoes of Armenian minorities all over the world. Let us imagine Minister Faurisson, General Faurisson, Ambassador Faurisson, Faurisson an influential member of the United Nations, Faurisson responding in the media every time the genocide of the Jews is talked about, in short a Faurisson of State with an international Faurisson look-alike and in addition, since 1943, Talaat-Himmler with his solemn mausoleum in the capital. No need to dwell on a historiography where everything is preordained.[1]

Holocaust denial includes a range of behaviours brought together within the family of a collective lie. First there is negation by omission. More or less innocent, this amounts to avoiding whatever is controversial. Then comes individual and isolated denial, which originates with 'historians' attached to a university or a research centre or an apprentice 'researcher' at odds with the system. The former hide behind their duty of criticism – a prerequisite for the profession of researcher. They forget that they base their narrative on a sampling of sources reputed as historical. Such an approach might be referenced as the variable nature of evidence-based research. As for junior researchers and assistants, who suffer from a lack of recognition, they may be prone to falsification to acquire status. Finally, there is official or state denial. In this family, there

---

[1]   Pierre Vidal-Naquet, *Les Assassins de la Mémoire* (Paris: Maspero, 1981).

is the Armenian exception. Besides Turkey, no other state has challenged the reality of an equivalent crime over such a long period and at the highest levels of the state's society and institutions. Turkey's state denial is so well practised that it has educated and inspired other states such as Azerbaijan, Pakistan, Iran and Sudan. One might mention Mahmoud Ahmadinejad in Iran, who contested the existence of the so-called Holocaust 'myth'. Others give the example of Sudan strongman Omar al-Bashir and his denial of mass crimes in Darfur.

It is not the role of this enquiry to narrate the story of state denial in Turkey, although it would be desirable if, in addition to the work of Fatma Müge Gokçek on official Turkish historiography, another academic sought to improve research into this specific technique of falsifying history. It is not a matter here of enumerating the major steps in the Turkish denial of the events of 1915. The attention given to negationism (formerly called revisionism), a term used for the first time in 1987 with reference to the Holocaust, is more an interest in the logic for and the mechanisms of denial. How does such denial, backed as it is by the state system, keep Armenians and, more broadly, history in suspense?

In Turkey, says sociologist Hamit Bozarslan, 'history, nation and honor are part of the same fortress'.[2] Turkish historiography is an example of national, state, traditional and negationist history. It is based on a Turko-centred approach, defensive and sometimes vague, especially that dating from the end of the imperial era. In a study in 2013 published in the Turkish journal *Cogito*, on the historiography of Turkey, the famous historian Edhem Eldem deplored, in broad terms, the nationalist account of the Osmanlis dynasty's rich history.[3] While denouncing the archaic methods of the first generation of historians, he shows that for almost three decades tremendous progress was made in the social sciences regarding the history of the Ottoman Empire in the nineteenth and twentieth centuries. Among these notable advances, he pays particular attention to the study of the Armenian genocide. According to him, the break occurred after the 1980 coup – a break that marked a turning point without ever overcoming the split between the majority who are loyal to the narrative concerning the denial of 1915 and a tiny minority which is favourable to the truth discourse. The treatment of the Armenian Question is at the heart of this confrontation between nationalist historiography and negationism on the one hand and post-Kemalist and globalized historiography on the other.

The former category is based on negationist institutions, such as the Institute of Turkish History (Türk Tarih Kurumu, TTK), created in the 1930s by Mustafa Kemal and publisher of the two main works of falsified history: Sinasi Orel and Süreyya Yuca's *Armenian Affairs: Telegrams from Talat Pasha, Historical Fact or Fiction?* (1983) and Kâmuran Gurün's *The Armenian File* (1983). It can also count on the Coordination Committee for the Fight against Unfounded Genocide Allegations, established in 2001 by the National Security Council, the highest police authority in the state. This committee includes ministerial representatives from defence, justice, interior, foreign

[2] Hamit Bozarslan, 'Les discours unionistes sur l'extermination des Arméniens' in *Histoire de la Turquie, de l'Empire à nos jours,* Tallandier, Paris, 2013.
[3] Edhem Eldem, '*Osmanlı Tarihini Türklerden Kurtarmak*', *Cogito*, 73 (Spring 2013), pp. 260–282.

affairs, education, culture and the military, as well as the president of TTK, the director of intelligence services, the president of the Higher Council of Universities and representatives from the national archives and various Turkish promotional funds. Official historiography is also relayed in the academic world overseas: the late Stanford Shaw, Heath W Lowry and Bernard Lewis in the United States and the late Gilles Veinstein in France. For these mainstream scholars, the use of the word 'genocide' is to be nullified to allow a glorious representation of Turkish history. Everything possible is done to turn attention away from the past and to rebuild the Turkish nation on new and uncontestable foundations. But how is this false propaganda orchestrated?

The second category is associated with the impact of the 'de-Kemalization' of Turkish historiography and remembrance initiated in 2002. The official position of the AKP Islamic government with regard to the genocide has not moved an inch. However, since the AKP has come under pressure from the international community, sections of civil society and courageous Turkish researchers, the end of Kemalism has been accompanied by a loosening of the Armenian taboo. The study of genocide has become the subject of new research which provides useful insights for measuring what this tragedy signifies on the banks of the Bosphorus. Can we, therefore, speak of a new historiography in Turkey? What is the profile of this community of researchers who are willing to defy the justice system in their country 'having undermined Turkish dignity' or simply for having reminded the country of its past?

Between official historiography and state industry

As the French historian Yves Ternon wrote in his book *Enquiry into the Denial of Genocide*

> The territory of the historian, when the liar enters it, is no longer the place of research but of manipulation. The genocide of the Armenians was a crime protected by untruth, accomplished in falsehood and guaranteed impunity by the remarkable duplicity of its authors. They provided their successors with all the weapons to defend themselves. They allowed them to carry out a strategy of avoidance by turning the real into the false. Under these conditions, academic debate is impossible. The historian is manhandled by the smooth talker. He believes he is engaged in an academic controversy but is precipitated into a conflict where the stakes are political.[4]

When the lies that emanate from civil society encounter lies from the political world, the negationism of the Turkish state is granted an unequalled power. This makes the work of those who work for truth even more difficult.

---

[4]   Yves Ternon, *Enquête sur la négation d'un génocide* (Marseille: Editions Parenthèses, 1989).

Turkish historiographical difficulty with genocide

Associated as it is with the study of the First World War, the Armenian genocide raises a major difficulty in Turkey from a historiographical point of view. To fully understand this tragedy and its impact on Armenian–Turkish relations, a specific factor must be taken into account. Examination of the genocide can only be considered by studying its origins prior to Turkish entry into the war, in November 1914, as well as its consequences long after the armistice of Mudros of 1918, during the war of liberation (1919–1922) and the 1923 proclamation of the republic. Hamit Bozarslan speaks of 'a double triptych' of denial in these three periods.[5] Before the republic, it was the Unionists' triptych for explanation of the events of the Armenian genocide: negation, relativization, justification. After 1923, with the installation of the republic, the justification became innocence, suffering and deliverance – but with a particular spin: even though the Kemalist state saw itself as the legitimate heir to the Ottoman state, the republican triptych absorbed and replaced the Unionist triptych. This had the effect of creating a negationism with entangled components, generating disjointed analyses. Thus, as Vincent Duclert writes:

> the major problem that occurs as a result of an historiography that denies the destruction of Armenian society is that of an interpretive narrative voluntarily divorced from the principle of knowledge and the ability to understand and whose main objective appears to be limited to the denial of genocide or to overthrow the concept as it is applied to the massacre of Turks by Armenians during the First World War.[6]

The Unionist triad of explanations goes back to the Hamidian policy of countering demographic changes in the eastern provinces of the Empire for the benefit of Muslims (whether sedentary or those who were refugees from military campaigns in the Balkans and in territories surrounding the Black Sea), which corresponds to a falsification of history over the short term. The resettlement of Armenians in the Syrian desert addressed the necessity of protecting Turkish interests on the Caucasian front (the argument of denial). Such deportations were localized and the Muslim populations would also have been affected (proportionality of suffering) but only marginally so. Finally, Muslims had to be protected from retaliation by Armenian revolutionary committees (justification). This narrative of denial was articulated by the leading personalities of the CUP regime (Talaat, Enver, Djemal, Azmi and Chakir) and confirmed in talks with allies in the Triple Alliance (Austria-Hungary and Germany) and in neutral countries (United States). It was also communicated officially, either in the form of press communiqués or as declaratory briefs at the end of the war, published without regard to their historical veracity (Djemal Pasha).

The republican triad of explanations is inscribed over the longer term. The victors and the Triple Entente spent their time breaking up the empire. Turkey had been

[5] Hamit Bozarslan, *Histoire de la Turquie, de l'Empire à nos jours*, Tallandier, Paris, 2013.
[6] Vincent Duclert, *L'avenir de l'histoire* (Paris: Armand Colin, 2010).

subjected to foreign aggression and should, therefore, not be responsible for defending itself when in a state of war (the innocence argument). Besides, Muslims had suffered badly in the decades preceding the great deflagration in 1914 (relative suffering). Like other Christians of the empire, the Armenians took advantage of this vulnerability to betray their historical protectors, the Turks, who nevertheless found the resources necessary to free themselves from the burden of foreign intervention, banishing the French, the Italians and the British from the sacred lands of the new Kemalist and Republican Turkey (rescue argument).

The combination of these scenarios determined the structure of contemporary Turkish history and assumed the form of a 'four-headed hydra' as Richard Hovannisian put it: 'negation, rationalization, relativization and trivialization'. This served as a bulwark against the onset of a phobia provoked among the Turks by the Treaty of Sèvres, a phobia that spanned two negationist approaches. Sèvres completed the dismemberment of the Ottoman Empire (first argument) and extinguished any Turkish renaissance (second argument). Eventually, this was given as the reason why the Treaty of Lausanne was not only the best reply to the 'conspiracy of Sèvres' but also the most powerful pillar of modern Turkey.

The architecture of the Lausanne Treaty, however, never allowed the ghost of Sèvres to be erased. Eldem goes against the grain in his analysis of this period, of the First World War and its treaties, in his study of the writing of history in Turkey. He explains the inability of Turkish researchers to determine the narrative of national history owing to their archaic historicism when compared with Western historians. For him, Turkish nationalism is so strong that it has managed to 'Turkify' Ottoman history by classifying 'good and bad Turks' into different categories. In such a classification, the nine members of the central committee of the CUP responsible for the genocide fall on the side of 'good Turks', so that the genocide of 1915 could then be classified as collateral damage whose narrative is the monopoly of the Turkish military; thus notes Alexander Toumarkine, in an article published in the review *Histoire@ Politique* in 2014. As such, historiographic production has always been under surveillance and has always emphasized the nationalist narrative of the pre-genocide period. Eldem considers that Turkish historians are not the only ones responsible for the 'Turkification' of Ottoman history. Their fellow Europeans must take their share of the responsibility when they mix up the terms 'Turkish', 'Ottoman' and 'Muslim' when speaking of the Ottoman Empire. The European powers have multiple references to these concepts, adopting them according to whatever suits their strategic interests. If as early as the seventeenth century, one speaks of 'Turkey', how much more should one then speak of Turkey in the eighteenth, nineteenth and twentieth centuries when studies strictly concerned the Ottoman Empire? In the historiographic context, however, use of the word 'Turkish' concerns the rise of nationalist sentiment in Constantinople beginning in the 1880s. From the birth of this nationalism embodied by the Young Turks movement, successors of the Young Ottomans, the pre-nationalist ideology was triumphant and enforced its universal 'scientific law'. Consequently, it is easier to understand why Turkish historians could not study the history and role of non-Muslim minorities in the Ottoman system or offer a critical appraisal of the history of the Ottoman Empire during the First World War. Beyond the

Turkish-Muslim world, other subjects were neglected, ignored or abandoned, even though Christians represented almost 30 per cent of the Ottoman population. Turkish historians did not speak the minority languages – Armenian, Hebrew, Greek and Aramaic – and had a real apprehension of foreign sources. They consecrated the potency of exclusively Turkish documents and totally underestimated materials available in foreign archives, many of which would have been ill-disposed towards the Turkish point of view. On the grounds, for example, that the telegrams of Talaat Pasha, studied by Andonian after the war, had been misinterpreted, the genocide deniers, inspired by the book by Orel and Yuca, concluded that they were fictional and that this 'fabrication' proves the authenticity of an international conspiracy against Turkey for which the Armenians were merely the executors. Dadrian and Akçam have shown, though, that these documents are authentic, albeit they have sometimes been misused. Moreover, Ternon reminds us that historians of the Armenian genocide no longer use the telegrams from Andonian as proof of the crimes: they contain errors and contradictions so it is better not to use them to avoid debasing the genocide as they are not needed to prove criminal intent by the CUP. As no Turkish official document directly states that 'the imperial government has decided to exterminate the Armenian population of the Empire', historians conclude that the genocide never took place or is pure foreign invention. However, as Raul Hilberg says in an interview with Claude Lanzmann published in *Shoah*, there is not a single German document clearly showing the order to exterminate the Jews. Rather, the design, planning and execution of the crime were the subject of a vast operation to destroy the evidence.[7] Similarly, official Turkish publications do not mention the Armenian presence before the arrival of the Turks. The Ministries of National Education and Foreign Affairs are in the vanguard of this: the first is responsible for filing archives and monitoring their access; the second for communication with the rest of the world. If we add to this the work done by the Ministry of Tourism and that of Justice and Domestic Affairs, we may infer that a system of denial is well deployed.

De-Kemalization and the Armenian Question

For almost three decades, study of the genocide has been remarkable both in its quality and quantity. This results from a multidisciplinary approach in the social sciences, which have brought additional and fundamental elements to research into the organization and execution of this crime. From Armenia, the United States, the European Union (especially France) and the Middle East (Lebanon, Israel) and, in particular, Turkey, these individual or collective research efforts have been concerted and sustained. The research literature continues to grow and the genocide is being studied from all angles, including the victims as well as the perpetrators.

---

[7] Quoted by Yves Ternon in *Enquête sur la négation d'un génocide*, Editions Parenthèses, Marseille, 1989.

Birth of a dissident historiographical trend

The credit for these developments should be given, first and foremost, to those researchers who have, tirelessly and often out of the spotlight, carried out a great deal of hard work. The perspective of studies and the resulting narratives has also changed. No longer is it simply a matter of reporting the stories of the men, women and children at the scene of the tragedy in 1915, but encompassing a wider field of study which covers the responsibility of the Ottoman state, the involvement of the CUP and the role of the nine members of its central committee. It is also a question of exploiting the archives of the foreign powers – Germany in particular – and studying the role of the forces of the Triple Alliance in the execution of the crime. The American and European archives as well as those from the Armenian Patriarchate of Constantinople have been studied and the results published.

The most significant research developments took place in Turkey after the collapse of Kemalism in Ankara in 2002. In 2005, researchers were granted access to the Ottoman archives of the prime minister in Istanbul as well as the account books for the security services attached to the Ministry of the Interior. This development radically changed the situation and gave rise to new opportunities, which the AKP intended as a means of moderating the Kemalist influence over the institutions of the republic. This may be so, but they gave a tremendous boost to unlocking the secrets of the twentieth century. Has this liberalization process come to fruition in the field of research? Probably not, because the process has been suspended and the Ottoman registry, digitized in 2005, remains inaccessible. The same is true for the archives of the Ministry of Defence. Historians working on the genocide have lamented this lack of access, emphasizing the importance of these documents for understanding the exact role of the Special Organization, the nucleus for Ottoman criminal activity. At the same time, on the Ministry of Defence website there is a general announcement that the archives have been accessible since 1990 to four categories of researchers: Turkish and foreign, those attached to official institutions and those attached to the Department of War History at the Ministry of War, now called the Presidency for Military History and Strategic Studies (*Askeri Tarih ve Stretejik Etut Baskanligi* or ATASE). In reality, when it concerns research into the Armenian genocide or the CUP during the First World War, difficulties accumulate for those wishing to access the national archives despite an official narrative overflowing with goodwill. In sum, state denial is still intact.

Yet a dissident branch within the Turkish research community, mostly working abroad, has recently emerged. This, which has been appearing over decades, is thanks to the work of sociologist Ragip Zarakolu, an author of books on the genocide. His effort to pry good information from state archives has fostered the emergence of thinkers such as Hrant Dink, whose fight for the truth but also for Turkish–Armenian reconciliation has won near universal support. In January 2007, he was shot dead by a Turkish extremist, triggering a widespread emotional outpouring from all sections of the community, including Armenian radicals. Nevertheless, the Turkish authorities took advantage of the 2004 reform of the penal code to monitor research in sensitive areas and to threaten prison sentences against anyone who undermines Turkey's fundamental interests. Among the first to be targeted were historians who were concerned with the recognition of the genocidal character of the Armenian massacres of 1915 (Articles 301 and 305 of the Penal Code).

It is precisely under these ambivalent working conditions – partial access to the archives and judicial supervision by the same authority – that dissident Turkish researchers undertake their profession in Turkey. Edhem Eldem has spoken at length about this ambivalence and its negative impact on Turkish historiography. For him, the blockage reflects a reality: the Islamist regime, although it has succeeded in negating the Kemalist influence in its institutions and continues to show evidence of neo-Ottomanism, has been unable to drag Turkey away from its nationalism. Quite the opposite has transpired. Just as historiography evolves midway between progress and conservatism, post-Kemalist history revolves around four 'isms': democratic statism, Ottomanism, Islamism and nationalism. Eldem writes:

> If we take into account the effects of the political and ideological liberalization of the most recent period, we see that the dominant advances related to our history have been not to question nationalism but rather to update it. By reconstructing if in a more participative form [...] Ottomanism has become a form of gradually reinforced nationalism [...] since the Turkish-Islamic synthesis brought about by the coup in 1980 [...] It is obvious, he concludes that such a state-controlled history has nothing to do with academic historiography.[8]

He, like so many other Turkish researchers such as Ragip Zarakolu, Taner Akçam, Füad Dundar, Sukru Hanioglu, Musfata Aksakal, Ugur Umit Ungör, Selim Deringil and Hamit Bozarslan, recognizes himself in this new academic historiography at the service of the social sciences, which must be free of nationalist interference. Like other Turkish or foreign historiographers of the Turkish nation, he celebrates the benefits that should flow from social liberalization and is poised to be freed from the official line to allow real history to emerge. Most of these 'marginal researchers', as Eldem calls them, some of whom continue to be constrained by judicial inquiry, share a common history as left-wing activists and campaigners against the military junta responsible for the coup in 1980.[9] In the study of the 1915 genocide, they have found sources for a challenge to the Turkish political system rather than armed struggle (PKK) or trade unionism (strikes and support for the working class). Most live overseas and, having access to their colleagues' research, they can connect their research to Western historiography about the genocide and complement genocide research with their own information, thus filling a large void on many aspects hitherto unknown. They were brought together at the first conference on the massacres of Armenians, held on 24 and 25 September 2005 in one of the private universities of Istanbul. It was initially planned to be held at Bogazici State University, but the government banned it, threatening to prosecute all those who planned to participate. This conference, according to Eldem, had the effect of giving a 'serious jolt' to the stranglehold on Turkish historiography and, for the first

8   Eldem (n. 3).
9   Ibid.

time, allowed dissenters from the state line to present their research findings in public. Since this two-day conference and the interactions surrounding it, public debate in Turkey has split into two radically divided camps. As a result of this conference, states Eldem, the expression 'so-called', which systematically preceded the word 'genocide' in the official narrative, has been removed and new research topics such as the critical analysis of Kemalism have been opened up for scrutiny alongside themes such as secularism, Islam, anti-Semitism, Atatürk and the Kurds. This expansion shows that Kemalism has become the indirect object or target of critics in breach of the sclerotic interpretations of the foundational ideology. However, it also reflects a new consideration of minorities. Excluded from the field of research for a long time, they have become an asset. A focus on pre-republican themes also follows the wishes of the Islamist power to rehabilitate Ottomanism in the public sphere, with a trace of nostalgia for the absent past. Here, also, divergent currents can be seen. On the one hand, there are those who want to hold the debate around an idealized image of an egalitarian and tolerant imperial Turkey. These endorse the idea of an Ottoman nationalism, a kind of neo-Unionist CUP and continue to think that Greeks, Armenians and Jews are foreigners, outside the Turkish-Ottoman social entity. On the other hand, there are those who emphasize the political conflict, social injustice and ethnic discrimination that have occurred since the time of the sultans. They tend to believe that these religious communities are a lost resource for a state incapable of taking responsibility for the protection of its own subjects.

This responsibility is one of the ideas developed by Hamit Bozarslan.[10] His work on genocide has emphasized the impossibility for the state to overcome structural violence.

In addition to these sociological contributions, critical historiography has extended analysis concerning the policy of extermination. According to Bozarslan, four complementary levels existed for appraising the deadly reasoning of the Unionist state. In the first place, there was the social Darwinism typical in all totalitarian reasoning and explored in the work of Hanioglu. In his books *The Young Turks in Opposition* (1995) and *Preparation for a Revolution: The Young Turks, 1902–1908* (2001), this Turkish researcher lists the racist politics of the CUP from the perspective of a struggle to the death between 'species' of human beings, where in the final analysis the strongest must be victorious and crush its opponents. Armenians lost this Darwinian struggle. Hence the second level, which was Turkish racial domination over the entire Ottoman social sphere as part of a master–slave or executioner–victim relationship. Armenians did not have the right to evade Turkish rule. The third level, largely covered in the work of Dündar, emphasizes the reasoning for ethnic-religious purification in the remote provinces of the Empire, the heart of Republican Turkey. His research brought to the fore a programme of demographic engineering. This aimed to eliminate almost all Armenians in the Asian areas, reducing their number to a given threshold (often 2 per cent, sometimes 10 per cent) among the majority Arab population. The remainder were to be relocated. Raymond Kévorkian and Taner Akçam have shown that the elimination of the 'surplus' in the Arab provinces was a Unionist objective put into

[10] Bozarslan, *Histoire de la Turquie* (n. 5).

action to respect the initial demographic plan. Finally, at the fourth level, to achieve demographic forecasts, the central authority gambled on a programme of 'Islamicization' and 'Turkification' of the economy. This occurred through the plundering of Armenian merchandise. Women were subjected to special treatment; they were often massacred like the rest of the population relocated as a 'procreational resource' for the benefit of the executioners. This forced Islamicization demographically strengthened the Turkish component of the population and enabled the development of a Muslim-based economy in Anatolia. The work of both Akçam and Zürcher focuses on the transition from empire to republic. Both authors strongly contest the historiography of the state. Official analyses have, for a long time, made no connection between Unionists and Kemalists. Yet Akçam and Zürcher's research into the process of state transition using exclusively Turkish sources has established both the ideological unity between the two systems and the employment of CUP managers in the Kemalist state apparatus. These revelations have detracted from the image of Kemal. Although he rose from the ranks, the father of the Turkish nation has always been portrayed as a fierce opponent of the CUP leaders, who had been refugees in Berlin since the end of the war in November 1918. Proof of an organic relationship between Unionists and Kemalists in the leadership of the secular state offers a new perspective on the origins of the 1923 Republic and the rivalry between these two factions. In the final analysis, they were ultimately more complementary than adversaries in the rise of Turkish nationalism.

This social history of genocide does not end with the importation of totalitarianism from Europe to Turkey. In a micro-historical approach using regional monographs, Üngor's work on the Vilayet of Diyarbekir and the process of modernization of the Turkish state between 1913 and 1950 reveals the division of labour between the Ottoman administration and the Special Organization during the genocide. Elsewhere, Akçam pays special attention to the Special Organization and the central committee of the CUP, the group of nine leaders. This work reveals the existence of different tendencies concerning the treatment of Armenians. The maximalists in the majority favoured the systematic extermination of the Armenians, while the others advocated the massacre of the populations living along the Russian front and the deportation of the remainder to the Arab deserts. According to this Turkish researcher based in the United States, it seems that the decision date for the implementation of the Armenian extermination programme was between 22 and 25 March 1915. Economic history also makes its contribution to this new historiography, thanks to research by Onaran on the lack of legal titles held by the 'new owners' of property plundered from the Armenians.

These dissenting voices can also count on the work of foreign researchers. The history of law has made great progress in the study of the evolution of crimes against humanity, thanks to the seminal work of Samantha Power, US ambassador to the United Nations (2013–2017). Dadrian and Akçam provided important studies of the trials of Unionists and the connections between these special tribunals in 1919 and international law, the Achilles' heel of historians and genocide legal experts in their desire to place 1915 within an international regulatory framework. Other noteworthy contributions come from the innovative research by legal experts, the Swiss-Armenian (Sevan Garibian) and Canadian and French experts, Katia Boustany and Daniel Dormoy respectively, on the evolution of the concept of crimes against humanity and the punishment thereof. The work of Raymond Kévorkian should also be mentioned: he investigated the archives of the Commission of Responsibilities at the peace conference held between February and April 1919, including conclusions that proposed the creation of an international tribunal to try war criminals and to define new categories of crimes, some of which found an echo in the 1948 Convention on the Crimes of Genocide.

In diplomatic history, Donald Bloxam's work on the impact of international relations on genocide is authoritative, just as Annette Becker and Jay Winter's research on mass violence brings important insights into the intrinsic relationship between war and genocide. And when we learn, as Alexandre Toumarkine reports,[11] that in Turkish historiography there is more work on the genocide than on the First World War, one naturally concludes that when really free access is given to the archives of the Turkish Ministry of Defence, they will undoubtedly provide ample new information as to how this crime was organized. In the meantime, between the citizen's campaign for history and the emergence of a critical and coherent historiographical trend, more and more works on the Armenian taboo have been published in Turkish. First, there is Talaat Pasha's *Black Book*, which was published in 2008 thanks to the efforts of the historian Murat Bardakçi, who was entrusted with the diary of her husband by Pasha's widow in 1982. In this diary, the former minister of the interior meticulously and coldly updated the deportation schedule with the number of deportees, the list of abandoned property, topographical maps and new interethnic statistics in accordance with the CUP policy of 'demographic engineering'. Talaat Pasha's revelations counterbalance the official thesis that deportations were carried out through methodical procedures in accordance with Ottoman law or that the deportees were successfully settled in the desert of Deir ez-Zor, today part of Syria. According to his notes, it appears that the total number of Armenians reported missing was nearly 1 million up until 1917. However, we know that the genocide carried on beyond 1917 and these statistics do not include all the regions subject to deportation.

Journalist Hasan Djemal, Pasha's grandson published *1915, The Armenian Genocide* in 2012. This testimony further breaks down the barrier of negationism in Turkey. The fact that this book, written by a famous Turkish journalist, is freely available in Turkey shows that things have changed in Turkish society. A few years ago, the use of the word 'Soykirim' would have sent Djemal straight to prison.

The impossible autonomy of history in relation to the state

Even as the wall of negationism begins to crumble in Turkey, successive governments, whether Kemalist or Islamist Unionists, persist with state dishonesty. A glimmer of hope is to be found, concentrated in a small community of dissident researchers that is backed up by a limited segment of society but enjoys important communication networks abroad. In short, the development represents a great leap forward for the development of social sciences in Turkey. That said, the return of the 'Unionist' attitude

---

[11] Alexandre Toumarkine, 'Historiographie turque de la Première Guerre mondiale sur les fronts ottomans: Problèmes, enjeux et tendances' (2014) 22 Janvier–Avril.

towards power in Turkey, as Bozarslan implies, does not bode well for critical historiography. Eldem has issued a caution regarding the dangers that exist for historical research in Ankara.[12] The revival of the half-nationalist, half-Islamist AKP regime that has held power since 2002 has been a source of frustration for researchers and placed two dangers in its path. There is a risk of the increased political instrumentalization of history.

In fact, in Turkey, history has never managed to distance itself from politics. Herein lies the entire ambition for the critical school of Turkish historiography, one that maintains that Turkey will never be at peace with its history until it has emancipated itself from its political masters. 'History', already held hostage to denial, becomes the instrument for the protection of an identity that is supposedly under attack. It is built on fragile foundations, notably the dead of a people whose descendants demand justice. This journey through historiography also helps us to understand the similarities between Turks and Armenians, especially in the way they write their respective national histories. Encouragement must be given to exchange and co-operation between Turkish and Armenian critical historians, while avoiding the trap of ceremonial commissions and committees of mixed historians which would only strengthen the Turkish and Armenian governments in their desire to exploit history. Thus, Armenians would no longer have a monopoly on their problem. The Armenian Question is, in its academic dimension, an Armenian–Turkish question. It has become universal through the rise of genocide studies.

With a Haitadist Cultural Revolution that refuses to die, an Armenian remembrance state of impoverished memory and a Turkey in full historical denial, the power of memory still has a bright future. But it is not infallible. Reversing the situation would be sufficient. But how? Until now, the idea of nation has flowed through official discourse and manufactured collective identity. Nationalism has spanned almost all the political forces in both countries. Armenia has huddled in the protective blankets of remembrance, whereas Turkey has refused to confront its past. The former believed it would find peace and loyalty in an enhanced, reassuring memory; one that holds no more secrets. The latter believed it could buy peace by rejecting memory of the Ottoman past, which was uncomfortable and full of unknowns. Both failed. They managed only to accumulate crises, depression, tension and other phenomena promoting disintegration. Nationalism has sustained and developed these social pathologies to the extent that the two societies have become the yin and yang of peace and reconciliation. In their differences, these civilizations remained faithful to a heritage. In their similarities, they can overcome their trauma if the effort is based on truth and justice. It is not the role of politics to interfere in this new challenge; it is not for states or political parties to go down this road. But it is incumbent on civil society to take advantage of globalization to empower and democratize. It is the responsibility of the international community to encourage these exchanges and of the academic community to promote social science research, the only area where truth and identity can co-exist.

---

[12] Eldem (n. 3).

9

The Armenian Memorial State, from February 1998 to April 2018

Following the resignation of President Levon Ter-Petrosyan on 3 February 1998, a new regime came to power in Yerevan with the ambition to correct the errors of the outgoing regime and to maintain and continue the liberal-inspired structural reforms. These adjustments aimed to create a break with the initiatives of the PANM which had held power since 1990 and to globally re-centre the Armenian identity, aligning it with universal values and removing any particularities. The break with Communism could not be violent. The country and the people were emerging from a fierce war, an appalling earthquake and the collapse of a system the effects of which were largely unknown. Armenia had to find its own pace of development, its own growth trajectory and its own historical reference points. In view of this context, the nature of Robert Kocharyan's regime – when he was prime minister for Levon Ter-Petrosyan, then in 1998 as elected President of the Republic of Armenia – was to fall back on the distinct features of the collective identity, Armenia's unique history and geography: the two pillars of national unity. The step back from normality allowed Kocharyan and his supporters to play the card of nation-state gathered around traditional values and Haïtadism. This process of consolidation of the bases for Armenian statehood, adopted the cover of the past as the unifying narrative for gathering Armenians around the world. Kocharyan, but also his successor Serzh Sargsyan, withdrew from the republican schema of national identity to embrace a nationalist dimension taking into account the broad influence of the diaspora. This approach was based on the distinctiveness of Armenian experience and transformed Armenia into a memorial state of out-sized remembrances.

If this essentially nationalist rather than republican approach had the merit of attenuating differences between Armenia and its diaspora communities, it prevented Armenian society from doing the work of memorialization. This was no time to doubt or relive history, but a time for social empowerment, of respect for the work of citizenship and the defense of individual rights. It was a time to promote the national ideal and consecrate the idols of the past. It was not a time to re-examine contemporary history but to strengthen national security around the all-important struggle for Nagorno-Karabakh. National security was threatened by emigration and widespread corruption which prevented the development of a social contract between the elites and the people. National disenchantment led to a loss of confidence in the future, confronted as it was by the outdated methods of an Armenian political system that was not fundamentally different from the Soviet regime. If one were to replace communist ideology with the nationalist ideology, one would find a Second Republic which functioned almost identically to the Soviet Republic. Recourse to a unique identity by virtue of glorified memory and patriotism undermined state sovereignty, damaged relations between Armenia and its diaspora and precluded any process of regional integration.

Consolidate the foundations of the state by the cult of the past

To continue liberal reforms through national inclusiveness, while pursuing the transition to a market economy, harnessing Armenian vitality for national recovery and transforming military success in Nagorno-Karabakh as the basis of a new Armenia – such was the credo of the Kotcharyan regime (1998–2008). To achieve this, Armenia was faced with providing itself with the means to consolidate its identity around several angles.

A national memory at the service of the State

The first was to make the past a strength. By drawing on collective memory of historical acts of bravery in support of religious values, the family and the memory of the genocide, it was possible to underscore Armenian uniqueness and allow it to find its place on the international stage while accelerating its exit from communism. The national honours accorded to the repatriated remains of two heroes of the revolutionary movement, true cult figures of the Yerevan warrior class, the generals Antranik and Drasdamat Kanayan aka 'Dro', bear witness to this. In February 2000, Antranik's ashes were transferred from Paris to Yerevan, to the Yerablour cemetery, the final resting place for fighters who had fallen in the Nagorno-Karabakh war. Three months later, in May 2000, Dro's remains were repatriated from Boston. His remains were transferred to the city of Sardarabad, Armenia, the scene of an epic battle against advancing Ottoman forces in May 1918. The Armenian victory in that battle was decisive for the constitution of the First Republic of Armenia. The return of these remains to their homeland set the tone: the State sanctifies those, often military heroes, who put themselves at the service of their people and whose strategic vision featured a balance between the pro-Russian and pro-Western. Here was one important reason why genocide recognition became central to Armenian foreign policy. Transformation of the tragedy of 1915 into a diplomatic principle allowed the Armenian Question to be placed on the international agenda. Reintroducing genocide into the government system also meant taking action on behalf of the children and grandchildren of genocide survivors, to ensure the inclusion and historicization of the genocide. Hence the steps taken to accommodate history but also the memory of the latter in the work for State reconstruction.

Pan-Armenian solidarity

The second dynamic, which stems from the first, is national solidarity between all Armenians. A logic which excludes the diaspora makes no sense when the task is to rebuild the country. The diaspora has proved its usefulness and potential for efficiency and responsiveness with its response to the earthquake and the Nagorno-Karabakh war. More so since Armenia does not enjoy access to natural resources like Azerbaijan, nor access to the sea like Georgia. Kotcharyan, therefore, chose to include the diaspora – through the recognition of dual citizenship – while respecting its autonomy – through diplomacy, striking a complementary stance towards both Russia and the West. He also set up a policy of alliance with the diaspora by integrating the recognition of genocide into the doctrine of national security. The principle was simple: because the Armenians were victims of a still-unpunished genocide, they cannot take the risk of endangering their compatriots in Nagorno-Karabakh, under threat from Azerbaijan and its Turkish ally.

Politics before economics

Preeminence of politics and security over the economy was the leitmotiv of the Ter-Petrosyan regime. By rehabilitating the ARF in 1998 and restoring them to the Armenian political game and by promoting personalities from Nagorno-Karabakh in the institutions, the Kotcharyan-Sargsyan duo intended to make the Armenian identity a force faithful to its past and recent history. An identity proud of the sacrifice of fallen soldiers on the Karabakh front. First and foremost, the state must guarantee the physical security of the Armenian people. It follows that the Nagorno-Karabakh peace process, which took place within the framework of the OSCE Minsk Group, had to take into account key principles: the security of the Armenian people is not negotiable, Nagorno-Karabakh will never again be administered by Azerbaijan, its self-determination is irreversible and even if Armenia does not recognize its independence, any return to the previous situation is impossible. The reunification process of Nagorno-Karabakh to Armenia is a founding principle of Haïtadist Armenia. Following the independence granted to Kosovo, Timor-Leste and other micro-states, nothing prevents Armenians from brandishing the right of peoples to self-determination. The military victory had to be transformed into a diplomatic victory. This was the route map for the new foreign policy of the Republic of Armenia.

A European horizon

The fourth dynamic refers to the projected inclusion of Armenia into the European area and, among other things, its membership within the Christian cultural space. Europe is an instrument of soft power and a space of intersection between Russian and Western history. Armenia had to rely on this democratic foundation to ensure its future, regional peace and economic development. Hence, the first step towards European integration was the accession of Armenia to the Council of Europe and its participation in the Eastern Partnership of the EU. This would have made sense if Armenia had reached an agreement to sign the EU Association Agreement at the Vilnius Summit, Lithuania, on 27 and 28 November 2013. However, under pressure from Moscow, Yerevan opted for Putin's Eurasian Union project with Russia, Belarus and Kazakhstan, thus putting a brake on the process of European integration.

A transnational diplomacy

Operating methods is the final remembrance principle. How to coordinate all this rebuilding on a global scale? Through transnationalism. This theoretical school of international relations promotes action, which although based on the state, upholds the emergence and role of other diplomatic actors from civil society in international relations. This is what Kocharyan diplomacy stands for, a form personified by Vartan Oskanian whose profile perfectly matches the complexity of the Armenian world. Born in Syria, Oskanian studied in Soviet Armenia and the United States where he settled before joining independent Armenia as a diplomat. He became deputy foreign minister in 1997 and was head of Armenian diplomacy from 1998 to 2008. Artizan of the complementarity between Armenia and the diaspora, he was one of the creators of the pan-Armenian conferences which began in 1999. Large gatherings, but with symbolic rather than tangible outcomes. The objective was simple: break the ties of intra-Armenian phobias and prejudices in favour of a double-headed identity with a single-purpose: national reconstruction. Robert Kotcharyan's Armenia was based on several vectors of influence. First a politico-economic vector: the corporation of oligarchs whose development the Republic would support; Second, the ARF vector, envisaging the promotion of its leaders within state institutions, allowing Kotcharyan to regulate Dashnak activity abroad while exploiting this unpredictable, but disciplined, active network, itself already well established in the Middle East, across Europe and America. The integration of the ARF into power politics would serve to co-opt and pre-empt internal discontent. Using the threat of judicial intimidation, the authorities were able to calm Dashnak zeal. We should also bear in mind that although the ARF was rehabilitated in 1998, its leaders could have been called upon at any time to answer for unresolved crimes. Third, there was a socio-cultural vector, through the Church and the Armenian General Benevolent Union (AGBU). The Armenian Church, led by Karekin II after the death of Karekin I in 1999, was used as an instrument of influence for government policy worldwide. By defending the candidacy of Krtij Nercisyan, the future Karekin II, as the supreme head of the Armenian Church, the authorities obtained the unwavering support of the AGBU. So, between the political instrument (ARF) and the socio-religious instrument (a combination of Church and AGBU), Kocharyan's policies came to dominate Armenian politics, stifled the potential loci of protest within the diaspora and gained strategic depth by securing an unprecedented network of influence and information. Another way to buy political and social peace.

When he took over from Kotcharyan in 2008, Sargsyan took a position halfway between his two predecessors. From Levon Ter-Petrosyan, whom he served as Minister of Defense, he retained the ability to work for a compromise over the Nagorno-Karabakh issue and to make overtures to Turkey, even with all the necessary cold blood this implied. Even though Ter-Petrosyan attended Turgüt Ozal's funeral in 1993 and met with the leader of the Turkish fascist movement, the Gray Wolves, Sargsyan adopted a policy of openness to Ankara using 'football diplomacy' around matches in the 2010 World Cup qualifiers. These efforts resulted in Armenia and Turkey signing two protocols for the normalization of bilateral relations on 10 October 2009 in Zurich. Even though the texts have not been ratified, as a declaration of intent they retain their moral force. From Kotcharyan, for whom he was prime minister, Sargsyan borrowed the idea of a garrison state, heavily armed and attached to the idea of respect for the national memory. The current Armenian president followed in the footsteps of his predecessors, pursuing liberal reforms and consolidating a patrimonial system around the oligarchy of important families. If Ter-Petrosyan had laid the foundations of this patrimonial system bedeviled as it was by endemic corruption and lacking redistribution of power or a social contract, Kotcharyan developed it to the point of industrializing the system and taking advantage of it for personal gain. Sargsyan, meanwhile, refined it, giving it an image of respectability. This is the connecting thread that binds the three Armenian presidents who have been in power since the independence of the Republic in 1991. We cannot examine the evolution of the political and economic life of the immature Republic if we ignore this 'liberal' lineage. They are from the same political camp and know each other very well. While the first is from the Yerevantsis clan (residents of Yerevan), the other two are from Karabakh (although Sargsyan was born in Tegh, an Armenian village bordering Nagorno-Karabakh which he left as a child to settle with his family in Stepanakert). The three presidents are set apart more by their behaviour than by their political orientations: Kotcharyan is more statist, Sargsyan is more conservative and Ter-Petrosyan, more separatist. The first president of the Republic of Armenia was an intellectual, distant from his fellow citizens and the media. Kotcharyan was an engineer with more rigid methods, equally distant from journalists and with a laconic style of communication. Sargsyan, also an engineer, developed a law enforcement vision of authority and an opacity through his experience as the head of several government ministries. He compensated for this by an easy interaction with the people. All three, however, were occasionally subject to paranoid notions of power. For his actions against the ARF, Ter-Petrosyan came close to ridicule imagining a Dashnak plot behind every political stumbling block. Since the terrorist attack of 27 October 1999 and the assassination of Prime Minister Vazgen Sargsyan and the Speaker of the Parliament, Garen Demirtchyan, Kotcharyan's name is mentioned in connection with those responsible for the massacre. Electoral violence followed the controversial election of 18 February 2008 and left 10 dead. Since the incident occurred shortly after his controversial election, Sargsyan and Kotcharyan, respectively prime minister and outgoing president, rejected any involvement with this tragedy. In reality, the three presidents depended upon a state that had not yet fully emerged from post-Sovietism. Palace intrigue, the settling of scores, nepotism, patronage, intimidation, manipulation and corruption are the words that come to mind when speaking of the early history of this Second Republic.

Sargsyan the chess player

In the wake of his two predecessors, Sargsyan took the logic of remembrance to the extreme, basing it on conservative values and traditional roots. A national sport in

Armenia (he is the President of the National Federation) his manipulative policies could be mistaken for a vast chess game,. A chess game internally, with his party and the opposition and with Armenian society along the road to empowerment. A chess game with Azerbaijan in the Nagorno-Karabakh conflict settlement process and with the diaspora through the ministry he created in 2008. A chess game with Turkey using diplomatic protocols and with Russia, but also Europe, the United States, Iran and Georgia. This is not politics in the true sense of the term because, alone at the controls of state, he remained quite unpredictable, even misunderstood, by his own entourage and among former collaborators. He followed his intuition, relied heavily on the vagaries of time and tests of strength. His non-standard verbal communication gave him great latitude and he was careful to leave an exit door open and to keep one step ahead. His was a personal method adapted from the ancient game of observation and strategic thinking.

Cynicism and manipulation complete Sargsyan's methods. To a greater extent than his two predecessors, he put into practice a combination of economic liberalism and domestic conservatism. He kept faith with IMF and the World Bank plans for the recovery of the Armenian economy, which was hard hit by the crisis of 2008 – Armenia being an extremely liberalized market to compensate for the blockade and its isolation. Serzh Sargsyan played up the role of the Armenian Church in the organization of civil society. A fervent Russophile, he counted on the support of his Foreign Minister, Edward Nalbandyan, trained at the Russian Diplomatic School and his wife, a relative of the influential Tarasov family, to iron out any differences with Moscow. A convert to Europe, Sargsyan affiliated his party, the Republican Party, with the European People's Party (EPP). A Nationalist, he aligned with the two main organizations of the diaspora, the ARF and the AGBU, establishing his authority and emphasizing the ethnic aspects of Armenian identity, an approach largely supported by the Armenians of the Caucasus who subscribe to a German concept of the nation (ethnicity, religion, language and territory). This approach caused problems in some countries, particularly in France, where the republican melting pot and the political conception of citizenship led to a rejection of this tendency as being incompatible with the ideals of equality and secularism.

The impossible work of remembrance

Besides the designation of remembrance state, Kocharyan and Sargsyan's Armenia contains another more problematic aspect: that of the negation of history. This negation of history can be considered in different ways.

Embellish the historical record by denying communist crimes

The negation of history is first and foremost political. Armenia refused to impassively confront its communist past. The denunciation of Stalin's crimes in 1956 and the collapse of the USSR in 1991 should have been a final settlement of any account of history. In common with other post-Soviet republics, Armenia was nostalgic for the communist era more than 20 years after it gained independence and continued to idealize the Brezhnev era when the country recorded strong growth in all domains. Two observations can be made about its inability to face its own recent past. On the one hand, Armenians tended to absolve themselves of any responsibility or complicity for acts of barbarity. Generally, they blamed all the crimes, misdeeds and failures of their system on the Soviet central authorities. On the other hand, there was a refusal to rekindle anti-Russian feelings in society, a factor which may have antagonized Moscow.

A refusal to face the dark side of the revolutionary movement

The negation of history also has a bearing on the treatment of the national question. Armenia and Armenians do not openly address the murky shadows of the revolutionary movement and its main personalities. The latest works on the revolutionary movement certainly provide new insights and innovative analyses of these decades of struggle. Consider Hratchig Simonyan's four-volume essay *The Orientations of the Liberation Struggle* published in Yerevan between 2003 and 2010 or the work on the ARF by Kevork Khutinyan, a member of the party and editor-in-chief of the magazine *Vem*. Neither, however, provides genuine critical analysis. Occasionally, the authors call into question the behaviour of certain leaders or combatants, but none evoke the dark side of the revolutionary movement by taking into account the historiography of the neighbouring populations. The Armenian-Georgian war of 1918 is examined purely through the Armenian prism, just as the Armenian-Tatar war of 1905-1906 is approached strictly from the national angle, never Azerbaijani. Admittedly, this is also valid for Georgian and Azerbaijani publications covering these events. This goes beyond regret, as the first thing to consider when talking about peace and regional integration is to create opportunities for cooperation, especially in social science disciplines that share a capacity to place actors on an equal footing without preconceived ideas or ideological posture.

The same can be said of the 2003 book by Stephan Boghosyan, the father of culture minister Hasmig Boghosyan, *Overview of the Past, in the Name of the Present Day and Tomorrow*, published in Yerevan. This explores in detail the role of the ARF before, during and after the First Republic of Armenia. Its publication aroused great emotion on the part of the Dashnak and their supporters in Yerevan because it challenged their own reading of certain events. After a few weeks of heated exchanges, including in the Armenian Parliament where Dashnak deputies denounced the book and its author, the entire manuscript was published online, on the site of *Fourth Power* (*Chorord Ichkhanutyun*), an opposition newspaper. A few years later the documentary film 'Sardarabad', dedicated to the Armenian victory of May 1918 and directed by Tigran Khzmalyan, was censored on the day of its release, 26 September 2008, at the Moscow theatre in Yerevan. The ARF, then a member of the presidential majority, lobbied the government to ban its distribution even though the project had been financed by public funds. The film mentioned, among other things, 'the incompetence of the members of the government of 1918–1920' and 'the ARF betrayal of certain fedayi chiefs, including General Antranik'. Three years later, the transfer of Antranik's and Dro's ashes to Armenia did not provoke the slightest negative reaction in Yerevan, except in some communist circles, who recalled Dro's pro-Nazi past during the Second World War. The historian Achot Nercisyan attacked Antranik's reputation by criticizing some aspects of his behaviour (eg his excessive anger or the time when he wanted to assassinate Hrair Tejork, the legend of Sassun). In the end, Nercisyan tells us, Antranik was disarmed for one month for disobeying Armenak Ghazarian. At the time, depriving a 'fedayi' of his weapon was a public humiliation. However, Nercisyan does not go further in his criticisms of Antranik, while other revolutionary leaders such as General Sebouh, Roupen Ter-Minassian and Simon Vratsian denounced General Antranik's megalomania and his tactical choices in their accounts.

Let us now turn to the fascination that Armenians hold for the nefarious Karekin Nejteh. In 2001, Armenia officially celebrated in Yerevan the 115th anniversary of his birth and the 80th anniversary of the founding of the Republic of the Mountains where he was the principal leader. If one were to associate a name with independent Armenia, inevitably Nejteh would come to mind first. Independent Armenia is unofficially a Nejtehian Armenia. He is known for his heroism during the liberation movement, the Balkan wars, the First World War and the defence of the Republic of 1918 and his lone fight against the Bolsheviks in 1921 at the head of his 'Republic of Mountains' in the Zanguezour region at the frontier with Iran. He enjoys a true cult following in Armenia. After the war, Nejteh became openly anti-Bolshevik and anti-democratic, identifying with fascist Italy and Nazi Germany, whose struggle he supported in 1939 in the name of the struggle against communism and the 'defence of the Armenian race'. In 1934, the the ARF youth organization in the United States was renamed as the Federation of Armenian Youth. Expelled from the ARF in 1921 after his surrender to the Bolsheviks, the Xth congress of the ARF rehabilitated him in 1924. He distanced himself of his own free will in 1937 after making contact with the intelligence services of Nazi Germany. In 1938, the ARF excommunicated him at its XIIIth Congress. However, the man and the revolutionary leader continued to exert influence within the party. Even today, there is at least one ARF regional committee named 'Karekin Nejteh' in California. The ARF is not the only place where this fascist ideologue has influence: on both the right and the left of the political spectrum, Nzhdeh's thoughts are recited as truths and adages: even Ter-Petrosyan's Liberals refer to his writing. He has become an icon for all generations and the reference point for the Republican Party. A branch of the Dashnak, embodied by the 2008 Dashnak presidential candidate and current ambassador to Germany, Vahan Hovannesyan and the Deputy Prime Minister of the Nagorno-Karabakh Republic, is Arthur Aghabekyan, who considers himself the heir to the 'eagle of Zanguezour'.

How can this phenomenon be explained? How is it that no initiative has been taken to date to question the thoughts and actions of this man? Two remarks may explain this 'Nejteh mania' in Yerevan. On the one hand, his selfless struggle for the preservation of his people. He fought the Hamidian regime and had always been against any collaboration with the Young Turks. Then he fought a desperate battle against the Bolsheviks allowing the Zanguezour to remain attached to the Soviet Republic of Armenia. Finally, alongside the Nazis, he fought remorselessly against Stalin's USSR during the Second World War. He was arrested by the intelligence services of the Red Army in 1944 and transferred to the USSR where he was tried and sentenced to 25 years in prison. He died in captivity on 21 December 1955. He remains a leading figure in the struggle against Stalinism and it is through this that we must clearly understand the hero worship that all generations of Armenians devote to him. Moreover, besides Nejteh, there are no theorists of the state among Armenians because of the lack of a tradition of sovereignty. Nejteh is, therefore, one of the only Armenian 'thinkers' to offer a comprehensive vision of what the power of the state should be, of the people and the supremacy of the national interest above all partisanship. His thinking is a combination of the philosophy of history, biology and law. His systematic, organic and integral approach to public power locates him closer to a Carl Schmitt or a Charles Maurras than to a Christapor Mikaelian. He claimed to be the founding heir to the ARF although he wanted to go beyond the limits imposed by its populist past. For Nejteh, the plan for the country's recovery should be part of the national revolutionary process and include the almost mystical struggle against the Turkish-Bolshevik enemy. Armenia must surpass itself in this hostile environment to find the route to its salvation and each individual had a responsibility to accomplish this. His emotionless vision of the relationship between Leviathan and society confines individuals to their natural state. Now, as we have already said, inspired exclusively by the German philosophy of the nation, Caucasian Armenians were not open to another conception of existence. So, in the absence of alternatives, it was difficult for them to escape 'nejtehism', a guarantee of independence and power of the state.

Accent on remembrance to avoid accountability to the population

There is another type of historical negation: the refusal to assume any responsibility for civil society. The two main events where the authorities kept scrutiny to a minimum are the massacre in Parliament on 27 October 1999 and the incidents of 1 March 2008. The identity of the true perpetrators of these tragedies, which frame Kocharyan's two mandates, has never really been revealed. Society has been won over by fear. However, if in these cases remembrance allows us to draw lessons from contemporary tragedies, it also licenses the easy diffusion of conspiracy theories. In the debates on these two major events, conspiracy theories are omnipresent. Terrorist theory? The commando members were arrested and confessed. They were tried and sentenced to life imprisonment. They say they acted in the name of the Armenian people to put an end to the ongoing betrayal. Yerevan was ready to concede the Meghri corridor on the border with Iran in exchange for the reunification of Nagorno-Karabakh to Armenia. Mafia theory? Sargsyan intended to wage war against corruption and, following victory, turn Armenia into an untainted country, but the mafia groups decided otherwise. Russian theory? Putin had recently come to power in Moscow and intended to regain control over all the current issues: Chechnya, the future for Russian bases in Georgia and Nagorno-Karabakh. By striking Yerevan and its leaders, he made it clear to the protagonists that he must now be included in the processes to resolve these conflicts. American theory? The main victims are Russophiles, so Washington would have had everything to gain by eliminating these troublemakers and thus facilitate the work of

Kocharyan. Internal theory on the ruling power? Sargsyan did not get along with Kocharyan, so he decided to eliminate him. Dashnak theory? Many of the ARF's leaders were released from prison just 18 months before the assassinations in parliament. The ARF was blamed because their commando leader Naïri Hounanyan phoned the General Secretary of the party, Hrand Markarian, to tell him that as the Parliament was under attack, operations to overthrow the rest of the Kocharyan regime could now be launched at other strategic sites. Let us be clear: all these theories are far-fetched for several reasons, with the possible exception of Russian. By losing two out of the three national figures at the head of the state apparatus, Armenia was politically weakened. Who had an interest in downplaying the political sovereignty of Armenia? By removing two of the three most rebellious figures in the Yerevan parliament, the perpetrators sent a message of intimidation to the entire Armenian people. How did the Russian anti-terrorist forces, the Alfa Group, arrive at the Parliament five minutes after the beginning of the hostage crisis? Were they already in Armenia? If yes, why? Finally, who would benefit from this carnage? Kotcharyan and Sargsyan, at the time chief of the Armenian KGB and a notable absentee from Parliament on that day. It is, of course, too early to advance any one of the above theories, even if the ex-colonel of the FSB (ex-KGB), Alexander Litvinenko, who was close to Boris Berezovski, both exiled in London fleeing Russian justice, said that 'the GRU, the intelligence service of the Russian army, was responsible for the October 27 massacre in the Armenian Parliament'.

Remembrance as a denial of reality

Finally, the negation of history finds expression in a denial of reality. By becoming embroiled in the cult of remembrance, Armenia can forget massive emigration, a low birth rate, endemic corruption and increasing poverty. This unique denial of reality coming from the Kocharyan regime and, more notably, during Sargsyan's time in power blinds the central authorities who take advantage of the accurate, but exaggerated to the extreme, risk to national security. Fatalism won over voluntarism and a sense of responsibility. Nothing was being done to counter the massive haemorrhage of the population to foreign countries, whereas emigration can ultimately undermine national security. Nothing was done to boost birth rates when fewer girls than boys were born. The fight against corruption had little effect among the political staff and the central administration. Finally, the government's economic policy was not effective enough to boost employment and reduce poverty (one-third of the population lived below the poverty line). For that to happen, the country would need double-digit growth, whereas it oscillated between 4 and 6 per cent, which is low for a post-Soviet state.

In this dark image of the memorial state, a glimmer of hope sparkles in the grey and polluted sky of Yerevan: the controversy around the erection of a statue in tribute to Anastas Mikoyan (1895–1978), the brother of Artem, the inventor of the Mig. Mikoyan was, above all, a former comrade of Stalin and the man who, until his death in 1978, held important positions of power in Moscow during the reign of Lenin and that of Brezhnev, including Soviet head of state. In 2014, Yerevan city council launched a project to honour him with a statue, a proposition which sparked an uprising from within the opposition and civil society leading some local powers to renege on this totally unexpected but worthwhile initiative. The honour was unexpected: there was nothing to indicate that Armenia cared at all about a man who was, if not hostile, at least totally absent from the history of independent Armenia. Worthwhile because, thanks to this initiative, civil society seized the opportunity to promote lengthy debates about the place that the former president of the Supreme Soviet of the USSR should be accorded in the national memory. The subject was so sensitive that even foreign states got involved. Poland, through its ambassador in Yerevan, considered the project an insult to human dignity, recalling that Mikoyan is cited in the Warsaw archives in connection with the massacre of Polish military and civilians in Katyn in 1940. Is the Mikoyan affair the sign of a beginning for remembrance efforts? For some, Mikoyan is one of the few Armenians to have held such a high position in the world and, as such, he deserves a tribute from Armenian society. For others, his name is associated with the death of several hundred Armenians during the purges of 1937 so any tribute should be made to those victims, not to their executioner! For some, Mikoyan saved the planet from a third world war in 1962 during the missile crisis by negotiating the de-escalation of the conflict on behalf of the USSR. For others, he was a loyal soldier for Stalin and carried out the most reprehensible acts against the First Republic, Nagorno-Karabakh and the Armenian nation. While the debate has rumbled on in Yerevan, what is most surprising is that the ruling powers defended him, yet another sign of the ambivalence of this memorial state. How could the Republican Party, member of the European People's Party (EPP) pay homage to a Stalinist leader?! How could the silence of the EPP be explained? Was it aware of the remaining elements? How could this initiative be supported by the Yerevan mayor himself, Daron Markaryan, whose father, former Prime Minister Antranik Markaryan, was a former nationalist dissident under Stalin's successors? Finally, how could the Republican Party support this project? A party which claims to be the heir of Nejteh, sworn enemy of the Stalinist Mikoyan! If the position of the majority party is incomprehensible to say the least, it is easier to understand the position of the remembrance state. In the name of remembrance, national security and the alliance with Russia, the situation has changed in Armenia, especially since the Yerevan turning point of 3 September 2013, where President Sargsyan announced from Moscow that his country had opted to accede to the customs union proposed by Putin. It is far too soon to speculate on the price to be paid for this sudden and full alignment with Moscow. But one thing is certain: by doing so, the remembrance state ignored the opinion of its own population and harmed its own sovereignty as the declaration was made from the Russian capital and not Yerevan. Being ready to join what some people called Putin's 'Soviet micro-Union' undermined independence. Between the decision of 3 September 2013, which caused shock waves to ripple out beyond Yerevan and a decision to erect a statue in honour of a murderer – a way to show Russia that if Stalin is the object of a new cult in Moscow, Armenia can adapt to the rehabilitation of Soviet personalities by glorifying one of its most emblematic personalities in Yerevan –, the remembrance state finds itself in dangerous territory. The sovereignty of Armenia will have difficulty in recovering, at least as long as Putin maintains his predatory and post-imperial policy towards what is dubbed his 'near foreign neighbour'. Under these conditions, is the remembrance state the guarantor of Armenian independence or the anti-chamber of its subservience to Russia? The heir of the first Republic of Armenia, an ephemeral but truly independent state or just the heir to the Soviet Republic of Armenia, a tributary of Moscow and a Russian satellite in the Caucasus?

The road to the 'Velvet Revolution' . . .

Authoritarianism, corruption, emigration and injustice, are the four pillars of the regime of Sargsyan and his memorial state. Armenia ws sinking into fatalism. But little by little, between 2014 and 2018, several signs of protest have overturned the process of resignation. First, between 2014 and 2016, social movements against economic injustice have arisen, with a peaceful will on the part of protesters to fight the government's policy of price increases. Then, as a consequence of the 'Four-Day War' in April 2016 against Azerbaijan, for the first time since independence in 1991, there is some feeling that the state does not protect either its citizens or the Armenian territory. Finally, after the desire of President Sargsyan to remain in power by amending the Constitution in 2015, changing Armenia from a semi-presidential regime to a parliamentary one, convinced Armenians they should break free from their passivity and become aware of their rights as citizens. At the end of his two terms (2008–2018) and the victory of his party in the legislative elections in 2017, Sargsyan wanted to occupy the post of prime minister and mainpower. This unilateral decision provoked an unprecedented wave of protest across the country. Under the leadership of opposition MP Nikol Pashinyan, Armenians took to the streets, demanding the resignation of Prime Minister Sargsyan, who had just been elected by Parliament. The Velvet Revolution was underway . . .

Part IV

Beyond the Genocide

As near the end of our research, the time has undoubtedly come to draw some observations of the mirror game that has been woven between the tandem history-memory and the Armenian socio-political universe in the twenty-first century. Four dynamics emerge. The first is that globalization is an unprecedented opportunity for three major reasons. The Armenia–Diaspora partnership is a real asset and its potentialities are far from being consumed by the national elites in Yerevan. The power of globalization also allows a reading of the future in breach with the domination of traditionalism. By its irreversibility and dimension of interdependence, globalization suggests overcoming the national level, brings people closer together and shapes identities against exclusion. Finally, globalization allows Armenia to emerge from its geographical isolation through information and communication technologies, a growing sector in Yerevan.

In addition to this process of integration, a second dynamic begins to surface: that of a paradigm shift among Armenians. The logic of identity, redistributing dangerous patterns, hazardous combinations and exclusion, has shown its limitations and revealed major failings in the proto-system of Haitadism. It is not a question of renouncing this dynamic of liberation and integration but of adapting it to our post-modern world by accepting the participation of non-state and non-traditional actors in the political arena where agents of civil society would enjoy recognized autonomy as such. The restoration of the sovereignty of the Armenian state – the longest period of independence since the Middle Ages – forced the traditional elites to operate this Copernican revolution in favour of post-Haitadism by privileging its social side. The examination of domestic and institutional problems based on an identity quest approach is no longer appropriate. The Armenians do not suffer from a lack of national benchmarks ; they suffer from an overflow of nationalist and memorial references, like all peoples who do not want to see their horizon outside the nation state. In our interdependent, interconnected and open world, the nation state is passing through an area of unprecedented turbulence since its appearance in 1648, the date of the birth of the Westphalian model.

The third dynamic is the inclusion of the 1915 genocide theme in the international system. The enactment of commonsense co-operation with the Turks would offer bilateral perspectives in the areas of recognition of a common past, exorcism of the present and normalization of a shared future around the issue of compensation. After all, the dispute with Turkey does not arise from a confrontation with the Turkish people or from the existence of Turkey as a State, but only from its official negationism. The stakes of rapprochement with Turkey are so crucial for regional peace and global equilibrium that this process cannot only be an inter-governmental monopoly. Societies have a say in this democratic transition and the work of mutual understanding, but they lack resources and encouragement. Hence the need to include the 1915 genocide theme in the international system. First, through sincere mediation by the international community in favour of justice. Second, by a multilateral involvement of the actors in the resolution of a problem inseparable from the security of the Armenians. Finally, with an investment by the world of social science research in the denationalization of history in order to make it an instrument of peace and sharing of knowledge and not a weapon of war and discrimination.

These three dynamics would be incomplete without mentioning the one which overshadows the whole of this new architecture of post-Haitadism: the Armenians' logic of projection. The 'eschatological' experience of the genocide, as Marc Nichanian put it, has long structured the group. The re-establishment of Armenia's sovereignty now proposes to go beyond it to find another thread to this common representation. Indeed, this process of empowerment began with a step back from the politico-religious model, which has already made it possible to question the place of hyper-memory in the public debate. Based on this principle of legitimate contestation, civil society, as a group and a sum of individualities, revisits national history and upsets the established order. These new expressions of protest take out the religious and ideological nature of the thought and process of national construction, for the benefit of history and individuals.

10

Democratizing Identity

The centenary year of 2015 offered an exceptional opportunity to raise the question of the state of Armenians in the twenty-first-century world. Armenians have never been more influential than they are today. For the first time since 1375, Armenia has seen its territorial base widen with the gradual integration of areas controlled by the forces of the Nagorno-Karabakh Republic – or rather the Republic of Artsakh since the Armenians of the province re-Armenized the name following the constitutional referendum of 20 February 2017 – as evidenced by the new political map of Armenia.[1] In the Caucasus, the Armenians won a military victory over Azerbaijan after a war that left 40,000 dead (35,000 on the Azerbaijani side, 5,000 on the Armenian side) and nearly 1 million displaced or refugees (600,000 Azerbaijanis, 350,000 Armenians). Armenia is the only state stemming from the Warsaw Pact to have won a war since the fall of the Soviet Union. With 70,000 men, if we add the 20,000 men of the defence troops of the 'Nagorno-Karabakh Republic', the Armenian army has a positive experience of Soviet security doctrine. But, despite the effects of the war in the collective Armenian psychology, there has been no sign of triumphalism or arrogance towards the vanquished. Since the signing of the ceasefire on 12 May 1994, Armenia has been a garrison state, over-armed and one whose defence capabilities are recognized by NATO forces. The key to regional security in the South Caucasus is through Yerevan and Stepanakert. However, to face all its security challenges, Armenia has embarked on the modernization of its armed forces in search of new projection capabilities, one of the challenges of which is to adapt them to its own, mountainous environment.

Armenia–diaspora relations to redefine

The two bastions of the pro-Armenian lobby

In France, pro-Armenian lobbying is active along the Paris–Lyon–Marseille axis. The French of Armenian origin – an estimated 450,000–600,000 people – rely on two

---

[1] The name Artsakh originated from the name of the King of Armenia Artaxias I, founder of the Artaxiade dynasty and the Kingdom of Armenia. The popular tradition sees another explanation: *Ar* (*Aran*) and *tsakh* (forest, garden), namely the 'Aran Sizakean Gardens', the first prince of North-eastern Armenia. A constitutional referendum was held on 20 February 2017 in Nagorno-Karabakh. The 'yes' to the new constitution, which opens the way for a presidential regime, won with more than 87 per cent of the vote.

France–Armenia friendship groups in parliament to defend their interests. In the National Assembly, the group comprised 64 representatives in 2014, or 11 per cent of the national representation. The France–Georgia friendship group included 24 members; the France–Azerbaijan group 32 and the France–Turkey group 78. In the Senate, the France–Armenia friendship group includes 26 senators, while the France–Caucasus group (Georgia and Azerbaijan) includes 39 senators and the France–Turkey group 34 senators. It is from these parliamentary groups that the legislative proposals on Armenia were launched (1998, 2001, 2006 and 2011; in 2016, it was a bill, therefore an initiative of the government). The pro-Armenian lobby is so important in France that it took a decision of the Constitutional Council in 2012 to invalidate a bill defended by Nicolas Sarkozy and the two main parties in parliament (the Republicans or ex-UMP and PS) on the criminalization of the denial of officially recognized genocides, punishable by one year in prison and a fine of €45,000. It also has representatives in the media, the intellectual and artistic worlds as well as the business world and society through the Armenian Fund of France, which brings together more than 50,000 donors. Among local authorities too, actions in favour of Armenia are far from negligible. Diplomatic decentralization has made it possible to strengthen the links between Armenia and the Paris-Ile-de-France, Rhône-Alpes, Provence–Alpes–Cote d'Azur regions and some departments of western France thanks to the tireless action of local elected officials, sometimes of Armenian origin.

In the United States, the pro-Armenian lobby is primarily located in California, Massachusetts, New Jersey, New York State and Florida. Established in 1995, the Armenian Caucus is one of the largest with 163 representatives out of the 435 members of the House of Representatives, or 37 per cent of the lower house of Congress for an Armenian-American population of about 1.2 to 1.3 million people out of 322 million Americans (0.37 per cent of the population). In the Senate, the pro-Armenian lobby is equally powerful, notably in one of the most important permanent commissions, that of foreign affairs led by the Democrat Robert Menendez until the victory of the Republicans in the mid-term elections of November 2014. On 10 April 2014, this Senate committee adopted, by a large majority resolution, S.410 on the recognition of the genocide. Systematically, the pro-Armenian pressure groups (ANCA and the Armenian Assembly of America) issue proposals for resolutions in the US Congress, a regular source of crises between Washington and Ankara. They have also succeeded in blocking the nomination of several White House candidates to ambassador positions in Armenia (such as Richard Hoagland to succeed John Evans, who had been reprimanded by the State Department for publicly recognizing the genocide of 1915) and in Azerbaijan (Matthew Bryza, for conflicts of interest between his official activities and his connivance with think tanks affiliated with the oil companies). In another sign of their influence, the US Congress pays more than $10 million a year in direct humanitarian aid to Nagorno-Karabakh, while the Freedom Support Act 1992 deprived Azerbaijan of all US technical assistance as long as Baku maintained its aggressive policy towards the Armenian province. After the 9/11 attacks, the United States repealed most of this law in 2002, at the request of Azerbaijan, who supported Washington in its fight against global terrorism. In addition, Armenia obtained $235 million over five years in 2006 from the United States under the Millennium Challenge

Corporation, a fund that supports states in their efforts to implement democratic reforms. However, since the semi-authoritarian turn of Sargsyan's regime in 2008, Washington has suspended the flow of this fund to Yerevan. Finally, in 2015, Armenia and the United States signed a framework agreement on trade and investment, thanks to the efforts of the pro-Armenian lobby.

The specific role of the ARF

The ARF has a special role to play in strengthening the interdependence between Armenia and the diaspora. As the only influential pan-Armenian organization in the diaspora and a member of the government in Armenia (2016–2018), the ARF plays a key role in the relationship between the two poles of the Armenian people. But since its legality was reinstated in Armenia in 1998, it has lost its source of inspiration. Its original vocation, its exceptional presence in more than 50 countries and its many resources, beginning with its role in the Socialist International, are under-employed by its centralized leadership in Yerevan. This 'Armenian International' faces three potential problems. First, Dashnakism and Haitadism, of which it is the main actor, pre-date the state and were destabilized by its restoration in 1991. Might they dissolve in the Armenian state? While Haitadism was propelled into the heart of the apparatus upon the arrival in power of the PANM, Dashnakism paid the price because of Levon Ter-Petrosyan's desire to overthrow the leadership of the party and recover for himself the Dashnak network – at the head of which he wished to appoint a more docile leadership. The whole issue of the twenty-sixth congress of the ARF in Beirut, in 1995, was to make Dashnakism *Levono*-compatible but, internally, the crisis continued between the different branches; following the change of regime in 1998–1999, the ARF moved from a *Levono*-compatible direction to a *Roberto*-compatible one.

When it returned to the political game, the ARF followed a strategy of integration into Armenian society from the top, whereas it would have been in its best interests to advocate its integration from the bottom, to consolidate its foundations. It could have insisted on socialization around the ideas of citizenship and a fight against inequality to propose a social alternative to the liberal policy of the government in conformity with the programmes of restructuring of the IMF and the World Bank. The ARF would have benefited from such social challenge, but instead its strategy has led to disappointment and disillusionment. By opting for integration from the top, the ARF has merged with the patrimonial system it is familiar with and the consequent introduction of corruption and monopolies. This has caused a stir inside the party, especially among American branches, who denounced the alignment of their leadership with the local political culture.

Its rehabilitation in Yerevan was marked by its allegiance to power. The Hrand Markarian–Vahan Hovannesyan duo at the head of the ARF sealed off internal debate. The first took charge of controlling Dashnak bureaucracy, the second took over the political aspect and relations with the Kocharyan and Sargsyan administrations. In exchange for some ministerial portfolios in the social sector (agriculture, health, education), official Dashnak discourse became sterile. This allegiance also resulted in the ARF's participation in the various coalition governments from 1999 to 2009, though its election results were persistently negligible (frequently 4 to 6 per cent of the vote). It should also be remembered that the two Dashnak leaders are former detainees and, in this respect, the Kocharyan and Sargsyan administrations have made it clear that any attempt by the Dashnak to revolt against the authorities could result in the reopening of old court cases. By playing the 'carrot and stick' strategy with the ARF, Kocharyan and Sargsyan bought peace inside and outside Armenia, which was not the case with their predecessor Ter-Petrosyan, who was unable to get the ARF to depend on him. The restoration of sovereign Armenia has thus emptied the ARF's message of its substance and, instead of anchoring itself in left-wing Dashnakism or social Haitadism, the ARF chose the path of normalization. However, as we have seen, this party is anything but an organization that fits into the normative framework of an institutionalized party.

Between vassalization and new breath

Armenia has been in a state of permanent war since the signing of a ceasefire agreement in May 1994. This conditions its political life and development strategies. Such circumstances are not conducive to a real economic take-off or an exit from post-Sovietism. With little room for manoeuvre, it develops in the international and economic life with an eye systematically fixed upon the sacred cause of Nagorno-Karabakh. Any comparison with other post-Soviet countries is biased, therefore, because of this obsession and the Turkish–Azerbaijani blockade. Both politically and economically, Sargsyan's strategy is to demonstrate that there is only one policy – his own – to ensure the security and stability of Armenia. In a way, this has largely succeeded, as evidenced by the absence of protest from the parliamentary opposition to the dependence of Armenia on Russia. This dependence characterizes the recent history of Armenia and dates back to the first signs of Moscow's presence in the Caucasus. Since then, ties have only grown stronger between the two nations against Turkey and pan-Turkism for the physical security of the Armenians and the strategic interests of Russia. Since the independence of Armenia in 1991, Yerevan has consolidated its relations with Russia: the accession of Armenia to the CIS in 1991, the signing of the Collective Security Treaty in Tashkent in 1992, the treaty of military co-operation in 1995, the accession of Armenia in 1999 to the Collective Security Treaty Organization, the bilateral agreement on the sale of the Armenian Energy Park to Russia in 2001, the 2010 agreement on the continued hosting of the Russian Federation military base of Gyumri for a period of 49 years from 1995, the accession of Armenia to the Eurasian Customs Union in September 2013, the December 2013 agreement on the sale to Gazprom of Armenia's shares in the pipeline with Iran and the accession in 2014 to the Eurasian Economic Union.

Armenia's political and economic dependence on Russia is part of a broad movement by the Russian power to recover its former Soviet buffer zone. Between the 2008 war against Georgia and the annexation of Crimea in 2014, Moscow intends to let the world know that the Yeltsinian period is a bygone episode: its return to the international scene is now irreversible and it will have to be reckoned with as an independent pole of stability in the new global balance. This Russian thrust into former Soviet territory or even beyond (eg in Syria) is making a hostage of the Armenian state, the only power allied with Moscow in the region, to the point that the debate about its sovereignty has resurfaced. Has Armenia become 'the southern Kaliningrad' of neo-imperial Russia or an 'autonomous republic' of the Russian Federation in the South Caucasus? Sargsyan's Armenia thus sails between national sovereignty and Russian domination.

This process of vassalization of Armenia, which is reminiscent of medieval Armenia under Arab rule, has aroused strong reactions from the parliamentary opposition and society at large. The four opposition parties – Prosperous Armenia led by the oligarch Gagik Tsarukyan, the Armenian National Congress led by Ter-Petrosyan, the ARF led by Hrand Markarian and the Heritage Party led by Raffi Hovannisian – have gathered around an economic and social platform to propose an alternative to what has been called the passive and fatalistic policy of Sargsyan's government. Their purpose is not to challenge the strategic alliance with Russia, even if Hovannisian, the unfortunate presidential candidate of 2013, is ranked among the pro-American leaders in Armenia. Their purpose is not to break the strong ties between the Russian and Armenian nations, but to strengthen Armenia's position and enforce its independence, making Moscow understand that Russia has every interest in relying on a politically strong and economically healthy Armenia to assert its influence in the region. Why did Sargsyan launch his invitation from Moscow to Turkish President Abdullah Gül to come to Yerevan in September 2008 for the Armenia–Turkey football match in the 2010 UEFA European Championship qualifiers? Why did the same Sargsyan announce from Moscow Armenia's decision to join the Eurasian Customs Union? As for Armenian Foreign Minister Edward Nalbandyan, why does he frequently use the Russian language when he speaks at joint press conferences when Russian officials visit Yerevan? For the opposition, such attitudes contradict the Armenian Constitution and offend the dignity of Armenians as citizens of an independent state. The opposition is also critical of the government's economic and social policy. They condemn the monopolistic practices of the oligarchs and the apathy of the authorities in the fight against poverty and emigration. For them, Armenians do not leave their country for lack of patriotism but in despair at such indifference, even incompetence, when it comes to solving the problems of poverty, housing, social security and jobs. In Sargsyan's Armenia, 34 per cent of the population live below the poverty line and rampant emigration has been increasing since the global financial crisis. The mere fact that these four parties have come to cooperate in the long term, while their history is marked by strong tensions – Ter-Petrosyan against the ARF, Hovannisian against Ter-Petrosyan, the Heritage Party against Prosperous Armenia – shows that it is no longer the time for legitimate quarrels over political orientation, but for national solidarity and a general interest to preserve the principle of sovereignty of the Republic of Armenia.

Is there a real political system in Armenia or is it just an extension of the Russian model? We have observed throughout this book that there is no autonomous political system in Armenia, while politics and religion are inextricably linked in the country. Since independence, the regime appears to be the only legitimate owner of the state and contempt for an opposition incapable of gaining credibility and preparing for power is significant. For a brief moment, the two consecutive two-round presidential elections in 1998 and 2003 looked like they would pave the way for the irreversible democratization of political institutions and practices. But this was not the case. Since 2008, Armenian political life has revolved around a single political force, the Republican Party, which dominates all resources and often practises intimidation to impose its authority. However, the opposition seems to have found in the deterioration of political life the reasons necessary to draw the blueprints for an alternative. Based on their experience of power, the four opposition parties, which account for nearly 40 per cent of the parliament, have shown a willingness to compromise, a sense of openness and the right approach to reconnect with a disenchanted society that is becoming increasingly suspicious of politics.

The beginning of the empowerment of civil society

Armenian civil society has anticipated this growing national awareness. After more than two decades of independence, a fringe of Armenian society has gradually become autonomous from the state apparatus. Better informed than their rulers, aware of the errors and abuses of their regime, the new generations (20-to-45 year-olds), educated in American and French universities, involved in non-governmental organizations (NGOs) in favour of civic action and open to the world of telecommunications, have taken the full measure of their rights as citizens and the threat to the sovereignty of their country. In the space of two years, social protest scored points and held back the government when no one expected such developments. In the spring of 2012, hundreds of protesters from all walks of life demanded that the authorities remove the stalls in Mashtots Garden in Yerevan. After a power struggle that lasted a few months, the Yerevan city council decided to dismantle them. Building on this momentum, the civic movement also managed to put an end to destruction of the Yerevan central market, one of the jewels of national architecture designed by Grigor Aghabadyan, in 1951, towards the end of the Stalinist era. Samvel Alexanyan, an oligarch backed by the mayor of Yerevan, had plans to destroy the monument and replace it with a shopping centre. As a result of popular demonstrations and legal appeals, the protestors won their case: at least the market enclosure is preserved. Finally, in 2014, the civic movement embodied by the group 'Dem'em' ('I am against'), supported by the parliamentary opposition, obtained from the Constitutional Council the invalidation of some articles of the pension reform bill promoting the principle of funded retirement. Following the overturning of the law by the Constitutional Council, Prime Minister Tigrane Sargsyan resigned in April 2014. His successor, Hovik Abrahamyan, the former Speaker of the National Assembly, agreed to meet his opponents and take their arguments into account. In reality, his government passed the bill on the sly after toning down the disputed articles without negotiating with the social movement.

This civic movement includes both social groups such as 'Dem'em' and political groups such as the Sardarabad movement within the framework of a pre-parliament that integrates Armenians of the diaspora, some of whom come from the small group 'Armenian Renaissance' installed in France. They are all part of a democratic and European perspective. Now independent from power and dissociated from corrupt practices, the new generations condemn Russia's authoritarian and post-colonial behaviour and strongly criticize the choice of the Armenian president to join the Eurasian Customs Union. They point the finger at Sargsyan's lies. For years, the president has been hammering home the message that 'Armenia must change to regain confidence' and that it relies on the talent of youth. He constantly evokes the need to professionalize the civil service, fight corruption effectively, sanitize economic life, create jobs, ensure the independence of justice and be accountable to citizens. Yet the reality is quite different: nepotism is king and impunity reigns. The government believes in the effectiveness of its programme, but the forecasting agencies are more pessimistic in terms of growth. The younger generations are removed from key positions of power despite the fact that inter-generational shock is the key to the country's future. Government personnel has been pretty much unchanged since 2008; as a result, the sons of rich families accused of murder or other crimes are protected by the regime, while innocent people remain in prison. In short, post-Soviet Armenia is a sluggish, inegalitarian, corrupt, poor, oligarchic and vassalized state – so much so that the Russian officials present in Yerevan no longer bother to publicly criticize the rise of anti-Russian sentiment in Armenia and demand that the Armenian government take action against NGOs acting there against the interests of Moscow.

Yet not everything is so dark in this republic in transition. At the regional level, Armenia has high expectations of the outcome of the Iranian nuclear crisis. If negotiations between P5 + 1 (the five permanent members of the Security Council and Germany) and Iran lead to a final agreement, Armenia could take advantage of the opening up of oil-rich Iran and find itself on a new route between Asia and Europe. On the domestic front, the civic movement and the 'group of four' opposition parties in parliament preserve an informal link, the basis of a hypothetical social contract. Finally, in society, women and young people with new ideas are working to change attitudes in Yerevan. In addition to the international and social movements, the civic movement promotes the idea of a new republic with modernized institutions – there is more and more talk of bicameralism in Armenia – but opposes constitutional reform projects aimed at transferring most of the presidential power to the prime minister. As a semi-presidential republic at present, Armenia would become a parliamentary republic, in accordance with the wishes of President Sargsyan, who intends to ensure his continued hold on power after his second term in 2018. Finally, the civic movement expects a lot from the diaspora, which is increasingly involved in the economic and social life of Armenia. Whether it is owing to sustainable investments or political crises (more than 10,000 Syrians of Armenian origin are refugees in Armenia), more and more Armenians from abroad are resettling in Armenia every day. Whether Armenia can meet these expectations remains to be seen.

What process for democratization?

From national security to common security

To ensure its security, Armenia now seems to rely exclusively on Russia. Moscow, of course, ensures the protection of Yerevan not for the benefit of the Armenian people but for its own ends. Therefore, when Russia feels powerful it weakens Armenia to the detriment of Azerbaijan. This alternative principle is simple: it is up to the Armenians to offer counter-solutions.

They could first invest in a long-term effort of convincing Russia to change the nature of the alliance. Even if Russia, as the heir of an imperial past, is not inclined to take into account the independence of its neighbours, it would be well advised, if it wants to reinforce its interests in a globalized economy, to take good care of its relations with the few ex-Soviet allied republics. If Moscow intends to play the card of a multipolar world by becoming one of the poles of regional stability, at a time when its influence in Georgia, Moldova and Ukraine is decreasing and as the Baltic countries have been emancipated since 1991, it would be in its best interests to respect the sovereignty of its neighbours and create a well-balanced relationship with them. Armenia should also improve its defence capabilities and adapt its military tools by taking advantage of its mountainous topography. Indeed, it does not lack resources for this purpose. It is therefore incumbent upon the central authorities to give real meaning to the value of the lives of their fellow citizens and, in the first place, of their soldiers.

But security is not just a realistic approach to international relations. Globalization has broadened the focus on issues of protection and integrity of the interstate system and populations. Armenia could thus find its place in a multilateral system of collective security. Its diplomacy based both on traditional actors (diplomats) and what are sometimes seen as 'intruders' from civil society, as Bertrand Badie calls them, would change its structure and help to find a new range of international integration, thus guaranteeing its sovereignty.

Finally, security is part of the democratic commitment. Without democracy, there is no security; without democracy there is no going beyond memory. It is up to the Armenians to widen the meaning of the concept of security and apply it not only to the national interest but also to society. Global or common security representative of the transnational school of international relations is based on the democratization of societies in the context of globalization. On this point Armenia has everything to gain, as long as it learns from the past.

Moving from a heritage model to a rational model of the state

This necessitates a paradigm shift from a patrimonial, arbitrary, post-Soviet model to a rational, modern, neutral model of power. By moving from a heritage system to a rational system, Armenia could choose modernity and progress. Since the only legitimate holder of the state is the people, not the regime – which confiscated it during the First Republic, under the Soviets or with the current Republican Party regime – the major task of educating society lies ahead.

As long as impunity reigns in the state apparatus and economic and social life, there is nothing to expect in terms of social contract between the state and society. State public services cannot act as agents of a regime, but they must change the order of priority. They are not serving a government or a party; they are serving a population whose only existing common good is the state. If Armenians show sympathy and respect for their army and if there is popular support for a branch of the national administration, then it is possible to extend this process of social contract to all other sectors of bureaucracy, to begin with education, justice and the police – three institutions riddled with corruption, unpredictability and allegiance to power. Cleaning up economic life, suppressing nepotism, destroying monopolies and fighting against the criminalization of political practices all requires citizen mobilization in the framework of the law and with peaceful methods, to prove to the powers that be that society represents an unlimited support for democracy and the stability of republican institutions; that it is not the enemy. This is the challenge undertaken by the new Armenian Prime Minister, Garen Garabedyan. Since taking office in 2016, he has been calling for action against 'rampant corruption' to clean up methods and practices in political life.

Bicameralism: a step towards institutional and strategic modernity

In addition to social transformations, a vast project of institutional reforms could promote an exit from post-totalitarianism and memory. The power of parliament must be strengthened not so much by a necessary yet insufficient transfer of power from the president to the National Assembly – as put in place by Sargsyan with the constitutional referendum of 2016 – as by the introduction of bicameralism. The principle of two houses is not restricted to federal states, as evidenced by the likes of France. Nor is such institutional prerogative limited to large states alone; indeed, Belgium's surface area is equivalent to that of Armenia, yet it has a house of representatives and a senate. In every respect, bicameral innovation with the creation of a senate would bring a momentum and modernity. Such a new house, based on local authorities, would integrate them into the system of institutions and create a collaborative interdependence that would restore balance in their relations with the capital, Yerevan. The power would be better distributed and the regions would finally make a name for themselves. The creation of a senate would also make it easier to write laws and enrich the legislative procedure, which is too rudimentary. This could even have strategic benefits, to the extent that a diplomatic bill, such as the recognition of the Nagorno-Karabakh Republic, would be less likely to be rejected than it is at present. On two occasions, the Foreign Affairs Committee of the Armenian Parliament rejected a bill proposed by the Heritage Party regarding the recognition of the Nagorno-Karabakh Republic on the grounds that its adoption would force the National Assembly meeting in plenary session to confirm the vote. This would have led to a breakdown in negotiations with Azerbaijan and a regional crisis. The rejection strengthened Azerbaijan's position in the ongoing negotiations, by demonstrating, with the evidence to prove it, that Yerevan does not favour the independence of Nagorno-Karabakh. In a two-house scenario, however, Armenia could have had a parliamentary commission pass a similar bill to dissuade Baku from pursuing aggressive policies. In the event of a repeat offence by Azerbaijan, the National Assembly would have confirmed the decision, even if the law could not be officially enforced as it had not yet been approved by the Senate. The Minsk Group would then have intervened to stop Armenia's proceedings, to which the Armenian executive could have replied that in the name of the separation of powers – France and the United States understand the institutional distinction quite well – the legislature prevails. As a result, neither Armenia nor Azerbaijan would have lost face.

The Nagorno-Karabakh Republic would not be recognized by Yerevan, but would not be ill-treated. The Armenian Senate could use the text to its advantage should the conditions at the front so require. The co-presidency of the Minsk Group would have nothing to condemn since the separation of powers is a guarantee of democracy. Moreover, as the democratization of states and societies is a promise to unblock peace negotiations, the process itself would emerge more strongly.

Bicameralism would also benefit social and political peace in the case of full proportional representation and elections by direct universal suffrage. All political forces would be integrated into the power game, thus avoiding repeated and violent street opposition. This would force the different trends in the National Assembly to find a compromise and reach a stable majority. The list of potential modernization proposals for the state and its institutions is long. The current Civil Council, headed by former prime minister Vazgen Manukyan, could indeed be given a constitutional status. For the time being, this Civil Council has no institutional ties; it is a kind of unidentified political object, not recognized by any authority, which gives opinions on whichever issue is being debated (eg on the Armenian–Turkish protocols which it approved). What authority gave it the status of Constitutional Council number two?

Participatory democracy within the diaspora

This paradigm shift, this reversal in the accepted meaning of politics, from bottom to top and no longer from top to bottom, also affects the diaspora's organization and relations with Armenia. It is undergoing a transformation from community order to multicultural order, in response to the new political, economic, social and cultural challenges that are affecting relations between states and societies. It is also involved in participatory democracy with the organization of elections in each of its branches. The project is under study by the Coordinating Council of Armenian Organizations in France (CCAF). Following a lengthy educational effort, the CCAF gave birth to a project called the Conseil franco-arménien (Franco-Armenian Council or CFA). The project, whose final review has not yet taken place, could be launched in the years to come. To reinforce the cohesion of the republic and avoid any interference in its internal affairs, the organization of the CFA elections will take into account the principle of extra-territoriality and republican integration as well as the principle of autonomy for the Armenian diaspora in France. Through the organization of democratic elections in diasporic micro-societies, Armenian identity will lose its memorial, abstract dimension and acquire a sense of responsibility. At the level of each state, this new organization around a bicultural democratic council renewable every three or four years would put different strands face to face – on the basis of projects of a political, social, humanitarian, economic or cultural nature and so on. At the end of its mandate, the incumbent majority would defend its title in a new ballot, from which a possible new team would emerge to head the council. There would be no communitarian threat or worry for public order. Indeed, the unity of the republic would be respected. Moreover, French authorities would have a democratic representative. The CFA example is unique and can serve as a pilot project for all Armenian diasporas. In France, no other religious or ethnic community enjoys such a representative instrument.

In the United States, reflection is also moving forward slowly. In addition to press articles that are regularly published on the possibility of democratic elections, new ideas emerge, such as those emanating from several personalities – such as the former American ambassador Edward Djerejian, the late singer-songwriter Charles Aznavour and the entrepreneur Serge Tchuruk – who, in a statement published in the *New York Times* on 28 October 2016,[2] laid the foundations of a new model, the 'Global Armenians', a perspective that aims to bring together the full potential of Armenians around the world with the purpose of adapting Armenian identity to globalization and developing the Republic of Armenia in all fields.

The principle of 'win-win-win'

The potential reorganization of the diaspora is obviously not intended as an action against either the adoptive state or Armenia. On the contrary, in the context of globalization, it would strengthen the interests of states, according to the win-win-win principle. For the diaspora: respect of its operational autonomy. For the adoptive state: the absence of Armenia's interference in its domestic affairs. For the Armenian state: no interference of the diaspora in its internal affairs. The Armenian state could thus benefit from these new forms of institutional interdependence and functional autonomy through rationalization of 'diasporic' aid and representative branches. The adoptive state could also rely on an Armenian diaspora to reinforce its interests in Armenia. Voices are already proclaiming that no state should be able to join the club of democracies in just 20 years when others, such as France, have taken more than a century to get there. Other voices declare themselves the guardians of memory and sweep away any project that would shake them out of their inertia. To the former, I should like to respond that while two decades may indeed not be enough to become a democracy, 20 years is plenty of time to put the Armenian state on track. To the latter, their record speaks for them: where did the power of memory lead them? They wander like museum pieces, browsing commemorative events.

Former Armenian defence minister Roupen Ter-Minassian was not wrong when he wrote: 'Do not look for the cause of Armenia's curse in its geographical position. It is

---

[2] The statement, published in the *New York Times*, was echoed by the Armenian press, such as *Asbarez*, a bilingual Dashnak daily in California. Available at: http://asbarez.com/156506/global-armenians-ad-in-ny-times-calls-for-inclusive-leadership-in-armenia/. This declaration, whose signatories' ambition was to represent 'Armenians worldwide', was signed by 22 men and one woman. In protest, dozens of Armenian women from around the world told them that 'the gender gap cannot be ignored. The letter itself calls on the Armenian government to adopt "strategies based on inclusion and collective action", but the process of writing and publishing the letter should have modelled these ideals. In an effort to prevent this type of exclusion and symbolism, we undersigned promise to condition our involvement in the forums of the Armenian community on the participation of other women. Only one [woman] is not enough.' Signatories include Armenian-Canadian actress Arsinée Khanjian, Armenian-Canadian director Aton Egoyan and American academics Houri Berberian and Khachig Tololyan (see http://armenews.com/imprimersans.php3?id_article=133732&nom_site=News%20d%92Armenie%20en%20ligne&url_site=http://armenews.com).

not the reason for its weakness. On the contrary, from its position springs the power of its people.'[3] The genocide may have destroyed the Armenian people, but Haitadism is trying to revive the process of Armenian integration. The Haitadist project must, therefore, be part of a democratic and social dynamic rather than an identity dynamic and move from a logic of recognition to a logic of healing with regard to Turkey. But what exactly do Armenians want? What authority is entitled to speak on behalf of the sons and grandsons of the genocide survivors – the Armenian state, the Church and the traditional parties? This book contends that the entry of Armenia and Haitadism into the twenty-first century depends primarily on a rapprochement with Turkey.

---

[3]   Roupen Ter-Minassian, *L'organisation de la FRA* (Yerevan, 1991), p. 7.

11

Building Dialogue with the Turks

More than ten years after the electoral defeat of the Kemalist parties in Turkey in 2002, the Armenian Question is no longer considered in age-old terms in Ankara, especially since the opening of the country's negotiations for accession to the European Union (EU) in 2005 and the pressures of Turkish civil society. Yet, while the wall of silence around the 'G-word' (G for genocide), as the Americans call it, collapsed in Turkey owing to the pressure of dissident intellectuals, the official position of Ankara remains negationism. It has even hardened since the coup attempt in Ankara on 15 July 2016 and the ensuing crackdown. Even if some statements issued by the troika in power in Ankara – Abdullah Gül, Ahmet Davutoğlu and Recep Tayyip Erdoğan – are steps towards recognition of historical events, the negationist barrier continues to resist the truth. This was recently evidenced by the cynicism of the Turkish government in deciding to organse the celebration of Gallipoli's victory over the Allies one day early, on 24 April instead of 25 April 2015, to overshadow the commemoration of the centenary of the genocide and incite public figures to visit Turkey on that day to pay tribute to the victims of the Battle of the Dardanelles. The situation has even stalled to the point that Erdoğan's authoritarian regime wants to enact a law banning the words 'Armenian genocide' in all public speeches and publications. The denial of history, however, has reached such proportions in Turkey that civil society is now split in two. Since the birth of the republic in 1923, bilateral dialogue has taken many forms in history before entering the Turkish public space in 2005 for the first time. Islamist Turkey has broken the nationalist stranglehold of Kemalism and has reconnected with the Ottoman past in which it laid the foundations of its legitimacy in the name of the great imperial, multi-ethnic state. Yet by setting out on the path to a post-Kemalist opening and restoration of an Ottoman memory, the Turkish government comes face to face with ghosts from the past. The issue of minorities (Kurdish, Cypriot and Armenian) both inside and outside Turkey touches the higher reaches of government after long decades of indifference (the Armenian Question), negligence (the Cypriot question) and ill-treatment (the Kurdish question). The new Islamist authorities, by building in Anatolia rather than Ankara, the political capital and Istanbul, the economic capital, have thus revived the spectre of the Armenian Question. While promoting the democratization of institutions and civil society in the name of de-Kemalization and adaptation of the country to European standards, the AKP regime intends to keep at a distance this pre-republican memory, rising dramatically against its neo-Ottoman strategy and the anchoring of society in the traditional values of Islam. But it may be too late: the thirst for freedom and knowledge in Turkey today goes far beyond the consideration of the Armenian Question.

Since this Islamic shift, the destiny of the Turkish–Armenian community has materialized in different ways. The best known is the diplomatic approach: protocols between Armenia and Turkey were signed on 10 October 2009, in Zurich, for the 'establishment of diplomatic relations between the two countries' and 'the development of bilateral relations'. It is an intergovernmental initiative supported by the international community in the context of transitional justice. This is not the first institutional effort. In 2001, while Turkey was still ruled by the Kemalists, a first attempt at transitional justice was initiated by former Armenian and Turkish diplomats meeting as part of a Turkish Armenian Reconciliation Commission (TARC) under the auspices of the United States. It was a successful attempt to put an end to the wall of silence, but it had no further effect for lack of follow-up and sincerity. The dynamics of the Zurich protocols or agreements are very different. It is the most comprehensive and advanced initiative, yet it is also the most problematic and incomplete. With the purpose of encouraging the first inter-social exchanges, the Zurich agreements have only slowed the process of rapprochement. Today, while the protocols are deadlocked, the dynamics of inter-social dialogue, remain strong.

Civil society against the Turkish state

Academics and intellectuals, from the Kurdish and Armenian minorities or from the militant and trade union left wing, elected officials and journalists, lawyers and artists all are today part of the Turkish democratic current and not the illegitimate children of Turkish values as nationalists would like us to believe. This current is neither a distortion of the social body, nor an improvised ideology. Its presence in the Turkish political and intellectual heritage is legitimate, even if it has long been stifled by the CUP and the Kemalist parties and is now under the surveillance of the Islamic regime of the AKP. The heirs to the philosophy of the Enlightenment, to the Tanzimat era and to the fathers of the Ottoman Constitution, its followers identify with the universalist and egalitarian principles of the old Itilaf party of Prince Sabahaddin (1879–1948), favourable to the creation of a federal and constitutional Ottoman Empire and consider that it is through history, respect of minorities' rights and their full integration into the social body that the Turkish state will achieve irreversible democratization. In their opinion, the handling of minorities is the indicator of democracy in Turkey. They demand equal rights for Kurdish citizens and respect for their traditions, culture and language in society and in the institutions. They call for a fair, respectful resolution of the Cyprus issue under international law. They are in favour of recognizing the 1915 genocide, although not everyone uses the word 'Soykirim', out of political caution rather than conviction. But they are all willing to face the demons of national memory sometimes at the cost of legal ordeals, professional complications and even a threat to their lives, as evidenced by the assassination of Hrant Dink.

Indeed, as Turkey relies on the structures of the state and its nationalist representations in society or the AKP regime and its supporters, it is far from yielding to internal and external pressures. The regime holds its penal code and its arsenal of judicial repression in one hand while, with the other hand, it threatens to leave NATO and retaliate against any state determined to legislate for the recognition of the genocide. Negationism is not just a diplomatic position or a structural pillar of the state, it is also an instrument that gives ultimatums and sometimes causes deaths – for example that of 26-year-old Sevag Balıkçi, a soldier of Armenian descent murdered near his Kozluk barracks in the province of Batman, in the heart of the Kurdish region, on 24 April 2011, by one of his roommates, Kıvanç Agaoglu. Dying on 24 April is not a coincidence for an Armenian in Turkey. A mock trial took place and the alleged killer was acquitted. Sloppy investigation, manipulation of witnesses: the death of Sevag Balıkçi is proof, once again, that impunity for crimes against Armenians is the norm in Turkey. The assassination, the second in four years after Hrant Dink's, came at a time when the AKP regime had reduced the scope of fundamental freedoms. Journalists and intellectuals, publishers and human rights activists are in the crosshairs of justice and are increasingly condemned for producing reports related to the Armenian or Kurdish issue, such as Ragip Zarakolu and his son Deniz – the father was released in 2013, while his son is still in prison at the time of writing. This tightening of the screw supports negationism in Turkey, which has been immune from criticism since economic experts classified it as an emerging power. However, the prospect of its accession to the EU is retreating as the regime lashes out (e.g. blocking YouTube and Twitter) and engages in repression, as in 2013 during demonstrations at Gezi Park and Taksim Square, a 'Turkish May '68' crushed by the police under the thumb of Erdoğan's arbitrary policy. This authoritarian swing by the government, which is also a reflection of the failure of Turkish diplomacy, goes hand in hand with obscurantism, despite a few well-intended statements with regard to Armenians – which are immediately contradicted by the power of denial.

The emergence of a Turkish memory to revive the Armenian–Turkish past

A number of intellectuals today fantasize about the Ottoman past, of the happy cohabitation of Turks and Armenians as if this community, then considered the most faithful millet of Constantinople, had not been subject to the unequal status of *dhimmi*. Today's descendants of the millet claim justice for those who were murdered secretly and without burial in the mountains of Sassun, the plain of Muş or the Mesopotamian desert. This was the purpose of the public academic conference held in Istanbul in 2005 where for the first time 'the word "genocide" was applied' according to the Turkish liberal daily *Radikal* in its 25 September issue, 'and the world continued to turn, Turkey is still on the map'. Turkish society then discovered that under the Ottoman Empire, Armenians continuously played a major role in the development of the state. The multilayered Armenian society, as evidenced by the upper caste of the Amiras, was consubstantial with the organization of the state. Armenians contributed imperial state ministers (Noradunghian), diplomats (Mirzayan Manuk Bey (1769–1817), Hagop Krdjikian (1806–1865) Krikor Odian (1816–1873) Sahak Apron (1823–1900) and

Harutyun Pasha Dadian (1830–1901)), deputies, magistrates, doctors, lawyers, architects, businessmen, tradesmen, artizans, workers and peasants. All contributed to the organization of the great bodies of the state, its economic wealth, its cultural and artistic influence and the development of its land. Today, the Turks echo what Armenians have been saying for decades: by decimating Armenians between 1894 and 1920, Turkey lost gigantic economic potential and incredible cultural wealth and condemned Anatolia to underdevelopment. Even the Armenian revolutionary movement, so denigrated by the Kemalist and Islamist governments in Turkey, defended at the time the interests of the empire and had a political project to stop dismemberment to transform it into a federal state, as Prince Sabahaddin intended. In 1914, the ARF called on the Young Turk government to choose neutrality as an official position in the conflict to preserve the unity of the empire. Ironically, in 1939, Turkey remained neutral during the Second World War, allowing it to attack Germany only a few months before its capitulation and thus become part of the victors' camp. This nod to history justifies our humble question: what would have happened in 1914 if the CUP leaders had listened to their former Dashnak comrades who advocated the neutrality of the empire?

Today, the status of the Armenian minority in Turkey, composed of 50,000–60,000 people, is governed by the Treaty of Lausanne, but Turkey does not comply with all the clauses, especially with regard to real estate titles and Christian Armenian cultural heritage. Therefore, the Armenians of Turkey are unlike other Turkish citizens. Their community exists in a state of dependence on the government in a climate of intimidation. Its official representative, the Armenian Patriarchate of Constantinople who is responsible for schools, hospitals, churches, cemeteries and newspapers, has no other choice but to abide by the government's position, sometimes going so far as to distance himself publicly from the Armenian cause, as was the case during the Armenian terrorism episodes (1975–1985) and, more recently, in Nagorno-Karabakh. However, since the 2000s, the religious community has evolved because of Hrant Dink. Thanks to him, the Armenian minority in Turkey has come out of its religious frozen status; the Armenian community has become independent of the power just as Turkish civil society has become independent of the state; the Armenian issue has moved from a religious dimension to a secular dimension; the Armenian voice has shifted from cultural content to psychosocial content; Armenians have gained a new place in the Turkish public space and ensured that their issues can enter politics in Turkey. Dink was anything but a nationalist. He advocated peace between Armenians and Turks based on values of equality, respect and truth. He endorsed a solid, rational, reasonable discourse against the Turkish and Armenian nationalists. He advocated a psychological approach to the Armenian–Turkish problem. However, this exercise forced him to constantly adapt his own discourse to the debate, sometimes at the cost of certain subtleties that were due more to the complexity of the Armenian–Turkish problem than to political calculations. Dink laid the foundation for *Dinkism*, a subsection of the Turkish democratic current. By murdering him, the Turkish nationalists intended to nip in the bud a cultural revolution incompatible with the idea of a republic one and indivisible.

The response came from Turkish society in two stages. On the one hand, the funeral of the Armenian journalist brought between 100,000 and 200,000 people onto the streets of Istanbul, gathered under the banner 'We are all Armenians'. Since 2007, every 19 January, his family, friends and human rights activists in Turkey pay him tribute and perpetuate his ideas through the Hrant Dink Foundation, created and led by his wife Rachel and his children. On the other hand, Dinkism has passed on and disseminated ideas throughout the Turkish territory. Now, every 24 April, more and more Turkish cities commemorate the 1915 genocide during public demonstrations, in silence of course, but gathering ever more people. In this respect, the city of Diyarbakır, the 'capital' of Turkish Kurdistan, plays a decisive role. More and more is happening in memory of 1915: conferences, exhibitions, the renovation of religious monuments and cultural exchanges with Armenian organizations of the diaspora. In 2005, the Turkish Nobel Prize winner Orhan Pamuk joined Dink in support of recognition of the genocide, which led to his receiving death threats in 2007 from Turkish nationalists. In the same spirit, a month before the second anniversary of the death of Dink, 200 Turkish intellectuals launched an internet petition on 15 December 2008 under the leadership of Ahmet Insel (an economist), Cengiz Aktar (a political scientist and diplomat), Ali Bayramoglu (a journalist) and Baskin Oran (a university professor) to ask Armenians' forgiveness for the silence that followed the 1915 Armenian massacres: 'My conscience does not accept the insensitivity showed to and the denial of the Great Catastrophe that the Ottoman Armenians were subjected to in 1915. I reject this injustice and for my share, I empathize with the feelings and pain of my Armenian brothers and sisters. I apologize to them.'

The appearance of this text was a seismic event that shook the Turkish world. Within a few weeks, 30,000 people had signed the petition. The international press echoed the subject and encouraged Turkey to step up its duty of remembrance. The word 'genocide', however, was not included: the initiators prefer the Armenian expression of 'Great Catastrophe' ('Mendz Yeghern') used in 2001 by Pope John-Paul II in Yerevan. But thanks to this initiative, the Turkish state no longer has a monopoly on Turkey's position with regard to 1915.

The memory of 1915 took a new turn when the issue of Islamized Armenians emerged.[1] More and more Turkish citizens have discovered Armenian roots in their own families. For example, lawyer Fethiye Çetin, a human rights activist, discovered the Armenian origin of her grandmother in 2003. She told her touching story in a book, *My Grandmother: A Memoir*, published in 2004 in Turkey. This biography, like other testimonies, echoes the book of Berdjouhi Barseghian, *Jours de Cendres à Istanbul* (*Ash Days in Istanbul*), published for the first time in Armenian as a series of articles between 1932 and 1939 and published in French in 2004 in Marseille. The wife of Sarkis Barseghian, a Dashnak revolutionary from Van killed during the raid of 24 April 1915, recounts how she and other Armenian women created a rescue network for children, often abducted girls, during the deportation in 1915 and placed them in Muslim homes (Turkish and Kurdish), either with infertile couples who longed to have children or to prevent them being locked in harems where they were exploited at will.

---

[1] According to Ayse Gül Altinay, since 2004, 14 books have been published in Turkish on this issue, *Gendered Silences, Gendered Memories*, Eurozine (eurozine.com), 12 February 2014. First published in *L'Homme* 2/2013.

Heranouch, Fethiye Çetin's grandmother, abducted at the age of nine, could have been one of the young girls rescued by Berdjouhi and her friends. Turkey may have hundreds or even thousands of Heranouchs and families regularly discover these 'invisible survivors', to use Laure Marchand and Guillaume Perrier's expression.

Once the first steps had been taken, the wave spread further into Turkey and entire villages publicly announced their Armenian roots. These Armenians, the Hemshin people, who had converted to Islam in the seventeenth century, formed an ethno-religious group estimated to number around 500,000–700,000 people, settled principally in the region of Trabzon and near the border with Georgia. In recent years, Armenia and diaspora organizations have been working on the issue of the Hemshin and the number of conferences, symposia and publications on the subject has increased. Attached to Turkey, these Hemshin defend their mixed traditions between Armenian culture and Muslim rites and several projects for the development of Hemshin identity were presented, such as the publication in Hemshin dialect of the monthly *Gor* ('Volunteer'), the first issue of which was published in September 2014. But the geography of Armenian memory in Turkey does not stop there. It extends into Dersim (currently the Tunceli Province), or the former Armenian Sassun, historically Armenian land and home to revolutionaries, where Kurdish people of the Alevi faith were massacred by Turkish troops in 1937–1938 by order of Mustafa Kemal. The purpose of central authorities was to quash a Kurdish revolt which resulted in the death of 15,000–20,000 people. It is now evident that the population of Dersim in fact included thousands of Armenians, hidden survivors of the 1915 genocide. Other research conducted by the sociologist Ismail Besikçi, the Dutch anthropologist Martin Van Bruinessen, the ethnomusicologist Hasan Saltik and by Hrant Dink and Sarkis Seropyan bolstered the theory of a Dersim population with Armenian roots. Ironically, one of the main executioners in the Dersim massacre was none other than Kemal's adopted daughter, Sabiha Gökçen, in the care of the Father of the Nation from the age of 12, when she was taken away from her Armenian parents who died during the genocide. Hrant Dink made this revelation in a series of articles published in 2004 in *Agos*. Gökçen obtained a pilot's licence in the Soviet Union and spent part of her life dropping bombs on thousands of Dersim Armenians, without knowing that she was killing her own people. Today, the 'cause of the Armenians of Dersim' is defended by an association created in 2010 in Istanbul by Mihran Pirgiç Gültekin, a former Alevi Muslim converted to Christianity. Turkish memory does indeed look like a matryoshka doll where each layer of a sequence of Turkish history contains the parchment of an episode from Armenian history.

In November 2011, Erdoğan acknowledged the Dersim massacres and formally apologized, on behalf of the Turkish state, to the victims and descendants of this savagery. While the descendants of the victims welcomed the government statement, they now demand justice and reparation. The Dersim case is therefore far from being closed and most observers see in this recognition a simple way for the AKP regime to spirit away Kemal's legacy. Indeed, repentance is an accommodating technique in Turkey.

Since the AKP came to power, no initiative by Turkish society has rattled the position of the central authorities. To this end, let us recall the existence of a counter-petition to the 'Request for pardon to Armenians' which, in the space of a few months, collected more than 600,000 signatures in Turkey in 2009. While they practise intimidation without restraint by using the power of the state, the central authorities have occasionally inflected their position, but they remain firm about the main point: no recognition of the genocide. This manipulation technique in the higher reaches of the state began in 2004–2005 when Abdullah Gül issued the first statements on the reality of massacres of Armenians and Turks committed in the history of the First World War, cautiously adding that we must leave this to historians. Following this, the head of Turkish diplomacy proposed to create a joint commission of historians to shed light on the 'events of 1915' and announced that the Turkish national archives would be opened, in exchange for the opening of the ARF's archives, stored in Boston, Massachusetts. But they are more likely to confirm the CUP's betrayal of its former ARF allies. A few months later, in 2005, this time by official letter, Turkey invited Armenian President Robert Kocharyan to create a commission of historians to establish the reality of the genocide. In 2008, as part of the 'football diplomacy' that marked the beginning of rapprochement between the two countries, Abdullah Gül, crossing the border declared: 'when I look up, I see Armenia facing me'. It was a way to say that the vicinity of Armenia is unavoidable, although the Kemalists never went beyond recognition in principle of the Armenian state. In 2009, Turkey and Armenia signed the normalization protocols after more than a year of negotiations. However, Turkish pre-conditions being unacceptable for Yerevan, Armenia decided to freeze the ratification process and Turkey refused to open its border – one of the essential stakes in the normalization protocols. In 2010–2011, Turkey called Armenia to reason: as a sign of religious tolerance towards Christians, it decided to renovate Armenian churches in Ani, near Kars and Agdamar, an island located in Lake Van. Until that date, Ankara had the shameful habit of turning Armenian churches and religious monuments (convents, monasteries) into stables or military targets during army manoeuvres. Today, the AKP government is initiating the renovation of Armenian sites in partnership with the World Monuments Fund to preserve the ruins of the two cathedrals. The restoration of part of the architectural heritage of Eastern Anatolia or Western Armenia is intended to be seen as a sign of new openings, to show Brussels its goodwill, to divide the Armenian diaspora and derive economic profit by promoting the wealth of 'Turkish cultural' tourism. Few have been fooled by the seduction policy of the Ottoman regime since Erdoğan authorized the MHP party nationalists to say their prayers in October 2010 in the Armenian Cathedral of the Blessed Virgin in Ani. On 24 April 2011, the government ordered the destruction of the monument celebrating the friendship between Turkey and Armenia that was located in Kars, a former Russian garrison city prior to the First World War, where Armenians were the majority.

After this frosty episode, relations warmed up again. In December 2013, Turkish Foreign Minister Ahmet Davutoğlu, on the occasion of a meeting of the Organization of the Black Sea Economic Zone in Yerevan, said that 'this wave of deportation under the Ittihatci (CUP) was an absolute mistake. What they did was a mistake and an inhuman act'. Never had a Turkish official gone so far in interpreting the tragedy of 1915. Never before had such an important member of the Turkish government been so explicit in condemning the 1915 deportations of Armenians. He added:

[One must] create collective consciousness between the two countries with a fair memory. What I mean by this is that we should know the facts [...] Our main goal is not only to open the Turkish-Armenian border, but to form a base that will pave the way for world peace [...] It should be supported by three pillars. The first is the relations between Turkey and Armenia. The second concerns relations between Azerbaijan and Armenia. This also includes relations between Georgia and Abkhazia. The third concerns relations between Turks and Armenians.

Here he is referring to Armenians in the diaspora, to whom Turkey would be willing to grant Turkish citizenship to facilitate their *return home*. Was he sincerely willing to solve the problem or totally cynical in recalling the long experience of Turkish rule over Armenians? The question remains. On 23 April 2014, on the eve of the annual genocide commemoration day, an official statement in eight languages on the Turkish prime minister's website declared the following: '[Turkey] wants the Armenians who lost their lives in the circumstances that marked the beginning of the twentieth century to rest in peace and expresses condolences to their grandchildren.' For the first time since the birth of the republic, the head of the government, the most important figure in the state, offered his condolences to the Armenians. While the community and the international press at first welcomed this unprecedented step in favour of the truth, most commentators pointed out issues still unresolved: the word 'genocide' was not included, nor even the object of condolences. For the past ten years, Turkish rhetoric has been about 'shared suffering' of the Ottoman Empire subjects, placing the fate of Armenians on the same level as that of the 'Muslim' victims of massacres in the Balkans and the Caucasus. Even if optimism invites us to believe in the good intentions of the Turkish power, pessimism sees a well-oiled rhetoric of sophisticated negationism – as evidenced by Erdoğan's statement of 28 April 2014, just five days after he offered his condolences. In an interview broadcast on the US television channel PBS, he said: 'This is no genocide, it can't be, because if it was a genocide, how could there still be Armenians living in the country [in Turkey]?'

In a column entitled 'Armenians and Turks, Let's Have a Dream Together', published on 29 May 2014 in the French daily *Libération*, a Turkish–Armenian collective including, among others, three initiators of the petition asking for 'Pardon to the Armenians', Cengiz Aktar, Ali Bayramoglu and Ahmed Insel, 'shared the dream that an era of peace between Armenians and Turks begins with respect for history and one another'.[2] All the respect, dignity, truth, justice, law and humanity contained in universal consciousness was part of this shared dream reminiscent of Luther's values. The signatories denounced 'the political culture of the Republic of Turkey [who] wanted to cover up a founding crime by blocking access to the past, thereby preventing a

[2] List of signatories: Samim Akgönül, Cengiz Aktar, Aprikian Gorilla, Ariane Ascaride, Sibel Asna, Serge Avedikian, Ali Bayramoglu, Marie-Aude Baronian, Rosine Boyadjian, Anaïd Donabedian, Denis Donikian, Claire Giudicenti, Nilüfer Göle, Robert Guédiguian, Defne Gürsoy , Ahmet İnsel, Ali Kazancıgil, Jacques Kebadian, Ferhat Kentel, Raymond Kévorkian, Michel Marian, Gerard Malkassian, Umit Metin, Aravni Pamokdjian, Manoug Pamokdjian, Izabelle Ouzounian, Armand Sarian, Betül Tanbay, Gerard Torikian and Serra Yılmaz. *Libération*, 29 May 2014.

sustainable rule of law to be built'. They paid tribute to the ongoing academic research work conducted in Turkey on 1915 and all those who act for the duty of memory of the Turks. And they presented their shared dream in those words:

> The memory of Turkey, through its stories and places, honors the Armenian dead by admitting that they have been victims of genocide and by pointing out the men and ideas that have initiated it. Its history books and street names praise the Righteous who saved Armenians rather than the rulers and executors of their annihilation. It gives back to the Church and to the Armenian foundations the monuments that they once owned. Turks and Armenians are proud of this common heritage.

> They also dreamed of Turkish citizen equality between Muslims and Christians who would all have access to public office in a country where justice would work with independence, impartiality and transparency.

> To symbolize this new era, they dreamed that both countries share the mountain of Ararat spiritually. Mount Ararat is transformed into a large natural park, declared World Heritage Site by UNESCO and opened as a sort of free zone cared for by Turks and Armenians together as a showcase. The place of the origins of humanity becomes a beacon of peace.

To achieve this, they wrote, 'only a word of truth from the authorities of the State will help heal the wounds of memory. Only a strong word of invitation will make it possible to create new links with towns and villages whose names cannot be heard without feelings of sorrow. And "the water will again dig its furrow," as Hrant Dink said'. This totally Dinkian text, both in substance and form, was published a few weeks after a colloquium at Saint Joseph University in Beirut, where most of the signatories gathered around the theme 'Rebuilding the Memory Dialogue: The Turkish-Armenian Case'. Never had a text signed by Turkish intellectuals so strongly taken into account the Armenian plea. Never before had Turkish intellectuals openly mentioned the Turkish–Armenian co-management of Mount Ararat. For the first time, Turkish intellectuals were calling for the unconditional opening of the border with Armenia. As we know, all thoughts are permitted in a dream – even the unthinkable. Since then, however, the position of the state has shown no sign of change. Why is it so difficult for Turkey to recognize it?

Why does Turkey refuse to acknowledge the genocide?

There are a number of reasons behind the Turks' choice to remain in a position of denial. Taner Akçam, in his preface to the work by Laure Marchand and Guillaume Perrier, reveals some,[3] to which we may add a few more.

---

[3] Laure Marchand and Guillaume Perrier, Preface, *La Turquie et le fantôme arménien, sur les traces du génocide, Solin, Actes Sud* (Paris, 2013).

The first reason is as simple as it is frightening: a majority of Turks are convinced that a genocide never occurred. They believe that the events of 1915 were the result of war operations that caused military and civilian casualties on both sides and all fronts. What is more, they believe that the Turks suffered the most from these horrors; that they are the victims of a 'genocide' perpetrated by Armenians. For the Turks, Armenians use these 'events' in a spirit of revenge and hatred against them while, at the same time, they have the blood of innocent Muslims on their hands. As for the international community, they are seen as exploiters of these sad facts whose aim is to weaken Turkey and prevent it from progressing at its own pace. This is indeed a case of absolute denial, yet it is the feeling that prevails today in Turkey.

The second reason is that recognition of the genocide by Ankara would delegitimize the Kemalist revolution and negate Turkish identity. To recognize the crime of 1915 would be to question national self-aggrandizement, the glue that holds together a single and indivisible Turkish nation and the very definition of Turkish collective psychology. The unity of the Turkish nation is the result of a long process of homogenization which, to free itself from any contingencies, jettisoned all that could hinder its achievement. But this argument does not withstand the reading of history, because on several occasions, in the interviews he gave to the press and in his writings, Kemal recognized the 'shameful act' of the CUP against Armenians. The expression was even borrowed by Taner Akçam as the title of one of his books. So then, if the national hero of the Turkish Republic personally recognized the heinous crime of 1915, why is it so difficult for his successors to admit it 100 years later?

The third and perhaps most problematic reason for Ankara is that recognition of the genocide would involve compensation and indemnification of a moral, material, political and territorial nature and of inestimable value. One may recall that the Turkish bourgeoisie of the 1920s was born from the spoliation of Armenian property. Ankara prefers to deny the genocide rather than initiate a process leading to the payment of compensation, even loss of territory – an issue that falls under international law. For the ARF and other political forces, reparation could make it possible for 'Armenian lands to be returned to their legitimate owner, the Armenian people'. In reality, this great claim is far from being shared by all Armenians. The Republic of Armenia recognizes Turkey's current borders but leaves lingering doubts as to bilateral normalization negotiations – a nebulous concept which fuels Turkey's denial. Recognition of the genocide would challenge the logic of Lausanne and awaken the ghost of Sèvres.

The fourth reason is historical. To recognize the genocide would be to admit that Armenians, these early Christians, were present in Eastern Anatolia before the Turks. Given the fact that Eastern Anatolia is the cradle of Turkish identity, we can better understand why the Ottoman authorities did everything to preserve this territory that threatened to be split by the Armenians with Russia's 'support'. The Turks have half-heartedly become accustomed over time to losing provinces in the Balkans, Africa or the Middle East, but the case of Eastern Anatolia is more sensitive. Moreover, the territorial recapture launched by Kemal at the end of the First World War began with Eastern Anatolia before reaching the European façade of a dying Empire. Eastern Anatolia is historical Armenia, the eastern extension of today's Republic of Armenia. Indeed, this historical argument should not be overlooked, as evidenced by Turkey's will to impose the expression 'Ancient Turkey' when it funds or participates in exhibitions on ancient Anatolia, as was the case in 2013 at the British Museum; the term did not fit any geographical reality since Turkey did not appear in Western Asia until the eleventh century. A collective of associations, the Forum of Armenian Associations in Europe, advised by Claude Mutafian, expressed their concern to the prestigious institution. After a few exchanges, Angela Smith, the director of the Middle East Department at the museum replied that she had renamed Room 54 'Anatolia and Urartu, 7000 to 300 BC'.

Another sociological reason refers to the direct relationship between Armenians and Turks, therefore to one's perception of the Other. For the Turks, recognition of the genocide would amount to considering Armenians as their equals. However, in history as in the Turkish collective unconscious, Armenians are at best a dominated people, at worst a people who must disappear. The scornful term 'son of an Armenian' or 'giaour', associated with infidels, refers to the notion of traitor to the nation. Today, in the press and public debates, suggesting any kind of affiliation with Armenians is still the preferred way to denigrate individuals, even going as far as attributing Armenian roots to President Abdullah Gül on his mother's side.

There is also a reason related to the rapport between the West and Turkey. At the time, Armenians were considered as the most Westernized minority in the Ottoman Empire. But Constantinople was very dependent on the European powers. By massacring Armenians, the Turks got rid of those who recalled them to their dominated status vis-à-vis the Concert of Europe. Recognition of the genocide would be a reification of these representations of Western domination over the Turks.

There is also a temporal and psychological reason. Since 1915, a lot of water has flowed under the bridge. Does it really make sense to recognize a crime a century after the fact? After all, this challenge to the history of the Turkish people has not stopped five generations from living peacefully. Is it really necessary to stir up the past? Why put the blame for these events on the new generations who are totally innocent? Turkey calls on the international community to turn the page of the past and look to the future of Turkish–Armenian relations. In an article published in the journal *Studies in Contemporary Genocide* in 1998, Akçam discusses this desire to forget:

> I would characterize amnesia as a social disease in Turkey [...] I hereby maintain that the 'wish to forget history' is directly related to the genocide of the Armenians. [...] It is incumbent upon us to 'remember' a reality that was treated in our history as a non-event [...] and to assign to it the proper significance. But what shape can or will this recovered memory take? [...] A start can only be made by way of discovering the meaning of belonging to the perpetrator group and of bearing collective responsibility'. 'The [Turkish] republic [...] believes that the entire dismal image can be suddenly erased and that the Turks can thus be delivered from a nightmare, from an extremely dangerous, fatal illness.

Thus, he continues, the genocide has plunged Turkey into a 'black hole', a social pathology that renders society psychologically incapable to emerge from a 'coalition of silence' and concludes that 'the difficulty we have in our country with speaking about the Armenian issue lies within this existence–non-existence duality'.

Finally, one last reason completes the formation of this 'black hole' in Turkey. A signatory to the Convention for the Prevention and Punishment of the Crime of Genocide of 1948,[4] Ankara recognized the genocide of the Jews and is well aware of Nazi barbarism. To this end, recognition of the Armenian genocide would mean being aligned with the Nazi genocide perpetrators. Turkey refuses such association and rejects any comparison between states and genocidal policies in the twentieth century.

The stakes of Turkish–Armenian normalization

If the Turkish–Armenian problem is so sensitive and raises so many concerns beyond the two peoples, it is because of its multidimensional vectors that range from global geopolitics to relations between national memories. The first pertains to the victory of memory and history. In this globalization, which unifies minds and links national historiographies, memory and history have become the stakes of power. The Islamic shift in Turkey in 2002 and the independentist shift of Armenia in 1991 had the merit of inciting Turks and Armenians to reflect on their conception of memory – a failing memory on the Turkish side and an atomized memory on the Armenian side. These two shifts have highlighted the two peoples' histories – increasingly analysed by their scholars, who are trying to write in parallel. This double clash of bothersome memories with national histories in the global arena has allowed Armenians and Turks to distance themselves from a natural tendency to think of the Other negatively. Turkish society has gradually freed itself from its amnesiac representation of the tragedy of the Armenians and integrated otherness into its efforts of introspection. Armenians are gradually becoming familiar with Turkish society and no longer see it as the archetype of anti-civilization. Henceforth, it may be posited that a fraction of Turkish society recognizes Armenians as their equals, just as some Armenians might consider the possibility of sincere communication with the Turks. The first inter-social exchanges and the entry of national histories into globalization have freed them from memory blindness. This liberation has allowed them to no longer see history simply as a whole but to consider that breaks in history are necessary to overcome differences.

---

[4] Here are the first three articles plus the sixth article of the Convention.

Article I: The Contracting Parties confirm that genocide, whether committed in time of peace or in time of war, is a crime under international law which they undertake to prevent and to punish. Article II: In the present Convention, genocide means any of the following acts committed with intent to destroy, in whole or in part, a national, ethnical, racial or religious group, as such: (a) Killing members of the group; (b) Causing serious bodily or mental harm to members of the group; (c) Deliberately inflicting on the group conditions of life calculated to bring about its physical destruction in whole or in part; (d) Imposing measures intended to prevent births within the group; (e) Forcibly transferring children of the group to another group. Article III: The following acts shall be punishable: (a) genocide; (b) conspiracy to commit genocide; (c) direct and public incitement to commit genocide; (d) attempted genocide; (e) complicity in genocide. Article VI: Persons charged with genocide or any of the other acts enumerated in article III shall be tried by a competent tribunal of the State in the territory of which the act was committed, or by such international penal tribunal as may have jurisdiction with respect to those Contracting Parties which shall have accepted its jurisdiction.

The second issue relates to the nature of the Turkish–Armenian dispute. Are we facing a religious conflict? Armenian history has long experience of submission to Muslim powers (whether Arabic, Persian or Turkish). It has more or less adjusted to this guardianship and has sometimes showed an adaptability that has given it enough autonomy to express the qualities of its people and ensure the protection of its cultural heritage in 'Muslim lands'. Turkish, Ottoman or Republican history, on the other hand, never experienced physical domination, except for a few years after the First World War – but it was a military, temporary domination. To overestimate the religious nature of the Armenian–Turkish conflict is an expression of historical narrowmindedness. To underestimate it is to forget that the Ottoman Empire and the Muslim states that stemmed from it have always placed religion at the heart of their social cohesion. At the time of the revolutionary movement, the Armenian socialist parties (ARF and SDHP) never gave their fight any religious purpose. They proved by their alliance with Muslim parties that they could make peace in the Caucasus (1905), in Iran (1906–1907) and in the Ottoman Empire (1908). They also expressed their solidarity with the Turkish and Kurdish peasantry, perceived as a social class and not as religious groups. This was with two reservations, however: on the one hand, the Armenian parties have never broken with Christian traditionalism and a large number of fedayis, beginning with Andranik, have always equated the enemy with Turks, Kurds and Muslims without distinction. On the other hand, the parties' strategy was confusing when they fought to overthrow the regime of the sultan and that of the caliph (Abdul Hamid II) – considered at the time as the highest religious authority of the Muslim world. The ARF structured its actions against the temporal power of the sultan. Is it possible to separate the temporal from the spiritual in the Ottoman chief of state? What could stop the Turks from interpreting the anti-Hamidian policy as an indirect way of attacking the symbol of Muslim power?

At the time of the Haitadist Cultural Revolution, the Armenian parties insisted on reaffirming their loyalty to the older generations, emphasized their secular dimension and staged a universalist, socialist and internationalist position to ensure the safety of the Armenian communities in the Arab States of the Near East. But this secular approach was not in tune with the religious reading of the Ottoman power. Therefore, the Armenian Patriarchate was the only Armenian authority recognized by the Ottoman power. When the Empire went to war in November 1914 and ordered the massacres of Armenians, was it not in the name of jihad? Prior to this conflict, Christians made up 30 per cent of the total population of the Ottoman Empire. After 1923, they were only a few thousand. Was this not the result of a Turkish-Muslim homogenization process?

Taner Akçam and Hamit Bozarslan have studied this religious aspect in the formation of the modern Turkish Republic in depth. 'The Republic', Akçam writes, 'has been constructed upon the removal of the Christian population living in Turkey, in other words, the annihilation of an existing entity'.[5] In this Islamist Turkey, once

---

[5] Ibid.

nostalgic of the Ottoman past, the AKP government, as Bozarslan explains, attempted to align with Ziya Gökalp, a theoretician of the CUP and pan-Turkism at the turn of the twentieth century. But in all three cases, the Gökalpian approach reopened old wounds. Kurds do not recognize themselves in Turkishness. Christians and Alevi cannot naturally identify with Sunni Islam. And Turkish society, for the most part, does not stand by Western values. Relations with Armenians are caught between these three tensions. Post-Kemalism, however, has reopened the inter-religious debate involving Armenians who, as a Christian minority, expect to acquire new rights, particularly since the opening of Turkey's accession negotiations to the EU. If Westernization means adaptation to European standards of freedom and universal human rights ethics, Armenians around the world could eventually move freely on Turkish territory and open branches of their associations in Istanbul, Erzurum or Van. Except Erdoğan has taken the issue of the genocide into a religious sphere. In 2009, when Turkey was to host Sudanese President El Bashir, prosecuted by international justice for genocide, the head of the Turkish government declared that 'a Muslim can never commit genocide'. The same year, he denounced 'a form of genocide' committed by China against Muslims in Xinjiang, showing his solidarity with the Uyghurs, one of the main liberation movements with headquarters in Turkey. How should these statements be interpreted? Should we see a desire to 'denominationalize' the theme of genocide in the name of pan-Islamism or a way to trivialize the term 'genocide' in Turkey, thus preparing people to ask for the Armenians' pardon?

If there is pardon, would it have the same value in Turkey as in Christian ethics? Presumably not: as Bozarslan explained, the request for 'pardon', as interpreted in Islam, can only be to God (*tawba*) and to Muslim believers. Relationships with non-Muslims are governed – we are here in a post-Qur'anic codification – by submission alone. Therefore, what is the value of the 'request for pardon' launched in December 2008? Incidentally, why did the initiators of the petition not use the word 'state' in the text? Did they want to exempt it from any responsibility? Did they intend to de-judicialize the Armenian Question? Why does the text include the phrase *Mendz Yeghern* translated as 'Great Catastrophe' to speak of 1915? Is it a reference to an expression used by Armenians? In that case, it would have been better to use the correct translation of *yeghern*, which is 'carnage', because 'catastrophe' in Armenian is *aghed*. Is it an attempt to depoliticize the Armenian Question by associating it with a natural cataclysm, thus excluding all human responsibility? Indeed, despite its symbolic significance, the text is filled with grey areas.

The third stake promotes regional integration. The Turkish–Armenian rapprochement could allow the opening of the border and should bring about a revival of economic activity beneficial to all the states and populations in the region, starting with the cities of eastern Turkey such as Van, Kars, Iğdır and Diyarbakır, whose authorities are urging the Turkish central government to open the border with Armenia to take advantage of the flow of goods and people. For Yerevan, this would open up the Armenian market and bring the South Caucasus republics closer to the EU, provided that Turkey's accession negotiations come to an end. Furthermore, Armenia is not hostile to the integration of Ankara, perceived as an act of democratization in Turkish society. As former Armenian Foreign Minister Vartan Oskanian said: 'I am not hiding the fact that for Armenia, the ideal neighbour would be a European Turkey.'[6] The Armenian–Turkish protocols are potentially encouraging for regional integration by opening the lines of communication. Armenia, for example, has renovated the railway line connecting Gumri (Armenia) to Kars (Turkey), despite the freezing of protocol negotiations.

The normalization of Armenian–Turkish relations also conditions the future of Haitadism in two ways. On the one hand, in the context of negotiations, Armenians are invited to reflect on the consequences of a possible recognition of the genocide by Ankara. What would the Armenians ask if this encouraging prospect came to fruition? At the time of writing, no one can answer this question, given the absence of any tangible official document – apart from the slogan about material and territorial reparation, whose principle is endorsed by traditional Armenian parties. Indeed, why would Turkey recognize this genocide if the consequences lead to territorial diminishment? Ankara justifies its reluctance by referring to these partisan programmes and the equivocal message of the Armenian state on the subject. Officially, the Republic of Armenia has no territorial claim against Turkey. It will comply with the treaty of Kars, as recalled by Vartan Oskanian, in an interview held on 25 January 2005 with the Turkish daily *Zaman* and moral recognition of the crime would be fully satisfactory. But, from one Armenian president to another and from one Armenian tendency to another, variations emerge. Robert Kocharyan set out on a different path from that of his predecessor Levon Ter-Petrosyan who, without underestimating the stakes of recognition of the genocide, would have been satisfied with a simple admission from Turkey. Kocharyan, however, was ambiguous about the management of a post-recognition and the lack of clarity continued with his successor owing to the absence of a normative framework governing the common border, even if the treaties signed in 1921 are still in effect. Yet, considering that the Republic of Armenia was not a signatory to these treaties, it cannot express more than a formal declaration of recognition of Turkish integrity. In other words, if Kocharyan could guarantee that recognition of the genocide by Ankara would not involve any territorial claim by Armenia, he could not guarantee that the Armenian state, let alone his successors, would not reopen the case during talks on reparation. In his turn, a few days before announcing the freezing of the ratification of the protocols, on 12 April 2010, President Sargsyan visited the grave of American president Woodrow Wilson in Washington and paid warm tribute to the one who 'revived our dream of the lost homeland [. . .] Ninety-five years after [the genocide], states and international organizations, including the United States, continue to act faithfully to that commandment of President Wilson of prevention of the crime of genocide and compassion through recognition of the Armenian genocide'. Never since the fall of the First Republic of Armenia in 1920 had an Armenian president endorsed so clearly the symbol of the Great Armenia of Sèvres in an official speech, without forgetting to highlight the link between genocide and sovereignty. Other organizations have since called on Armenians to change their concept and shift from a claim of recognition claim to one of reparation. While the Collectif 2015 réparations association

---

[6] Interview with Vartan Osakian, 'Le rêve arménien' (2004) 104 *Politique Internationale* 97–107.

was created in Paris in 2004, by citizens of European states brought together by Kegham Kevonian, president of the Land and Culture Organization, the ARF, through the voice of the international leader of their Armenian National Committee, Guiragos Manoyan, declared: 'We believe that Armenia is unable to make such demands today, But this doesn't mean that it will be unable to do so tomorrow. So it must not take any steps that would hamper or inhibit us tomorrow.'[7] This is a sign that the body of the Haitadist Cultural Revolution is still in motion. The International Center for Transitional Justice (ICTJ), based in New York, has also been seized upon by the TARC to shed light on a possible link between recognition of genocide by Turkey and territorial reparation. In its conclusions, the ICTJ specified that there is no automaticity and added that if the term 'genocide' is pertinent for the tragedy of 1915, Armenians cannot use it to voice 'a claim of a legal, financial or territorial nature against Turkey', since the 1948 Convention does not include provisions leading to retroactive application of its content. This preventive measure, taken by experts in search of a balance, clears the way for Turkey, now freed from the burden of reparation, to abandon its position of denial. The Armenians have objected, stating that the decision of the ICTJ does not come under international law, that it is part of a legal debate and they continue to think, as does former Armenian ambassador, Ara Papyan, director of the think tank Modus Vivendi in Yerevan, that international law is far from being categorical on the subject and that the door of negotiation and therefore of claims, remains open.

The other effect on the future of Haitadism is systemic; because the Turkish–Armenian rapprochement allows it to be based in its two original spaces: the Caucasus and Anatolia. This is a novelty in the Haitadist system, deprived of a land base in Ankara since 1920. The first signs of reintegration into the Turkish space are already apparent. In addition to the commemorative events of the genocide on 24 April in major Turkish cities, in the presence of an increasing number of Armenians of the diaspora, the projects of co-operation between the Turkish and Armenian civil societies are multiplying in various places. Armenian organizations based in Europe, such as the AGBU, are preparing to open branches in Istanbul. A delegation of the ARF led by Mario Nalbandian, vice-president of Socialist International and Guiragos Manoyan met on 12 November 2013 with a delegation of the Kurdish party BDP (Peace and Democracy Party) led by its head of international affairs Nazmi Gür, a Turkish Parliament representative. This was the first bilateral meeting on Turkish soil since 1923. Both parties spoke of Kurdish–Armenian collaboration in 'Western Armenia and Kurdistan', according to the terminology of the Dashnak press release and of the national democratic aspirations of the two nations and they reminisced about the past Kurdish–Armenian alliance of 1927 between the nationalists of the Khoyboun League and the ARF against Kemalist Turkey. Finally, in this logic of relocating Haitadist organizations in Turkey, the ARF sent several activists to Hemshin villages in order to awaken national awareness and regenerate Armenian identity in the field. These manoeuvres were reminiscent of the days when the Dashnak 'kordzich' political leaders

---

[7]   Emil Danielyan, 'Dashnaks Fear Genocide Recognition "Without Consequences"', Radio Free Europe/Radio Liberty, 4 April 2005.

were sent to the eastern vilayets of the Ottoman Empire at the turn of the twentieth century to train the Armenian people for the revolution.

Last, but not least, the Armenian–Turkish dialogue has a global geopolitical dimension, to the extent that normalization would favour a relocation of the South Caucasus on the Western side. In their strategy of penetration of this sensitive region, Americans and Europeans come up against Russia, which relies on Armenia to block the global opening of this space. Breaking this deadlock would imply that Westerners are heavily involved in the Armenian–Turkish dialogue. This is the context behind the US State Department's support of the TARC's mission and normalization protocols. In addition to the recovery of the South Caucasus and its wealth, Westerners would finalize the transformation of this former Soviet cul-de-sac into a crossroads of globalization. However, Russia has not remained inactive. Since the turn of the century, Moscow has laid the foundations for a strategic partnership with Turkey and strengthened its relations with Iran. These three former imperial powers are planning to build a multipolar world in which the South Caucasus, not Europeans and Americans, would be under the influence of these emerging powers. Since 2008, Russia has embarked on four projects for deactivating the US presence in the South Caucasus. First, by signing gas agreements with Baku to prevent Caspian gas from going to the European markets. Second, Russia's victory in the Five-Day War against Georgia demonetarized the country as a regional hub and facilitated the coming to power of Mikheil Saakashvili's opponents in Tbilisi. In addition, Russia is trying to impose its leadership in the co-chairmanship of the Minsk Group over Nagorno-Karabakh. Finally, it initiated the rapprochement between Turkey and Armenia in 2008 to prevent the Americans from taking over the issue of the opening of their common border. This is why Russia has no interest in the United States recognizing the genocide of the Armenians. It would be a victory for American soft power and would upset Russian interests in the region. One question remains: the outcome of the Iranian nuclear issue. If the international community and Iran reach an agreement, the resulting peace process is likely to turn the South Caucasus into a global economic hub, a prospect that would put Turkey and Armenia at the forefront of beneficiaries. Assuming, of course, that the two states decide on a roadmap towards peace.

Actors involved in the dialogue

Several trends have emerged on both sides. On the Armenian side, the first is that of the *optimists*. Embodied by former President Levon Ter-Petrosyan, the movement became known in the 1990s and through the Armenian delegation of TARC whose members all worked under his responsibility. It has support in the diaspora, from such figures as the historian Gerard Libaridian in the United States and the philosopher Michel Marian in France. They have regular exchanges with Turkish society and consider this dynamic of dialogue as a way to complement intergovernmental relations. They want to end the isolation of Armenia and invite Yerevan to distance itself from Moscow. Their demands are moral, democratic and peaceful. The second movement is that of the *pragmatists*. Led by the Sargsyan-Nalbandyan duo, this trend is responsible for the

Turkish–Armenian protocols and considers that any litigation about the past can be settled around a table. Pragmatists play the card of economic development and took a major risk in accepting the principle of a commission of historians in charge of examining the past. They also seek to break the Turkish–Azerbaijani alliance. They defend a strategic and economic approach to normalization. There is also a third trend: the *sceptics*, made up of the two major organizations of the diaspora (ARF and AGBU) supported by former president Robert Kocharyan. Since the Armenian–Turkish question affects the security of Armenia and because the balance of power is a priori favourable to Turkey, the cost of the dialogue seems too high to be satisfied with an ill-defined discussion. According to this trend, Turkey unilaterally decided to close its border with Armenia. It is therefore up to Turkey to reopen it unconditionally. The group is not opposed to dialogue with Ankara, but refuses any process that casts doubt on historical truth. Its claims involve financial (AGBU), political (Kocharyan) and territorial (ARF) reparation. There is one last trend, that of the *hostiles* who are against any exchange with Turkey. It is a minority in the institutions, but it is, to some degree, popular in society, especially in the diaspora. It preconditions any dialogue with Ankara on recognition of the genocide, which it considers improbable given that Turkey is stronger economically today and has become considerably closer to other emerging powers (China, Russia) and is therefore less inclined to acknowledge its past.

On the Turkish side, three trends have emerged. First there are the *traditional deniers*. For this majority nationalist group, Turkey has not committed any crime. The trend, which is believed to be close to the nationalist Ergenekon network, dismantled by the AKP government and currently on trial for conspiring against the state, is against the reopening of the border with Armenia. For this group, the Armenians killed many Turks as part of an international plot against the Ottoman Empire. There are also *modern deniers*. This trend recognizes the reality of the massacres of Armenians and favours the formula 'events of 1915' formalized in 2009 by the board of national education to qualify the genocide. It considers, however, that the Turks also suffered during the First World War and thus calls for the respect of a 'just memory'. This dark page of the past should not poison bilateral relations in the name of peace and development. It is not up to politicians to investigate history. This trend hides behind Articles 301 and 205 of the Penal Code, which penalize any person who attacks the dignity of Turkey. Finally, the third trend is inspired by the ideas of Hrant Dink. Originating in civil society, it has taken hold of history to include 1915 in the public debate. It initiated the rapprochement with the Armenians and took essential measures to bring down the Armenian taboo in Turkey. This trend is grouped under the banner of the People's Democratic Party (HDP), which has a parliamentary group in the Turkish National Assembly but whose main leaders are now in prison accused by Erdoğan's government of 'treason' and 'terrorism'.

Which Modus Operandi?

In its contemporary history, Turkey, whether imperial or republican, has systematically blown hot and cold in its relations with the Armenians, as evidenced by the following examples. In 1878, the Ottoman Empire signed the treaty of Berlin and pledged to implement reforms in the eastern vilayets; the Sublime Porte replicated with the massacres of Armenians in 1894. In 1895, Sultan Abdul Hamid II promised the Concert of Europe he would put in place the said reforms; he responded with new massacres until 1896. In 1908, the Young Turks revolution rehabilitated the constitution and called for the equality of the peoples of the Empire; in 1909, the Ittihadist government organized the Adana massacres. In 1912, Constantinople signed the European Agreement on Reforms in Eastern Anatolia and approved the sending of two European Commissioners to the six Armenian vilayets; three years later, the CUP government launched its plan to exterminate Armenians. In 1918, the Ottoman Empire recognized the First Republic of Armenia but waged an almost permanent war until its fall. In August 1920, the Ottoman Empire signed the Treaty of Sèvres, which imposed in writing the creation of a Great Armenia; in 1923, the Republic of Turkey replaced the Treaty of Sèvres with the Treaty of Lausanne. In 1991, Kemalist Turkey recognized the young Republic of Armenia; in 1993, it unilaterally closed its border with Yerevan. On 10 October 2009, Turkey and Armenia signed the normalization protocols; that same evening, Turkey set conditions to their ratification. In April 2014, Erdoğan, in an apologetic gesture, offered his condolences to the Armenian descendants of the victims of 1915; in May 2014, he declared that there never was a genocide. This list of examples of a 'one step forward, two steps back' approach could be continued indefinitely. On a global scale, the Turkish Ministry of Foreign Affairs acts as the main player in this *danse macabre* by putting pressure on the foreign media, publishing houses and the political class of the states and by facilitating the creation of levers of influence abroad, such as the Institut Bosphore in Paris. Because it is the most exposed to the pro-Armenian lobby in the world, this ministry is a fortress of state negationism. This may also be thanks to the high price it paid for this denial, with the loss of about 50 diplomats felled by Armenian terrorism during the years 1970–1980 whose faces are exposed at the entrance of the ministry's headquarters in Ankara.

On the Armenian side, the technique used by the negotiators is rather one of diplomatic solos. The Armenians of the Caucasus have always excluded from negotiations with Turkey their brothers of the Ottoman Empire as well as those of the diaspora. In 1896, Russian Dashnaks in Geneva negotiated with the sultan's missionaries an agreement to stop assassination attempts in Constantinople. In 1907, the Dashnaks of the Caucasus signed an agreement with the CUP at the Paris Congress. In 1918, Caucasian Armenian ministers negotiated with the Talaat-Enver-Pasha triumvirate the nature of bilateral relations. In the 1920s, two Caucasians (Roupen Ter-Minassian and Simon Vratsian) participated in the negotiations within the framework of the 'Prometheism' project, the anti-Bolshevik group also comprising Azerbaijanis and Turks. Finally, in 2009 the authorities of the Republic of Armenia negotiated and signed the protocols with Turkey. The diaspora Armenians hardly tolerate the supremacy of the Caucasians, which has always proved to be unproductive – and they let it be known, as demonstrated by historian Vahakn Dadrian, who, during public interventions, recalled that he never stopped telling Yerevan about the need for Ankara to negotiate with the Armenians of the diaspora. Despite the Nagorno-Karabakh war, the 1988 earthquake and the economic difficulties resulting from the collapse of the

Soviet Union, the Armenian authorities have never thought of launching a major consultation with Armenians worldwide to present Turkey with a list of grievances. As long as Turkey does not give up its favourite dance and Armenia does not stop playing its favourite solo, there is no point in waiting for an unblocking of the Turkish–Armenian peace process, impaired as it is today by a significant deficit of trust.

A failure of peace protocols

There is always something good to be gained from a peace initiative, especially when it is prepared by the international community. But the two protocols for restoring bilateral relations that were signed on 10 October 2009 ultimately failed.

How were they designed? The initiative was exclusively Russian. From 23 to 25 June 2008, a few months after Serzh Sargsyan's controversial election as head of Armenia, the new head of state went to Moscow to meet, among others, his newly elected Russian counterpart Dmitry Medvedev and the Russian prime minister, Vladimir Putin. On 23 June, Sargsyan participated in a meeting of Russian businessmen of Armenian origin where he announced that he would invite Turkish President Abdullah Gül to attend the Armenia–Turkey football match in September 2008 in Yerevan on the grounds that 'there should be no closed borders between two neighbouring states in the 21st century'. On 9 July 2008, in a *Wall Street Journal* column, Sargsyan announced that he was 'ready to talk to Turkey'. 'As president of Armenia, I take this opportunity to propose a fresh start – a new phase of dialogue with the government and people of Turkey, with the goal of normalizing relations and opening our common border', he added. 'There is no real alternative to the establishment of normal relations between our countries', he then said, before acknowledging that: 'There may be possible political obstacles on both sides along the way. However, we must have the courage and the foresight to act now. Armenia and Turkey need not and should not be permanent rivals. A more prosperous, mutually beneficial future for Armenia and Turkey and the opening up of a historic East–West corridor for Europe, the Caspian region and the rest of the world, are goals that we can and must achieve'. Thus, it is from Moscow that this 'football diplomacy' was initiated and it was through an influential American newspaper that Sargsyan set out his intentions. For the Armenian president, his Turkish counterpart was one of the first heads of state to congratulate him after his election on 19 February 2008. Admittedly, he added that 'Erdoğan suggested that the doors are open to new dialogue in this new period'. In an effort to break any US initiative on the Turkish–Armenian border, Russia had indeed moved closer to Turkey by exerting pressure on Yerevan to make this gesture of openness. For Moscow, after the failure of the TARC – launched by David L Philips, director of the Program on Conflict Prevention and Peace-building in the United States, a think-tank close to the US State Department – leaving this field of Turkish–Armenian normalization open to a new American adventure was out of the question.

The Russian intervention was not enough, however, to explain this attempt at pacification. Sargsyan followed his own logic. The incidents of 1 March that marred his controversial election – resulting in the deaths of ten people including eight demonstrators – placed Armenia under significant international pressure. Indeed, in the name of democracy and human rights, Westerners severely condemned the clashes of 1 March and demanded that the Armenian government open an investigation into these tragic events. The sanctions procedure in the European Parliament and the Council of Europe was set in motion in Brussels and Strasbourg based on the various post-election reports of the 19 February ballot observation missions, who denounced election irregularities without recommending challenging the results, according to the usual formula. While the Russians sought to fully take over Armenia, Westerners intended to encourage a kind of colour revolution in Yerevan and unblock the Nagorno-Karabakh peace process for which they consider the position of Armenia too strong and the source of the diplomatic impasse.

In making this invitation to Abdullah Gül, Sargsyan killed three birds with one stone: he responded favourably to a Russian request and nipped in the bud any hint of a colour revolution in Yerevan; he pulled the rug from under the Westerners who intended to reprimand his country by inviting them to support the perspective of a Turkish–Armenian peace; and he thwarted Azerbaijan, Turkey's ally, inasmuch as the goal of reopening the border with Turkey would allow it to put an end to the policy of strangulation of Armenia. While Turkey was initially suspicious, it finally encouraged this rapprochement, because the dialogue with Armenia was part of the 'zero problems' at the borders strategy valued by the AKP. Ankara relied on the support of foreign governments to play the card of a Turkish–Armenian dialogue to the detriment of genocide resolutions. Finally, as a member of the Minsk Group, Turkey hoped to be able to use this normalization to obtain Yerevan's final recognition of its border and unblock the negotiations around Nagorno-Karabakh. Russia was also triply satisfied: it took control of the Turkish–Armenian border, made the initiative part of its partnership policy with Ankara and took advantage of Azerbaijan's dissatisfaction with Turkey by signing several gas agreements with Baku. Westerners were also happy. They saw the Turkish–Armenian rapprochement to be a result of Turkey's EU accession negotiations; as a way to free themselves from the pressure of the pro-Armenian lobby on the recognition of the genocide which thwarted their relations with Ankara; and also the possible opening of the South Caucasus. Thus 'football diplomacy' allowed Sargsyan to obtain the international legitimacy he had been longing for since his 2008 election – when no Western head of state had congratulated him.

Only two actors remained opposed, for different reasons, to any process of normalization: Azerbaijan and its President Ilham Aliyev, on the one hand, who ordered the slowing down of energy negotiations with Ankara and encouraged the diversion operations conducted by his army along the line of contact with Nagorno-Karabakh. The ARF, on the other hand, caught unaware by the Armenian initiative since the theme of rapprochement with Turkey, had never been mentioned during the presidential campaign of 2007 by the then candidate Sargsyan. Had it been the case, the ARF would not have signed the March 2008 coalition government agreement with the Republican and the Prosperous Armenia parties. The initiative also undermined its lobbying in Europe and the United States over the genocide, as Turkey's EU accession process showed some signs of tension and was becoming less and less popular among the 27. Finally, it hampered the future of Haitadism's claim: the ARF left the government on 27 April 2009, owing to 'insurmountable differences' and, five days after, under the mediation of Switzerland, Armenia and Turkey announced at midnight on 22 April the existence of a 'road map' called the 'Bern Declaration'. As part of the opposition, the ARF led the international 'no' movement.

What exactly was this declaration, made public as the 'Protocol on the Establishment of Diplomatic Relations Between the Republic of Armenia and the Republic of Turkey' during the night of 31 August/1 September 2009 and scheduled to be ratified in Zurich on 10 October, four days before the second leg of the Turkey–Armenia football match on 14 October in Kayseri? The two states undertook to 'respect and ensure respect for the principles of equality, sovereignty, non-intervention in internal affairs of other states, territorial integrity and inviolability of frontiers'. They pledged to maintain 'an atmosphere of trust and confidence between the two countries that will contribute to the strengthening of peace, security and stability of the whole region, as well as being determined to refrain from the threat of the use of force'. They confirmed 'the mutual recognition of the existing border between the two countries as defined by relevant treaties of international law'. They also recalled 'their decision to open the common border' and agreed to 'implement a dialogue on the historical dimension with the aim to restore mutual confidence between the two nations, including an impartial scientific examination of the historical records and archives to define existing problems and formulate recommendations'. To implement all measures, the two states created an inter-governmental commission. A timetable was also proposed for the first measures. These protocols 'shall enter into force on the same day, i.e. on the first day of the first month following the exchange of instruments of ratification between the two Parliaments'. Thus, Turkey and Armenia decided to engage in transitional justice. These protocols gave three indications and raised three questions.

First, the Armenian–Turkish border was recognized by both states. Yerevan vouched for the territorial integrity of Turkey, which would amount to ratifying the Treaty of Kars signed on 13 October 1921 between Ankara and Moscow, who then represented the three Transcaucasian republics only recently Sovietized. Would this mean the end of the dream of a Great Armenia? Without doubt, unless in the context of bilateral negotiations the two parties agreed on derogations about the co-management of Mount Ararat and retrocession of the territories of Kars and Ardahan. Who would imagine that Turkey could accept to lose part of its territory, or even place it under co-management with Armenia? As for Yerevan, the opening of the border would be very favourable in terms of strategy vis-à-vis Azerbaijan, politically for the dividends it would draw from this rapprochement with the EU and economically owing to the reduction of import costs and free movement of goods. For the 'no' side, this first step was a mistake: to recognize the border with Turkey as a prerequisite for negotiations was to shoot oneself in the foot and cut short any benefit that could be claimed at the end of the talks. In other words, one should not give up one's main asset until the final phase of negotiations.

Second, the two states agreed to analyse the 1915 issue by accepting the principle of an 'intergovernmental sub-commission to implement an impartial scientific examination of the Turkish historical records in the presence of international experts'. Did this mean that Armenia agreed to question the reality of the genocide? Indeed not and the Armenian negotiators retorted to their opponents that they were simply repeating the proposal of former Kocharyan in his response to Erdoğan about the creation of a commission of historians, when he stated that he 'preferred that an intergovernmental commission be created' in which 'historians may be invited to participate'. This was tantamount to placing the responsibility on the ARF: were they not part of Kocharyan's government when he sent his response to Ankara? Yet the president's letter was ambiguous. Another interpretation, different from Edward Nalbandyan's, could be suggested. Indeed, Kocharyan may have meant that the 'intergovernmental commission' was not a commission of historians. It was not entitled to open the case of 1915 but its members could include historians by training. Moreover, the recognition of the genocide by the Parliament of Catalonia in Spain (26 February 2010), the Foreign Affairs Committee of the US House of Representatives (7 March 2010) and Sweden (11 March 2010) seems to prove, according to Sargsyan, that this strategy was the right one.

Third, the frozen conflict of Nagorno-Karabakh was only referred to in the form of allusions to 'regional stability', 'refraining from the use of force to settle regional disputes', 'respect for territorial integrity' as well as 'principles and norms of international law'. However, for the ARF, the phrase calling on both parties 'to respect the principles of equality, sovereignty, non-intervention in internal affairs of other states, territorial integrity and inviolability of frontiers' amounted to saying that Armenia would respect Azerbaijan in its current configuration – in other words, that it would give up Nagorno-Karabakh. This was a maximalist interpretation, according to some, considering that the phrase was, in fact, a summary of excerpts from the UN and OSCE charters signed by the two states and that there was nothing compromising for Nagorno-Karabakh. There was a blurring of boundaries, according to others, because this phrase may have referred as much to the unity of Azerbaijan as to that of the island of Cyprus – in which case one may wonder why Turkey approved it. In the event that the ARF's fears were justified, why did Baku refuse to support the protocols, considering them as 'contradictory to the national interests of the country', according to a statement issued by the spokesperson of the Ministry of Azerbaijani Foreign Affairs, on 1 September 2009?

Why did they fail? Six reasons come to mind. The first is that Turkey had assumed for too long that the negotiations concerning Nagorno-Karabakh were in a dynamic of resolution, failing to understand that it was necessary to approach in pacific terms to make progress in the Caucasus.

The second reason was that to satisfy its Azerbaijani ally, Turkey had back-pedalled since the signing of the protocols by indexing their ratification to 'the withdrawal of Armenians from the territories of Azerbaijan'. On the day of signing, Turkey did everything to ensure that Foreign Minister Ahmet Davutoğlu make a statement to this effect. His Armenian counterpart protested and threatened to withdraw from signing the document. It took all of Hillary Clinton's diplomatic skills to defuse the situation and let the ceremony progress without further announcements. Armenia has consistently condemned these preconditions and recalled that the two situations (Armenia–Turkey and Nagorno-Karabakh) are two different issues. The United States, Russia and France have agreed – though Washington and Moscow follow Paris's intermediate position, suggesting that the unblocking of one or the other issue would have a positive influence on the other. So, it is no coincidence that the three foreign ministers of the states co-chairing the Minsk Group attended the protocol signing ceremony on 10 October 2009 in Zurich.

The third reason for the failure was that on 12 January 2010 the Armenian Constitutional Court declared the conformity of the protocols with an attachment that stated that they could not be the object of contradictory interpretations. According to paragraph 5 of its decision,

> the Constitutional Court finds [...] that the content of the protocols signed between the Republic of Turkey and the Republic of Armenia cannot be interpreted or applied in the legislative process and application practice of the Republic of Armenia as well as in interstate relations in a manner that would contradict the provisions of the Preamble to the Constitution and the requirements of paragraph 11 of the Declaration of Independence of Armenia.

Paragraph 11 of the Declaration of 23 August 1990 provides 'for the Republic of Armenia to lend support to the efforts for international recognition of the 1915 Armenian Genocide in Western Armenia and Ottoman Turkey'. This is tantamount to saying that the Constitutional Court granted the legislator full responsibility to interpret these texts, while implying that to subject them to ratification by the Parliament was likely to provoke a *casus belli* given that their content – nebulous where history was concerned – could be the object of contradictory readings. After this decision, Sargsyan considered that it was up to Turkey to show its goodwill. 'Now, the ball is in Turkey's court', Hillary Clinton said on 5 July 2010, during a visit to Yerevan as part of a tour of the South Caucasus.

Another reason: the secrecy of the negotiations and the cynicism of both governments, who kept their respective publics uninformed about the exchanges, weighed heavily in the rejection of protocols on either side of the border and even beyond. Indeed, the diaspora, as the repository of the tragedy of 1915, was offended to learn, on the day before the anniversary of the genocide, of the decision of Sargsyan and Nalbandyan to make public the Bern Declaration. Instead of learning their lesson after the diaspora's reaction, Sargsyan and Nalbandyan repeated the experience by announcing the content of the protocols in the middle of a summer night. If the 'no' movement was popular among the diaspora communities and if it went as far as inciting hostile demonstrations against Sargsyan during his visits between 2 and 6 October 2009 in Los Angeles, Paris and Beirut, it was as much a protest against the form as it was against the substance. Sargsyan had just lost the support of public opinion.

The fifth reason was that the Armenian oligarchs, usually so quick to pressure parliament for special favours, had shown no real support here because opening the border could put an end to their monopoly advantage and jeopardize the sale of their goods on the Armenian market to the advantage of cheaper, better-quality Turkish goods.

Lastly, the content of the documents left too much room for interpretation and indeterminacy. Interpretation, because Turkey hardly waited after the protocols had been signed to suggest, with reference to the sensitive matter of the past, the creation of a 'joint commission of historians', while Armenia spoke of an 'intergovernmental sub-commission'. When the two signatories of a text do not reach a decision on its official content, why expect public opinions and observers to agree? Indeterminacy, because there was no deadline for the ratification of the texts by parliament. The only date mentioned was that of the obligation of both parties to open their border: within two months of the ratification of the protocols. In other words, as long as the Turkish and Armenian legislators had not ratified the texts, the border would remain closed and the protocols would remain topical. Under the circumstances, Armenia decided, on 22 April 2010, to freeze the protocols on the grounds that 'the Turkish side refused to ratify the documents without pre-conditions and within a reasonable time'. This decision came ten days after the meeting between Sargsyan and Erdoğan, at a summit on nuclear security in Washington. To make it clear that the momentum of hope was no longer there, the protocols were removed from the agenda of the Armenian Parliament in 2016. Admittedly, Sargsyan needed to satisfy a condition set by the ARF to encourage its return to the government.

Who was responsible for this fiasco? Essentially, the Turkish and Armenian states – in two main areas. First, they intervened much too early in the process of rapprochement between the two peoples and, without communication being relayed to society at large, the two diplomatic cohorts set about the Turkish–Armenian normalization process with too great an alacrity: so much so that former US ambassador to Armenia John Evans was right to say in an interview with *Nouvelles d'Arménie* magazine that 'when establishing such protocols, both sides had eyes bigger than their stomachs'.[8] Moreover, Russians and Americans rushed negotiations on this issue and refused to see the obvious obstacles along the way. For the Russians, it was necessary, at any cost, to save the text and prevent any alternative offered by the Americans. For the Americans, it was vital to obtain the ratification of the text to have something to show for these very meagre diplomatic years (2009–2010).

Today, the protocols are obsolete but not yet officially dead. Turkey knows all the advantages it can derive from diplomacy of empowerment towards the United States and rapprochement with Russia. Armenia, for its part, wants to show goodwill, to the point of playing with fire on occasion and wants to believe that by announcing the freezing of protocols it will gain the respect of the international community at the risk of losing that of its civil society, better positioned than the state to defuse tensions and prepare the ground for true normalization.

Fostering inter-social dialogue

Giving a social perspective to the bilateral dialogue seems essential today, so that the states can intervene with strong social backing. The first manifestations of the Armenian–Turkish dialogue came from civil society. In the 1980s, Jean-Claude Kebabdjian, director of the Centre de Recherche sur la Diaspora Arménienne (Armenian Diaspora Research Center) initiated a debate between Turkish and Armenian civilians in the diaspora. A pioneer in inter-social debates and marginalized

---

[8] Interview with John Evans, *Nouvelles d'Arménie Magazine*, October 2013, pp. 38–39.

by the rest of the diaspora in France, Kebabdjian showed courage when he made contact with Ragip Zarakolu and the human rights circles in Ankara at a time when Kemalist Turkey was recovering from the coup and the power of the military. Inter-social debates have the advantage of not being driven by an interest in power. Detached from the notion of power, the inter-social debate places the parties on an equal footing, while the political debate is based on the principle of the hegemon. Therefore, it can address all subjects, whereas the political debate may privilege certain elements and neglect others in the name of the reason of state. Finally, the inter-social debate has the capacity to democratize minds, which states, in this case Turkey and Armenia, cannot necessarily do. The social approach may rely on the intercultural debate where artistic and cinematographic creation promotes peace – as bicultural documentaries such as Serge Avedikian's have demonstrated for some time.

This approach avoids applying conflict resolution models to the Armenian–Turkish case. For example, former French prime minister Michel Rocard's suggestion to draw inspiration from the Franco-German model to resolve the Armenian–Turkish question proved historically gauche. France and Germany are two old powers and, in contemporary times, one has never been absorbed by the other. Furthermore, as tragic as Franco-German relations were in the past, they have never been categorized as genocide; disputes took place in a climate of interstate wars. The Armenian–Turkish case is the opposite. The Armenians were under Ottoman rule in a single state, the Ottoman Empire. There was no Armenian state before 1918. The Armenian–Turkish problem does not fall within the scope of interstate warfare; it is the result of a dominant–dominated relationship. A culturalist approach versus the principle of a ready-made external recipe for conflict resolution promotes an inter-social approach, whereas the export of the Franco-German resolution technique puts politics at the heart of the problem.

Likewise, the creation of a commission of historians as a cure-all would be misguided, because it would amount to politicizing history, even instrumentalizing research through history. When the TARC commissioned the ICTJ to determine the genocidal nature of the massacres of the Armenians, the Turkish delegation fully joined in the request. But as soon as the ICTJ reaffirmed, in its conclusions delivered in February 2003, that the events perpetrated against Armenians included all four elements of the crime of genocide as defined in the Convention of 9 December 1948 on the Prevention and Punishment of the Crime of Genocide, the Turkish delegation immediately left the TARC.

An approach that deals frankly with the events of the past should help restore confidence, as well as open, transparent and inclusive diplomacy to ensure the involvement of public opinion and the media coverage of the issue. In this logic of confidence, it is particularly important to pacify the relations between the Dashnaks and the Turks. Indeed, the memory of the ARF–CUP agreement of 1907 is still very much alive. The Dashnaks are aware that the alliance was unnatural and, nearly 100 years after the agreement, they are willing to redeem themselves. The assassination of Talaat Pasha and other senior genocide leaders between 1921 and 1923 was not enough to lessen their feeling of guilt. This explains their maximalist position and the fact that they have embodied the 'no' to the protocols and the establishment of an open, uninhibited diplomacy. Attention to the choice of places where bilateral meetings are held is also an important factor, based on inter-social logic. The geography of dialogue must be associated with a chronology of peace so as not to choose sensitive dates reminiscent of painful events on both sides. For many Armenians, it was an unforgivable mistake to make the Bern Declaration public in 2009 on the eve of 24 April. The signing of the Zurich Agreement on 10 October, three days after the disastrous Kars Treaty of 1921, was again an aberration. What sort of message did Erdoğan send to the Turks and the Armenians when he destroyed the monument of friendship between Turkey and Armenia on 24 April? On the other hand, when 36 Turkish intellectuals and elected representatives asked the Royal Danish Library in 2012 to call off Ankara's 'alternative exhibition', 'in response to' an exhibition on the genocide of the Armenians, which had taken place shortly before in Copenhagen, their initiative was part of citizens' practice of respect for history. In their letter, they denounced 'the blatant denial' of the Turkish government and the complicity of Denmark, who 'supports their policy of suppression and intimidation [...] a support equivalent to supporting a regime of apartheid'. Indeed, for the signatories, 'it is incorrect to suggest that two different views of what happened in 1915 are possible'.

To neglect the importance of symbols (numbers and places) does not promote normalization. For example, when the TARC consisted of ten members including six Turks and later 12 members including eight Turks, the initiators of the project committed a faux pas by not respecting equality. According to Dorothée Schmid, research director at the French Institute of International Relations and head of the 'Turquie contemporaine' programme: 'When you hear a Turk speaking with [...] an Armenian, you understand by listening to him that he feels in a position of weakness. He does not see himself as dominant at all.'[9] This is typical of representations of the Armenian–Turkish relationship. Face to face, the Turk feels dominated by the Armenian. He even feels a kind of fascination with him: the Turks, who waited until the end of the nineteenth century to project themselves into a process of national homogeneity, are indeed intrigued by the issue of a stateless people able to preserve their language, religion, culture and identity during centuries of domination. But in the context of missions, Armenians feel dominated by the Turks because history is written by the victor and the Turks had dominated the Armenians for centuries.

The debate about the Turkish unsung heroes who acted 'justly', those high-ranking Ottoman officials who refused to execute CUP orders to massacre the Armenians – Celal Bey, governor of Konya, Hüseyin Nesimi, sub-prefect of Lice or Mustafa Aga, Mayor of Malatya – is also very important. Recalling this history is to turn one's back on the message of the state and appropriate positive figures to protect society as a whole from guilt. Furthermore, the 'de-Ittihadization' of the Turkish public space – including the streets and schools named after or the mausoleums constructed in memory of those responsible for the genocide – could aid in ending the denial of history and the veneration of the executioners.

[9] Interview with Dorothée Schmid, 'Les Turcs sont en train de recomposer leurs Etats-nation' (The Turks are recomposing their nation-states), in *Eurasie*, 'au coeur de la sécurité mondiale' (at the heart of global security), under the direction of Gaïdz Minassian, *Autrement*, Paris, 2011, pp. 79–87.

In 2014, on the initiative of eight organizations – four Armenian, four Turkish – from Turkish and Armenian civil societies grouped in a consortium sponsored by the European Union (EU), a normalization programme was set up.[10] This programme is part of a non-political approach supporting the promotion of economic, cultural and educational exchanges to facilitate access to information between the two civil societies. For the first time, Armenian–Turkish dialogue has a balanced approach, reasonable objectives and egalitarian operation. The foundations of normalization are thus being laid. Soul-searching has begun in Turkey, without challenging the infamous national pride. Why should this feeling of pride express itself exclusively in a context of conquest and power? Is it so difficult to recognize the genocide of the Armenians? Hope has given way to desolation in Turkey since the aborted coup of 2016. The democratic debate no longer exists, the regime of Erdoğan has taken control of all the levers of power, locked in the opposition and imposed a constitution – following a controversial referendum – formatted for him.[11] Turkey, now open to the West, is entering a dictatorial process, according to even the most sceptical observers and cultivates a fear that pushes the country beyond reason; the ban in public spaces of the words 'Armenian genocide' and 'Kurdistan' also testifies to the evaporation of sense. Yet, should we not feel in Turkey a pride in admitting it and helping every Turkish citizen understand that they are not *personally* responsible for the genocide, not to make them feel indifferent, but to free them from guilt. Turks and Armenians must find the resources to confront the demons of the past and thus achieve peace: first for themselves, then for their respective states and, finally, for the international community.

---

[10] Civilitas Foundation, Eurasia Partnership Foundation, Public Journalism Club, Regional Studies Center for Armenia; Anadolu Kültür, the Economic Policy Research Foundation of Turkey, the Helsinki Citizens' Assembly and the Hrant Dink Foundation for Turkey.
[11] The 'yes' vote won by 51.41 per cent – a small victory mainly because the Turkish Electoral Council, mostly led by the supporters of the Erdoğan regime, validated the ballots not bearing an official stamp in favour of the 'yes' camp. There were 2.5 million of those ballots.

12

Encouraging the Commitment of the International and Academic Communities

In the world arena, the question of the Armenian genocide faces a major handicap. At the time, international law was not equipped to deal with crimes against humanity, nor was the international system integrated as it is today. Attempts to legislate international justice universally failed after the First World War. As the former President of the French Constitutional Council Robert Badinter reminds us, from a legal point of view 'the expressions "crime against humanity" and "genocide" have only existed since the Second World War'.[1] Historically, the first use of the expression 'crime against humanity' outside a treaty context dates back to a joint statement of the members of the Triple Entente (Britain, France and Russia) of 24 May 1915, condemning the Ottoman treatment of the Armenians. The phrase was used again in 1920 in the Treaty of Sèvres, by which time the genocide of the Armenians had been proved, recognized and condemned, even though the concept failed to gain traction legally because it lacked a basis in international law. Despite the fact that the inventor of the concept of genocide, the Polish jurist Raphael Lemkin, conceived this term partly in relation to the record of the Armenian massacres and the fact that the courts-martial that tried and condemned the Unionists in 1919 and 1920 are widely known, the Armenian demand for recognition has continued to face a legal vacuum. The trials of those responsible for the genocide do not fall under international law, but Ottoman domestic law that has been invalidated by Republican Turkey. European law has reintroduced the genocide of Armenians into its legislative arsenal and individual states have done the same in their domestic law. But since international law depends mainly on states, the international system has never had reason to consider the 'law of genocide' in the case of Armenia. With the entry of the Republic of Armenia into the international order in 1991 and with Turkey watching to ensure that its past crimes remain away from the public agenda, the recognition of genocide remains in limbo, caught between the political and the legal.

The difficulties surrounding the question of genocide are not limited to legal inadequacies. The question also lacks a grand design, a perspective of inclusion in which

---

[1] Robert Badinter, *Fin des lois mémorielles ?*, Le débat, Gallimard, no 171, September–October 2012, pp. 96–100.

all actors can find a place – the Armenian and Turkish states, their civil societies and the international community. The real issue is that all parties must cease to conceive of genocide recognition as the only factor to take into account regarding the normalization of relations between Turks and Armenians and the resolution of the Nagorno-Karabakh conflict, a Caucasian expression of the ethnic conflict. Genocide and the Nagorno-Karabakh war are linked in that they are part of the past (the fall of empires), the present (questions of global security) and the future (peace). They are all the more linked as Armenians draw the lesson from comparative studies of the genocide that they are no safer in the twenty-first century – with a repeat of crimes against humanity in the Caucasus, where massacres of Armenians have been a repeated occurrence since the fall of the Soviet Union. To make sense of the 1915 genocide is to act to prevent a repeat of ethnic cleansing in Nagorno-Karabakh. Indeed, according to Eric D. Weitz, the most recent historical studies 'very firmly place the genocide of the Armenians in the wider history of the Balkans, Anatolia and the Middle East from the last third of the nineteenth century until the First World War'.[2] By its history and geography, the logic of the genocide was dependent upon the upheavals in the Balkans, even if the crime was carried out between Anatolia and the Caucasus via the Near East (Deir ez-Zor). In this way, all four regions were linked in a single crime scene familiar to the populations of these regions who know what happened in 1915. The European Union (EU), the United States and all the states that arose from the ruins of the Ottoman Empire would be well advised to seize the theme of genocide and make it the basis for regional peace and dialogue between peoples. If Europe can see in the Holocaust a fundamental element of peace on the continent, it is possible to do the same for the Armenian genocide. By promoting such a prospect for peace, the international community would contribute to removing state violence from regional structures, including from Armenia. By promoting such a perspective for peace, it would invite a Turkey now in step with its history to positively use its power in the service of democracy and stability in that country's unique space, straddling three continents. Finally, the international community would fulfil its responsibility regarding the prevention of crimes against humanity.

Such a global perspective requires a total commitment to globalization, including the removal of barriers and historical obstacles that slow the development of national groups active in international relations. This vital expansion by autonomous groups within sovereign states has been accompanied by explosive developments in social sciences and a massive disruption of the architecture of international systems. It is within this dynamic of global history that the study of the Armenian genocide, beyond mere comparison with other holocausts, provokes a renewed interest, echoed by historian Jay Winter when he declares that 'today the Armenian genocide is at the center of the history of the Great War. Why? Because this is the extreme case of the war against civilians'.[3] Turkish dissident historiography is part of this global approach.

Globalization has also led to a re-centring: Westerners no longer hold the pen that writes the book of world history, nor do they hold the reins of power exclusively,

---

[2] C Delacroix, F Dosse, P Garcia and N Offenstadt, *Historiographies I et II, concepts et débats,* Gallimard, Paris, 2010 vol 2, pp. 1046–1061.

[3] Interview with Jay Winter, *Le Monde,* special issue, February–April 2014, 96–97.

since competition from emerging states raises the matter of solidarity among the downtrodden in the fight against Western (Euro-American) dominance. The former imperial powers are left to claim another source of history that is based on the grandeur of a now sublimated imperial past and a revisited present. Today's Turkey remembers the Ottoman power and seeks to impose its own conception of global history by confronting its own ideas, which it does not see as negationist, with those accepted in the West concerning the reality of the 1915 genocide. This forward movement in global history fits well with the challenge of normative developments by emerging powers in terms of human rights, interventions, civilian protections, peace and genocide and so forth. Turkish official historiography is rushing dangerously in this direction. It is understood that the Armenian Question has become a global issue. Today more than ever one cannot dissociate the international from the inter-social, legal politics and national interconnected history. It is in this global context that legislation challenging the genocide has its place and can be considered. Not to understand this complementarity between international relations and the social sciences is to fail to grasp the systemic breakdown of world architecture, one whose maintenance is increasingly slipping from Westerners' fingers and those who are destined to legislate for and safeguard the edifice of universal norms. Not to see this shift and by so doing to limit the criminalization of genocide simply to 'memorial laws' is to restrict the field of history to a national sanctuary. It also misuses a formula that concerns real international issues. Above all, in the globalized world of the twenty-first century this expression still has meaning.

When security does not accord with peace

The security of the Armenian people, as we have already said, is the priority of the Republic of Armenia and its diaspora. Wedged between two negationist states – a post-Kemalist Turkey and a racially discordant Azerbaijan – the Armenians are consumed by this security logic that links the memory of the dead to the climate of hostility which characterizes their environment. Everything suggests that nothing can relieve their anxieties as long as the international community does not energetically stand behind the democratization of the South Caucasus, for example by publicly denouncing unacceptable remarks. It was not until 2012 that the international community became aware of the racist drift of Azerbaijan. In that year, Hungarian President Viktor Orban authorized the extradition to Baku of Azerbaijani officer Ramil Safarov, who had been sentenced by a Hungarian court to life imprisonment for the assassination by beheading of Armenian lieutenant Kourken Markaryan. Both had attended a NATO language workshop in Budapest under the auspices of NATO's Partnership for Peace programme in February 2004. The Azerbaijani government gave assurances to Budapest of his continued detention, but Safarov was pardoned by President Ilham Aliyev and acclaimed as a 'national hero'. At liberty, he was also promoted to captain, receiving a number of material advantages (apartment, car, etc.). The international media immediately denounced this political scandal, while some heads of state simply expressed disappointment upon learning of the presidential pardon. The rare international condemnations of this racism are inversely proportional to the long list of public or official anti-Armenian acts by Turks and Azerbaijanis. If Armenians are not themselves totally free from racist or xenophobic remarks against Turks and Azerbaijanis – and it is absolutely necessary to condemn them for such – these official or public expressions have never reached the threshold of hatred and intolerance that prevails in Baku or Ankara. These claims are confirmed by reports from international NGOs. If any nationalism can be said to be potentially racist, those of Azerbaijan and Turkey are particularly virulent towards the Armenians.

The international community cannot, of course, denounce all official racist announcements. But where the international community is directly involved, its responsibility is engaged. This is so in the Armenian–Azerbaijani case in which France, Russia and the United States, three permanent member states of the Security Council and co-chairs of the OSCE Minsk Group, have agreed to mediate the Nagorno-Karabakh conflict to bring peace to the South Caucasus. Defined in 1992 by the Conference on Security and Co-operation in Europe, the Nagorno-Karabakh conflict has taken on a global dimension. By 'global', we must understand that it affects different transnational processes and that it concerns the social integration of societies, with social and historical consequences.

Since the signing of the ceasefire in 1994, the peace process has been deadlocked. Armenians and Azerbaijanis do not agree on anything and both states have embarked on a mad arms race. But security is not peace. It is at best a 'negative peace', according to Johan Galtung's definition, namely a configuration that 'results in the absence of war, conflict and repression and is defined only by emptiness and opposition to war', while 'positive peace' means 'the presence of both a state of harmony and a dynamic process for a culture of peace to replace a culture of violence and develop lasting harmonious relations imprinted with humanity'.[4] The South Caucasus is still far away from achieving this. The main creators of this 'negative peace' are Armenia and Azerbaijan, but they are not the only guilty parties. The other powers who share a responsibility include Russia, who, as the former tutelary state for both states, is keen to promote equilibrium between Armenia and Azerbaijan by facilitating their rearmament by delivery of military equipment to Yerevan under the CSTO agreement and via arms sales to Baku. When the co-chairmanship of the Minsk Group asks 'the Presidents of Armenia and Azerbaijan to prepare their people for peace and not for war', a message that translates on the Russian side into the sale of arms to both parties, any observer is entitled to doubt the *peaceful* character of Russian mediation. The horizon of peace moved a little closer when Armenia decided to join the Moscow Customs Union on 3 September 2013 at the expense of an association agreement with Brussels under the Eastern Partnership of the EU. By choosing the Eurasian Union, Armenia turned its back on European integration, renouncing any ambitions beyond the post-Soviet model of the state. It is within this new strategic context that we must note renewed tensions between Nagorno-Karabakh and Azerbaijan and on the border between Yerevan and Baku.

---

[4] Johan Galtung, *Peace by Peaceful Means: Peace and Conflict, Development and Civilization* (London: Sage, 1996).

Nagorno-Karabakh: A global crisis

Negotiations around Nagorno-Karabakh have progressively deteriorated from year to year, to the point where, between 2 and 5 April 2016, the region experienced what has come to be known as the 'Four-Day War', a conflict initiated by Azerbaijan in which more than 200 people died on both sides. Following a truce brokered by Russia and diplomatic mediation by the Minsk Group, new provisions were adopted – the Vienna and St Petersburg Agreements – which called for an increase in the number of OSCE observers along the border and the installation of a video surveillance system for the front line. Armenia immediately accepted these provisions; Azerbaijan rejected them.

The positions of Armenia and Azerbaijan are, in fact, diametrically opposed in all areas. For Yerevan, it is an infra-state conflict between Azerbaijan and the Armenians of Nagorno-Karabakh, an ethno-territorial and post-colonial type of conflict which calls for the application of a population's right to self-determination. In the circumstances, Armenians were forced to war. They won and Azerbaijan must now bear the consequences. For Baku, the conflict is between two states, Armenia and Azerbaijan and only the principle of territorial integrity can be applied, in accordance with UN Security Council resolutions No 822 (30 April 1993), No 853 (29 July 1993), No 874 (14 October 1993) and No 884 (12 November 1993), which require the withdrawal of Armenian forces from territories under Azerbaijani control since 1993. Yerevan replied that these four resolutions were not conflict resolution documents, but texts aimed at ending hostilities. Thus, for Yerevan and Baku the conflict is not of the same nature. For Armenia, it is part of the traditional liberation struggle against foreign domination. For Azerbaijan, it is a classic conflict of sovereignty between rival states.

De facto independent, the Republic of Nagorno-Karabakh is not recognized internationally, including by Armenia, which opted for a negotiated political solution. Azerbaijan demands an unblocking of the situation by any means, including the use of force, to recover its territories under Armenian control, a threat that Armenia and the Republic of Nagorno-Karabakh have declared themselves ready to defend against, the former vouching for the security of the latter.

In terms of mediation, the Minsk Group troika advocates a compromise built around 14 principles preceded by a preamble with four points: the right to self-determination, territorial integrity, the avoidance of force and equality between communities. Six of the 14 Principles of Madrid were made public in 2007. These are Armenian withdrawal from the seven provinces they control in Nagorno-Karabakh (Aghdam, Fizuli, Djebrail, Ghoubatli, Zanguelan, Kelbadjar, Lachin), the creation of a provisional status for Nagorno-Karabakh, the creation of a corridor connecting Armenia to Nagorno-Karabakh, a commitment to seek a final status agreement based on a popular referendum, the creation of an international peacekeeping mission and the return of internally displaced persons and refugees. Officially, Armenia and Azerbaijan declared themselves unilaterally in favour of these principles. They have since failed to make progress at any of the various summits and meetings organized mainly under Russian auspices but with the full agreement of the United States and France.

The Minsk process has fallen prey to a series of dysfunctions. First, the mediators failed to invite representatives of the Nagorno-Karabakh Republic to the conference, although the republic is frequently consulted by the mediators. While in most post-Soviet conflicts all the protagonists are gathered around the table, the 'HK' file (Haut-Karabakh), as the Quai d'Orsay diplomats call it, is an exception. Azerbaijan formally opposes the inclusion of Nagorno-Karabakh. Yerevan prefers to negotiate for the Armenian point of view, instead of Stepanakert, presenting this as a show of goodwill and despite the fact that of the four UN resolutions concerning the conflict only one mentions Yerevan in the context of 'using its influence' to make the armed forces of Nagorno-Karabakh understand reason. Yet it was the latter that signed the ceasefire agreement with Azerbaijan in May 1994 and which advocated for the participation of all actors as a gauge of dynamic dialogue, stability and appeasement. Second, the absence of civil society as a party to settlement testifies to delays in the democratization of minds. By limiting negotiations to an intergovernmental framework, the parties run a double risk that potential failures will be blamed on the public, thus widening any perceived gaps between governments and societies, who follow the process at a remove via the press. Such a format feeds local nationalisms and creates a climate of suspicion with regard to the authoritarian regimes that are in place. In addition, the lack of clear resolve among members of the work group casts a shadow over the negotiation outcomes. When France and the United States sign the declarations at the end of the NATO summits in which the Alliance recognizes the territorial integrity of the South Caucasus states, they also recall, as co-chairs of the Minsk Group, their commitment to the right to self-determination. Finally, the contradictions among the member countries of the Minsk Group, who on the one hand call the parties to the conflict to prepare their people for peace but on the other hand sell arms to Armenia and Azerbaijan, exacerbate the climate of distrust. This does not help the peace process. Beyond such contradictions, the process is ambivalent, beginning with the six Madrid Principles, which are themselves more a source of tension than of compromise. Will evacuation of the territories be accompanied by a demilitarization of the zone? If so, where will the demilitarized perimeter fall; the current front line or the former Nagorno-Karabakh administrative region? What guarantee of security will be offered to Armenians in the case of unilateral remilitarization of this area by Azerbaijan? What clarification will be needed between the evacuation of territories and the recognition of their status? When will the provisional status of Nagorno-Karabakh be determined? Under whose authority will the corridor connecting Armenia to Nagorno-Karabakh be placed? How will this authority be composed? How will the final status of Nagorno-Karabakh be determined, especially since the principles do not mention the word 'referendum'? Who will participate in this 'consultation respecting the general will'? In Azerbaijan, the constitution stipulates that any change of territory can only take place through a national referendum. Suffice it to say that a 'no vote' will prevail. On the Armenian side, the constitution of the 'Artsakh Republic' (the former autonomous region plus the security zone) has integrated the territories that make up the security zone. When will this consultation take place? Who will compose the international observation mission? According to both sides, neither the co-presidents nor the neighbouring states should be allowed to deploy troops in the region. This means that European countries could deploy forces on the ground, possibly NATO member states. Will Russia accept such a deployment? How will Iran react? Iran has already announced that it will oppose the presence of NATO or foreign troops in the region. Where will this possible observation mission be deployed? Will it be on the current front line or along the boundaries of the former autonomous region? Finally, how will refugee and displaced person status be attributed, despite the fact that within the Soviet Union Armenians from Azerbaijan and Azerbaijanis from Armenia were transferred at will within the single state?

These are some of the questions that revolve around the Nagorno-Karabakh imbroglio. Under the guise of consultation, compromise and the construction of peace, this puzzle is full of contradictions. For today, the Nagorno-Karabakh issue is more of a global than a local conflict, its outcome being associated with external dynamics. Among all the conflicts of the same type in the former Soviet Union, that of Nagorno-Karabakh has a particular status, because the territory borders on a non-member state of the former Soviet Union – Iran – a factor that binds the destinies of the two states. The Armenian diaspora is also directly involved in the development of the province as it is represented in France, Germany, Russia, the United States, Lebanon and Australia. As a result of its tensions with Azerbaijan, Nagorno-Karabakh is also dependent on the energy map of the Caspian Sea and the status of this enclosed body of water. Western companies are doing their utmost to dissuade Baku from taking up arms because they know that if hostilities were to reopen, Armenians would target Azerbaijani oil and gas projects. Moreover, the Five-Day War of August 2008 between Russia and Georgia strongly influenced the negotiations around Nagorno-Karabakh. Three months after the conflict, to restore its reputation, Russia launched a unilateral initiative under the aegis of President Dmitry Medvedev for Armenia and Azerbaijan to speed up the talks. Under his patronage, Presidents Sargsyan and Aliyev met 11 times between 2008 and 2011, while Turkey tried in vain to obtain Russian intercession on behalf of Baku. Furthermore, even if NATO does not interfere directly with this conflict, its strategy of enlargement to the East and its co-operation with the three South Caucasus states is likely to complicate the situation and upset Russia. Finally, any international process evoking the right to self-determination (Kosovo, Abkhazia, East Timor, South Sudan, Catalonia, Scotland) would resonate with Nagorno-Karabakh, not to mention the effects of the Crimean crisis in Stepanakert.

In these circumstances, between complex peace negotiations and global processes that are no less complicated, it is difficult to imagine a resolution of the conflict in the short or even the medium term. Both sides know it and apply different strategies. Armenia insists on the political solution and applauds each and every international declaration in this sense. As a sign of goodwill, Yerevan called for the withdrawal of snipers from the line of contact and has asked the OSCE to take responsibility for it. Azerbaijan, meanwhile, is betting on the end of the status quo. In the name of international law, Baku is demanding the application of UN resolutions, refuses to withdraw its snipers and blocks all OSCE budget estimates that take into account this item of expenditure, as it would then be obliged to negotiate with the Nagorno-Karabakh authorities over this delicate operation, which would amount to a form of recognition. Not to mention that Azerbaijan managed to force the closure of the OSCE office in Yerevan, more than a year after obtaining an office in Baku. Since the office established in Georgia was closed in 2008 following the Five-Day War, the OSCE no longer has any representation in the three states of the South Caucasus, with the exception of observers based in Nagorno-Karabakh.

Since the Four-Day War, Armenia has hardened its diplomatic position and systematically responds to Azerbaijani shootings and incursions. It requires the implementation of the Vienna and St Petersburg agreements to launch concrete and unhelpful negotiations. But Baku does not want to hear about this, because these measures would reinforce the status quo.

In fact, Armenia and Azerbaijan both play the time card. Yerevan is counting on the outbreak of a social protest movement in Baku and a deterioration of its image abroad. Baku, however, is betting on the economic collapse of Armenia. They both blame each other for leading diversionary operations along the line of contact that result in more than 20 deaths per year on either side of the front. Baku pushes the bidding up to question the legitimacy of the 'Republic of Armenia built on former Azerbaijani territories', according to President Ilham Aliyev. Far from being a 'frozen conflict', Nagorno-Karabakh sits awkwardly between impossible peace and improbable war.

The volatility and longevity of the conflict raises two questions. The first concerns how one should approach the conflict. Would it not be possible to settle this dispute if the mediators preferred a technical rather than a social approach? The addition of generic principles rarely, if ever, favours conflict resolution. Hence the second question: if there is no linear model of independence and no more than a normative framework for all conflicts of self-determination, why not allow oneself to be inspired by the micro-states? Such micro-states among the world's five continents number only six (Andorra, Monaco, Singapore, United Arab Emirates, Djibouti, Costa Rica) and the only area that remains closed to this special sort of guiding presence is the former Soviet space. Why should the right to independence of Abkhazia, South Ossetia, Transnistria and Nagorno-Karabakh be considered an aberration, while sovereignty status is granted to Malta or Monaco? The logic of peace sometimes finds its way to exceptional solutions; at other times, it finds peace by default. For instance, Georgia knows that joining NATO will only happen if Tbilisi gives up on the recovery of both provinces. Stuck between several states turned towards the EU, Transnistria could find a place equivalent to that of Bosnia and Herzegovina surrounded by EU Member States (Croatia, Slovenia and Greece) or those in the process of joining (Serbia, Albania and Macedonia). As for Nagorno-Karabakh, its independence would probably only be provisional: a process of integration into the Republic of Armenia would be immediately triggered, which would be neither more nor less than a fidelity to the initial claim of the province, its attachment to Armenia. We are still very far from such a denouement, but the crisis between Ukraine and Russia is forcing Europeans to rethink the ways of peace on the continent.

Russia or the West?

Where do populations of Eastern Europe look if they are settled on the plains that stretch from the Baltic to the Caspian? Do they look to the prosperous European markets or to the old Russian tutelary power? In other words, what is the future for these states located in this maritime arc (Baltic, Black Sea, Caspian Sea) and to whom the Ukrainian crisis is the most pertinent (but also the most dangerous) example for regional peace? This is the rivalry between the Eastern Partnership (Moldova, Ukraine, Armenia, Azerbaijan and to a lesser extent Belarus) of the EU and the Russian Customs

Union. Should we consider the leadership of the old powers as a pledge of maturity against younger states unable to ensure stability and peace, or should we see there a return of the domination of the larger powers? Should we consider the turn of events in Ukraine as an illustration of an increasingly multipolar world, with Russia as a pole of stability? Is Russia a reliable partner or a future enemy power of the Europeans? How should the states concerned behave in this new geopolitical configuration at a time when the United States has decided to shift its strategic centre of gravity from the Atlantic to the Pacific?

All Eastern Partnership states have ventured freely into the post-bipolar world, trying to find their place in the international system. They have more or less identified with the European values of democracy, human rights and market economics, seeing in European integration the salvation of their political transition. It is from this perspective that, a few months after the Five-Day War, the EU, surprised by this flash conflict, signed in Prague the Eastern Partnership with six former Soviet republics in May 2009. Its objective is to stabilize this buffer zone, create a new mode of regulation, improve the governance of these states and link them to European construction. Since then, Brussels has launched negotiations, with the aim of signing association agreements on new political, economic, energy and cultural developments. These exchanges were finalized by an association agreement signed at the Vilnius Summit in November 2013.

The Ukrainian crisis has changed the situation. Russia has promoted its proposed customs union with Kazakhstan and Belarus and is lobbying the partnership states to refrain from entering into association agreements with Brussels. Following the Maidan Revolution of February 2014 in Kiev, Ukraine aligned itself to Brussels, joining Moldova and Georgia in the camp of European integration, while a pro-Russian separatist movement broke out in East Ukraine inspired by the secession of Crimea. Azerbaijan has limited its involvement with the Eastern Partnership since it signed a memorandum of understanding on energy with Brussels in 2006. Belarus quickly joined the Moscow project. Armenia, against all expectations, announced on 3 September 2013 that it would apply for membership of the Russian Customs Union, putting an end to four years of negotiations with Brussels.

The Ukrainian crisis made it clear that the European integration process was not necessarily irreversible and that the parenthesis of sovereign choice opened in 1989 with the fall of the Berlin Wall could be closed. In short, nothing is more uncertain for these countries than their future as sovereign states. How, then, can a state such as Armenia emerge from this game of great power rivalries to impose its own overarching interests?

Since 3 September 2013, Armenia has been faced with new challenges. As a geopolitical challenge, tensions between the West and the Russians have delayed development. As a strategic challenge, the Russian annexation of Crimea and the resulting international condemnation has forced Armenia to take a stand. As a military challenge, the Ukrainian crisis produced a clear rapprochement between Russia and Azerbaijan, reviving fears of a resumption of hostilities in Nagorno-Karabakh. The political challenge, however, translates as opting for the EU and the rule of law, whereas joining the Eurasian Customs Union means remaining within the post-Soviet state model. Economically, Armenia must evaluate the impact of the Customs Union in terms of the transit of Armenian goods through Russia. There is a technical challenge in figuring out how to join the proposed Customs Union when Armenia has no common border with its member countries. Finally, there is the matter of the social challenge: if Armenia were to choose the Customs Union, would that not risk the aggravating emigration issues with Russia?

Among Armenians, history does not repeat itself, but it has an unfortunate tendency to stutter. Indeed, how not to draw a parallel between 1920 and 2013? In 1920, the Dashnak Republic opted for Sèvres as ideal for a resurrected Armenia – a miscalculation that accelerated its collapse. In 2013, Sargsyan's post-Soviet republic decided to join the Customs Union, at the risk of interrupting negotiations with Brussels and losing the confidence of his European interlocutors. A succession of events convinced Sargsyan to readjust his choice, including the announcement by Moscow of new arms sales to Azerbaijan worth more than a billion dollars. Officially, Yerevan played the card of 'both and', signing both the Customs Union and the Brussels Association Agreement. If Moscow did not seem to care, Brussels proved hostile to dual membership. Sargsyan nevertheless continued the European reforms with a view to signing a reduced version of an association agreement. He was counting on support from France and Germany, both of whom advocated for a special status for Armenia under the Eastern Partnership.

To these ambivalent exchanges with Brussels a further source of complication was added for Yerevan: Russia, Kazakhstan and Belarus launched the Eurasian Union in May 2014 without inviting Armenia to join them as founding members. Azerbaijan reportedly sent a letter to the three Eurasian Union capitals urging them to consider Armenia's candidacy exclusively within its internationally recognized borders at the UN. Moreover, the Russian, Kazakh and Belarussian presidents would have given the Republic of Armenia until the end of June 2014 to comply with international law and publicly announce that it would register its membership in the Eurasian Union within its present borders. This was aimed at imposing a customs barrier with the 'Nagorno-Karabakh Republic', thus precluding any possibility of reunification. While Armenia also technically complies with the requirements of the Eurasian Union, the case of Malaysia Airlines Flight 17, shot down over Ukraine on 17 July 2014 by a Russian BUK surface-to-air missile operated by Russian-backed Ukrainian separatist forces, released the political pressure to join the Eurasian Union, while indefinitely postponing Armenia's official entry into the Eurasian club. After more than a year of negotiations, Armenia officially joined the Eurasian Union in October 2014.

Although officially joining the Customs Union, Armenia remained hopeful that it would sign an association agreement with the EU in 2017. In fact, Armenia found itself in limbo, without a plan or a rudder. Since September 2013, state foundations had weakened as the Armenian government moved from the pro-Western orientation of Tigrane Sargsyan to a pro-Russian orientation under Hovik Abrahamyan. Armenian diplomacy was in retreat and security was strained by a succession of incidents on the Nagorno-Karabakh front line as well as in Nakhchivan. Since September 2013, Armenia was no longer only a memory state – but it has become a republic whose future is uncertain on several issues.

It is no coincidence that Russia first put pressure on Armenia and Ukraine to sign the Customs Union agreement. These are the two paths by which Iranian oil and gas could possibly transit if relations between the international community and Iran are normalized in light of the signing of the agreement of 14 July 2015 on the Iranian nuclear programme. However, having been bypassed by pipelines on the East–West corridor in the 1990s, Russia does not intend to miss the opening up of the North–South corridor. In accordance with the Russian-Armenian agreements signed in December 2013, Armenia must apply to Gazprom for approval for any new energy project over a period of 44 years. That said, Iran has signalled through its energy ministry that the Armenian (then Georgian) road is the safest and most profitable option for its gas and oil exports to Europe. So, the United States has invested $180 million in the purchase of an Armenian hydroelectric plant and other countries are trying to move from a fraternal relationship with Armenia to a geo-economic partnership.

In its quest for neo-imperial power, Russia must reckon with Armenia and bring it into its fold. In the Middle East, if the Baathist regime in Damascus were to be overthrown, Russia's only ally would be Armenia. Armenia, however, recalled that its co-operation with NATO was being strengthened. Yerevan even pledged to remain in Afghanistan after the departure of US troops in 2014. Following its experiences in Central Asia, Kosovo and Iraq, Armenia is preparing to send a contingent under the UNIFIL II programme to Lebanon. Since 1991, though, the topic of Armenian sovereignty has never been discussed as much as it has in recent times, with slogans such as 'Armenia is a prisoner of its history' and 'Armenia is a vassal state' – although the question of its independence has been raised yet again after Russia's latest verbal chastisements. Armenian diplomacy is now reinforced by the support of the latest crop of NATO recruits, such as Poland and the Baltic states and also the EU.

The final problem is that Armenian society hardly reacted to Sargsyan's about-face of September 2013. Armenians considered that the relationship with Russia had to be preserved. What would be the good of turning away from Moscow? Georgia and Ukraine crossed the yellow line: the former had two of its regions stripped from the national territory, the second lost Crimea and found its eastern territories tipping into a grey area. To escape such a scenario, it appears that Armenia has only two alternatives. On the one hand, there is the non-peace security approach, whereby Russia considers Yerevan as the hub of its Caucasian policy, without being in favour of opening it up. On the other hand, there is the peaceful but insecure approach that relies on opening up to Iran. In Yerevan, there are already some who imagine Armenia becoming the 'Singapore of the Caucasus', connecting China to Europe via Iran. Yet there may be a third way, beyond the binary of security. If Armenia can engage fully with the new knowledge disciplines, outlined below, there may be a guarantee of a secure peace.

Placing social sciences at the service of secure peace

After Europe and North America, then Latin America, Africa and Asia, it is the turn of the Near East (Turkey) and the former Soviet Union (Russia, Caucasus) to institutionalize subjects such as genocide or post-colonial studies and thereby adopt a global approach to knowledge. The latest volume by Jay Winter, *The First World War*, is considered its first global history. This transnational approach places, at its heart, the issue of the Armenian genocide with its mass violence and forced relocations, whereas until now the international history of the war evoked the tragedy of 1915 as a peripheral event on the secondary fronts of the East. The social sciences, which have become global, deconstruct the Eurocentric vision of the past. Thanks to genocide studies, the 1915 genocide escapes from its national or binational straitjacket and finds its own narrative pace and proper meaning, its own conceptualization. Without the social sciences and globalization, any examination of the genocide would not have emerged from its teleological and political character. This allows us to take a new look at the full range of Armenian historical productions and to insist on a multidisciplinary approach. Today it is not enough to be a historian to describe the history of genocide; one must also be a sociologist, something of a geographer, a lawyer, an anthropologist and a philosopher. Research into the human science of genocide adds depth to the conception of the crime, the strategy of actors and its social dimension. Globalization of the social sciences also fulfils a citizenship function. It provides public opinion with knowledge tools and offers historical and sociological benchmarks that allow individuals to overcome their own demons from the past.

The global shift in the social sciences therefore acts against nationalism and war. Just as a global view struggles against national histories, *connected history* or *cross-history* mocks colonialism and the spirit of Western domination – unless these virtues of global thinking are diverted.

Different stages of the historiography of the genocide

To fully measure this global shift in the evolution of the Armenian problem, we shall first look at the historiographical legacy. In its February 2015 issue, the French magazine *L'Histoire* launched a series on the archives of the first genocide of the twentieth century, leading with an editorial stating: 'The research on the genocide of the Armenians is already 100 years old and yet it is still very young.'[5] Indeed, studies date back to the First World War, but they have really only progressed since the 1980s, with the two main contributions to the historiography of the 1915 genocide by historians Raymond Kévorkian and Richard Hovannisian.[6] To date, studies have far from exhausted the wealth of subjects and materials presented in this tragedy, in the sense that Armenian historiography enjoys certain peculiarities that complicate the researcher's task: the lack of a tradition of sovereignty among the Armenians has mitigated against acts that would be second nature to an independent state, notably the back-up and safeguarding of archives and some form of official record. Stalinism did nothing to support the archiving of primary sources; on the contrary, according to

---

[5] *L'Histoire*, 'Arméniens: le premier génocide du XXᵉ siècle', No 408, February 2015.
[6] *The Armenian Genocide: Cultural and Ethical Legacies*, Richard Hovannisian, ed (New Brunswick, NJ: Transaction Publishers, 2006). 'Un bref tour d'horizon des recherches historiques sur le génocide des Arméniens : sources, méthodes, acquis et perspectives', Raymond H. Kévorkian, 'Se souvenir des Arméniens, 1915–2015, Centenaire d'un génocide' in *Histoire de la Shoah*, No 202, March 2015. See also, Proceedings of the symposium, *L'Actualité du génocide des Arméniens*, *Comité de défense de la cause arménienne* (Créteil: Edipol, 1999) and Nos 177–178 of the magazine *Histoire de la Shoah*, 2003, Paris.

some post-Soviet observers, in the Stalinist 1920s and 1930s, custodians even went so far as to destroy genocide archives and it was only with the resurgence of national memory in post-Soviet Armenia that there was renewed interest in the genocide from an academic point of view. Translating the Armenian language is a second obstacle for non-Armenian researchers. Armenian sources on the massacre have existed since 1915, however, very few people (and these, only Armenians) have had access to or have exploited them. This obstacle course regarding access to documents makes the task of the researcher very complex and gives the feeling that little, if anything, exists prior to the researcher's own work. Yet the archival records are there. To the difficulty of defining Armenian historiography is added another obstacle: the method of writing.[7] Do French or American researchers of Armenian origin write Armenian historiography or do they do write a French or American historiography of the genocide? Ideas, authors and writing methods circulate in Armenia and the Orient and are shared between several powers, this being especially the case in the era of sovereignty since the mid-seventeenth century. Finally, the historiographic interaction between the genocide studies of the events of 1915 and those on the Armenian Question closes this list of peculiarities. Here, it is a matter of continuity that should not be taken for granted and which at the very least deserves further examination.

The historiography of the genocide is initially of a dual nature. On the one hand, there are foreign sources concerning the crime, which are unprecedented in scale and organization.[8] As the international system is not integrated and Kemalist Turkey was triumphant, these foreign sources (both official and fictionalized) have either fallen into oblivion, especially during attempts to create international justice from the treaties that ended the war, or have been classified as ancient history or literature – that is to say, pertaining to the imaginary. On the other hand, there are Armenian sources that stretch from the 1920s to the early 1950s.[9] There is a desire to compile the documents, to leave a written record that consists of the collection of testimonies and memories

[7]　Gaïdz Minassian, *Trois mille ans d'historiographie, marquer le temps et l'espace* (CNRS Editions, 2015).

[8]　Arnold Toynbee, *Les massacres des Arméniens, le meurtre d'une nation* (Payot: Paris, 1916); Johannes Lepsius, *Rapport secret sur les massacres d'Arménie*, Paris, 1918; Henry Morgenthau, *Ambassador Morgenthau's Story*, New York, 1918 translation into French under the title *Memoirs of Ambassador Morgenthau*, (Paris, 1919); *The Trials of the Unionists*, Constantinople; Franz Werfel, *Les 40 jours du Moussa Dagh*, Berlin, 1933 (Paris: Albin Michel, 1936); Paule Henry Bordeaux, *L'immortelle de Trébizonde* (Paris: Albin Michel, 1930); Jacques de Morgan, *Histoire du peuple arménien depuis les temps les plus reculés de ses annales jusqu'à nos jours*, Paris, 1919; André Mandelstam, *Le sort de l'Empire ottoman* (Payot: Paris, 1917); Frédéric Macler and Antoine Meillet, founders of the *Revue des Etudes Arméniennes* in Paris in 1919.

[9]　Sebouh Akuni, *Histoire du massacre d'un million d'Arméniens, Constantinople*, 1921; Aram Andonian, *Souvenirs du génocide arménien*, Boston, 1919 and Official Records regarding the Armenian Massacres, London, 1920. Stepanos Sabah-Gulian, *Les responsables, Jeune Arménie Publication* (Providence, USA, 1916); Zabel Essayan, *Hayg Toroyan, L'Agonie d'un peuple* (Paris: Classical Garnier, 2013); Krikor Balakian, *Le Golgotha arménien*, Vienna, 1922; Alboyadjian; Yervant Odian, *Journal de Déportation* (Marseille: Editions Parenthèses, 2010); Archag Tchobanian, *Histoire des Arméniens de Tokat* (Cairo, 1952); Leo, *History of the Armenians in three volumes*, published 1917–1947; Armenian writers united in the 1920s around the magazine *Menk (Nous/Us)* or elsewhere and all the former leaders of the Armenian revolutionary movement who wrote their memoirs, especially in the magazine *Haïrenik Amsakir* (*MensuelPatrie*), Boston.

referring to the Great Armenian Tragedy (a method characteristic of traditional Armenian historiography), but this is not proper history.

The link between the *Yeghern* (Great Carnage) and the Armenian Question became inseparable only in the 1920s. It became more a matter of demonstrating for the record that Armenians would fight against extermination than a question of explaining the mechanisms of national extermination. The image and memories of the genocide were set – not so the history of the crime, which remained to be written, the times being preoccupied with survival and the ideological struggle between Dashnakism and communism. The publications deal more with the long history of this old civilization than with the crime against humanity itself. Between 1946 and 1949, the works of Nicolas Adonts, René Grousset and Hrand Pasdermadjian raised again the issue of Kars-Ardahan (the Treaty of Kars) and the reestablishment of the international system with the UN as part of a desire to remind the Great Powers of the existence of old questions that remain unresolved.[10]

From 1947 to the 1970s, the Armenian historiography of genocide was progressively divided between a post-Stalinist Soviet–Armenian branch, especially after the fiftieth anniversary of the genocide in 1965 and a branch among the diaspora that was evolving in a democratic context (France and the United States) and was marked by the Nuremberg Trials and the 1948 United Nations Convention on the Prevention and Punishment of Crimes Against Humanity and Genocide. These two currents in Armenian historiography shared a common idea that there should be a continuity between the historiographies of the genocide and that of the Armenian Question.

The Soviet–Armenian branch expanded its work by targeting its attacks on Turkey, a member of NATO. Repeatedly evoking the genocide and liberation of Western Armenia, Armenian historiographers leveraged the political and ideological arsenal of the Soviet Union in the middle of the Cold War, even when by doing so they risked promoting an ethnic approach to criminality. They systematically defended Russia, their 'older sister and protector of the Armenians' and took down anything that was not communist. Soviet Armenia thus acquired instruments for storing memory and a unique proto-history of the genocide, even though these studies seriously lacked rigour. One exception is the *History of the Armenian People*, which was published in the Brezhnev era and whose historiography is authoritative up to the early nineteenth century.[11]

The diaspora community, mainly in the United States, engaged in the creation of university chairs in Armenian studies.[12] In France and the United States, both countries marked by the memory of the Shoah, the first academic studies were published in the

[10] Nicolas Adonts, *Etudes historiques* (Paris, 1948). Hrand Pasdermadjian, *Histoire de L'Arménie depuis Les Origines Jusqu'au Traite de Lausanne* (Paris: Librairie Orientale H Samuelian, 1949). René Grousset, *Histoire de l'Arménie des origines à 1071*, 1947, Paris.
[11] S Eremian, P Arakelian, MS Hasratian, *Histoire du peuple arménien* (Yerevan, 1956). A first edition in Russian was co-authored by P Arakelian, M Hasratian, A Hovanessian (1951). A third edition was published in eight volumes from 1967. It was co-edited by Tz Aghayan, P Arakelian, G Galoyan, S Yérémian, L Khatchikian, A Hakobian and M Nerseian.
[12] *Rethinking Armenian Studies*, (2003) VIII(2) *The Journal of Armenian Studies*.

years 1960–1970 – for example, by Louise Nalbandian, Anahide Ter-Minassian, Ronald Grigor Suny, Arthur Beylerian and Richard Hovannisian,[13] the first three dealing with the revolutionary movement, the fourth with diplomatic history (as a compilation of documents) and the last producing a four-volume history of Armenia, *The Republic of Armenia*, which avoids dealing directly with the history of the genocide while contextualizing the crime. Among these authors there is a desire to go beyond the 1915 turning point to show that there was a before and an after. The link between genocide and the Armenian Question has been made stronger and stronger. It is ideologically even-handed and often borders on the nationalist approach. The great difference between the Armenian and the diaspora branches concerns critical history and professionalization. In Soviet Armenia there was no critical history and historians, aware of the weight of the regime, were not empowered in their work. In the diaspora, although critical history was taking its first steps, young, well-trained historians and professionals remained prone to the temptations regarding the ideologies which are at the root of the process of universalization of Armenian history.

The movement towards openness and empowerment took place nevertheless.[14] To understand this, we need to explore why scholars write in the first place and how an emergent autonomous genocide historiography compares with the historiography of the Armenian Question. Scholars write primarily to inform and convince, using as proof the reality of the crime committed, in accordance with the language of the Convention of 1948. They amplify the arguments of those who defend recognition by European and American legislatures in the face of Turkish denial. It is then that they methodically document the research by turning to the social sciences; the concept of a genocide therefore becomes a research object in its own right. They write to not forget the unforgettable, to ensure that humanity does not accept the impunity of the crime and to better protect the precarious populations of tomorrow, because these stateless minorities are themselves threatened with extinction and assimilation, their rights having been violated by history and for reasons of state. Among other reasons, they also write to show that the Armenians still exist and thus pose a problem to the whole world. They write to remove this problem from its memorial dimension and to escape the darkness of 1915's memories with proven facts, not just the oral testimony of the victimized. Finally, they write to empower the historian's profession.

[13] Louise Nalbandian, *The History of the Armenian Revolutionary Movement* (Berkeley: University of California, 1967). Ter-Minassian Anahide, *La question arménienne* (Marseille: Edition Parenthèses, 1983). Arthur Beylerian, *Les Grandes puissances l'Empire ottoman et les Arméniens dans les archives françaises (1914–1918)*, collection of documents (Paris: La Sorbonne, 1983). Richard G Hovannisian, *The Republic of Armenia*, vol 1 (Berkeley, Los Angeles: University of California Press, 1971). Richard G Hovannisian, *The Republic of Armenia*, vol 2 (Berkeley, Los Angeles: University of California Press, 1982).

[14] Jean-Marie Carzou, *Un génocide exemplaire : Arménie 1915* (Flammarion, 1975). Yves Ternon, *Les Arméniens. Histoire d'un génocide*, Paris, Seuil, 1977. Ronald Grigor Suny, *The Baku Commune, 1917–1918: Class and Nationality in the Russian Revolution* (Princeton University Press, 1972) and *Armenia in the Twentieth Century* (Scholars Press, 1983). Christopher J. Walker with David Marshall Lang, *The Armenians*, London, Minority Rights Group, MRG Report No 32, 5th edn, 1987. Vahakn Dadrian, Histoire du génocide arménien (Stock, 1996).

However noble and innovative such initiatives may be, we must face the fact that our stories are based only on partial use of archives and official documents. Authors recycle ever-more documents published in the years 1916–1920 without bringing in new official sources. These researchers describe the fabric and conditions of the crime – the state of the Armenians of the Ottoman Empire before the war, the Armenian revolutionary movement, the international context. They denounce what is publicly known about the decisions of the Young Turk Party, the Committee on Union and Progress in Constantinople during the war and those responsible for the genocide.

Despite these advances and access to the archives of the Armenian state and institutions, academic research is still in its infancy. Much remains to be done. The years 1970–1980 constituted a transition period of sorts between the relative absence of rigorous work on the genocide prior to 1975 and the proliferation of historical work that followed the collapse of the Soviet Union. To tell the story of the Armenian genocide is to explain how it happened, how it was organized, what methods were used, the difficulties encountered by the Ottoman State, its authors, its geography, the history of its victims, the treatment of children, the forced conversions, the question of women; it is to be interested in the post-genocide period, including the fate of the refugees, the trials of the Unionists and the transition of power from empire to republic. For this we must resort to archives – as Yves Ternon wrote in 1977, 'the archives of the Sublime Porte remain impenetrable to researchers', most notably those of the Triple Alliance, beginning with Germany, Turkey's ally during the conflict.[15]

By the early 1990s, two new factors had appeared in the historiography of genocide: the passage from a descriptive to an analytical approach and the popularization of the comparative studies approach. Thanks to the pioneering work of Richard Hovannisian and especially in France of Yves Ternon, Jacques Semelin, Pierre Vidal-Naquet and Robert Melson,[16] genocide research switched to comparative studies, where events were compared with those of Rwanda and Srebrenica. With this shift, the academic view of the concept of genocide also became more innovative. It became a question of universalizing the Armenian genocide, of removing it from the ghetto and from memory, to identify the specificities of each massacre and to explore potential continuities in the criminal methods used. Then the question became whether, in considering genocide, the historical approach should take precedence over the legal. Revisiting international law on 'crimes against humanity', is it possible to differentiate genocide from a crime against humanity? How should one distinguish intentionality and functional character among the various experiences of genocide, reflecting on the criminalization of the leaders and responsible states? Ought denialism to be punished? What about the role of judges in the trials for crimes against humanity? These questions were asked as early as the 1970s, but overall their answers awaited the development of

---

[15]   Yves Ternon, ibid.

[16]   Yves Ternon, *Empire ottoman. Le déclin, la chute, l'effacement* (Editions du Félin, éditions Michel de Maule, 2002); *Du négationnisme mémoire et tabou* (Paris: Desclée de Brouwer, 1999); *L'Etat criminel, les Génocides au XXᵉ siècle* (Paris: Editions du Seuil, 1995); *Enquête sur la négation d'un génocide* (Marseille: Editions Parenthèses, 1989). Jacques Sémelin, Claire Andrieu, Sarah Gensburger (under the direction of), *La résistance aux génocides, de la pluralité des actes de sauvetage* (National Foundation of Political Science Press, 2008). Robert Melson, *Revolution and Genocide. On the Origins of the Armenian Genocide and the Holocaust* (University of Chicago Press, 1992).

a genocide historiography following the end of the Cold War. Indeed, today, twenty-nine years after the fall of the communist bloc, three major historiographies of the genocide and a different age are face to face. The oldest is Armenian historiography, that of the vanquished who is characterized by the interaction between Armenian Genocide and Armenian Question. We talk about restorative history. The second is international historiography, the one that inherently links genocide to the Great War. It's the universal and cultural history. Finally, the youngest is Turkish historiography "dissident" in the words of Hamit Bozarslan[17] in relation to the history of the conquerors of peace in 1923, Turkey. The studies of this "marginal" school, according to Edhem Eldem's formula[18], completely correspond to the canons of research, rid of the mantle of official historiography, namely of negationism. What has happened over a century? How do these three branches of the Genocide Studies family evolve? And what are the prospects?

Genocide in the global turn of history

Displacement of the genocide as the central subject in Armenian history is not intended to belittle the crime, but to provide a context over time. Genocide refers to concepts, ideas and elements related to a society, a state or a world in crisis, over a long period that is marked by successive warnings, often underestimated by potential victims and the international community.

The use of the human sciences at first made it possible to encourage comparative approaches in studying various genocides. This process of 'de-ethnicizing' the crime consists in enriching the conceptualization of genocide beyond the definition given in the United Nations International Convention for the Prevention and Punishment of the Crime of Genocide 1948. Indeed, the comparative approach seeks above all to understand whether a criminal genocide is an exceptional failure of the interstate system or a recurring crime in history. For this, specialists have reviewed the dossiers of mass crimes to examine conformity with the definition of genocide of the 1948 Convention. The examiners concluded from the study of three genocides – the Armenian, Jewish and Rwandan cases – that 'the twentieth century was an era of genocide', according to the expression of Roger W Smith,[19] an American professor of political science. In addition to these objective findings, which serve as a backdrop to the concept of genocide over time, the comparative approach proved useful in identifying subjective elements that were common to the three examples studied. For instance, there was no genocide without war. War, it turns out, provides a convenient screen for massacres behind the front line. Policies of destruction were enacted in the name of ideologies claiming an academic approach and utilitarian vision of policy objectives. The executioners conceived their crimes in the name of a vital need and a public good. For them, their actions responded to a public need and pressures to modernize. It was no coincidence that those responsible for the three genocides

---

[17] Bozarslan Hamit, Histoire de la Turquie, de l'Empire à nos jours, Tallandier, Paris, 2013.

[18] Edhem Eldem, « Osmanlı Tarihini Türklerden Kurtarmak », Cogito, 73, Printemps 2013.

[19] Roger Smith, 'Pouvoir étatique et intentions génocidaires. Les usages du génocide au XXe siècle', in *L'actualité du génocide des Arméniens*, Comité de défense de la cause arménienne (Créteil: Edipol, 1999).

mentioned shared the particularity of having been schooled in the positivism of Auguste Comte; they justified their actions in the name of the science that they served.

The degree of intentionality makes it possible to distinguish genocide from other widescale criminal acts. The greater the intentionality, the greater the state's involvement in committing the crime. In the Armenian case, scholars long sought to know whether the crime of 1915 was functionalist or intentionalist. If the experts determined that the massacres of 1915 were functionalist, they did not differentiate the massacres of 1894–1896 from those of Adana in 1909 or the carnage of 1915. However, as the design and execution were exceptionally large, given the extent of the atrocity, genocide systematization, its academic character and strong state involvement, the experts concluded that the crime of 1915 had been perpetrated intentionally. The intentional component is doubly important. On the one hand, this is because the comparative approach distinguished between total responsibility of the state for the conception of the crime and the involvement of a circle of power acting outside their roles as representatives of state authority to execute the intended crime. On the other hand, it is because the comparative approach made it possible more fully to understand the extermination logic behind the state executions: motive for the crime, preparation and execution. The comparative approach also makes it possible to highlight the bureaucratization of crime with its own hierarchy and functional organizations – the Teskilat-i Mahsusa (Special Organization) in the Turkish case was totally devoted to the execution task. Finally, all genocides are unfortunately accompanied by denials and falsehoods. Each genocide engenders its own negationism.

Global history rejects the academic domination of the West and distributes equally the various approaches to history. For the Indian historian Sanjay Subrahmanyam, it was not only Europeans who broadcast the Enlightenment:

> What I find problematic is that every time we discover more or less fascinating ideas in the world, Westerners hasten to say that it does not come from them. It is as if only the Enlightenment came from the West! The reality is that there have been admirers of Benito Mussolini (and a bit of Adolf Hitler) in the extra-European world. For us, this too was the West! We cannot decide that only what is democratic and positive comes from the West and reject the rest of the heritage, claiming it is the product of cultural differences.[20]

Finally, the global approach taken by social sciences on the subject of genocide must take into account the evolution of the law. When Pierre Nora mentions the lack of consensus on the definition of genocide, he refers to the multiple meanings of the concept proposed by international and national law. Since 1998, universal justice has come a long way, with a recognition of the superior interests of the International Criminal Court (ICC). The end of the Cold War, and legal progress through the International Criminal Tribunals for the horrors in the former Yugoslavia (1993) and Rwanda (1994) have allowed this. However, these advances in international justice are not without ambiguity. Article 5 of

---

[20] Interview with *The World*, 7 September 2013.

the Rome Statute of the ICC reduces the jurisdiction of the Court to four criminal offences: the crime of genocide, crimes against humanity, war crimes and the crime of aggression (there is still no definition for this last category). Article 6 of the Statute, which defines genocide, reproduces word-for-word that of Article 2 of the 1948 Convention, but deletes Article 3 in respect of the acts to be punished. Article 24 states that 'no one is criminally liable [...] for conduct prior to the entry into force of the Statute'. Thus, the genocides perpetrated in the twentieth century do not fall within the jurisdiction of the ICC, since the latter did not begin to sit until 2004.

With these three approaches – comparative, historiographic and legal – the theme of genocide crosses an area of turbulence to face three main risks of perversion. This confusion around the word 'genocide' in international and national law weighs in three ways on the Armenian problem. First, it is used by those who, in the context of the debate around the labelling of 'genocide', give priority to the approach of law at the expense of the approach of history. Since the law proposes different interpretations, it is easier for them not to recognize the crime of 1915 as genocide.

This legal confusion was then used as an opportunity on the part of the emerging powers against the Western powers. Emerging states denounced the historical humiliation inflicted by Euro-Atlantic domination to challenge the legitimacy of international standards, essentially enacted by Westerners. Behind this questioning of international rules lies a critique of the Western values that shape the international system. In law, as in international relations, some emerging powers advance a more accommodating interpretation of the universal foundations of the world order. Sometimes, for example, when it comes to defending the principles of state sovereignty and non-interference in internal affairs, such foundations are the guarantors of the system. Sometimes, they vigorously challenge the position of Westerners when it comes to defending human rights and democracy in the world, including a limited interpretation of the concept of 'responsibility to protect'. When, for example, Erdoğan described as 'genocide' the events taking place in Gaza in 2008 or 2014 (Palestine) or in Xinjiang (China), he reformulated the Western concept to fit the challenge to international standards. When Russia justified its intervention in South Ossetia (2008) and Crimea (2014) to prevent the genocide of local populations, it wanted to show that there is not just one form of genocide. When Russia and China vetoed the UN Security Council resolution calling for armed intervention in Syria, they not only expressed support for the Bashar al-Assad regime, but they also challenged the right of the international community to intervene in Syrian affairs. On what basis other than a challenge to universal values do Turks, Russians and Chinese justify their hostility to intervention?

Finally, this legal confusion is the game of deniers. This is true of Turkey, which perverts Paul Ricoeur's expression, 'just memory', to express its disapproval of the theses commonly accepted in the academic and political worlds concerning the authenticity of the Armenian genocide. In fact, Turkey would have liked the international community to recognize equally the tragedy of Turkish civilians as well as the Armenian civilians in the First World War. This argument would be tantamount to those who want governments and nations to pay tribute to the German civilian and military casualties of the Second World War, including those who died in the

Allied fire-bombing in Dresden. 'Just memory' also contains the misconception that the misfortunes of war are responsible for the tragedies, as if there were no Ottoman central government during the conflict, as if the Ottoman state had not existed. In fact, in its effort to escape the judgement of history, Turkey does not relinquish the role against which it claims to fight, namely the status of a dominated power and victim of Western subterfuge. Not to recognize the genocide of the Armenians is to remain under pressure from the international community, just as the Ottoman authorities were dependent upon the European Concert. In this, Turkey's position is doubly weak.

Legislation against historical negationism

In the United States, a resolution recognizing the genocide of 1915 regularly finds its way onto the congressional agenda, but never gets past the stage of adoption in parliamentary committee. Beyond particularities on either side of the Atlantic, if the community of historians is unanimous in describing the 1915–1917 massacres as genocide, the criminalization of the denial of this crime poses a problem for historians. For opponents of criminalization, history is neither a religion nor morality. It is not up to parliament or to the judiciary to define historical truth. For defenders of the law, historians are not above the law: these so-called memorial laws can appear as public affirmations of a society that is compatible with a state's democratic traditions; especially as, in the case of the Old Continent, the EU encourages Member States to legislate on this point. Indeed, was it not the EU that in 2008 adopted in the Council of Ministers a framework decision on the fight against racism and xenophobia,[21] condemning to sentences punishable by imprisonment any vulgar trivialization of genocide, crimes against humanity and racist war crimes?

In fact, beyond the arguments in favour or against the criminalization of denial of a crime against humanity and the political or strategic obstacles to the adoption of such a text, the real issues are elsewhere: just who is entitled to describe a crime against humanity as a genocide, the judge or the historian? How can one fight against state denialism? Is it up to the politician to intervene against this official falsification of history?

The relationship between law and history, judge and historian goes far back in time. There are two approaches, two functions for the use of the same word 'genocide', invented by a jurist, Raphael Lemkin, who worked on the exterminations of Armenians, Ukrainians and Jews to give birth to this neologism. The legal approach is forward looking. The judge endeavours to bring together under the same category types of crimes and offences that may arise in the future. He is called to rule upon the responsibility of an individual accused of genocide. He is not there to tell the truth, but render a verdict based on what the normative texts contain. The historical approach is different. It examines the past, looking for evidence of the truth. The historian is not

---

[21] 'Racist and xenophobic behavior [such as public apology, public denial or trivialization of crimes of genocide, crimes against humanity or war crimes] must be an offense in all Member States and be punishable, effective, proportionate and dissuasive criminal penalties of not less than one to three years' imprisonment' (EU Framework Decision).

obliged to respect a legal framework to express himself on specific events. He conducts his investigation using research instruments and comparative methods to produce an opinion from which he is able to say whether a genocide is factual. For all of that, are the categories hermetic? If the judge does not examine the history, he can, nonetheless, from contradictory versions of a fact, raise the issue of a historian's ethics. The judge can sanction the historian if his defence lacks rigour or if the historian wilfully neglected historical sources to present his own version of history. The judge thus formulates his own decision according to personal conviction.

A mixed record of the centenary of the genocide

For the first time, in 2015, humanity commemorated the centenary of a genocide. One hundred years after this international tragedy, Armenians around the world, but more broadly all consciences concerned with human rights and justice, shared this moment of meditation and protest, memory and struggle. While the candles of memory are now extinguished, the time has come to draw the outlines of a balance sheet around four complementary poles.

Academia

There has never been so much well-researched and cultural data on the genocide as there is now. Today, any historian worthy of the name recognizes this crime as the first genocide of the twentieth century. Between books, documentaries and fiction, including *The Promise*, a Spanish-American film directed by Terry George, released in America in early 2016,[22] there are nearly 100 cultural products on the subject that have flooded the market in France and the United States. This is all the more true, given that the cultural production does not take into account the press, with its special issues and its dossiers. There was neither a newspaper, nor a television or radio broadcaster that did not include Armenian subject matter. The result of this was such extraordinary coverage of the genocide that one must ask how it was possible in earlier times to present this question of genocide as an exclusively Turkish–Armenian problem? It is the opposite that has come to pass; the genocide record is of interest to all of humanity.

Beyond 50 years of political determination, the process of exposing the events of 1915 is the result of long and patient research. On this point, the progress is impressive. Thanks to the advances in research, including the work of members of the Conseil scientifique international pour l'étude de génocide des Arméniens (International Council for the Study of the Armenian Genocide), organizers of a four-day symposium in Paris in March 2015, in the presence of 60 researchers including 16 Turks, the genocide of 1915 began to be viewed as one of the major events in world history. On this occasion, at the opening of the symposium on 25 March, the French government launched a ministerial study mission on the research and teaching of genocide and mass crimes.

---

[22] The film had some difficulty finding a distributor in the United States and France, seemingly under pressure from Turkish diplomacy, according to film producers and Armenian organisations.

Another important step was the establishment of a commission of the French judicial archives on the genocide of the Armenians, entrusted to the historian Raymond Kévorkian. This is intended as a reminder that it was the tragedy of the Armenians that set out the premises for a legal treatment of genocide and crimes against humanity in the twentieth century.

The political aspect

The two states mainly concerned, Armenia and Turkey, missed their historic rendezvous. Armenia, which contented itself with a Pan-Armenian Declaration on the centenary of the genocide, for the first time since 1920 raised the question of the Treaty of Sèvres and reparations. Of Dashnak inspiration, the text that was presented on 29 January 2015 assembled into a single profession of faith the outline of the Armenian cause. The document did not fail to raise protests from Levon Ter-Petrosyan, who refused so much as a solemn declaration without having first consulted the Armenian people. President Ter-Petrosyan then criticized the Armenian authorities for not creating channels of dialogue with Ankara. But if the opportunity for dialogue between the states was missed, the blame lies squarely with Ankara, which in 2013 made it clear that it would not change its position on the genocide. As discussed earlier, in that year Turkey announced that the commemoration of the victory of the Dardanelles, traditionally organized every year on 25 April, would be advanced by one day, to 24 April, as a means of upstaging the centenary celebrations without any consequence for the Turkish denialist position. As a result, the celebration of Gallipoli's victory not only was a fiasco for Ankara, but also the hoped-for meeting between the two states did not take place.

We are very far from the wobble in 2005 around recognition of the genocide on the part of the Turkish government. At that time, Erdoğan not only reaffirmed his intransigence with respect to the historical truth of his passage – in force – to the presidency, but he also multiplied the provocations and conducted himself according to a double standard with representatives of the Islamic State (Daesh) in Iraq and Syria. We know that Armenian sites in Syria were destroyed, not so coincidentally following the appearance of Armenia in the news or on a notable Armenian anniversary. On the electoral front, Erdoğan achieved his ends, but at what cost? Nearly two years after the coup attempt of 15 July 2016, the country is on the verge of implosion, plagued by radicalization and tension between Turkish and Kurdish nationalists marked by a narrow authoritarianism which prevails at the highest levels in Ankara. Fortunately – and this is a lesson whose scope remains to be measured – the HDP, considered to be pro-Kurdish, made a notable entry into parliament with nearly 60 deputies. The Turkish Parliament now has three Turkish–Armenian deputies and the Armenian Question has finally been introduced into the Grand National Assembly of Turkey, despite previous attempts at repression. This is far from negligible when one considers the weight of denialism in Turkey and the risks incurred by defenders of historical truth in Ankara. However, the presence of these three deputies is relative if they cannot rely on a mobilized Turkish civil society. Times are hard on the banks of the Bosphorus. As long as the regime does not relax, there will be little to expect from public opinion regarding their relationship to history, so the Turkish–Armenian dialogue is now frozen.

The sociological component

The centenary saw the old Armenian world give way to a new one that was hardly ready to stand on its own two feet. This is the challenge for Armenians in the twenty-first century: how to move from a traditional, associative and memorial identity to a modern, democratic and forward-looking country. No one denies that a new paradigm of identity has been born, yet it seems too early to say whether the new Armenia is sufficiently mature to endure in the long run and is able to assist with the passing of the old.

And yet Armenians have no choice. In 1965, with the fiftieth anniversary, they moved from a logic of recollection to a logic of recognition. In 2015, with the centenary of the genocide, Armenians went from a logic of recognition to a logic of reparations. It is a big new construction site that opens up for them. But what to do? Working groups have been labouring for years on the best conditions for repairs. To date, none is credible and consensual. Two approaches stand out. First might be a more political approach that is articulated based on the Treaty of Sèvres to justify a request. However, this Treaty of Sèvres has never been ratified. It is as if citizens of EU Member States consider that the 2005 Treaty on the European Constitution adopted by Member States' parliaments should be applicable on the sole grounds that they adopted it. The EU Constitutional Treaty has no official value at a European level since neither the French nor the Dutch have ratified it. The treaty has become obsolete and the constitutional articles have been incorporated into the Treaty of Lisbon.

The other approach, more legal than political, is based on Turkish law and uses the Ankara judiciary to advance the issue of compensation and reparations. This approach has materialized through trials in Turkey but here, too, there is a risk of the genocide not being recognized by Ankara. In sum, if the first approach politicizes everything and makes recognition of the genocide a point upstream of the process, the second 'judiciarizes' the practices and does not resolve the issue of recognition.

Another problem considers who is in a position to represent Armenian rights. The Armenian state? Partly, but only because the diaspora (ie the direct descendants of the genocide victims) should have its say. The Armenian Church? But this is also insufficient, for other than religious property there is a far greater quantity of secular property to be claimed by private individuals. Political parties formerly in exile? They all returned to Armenia and so depend on the state apparatus. Who then? All Armenians, but no one in particular. Here is the root of a new problem.

In this respect, the idea of turning the Centenary Commission into a pan-national commission with a view to bringing the two Armenian poles closer together is fraught with ambiguities. If the object is to open this space to democratize practices based on the principle of 'one person, one voice', then the debate is open. But if, as seems to be the case, this Armenia–Diaspora commission is to be composed exclusively of representatives of churches, parties and large organizations, this practice would be a serious mistake and a matter of collective irresponsibility. Times have changed. Indeed, any pan-Armenian approach that proceeded, as usual, from top to bottom while civil societies based on individual rights were increasingly present, demanding and uninhibited, would be doomed to failure and, at the very least, to significant mistrust. Fostering links between the two Armenias is a legitimate and important concern and would require a multitude of new regulations and modes of communication between Armenia and the diaspora. The way to begin would be by streamlining co-operation from the bottom up, without interference from Armenia in the internal affairs of states that host a diaspora community. In the United States, reflection on the same theme has just begun and the idea is gaining ground in communities across the five continents. Behind this binational council hides another idea: that of making France a laboratory to inspire identical initiatives in Argentina, Canada, the United States, Greece, Australia, Russia, Lebanon and so on, to create a world congress of the diaspora in direct relation with Armenia. This is a new challenge for Armenians looking to the future without denying themselves. That being said, the time when Armenians were asked to participate in public demonstrations so that they could contribute to political actions without so much as asking for an opinion is over. Armenians are not a portfolio (financial participation) nor an umbrella (physical participation). They may also have the right to vote (democratic participation). Indeed, the democratization of practices and minds now means taking into account the views of citizens exhausted by the paternalistic and amateurish regime that has been the norm for a century. Armenians feel they deserve better and that they have the right to be represented at the height of their ambition by the public authorities of the republic.

In this new pan-national Armenian order, Nagorno-Karabakh's defence must become the priority: the drums of war were already heard in April 2016 during the Four-Day War. In this area of identity, 2015 was a crossroads. Either the traditional state, the diaspora communities or the political and religious institutions accept the democratic game and make Armenian identity a model adapted to the twenty-first century connected and engaged with the realities of globalization, or they wrest modernization of the Armenian identity to launch a unilateral offering that is conceived as an oligarchy and hatched in the greatest secrecy without considering the opinions of individuals who are kept away from the process. As long as there is no inclusive approach between Armenia and its diaspora communities but also between those institutions that have evolved among the diaspora and expatriated individuals, there can be no social contract and therefore no mutual trust. As everyone knows, solidarity and mobilization have their basis in trust and self-esteem.

The international aspect

As Georges Clemenceau, the 'Father of Victory', wrote in 1916, 'Is it true that, at the beginning of the twentieth century, five days from Paris, atrocities were committed with impunity, which covered the country in horror – such that worse could not be conceived at a time of the blackest barbarism?'[23] Why should the Turkish crime against

---

[23] Preface by George Clemenceau, from the book *Les massacres d'Arménie*, 2nd edition (Mercure de France, 1916), p. 6.

humanity not be considered at the height of its unprecedented character? In less than a decade, let us remember, the Armenians became orphans of the international system set up in the years following the First World War. If we take it even further, from 1878 to 1923 the European Concert cynically did not do anything concrete to prevent the extermination of a nation, considering what we now know not just about the role of Germany in the genocide, but also that of Russia and Britain in the massacre of Armenians between 1894 and 1896. Today, it is time to say loudly and clearly that a minimum of international justice must be shown to Armenians. Since 1923, Armenians have been wading against the tide of an international system that was reconstituted without them in 1920 and strengthened again in 1945. It is only since independence in 1991 that some of the rights of Armenians have been recognized. For the rest, the people demand justice and reparations.

If the international community is directly responsible for what happened in this part of the world in 1915, not all states have the same degree of involvement and not all have made progress in their work of introspection and self-analysis. Russia and France are doing well. It is enough to highlight the identity of the heads of state present in Yerevan on 24 April 2015 – Vladimir Putin and François Hollande – to realize that these two countries have been engaged in this work of recognition for some time. If one can criticize Putin's hollow speech that day, Hollande's offering was unequivocal on the exceptional dimension and the historical depth of the moment but forward looking and focused on peace.

A similar but more forcefully symbolic approach has been launched in the Vatican and Germany. Pope Francis, known for his boldness, openly admitted the genocide of 1915 as the first genocide of the twentieth century. Austria and Brazil, Catholic countries par excellence, but also Germany, instantly followed the Pope's lead. Indeed, the Bundestag even acknowledged Berlin's co-responsibility in organizing the genocide. So here is a new project for organizations and the Armenian state: using the German case to intensify the logic of reparations and to symbolically give full meaning to the trial of Tehlirian, Talaat Pasha's executor, on 15 March 1921. From this point of view, Germany's statement enhances Tehlirian's history and opens up new prospects for reparations. Should we seize these? Angela Merkel has personally engaged in this memory work, at the cost of a serious crisis with Turkey, despite the agreement on migrants agreed between Berlin, the EU and Ankara.

From the United States, another tune is heard, more muffled this time but promising and moving in the right direction, even though Barack Obama proved more sensitive to the alliance with Turkey than to humanitarian ideals. Should we expect a strong gesture from the Trump administration? For the moment, the new president has taken up the rhetoric of his predecessor: recognition and condemnation of the crime of 1915 without use of the word 'genocide'.

Finally, nobody really noticed it, but the presence of the heads of state of Serbia and Cyprus, Tomislav Nikolić and Níkos Anastasiádis, at the centenary commemoration in Yerevan was of particular importance. Indeed, through their act of solidarity, these two presidents acknowledge that the genocide of the Armenians was not strictly a Turkish and Armenian affair, but also concerned the former Ottoman provinces (eg Serbia and Cyprus). In fact, the genocide of 1915 cuts across three complementary spaces that have been talked about since the fall of the Soviet Union: the Balkans, the Caucasus and the Middle East – three areas at war. Therefore, if we associate these former areas under the Ottoman administration, a new reflection is needed: just as Europeans managed to use the Holocaust to remove structural violence from European states, transforming Europe in the process and proclaiming 'Plus jamais ça' ('Never Again'), would it be possible – and the presence of Belgrade and Nicosia in Yerevan memorial accredits the idea – to do the same with the genocide of 1915 to the states that extend from the Balkans to Caucasus via the Middle East? All states that were born amid the ruins of the sultans' empire know what happened in 1915. They are all aware, including the Arabs, that Armenians were slaughtered because they were Armenians. All these states could therefore make this genocide a kind of 'Never Again' to extract, in turn, this structural violence of states and trigger a liberalization of state apparatus and a surpassing of nationalism in the region, with a view to creating at best a climate of peace and, at the very least, a positive dynamic for the rule of law.

But we remain a long way off. In the Middle East, the barbarism of the Islamic State in Syria and Iraq, 100 years after the genocide, can only awaken the memories and the memory of genocide among Armenians. Same scene, same violence, same barbarism and almost even the same victims and actors, when we consider Ankara's double game in this Syrian–Iraqi tragedy. Beyond the crimes committed since 2014, the future of Armenians in the Middle East is openly questioned because after the departure of those from Egypt, Iraq and Syria, the fate of Armenians in Lebanon is fragile. What will be the status of Beirut in ten or twenty years? This is a challenge that Armenians would be well advised to take up, demonstrating not only to the peoples of the region but also to Europeans that the recognition of the Armenian genocide is not only symbolic, moral or bilateral; it has universal, strategic and world peace value. Armenians are in a position to refresh the memory of the international community, change their discourse and use all available levers to advance culture, justice and truth.

The future

On the basis of these lessons, what are the prospects for the Armenian Question as the world nears the end of the first quarter of the twenty-first century?

Despite all the political, economic and social difficulties, Armenians have never been so influential as today. Through the development of their state, the evolution of their diaspora, the irreversible recognition of the genocide and the assumption of responsibility for the Nagorno-Karabakh conflict by the OSCE, all the planets seem to be aligned for a return of the Armenians to the great family of the international community. Armenia is a member of several international and regional organizations and has made multilateralism a principal strategy in the pursuit of visibility, sovereignty and stability. Abroad, especially in the West, Armenians see their governing bodies better recognized by the public authorities. In France, for example, the representation of the CCAF has been considerably institutionalized since the last two presidents and the commemorations of 24 April are about to join the republican calendar. In the United States, the process is less advanced but relations between the various federal institutions (eg the White House, State Department, Pentagon and Congress) and pro-Armenian interest groups are firmly established.

It is in this context of restoration of a collective identity that three problems arise for the Armenians. The first is the security of ethnic Armenians in Nagorno-Karabakh but also in the Middle East. As long as the genocide of 1915 is not recognized and condemned by the international community, Armenians cannot collectively refrain from making reference to this tragedy and thus run the risk of being stuck with painful memories of injustice from over a century ago. The reflection is all the more relevant as barbarism again struck Mesopotamia in 2014–2015 with the genocide of Yazidis and Iraqi Christians by the Islamic State, whose images and terror recall that great savagery. Under such circumstances, what Armenian would possibly risk endangering his electors by renouncing the legitimate rights of Artsakh, especially while the wound of 1915 remains open because of state denial cultivated by the Ankara–Baku axis? After the injustice of 1915, no authority would intentionally expose its people to a second major injustice because officially, Azerbaijan rejects compromise and promotes anti-Armenian racism, walking in the footsteps of ultra-nationalists in Turkey.

Indeed, in Turkey, as long as Erdoğan's paranoid regime provokes its people to hysteria, stifles the opposition, sees conspiracy at every turn and refuses all criticism, should we await a gesture of redemption or reconciliation from Turkish leaders? On the contrary, Turkey organizes its diaspora communities as a political force ready to interfere in the internal affairs of host states. The strong alliance with Azerbaijan, NATO membership and strategic partnership with Russia all suggest that Ankara would neutralize any Armenian initiative, isolate Armenia and fantasize about a Pan-Turkic South Caucasus without Armenians. It is well known that there is no security without justice.

The road linking genocide to security also goes through the repair phase in the broad sense (penalization of negation and symbolic, financial and political compensation), with a roundabout perception of the Treaty of Sèvres signed on 10 August 1920. What does this treaty mean? How should one understand the Unionist trials of 1919–1920 that ended the long story of the Ottoman Empire? The first is a matter of history and treaty law, although the treaty was never ratified. The Treaty of Sèvres cannot be introduced into the legal texts in force, even if it is based on the work of the Paris Peace Conference of 1919 and it advanced the history of law by coining the notion of a crime against humanity. The latter proves that competent courts heard the trials and ruled on the Armenian massacres by Ottoman forces. Here too, history decided otherwise, since Mustafa Kemal abolished the courts in 1921 and granted amnesty to those responsible for the crimes in 1923. However, to affirm, as Robert Badinter does, that the genocide of the Armenians was 'not the subject of any decision emanating from any international or national jurisdiction whose authority would be binding on France' is doubly problematic. On the one hand, French law recognized the massacres of Armenians as a crime against humanity in the Lewis and Sezgin cases.[24] On the other, it would be difficult to find a serious judge or historian capable

---

[24] CDCA case against the Turkish Consulate and Wanadoo. Read Jean-Baptiste Racine, *Le génocide des Arméniens, origine et permanence du crime contre l'humanité* (Paris: Dalloz, 2006), pp. 134–138.

of challenging the existence of the genocide of the Jews, while the very concept of genocide was invented using the Armenian, Ukrainian and Jewish examples studied by Raphael Lemkin in 1944 and legally consecrated only in 1948.

As for criminalization of genocide denial, no procedure has been engaged in the United States on behalf of the First Amendment (freedom of expression) of the constitution, whereas the file is blocked in France as a result of the invalidation of the 2012 and 2017 legislation and the opinion of the Constitutional Council. The CCAF has very limited room for manoeuvre, even less since the Grand Chamber of the European Court of Human Rights (ECHR), in its final judgement of 15 October 2015, ruled in favour of Dogu Perinçek against Switzerland; the latter did not respect the principle of Perinçek's freedom of expression. Despite the personal success of the Holocaust denier, readings of the judgement of the ECHR appear to be contradictory. Armenian and human rights organizations have had difficulty accepting this defeat because they see it as an encouragement of denialism in Europe. However, for the representative of the Republic of Armenia, British lawyer Geoffrey Robertson, the judgement of the Grand Chamber of the ECHR is more nuanced and complete than the decision of the Lower House of 2013. 'This is a great day for Armenia' he said, 'because the Court was satisfied that Dogu Perinçek had not made a racial hate speech by denying the Armenian genocide.'[25] For Armenian Vice-Minister of Justice Arman Tatoyan: 'Armenia's goal as a third party was to ensure that the Grand Chamber did not reuse the wording of the 2013 decision because it could question the very fact of the Armenian genocide.'[26] According to Robertson, the final judgement of the ECHR states that 'the court does not have jurisdiction to provide definitions and estimates concerning the occurrence of the genocide, which was very weakly presented in the previous decision.'[27] The issue of criminalization is all the more confusing in that the countries of the EU are at the same time called to apply the Brussels Framework Decision on the fight against racism and xenophobia. In Articles 1(c) and (d), the Framework Decision states that 'criminal offences' include:

> 'public apology, denial or trivialization of crimes of genocide, crimes against humanity or war crimes as defined in the Statute of the International Criminal Court (Articles 6, 7 and 8) and the crimes defined in Article 6 of the Charter of the International Military Tribunal, where the conduct is intended to incite violence or hatred towards a group of persons or a member of such a group'.

From one centenary to the next, following the extermination, chaos and desolation of 1915, it is time to turn to rebirth, hope and life as in 1918. In 2018, three years after the commemoration of the genocide centenary, Armenians celebrated the restoration of their sovereign state. This was for Armenians first a moment of truth and reflection on

---

[25] Available at: www.lepoint.fr/monde/la-cedh-doit-se-prononcer-sur-la-negation-du-genocide-armenien-15-10-2015-1973721_24.php
[26] See http://armenews.com, 4 November 2015.
[27] Ibid.

their identity, their destiny, their transmission and their future. It is impossible to think and act as if the world had stopped in 1915 or 1965, as if ritual commemorations were the only possible perspective. It will therefore be necessary to rethink the basis of identity to respect individuality and promote inclusion. The idea that memory is just a lantern for the future has had its day. It can no longer freeze thought; it must find a meaning inscribed in real time. To give meaning to memory is to modernize discourse and ideas and place these in the service of history, not the other way around – because the future cannot be built on the worship and tyranny of memory, but on democracy and respect for differences. Therefore, it is up to the Republic of Armenia and its diaspora to search for and find a new paradigm of identity, one that goes beyond the memory of genocide but which is also rooted in the common heritage to promote the individual rights of the Armenians.

Conclusion

By overthrowing Serzh Sargsyan's regime in April 2018, the 'Velvet Revolution' put an end to the Armenian memorial state. The Armenians advocated openness to the world, hope for a better life and cleared a horizon hitherto obscured by corruption, opacity and authoritarianism. Above all, they appealed to a sense of civic responsibility and to a better understanding of their history. Indeed, history is a process of maturation, empowerment and liberation; memory entails infantilization, guilt and domination. 'The order of priority being undecidable', as Paul Ricoeur said, the Armenians do not favour either. In uncertainty and as often by precaution, they remained in-between, not unlike the image of their doctrine of Ephesus and the political-religious tandem that fuels their national identity. Collectively, Armenians do not go beyond this halfway line. They have every reason to hate history, cruel for past ministrations and yet they have a passion for discipline. However, they have every reason to snuggle into the arms of memory even while they suffer from servitude. As Kevork Khutinyan said:

> 'the rationalization of memory is as dangerous as the mythification of history and only a parallel coexistence between our will and our reason will in the years to come prevent, on the one hand, the reminiscence of the Armenian genocide from being perceived as a single fact of the past and, on the other hand, our failure to take into account the lessons of Armenian history (. . .) A hundred years ago, our enemies criminally stopped the political and economic development of Armenians, we must now, before we can claim compensation or even, before we can receive compensation, prove our own vitality, transforming the living memory of the nation into a powerful asset for the progress of Armenia. The current heated debate between memory and history will, at the dawn of the Armenian genocide centenary, allow us to plan the future by being aware of the past and avoid the danger of falling into the trap of enemy aspirations'.

To dwell upon the ambiguous relationship between history and memory is to reject the idea that truth liberates minds and fidelity involves constraint. History is a right to know and access knowledge, while memory is an imposed duty of transmission and beliefs.

However, to not choose is not to forego evaluation of the history-memory duo. The exercise is not new and Armenians, under the leadership of Christapor Mikaelian, experimented with it at the turn of the twentieth century. The founder of the ARF embodies this movement of ideas, this dynamic of innovation without renouncing the past. His success at creating his Federation was based on the use of social sciences, booming in his time. His success also relied on his achievement in creating political unity around his – incorporeal – person in the service of the revolution. Finally, his success was due to the pyramid he built based on the French and German – therefore contradictory – conceptions of the nation and from social and sometimes identity determinants. As a reminder, Christapor Mikaelian was at once Hobbesian and Durkheimian, Kantian and Bergsonian, Owenian and positivist, Hegelian and nihilist. But his accidental death interrupted his undertaking, leaving his heirs without a prophet or a strategic plan. Only his identity and Hobbesian approach is remembered, yet he was fundamentally Durkheimian when he considered, like Durkheim, that a 'social fact can only be explained by another social fact' and when he trusted more in society than in the State, more in solidarity than in selfishness. In his 'Revolutionary Thoughts', his occasional mention of the idea of the Nation was in line with a political, French citizen inspired methodology, not a cultural, ethnic German inspired approach.

That is why, taking advantage of the centennials commemorating the creation of the Armenian state in 1918 and three years earlier, the centennial of the 1915 genocide, it is difficult to resist the temptation to invite Armenians to walk in the footsteps of Christapor the Durkheimian to the detriment of Christapor the Hobbesian. Reassessing the relationship between history and memory requires such a Christaporian shift, because he subscribed very early to a global approach to political thinking. Christaporism is not an ideology but a unique sociological method that involves the variables of time and space coupled with a multidisciplinary approach to social sciences. Mikaelian was an historian, geographer, sociologist, philosopher and anthropologist. He was not a nationalist nor was he a Marxist, sectarian or even an ideologist. He was a pragmatic and ambitious man. He was a natural leader who had the reflex of audacity, a sense of history and an understanding of the balance of power. Is it too late, 110 years after his death, for Armenians to draw inspiration from his global approach? We believe it is not, subject to taking this shift in the global social sciences in four directions.

First direction

By shifting from Hobbes to Durkheim, we go from identity processing to social problem-solving. Let us take two examples to illustrate our point. In 1859, the year of the birth of Mikaelian, writer Stepan Vosgan urged his comrades 'to rally around the concept of Haiastan [Armenia], not religion', which can be understood either as a sterile nationalist position (identity approach) or as a desire to free oneself from the logic of domination (social approach). Another example, an identity approach to the Armenian Question, as it was posed in the Ottoman Empire, refers to the liberation of the territories of Western Armenia, whereas a social approach is based on the impossible agrarian reform and the equality of rights. This social perspective makes it possible to apprehend problems with better hindsight, in a less 'crisis-provoking' way, by breaking with a tendency to ethnicize behaviours. This social approach stems from positive chemistry between individual empowerment (release) of and the gravity of constraining forces. This valorization of individual conscience helps to create new spaces of expression and recognition of actor strategies. Mikaelian understood this perfectly and emphasized the place of the individual in history – man or woman, rich or poor, urban or rural – when he wrote the Manifesto of the Federation. If the identity approach was sometimes totalitarian, the social approach took into account the specificities of each and the permanent relationship between the actors and the general fact.

Second direction

By shifting from Hobbes to Durkheim, reflection enters directly into the social space of politics and breaks with the Armenian tradition that has always favoured the cultural aspect over the political. Indeed, as the Federation Manifesto mentions: 'For centuries, our people thought they could persuade humanity that the paths of cultural emancipation were the only way to guarantee their political freedom.' In other words, the Armenians have projected themselves into history with a cultural, not a political governing principle for development. In the absence of a traditional sovereign State, culture has been a way to overcome the inability to achieve the construction of politics. The only possible development for the secular-religious elites was cultural, because a political development would be fragile, therefore too dangerous and likely to create dissension, therefore too uncertain. Faithful to the tradition of their elders and to untouchable memory, the Armenians have maintained an ambiguous relation – to say the least – with political issues, leading them to believe that it is better to be dominated and 'secured' than sovereign and exposed. More than 100 years after this call for emancipation, the sociological picture is clearly unchanged: the Armenians remain collectively prisoners of domination mechanisms although they now enjoy the privileges of a sovereign state, the pre-eminence of politics and the benefits of globalization. Over 100 years ago, Mikaelian attempted to redress the balance between cultural and political in favour of the latter, insisting that Armenians could no longer legitimize domination and indulge in servitude. They could no longer, since the Enlightenment, identify exclusively with a religion or a language. He invited Armenians to make a qualitative leap and to explore the possibilities of projecting oneself into another community of destiny. Yet, ironically, when Mikaelian pointed to the horizon of the political, his comrades and successors only saw a finger, that of ideology and messianism.

Third direction

To come out of messianism: Mikaelyan was never a hard liner. He had integrated the force of reality and a sense of proportion into his plan of conquest of the spirits. However, he was resolutely determined, both courageous and aware that the revolutionary movement had arrived too late – at the turn of the 1880s – to achieve unanimity. His representation of the balance of power had internalized the interests of other actors, including those of the enemy. In his letter to Mikael Varandian, on 24 December 1900, he said: 'The powers are all hostile to us, we cannot align ourselves with any of them, that's our formula until we know which among them sees in our interests its own interests.' His heirs confused politics and ideology, means and ends or independence and freedom. Staying in the political arena required accounting for obstacles, especially those of rivals but also the existence of a social contract between the revolution and the base, the elites and the people. Henceforth, Armenian political actors could no longer act as if their adversaries' demands did not exist, as if the objectives of the cause did not need to be revised. Nor was Mikaelian heard by his opponents. The religious and conservatives saw in him the messenger of politics, the symbol of the catastrophe and the champion of socialism, whereas he embodied only a new method of identification. Internationalists and communists saw him as an agent of a tearful nationalism, a symbol of a petty bourgeoisie, whereas he believed more in sociology than in Marxism to deal with the social question.

Finally, his heirs who, for a long time, considered that the movement he had created was traversed since its origins without any historical break, as if social realities, mentalities and modes of action were identical from one era to another, from one continent to another, from one regime to another, from one generation to another, from one man to another. The hyperpower of memory is the main reason for this blindness. To be rid of it is to accept the revolutionary movement as an aggregation of elements independent of each other and not as a monolith, inseparable whole, subject to some mnemonic power.

Fourth direction

All this would be much simpler if the Armenians accepted, individually and collectively, a belief in their own singularity and by so doing, better understood their historicity. They must be told that the world of the Vienna Congress of 1815 is over even if they continue to perceive their Question as an issue before the European Concert. Governments, media and opinion leaders must also tell Turkey that denial of 1915 will never defeat history, that any attempt – even by civil society – to relieve Armenian suffering without first recognizing the historical truth may be understood as a misguided attempt to dominate them. The twenty-first century, the globalized world, is hardly compatible with the principle of domination. Moreover, if, like most emerging powers, Turkey denounces the historic humiliations to which the Western States have subjected her, she must find the dignity and the courage to condemn the humiliation she inflicted on the Armenian people when they were under her protection. A Christoprian turning point is therefore urgently awaited to lay the foundation for a New Armenian Question, a neo-haitadism built on the individual, a society of law and global thought. To see in the deep wound of 1915; a wound deeply disfiguring all of humanity and not just one of its branches. As the famous British journalist and author Graham Hanock wrote in July 2014: 'There is a huge history of humanity's past hidden in Armenia.' So, even if the smell of gunpowder remains in the air of the Caucasus and the drums of war sound a martial roll around Nagorno-Karabakh, as they did in 2016 for the 'Four-Day War', without any doubt the time has come for Armenia to reveal the treasures created by the suffering of some one-and-a-half million men, women and children, victims of the genocide, in the name first of history and of their memory.

Bibliography

Books on general themes

International relations

Badie, Bertrand, *Le temps des humiliés, pathologie des relations internationales*, Odile Jacob, Paris, 2014.

Badie, Bertrand, *La diplomatie de connivence, les dérives oligarchiques du système international*, La Découverte, Edition Poche, Paris, 2013.

Badie, Bertrand, *La fin des territoires*, CNRS Editions, Paris, 2013 (Fayard, 1995).

Badie, Bertrand, *L'impuissance de la puissance*, CNRS Editions, Biblis, Paris, 2013 (Fayard, 2004)

Badie, Bertrand, *Quand l'Histoire commence*, CNRS Editions, Paris, 2013.

Badie, Bertrand, *Culture et politique*, Economica, Paris, 1993.

Badie, Bertrand and Marie-Claude Smouts, *Le retournement du monde, Sociologie de la scène internationale*, PFNSP, Paris, 1992.

Brown, Seyom, *International Relations in a Changing Global System: Toward a Theory of the World Polity*, Westview Press, Boulder, San Francisco, Oxford, 1992.

Chaliand, Gérard *Anthologie mondiale de la stratégie, des origines au nucléaire*, Editions Robert Laffont, Paris, 1990.

Combacau, Jean Serge Sur, *Droit international public*, Montchrestien, Paris, 1997.

David, Charles-Philippe, *La guerre et la paix, approches et enjeux de la sécurité et de la stratégie*, Sciences Po, Les Presses, 3ᵉ édition, Paris, 2013.

Devin, Guillaume, *Sociologie des relations internationales*, La Découverte, Paris, 2013.

Durand, Marie-Françoise, Jacques Lévy, Denis Retaillé, *Le monde: espaces et systèmes*. Paris, 1992, PFNSP & Dalloz, Paris, 1993.

Duroselle, Jean-Baptiste, *Tout empire périra, Théorie des relations internationales*, Armand Colin, Paris, 1992.

Flory, Maurice, Bahgat Korany, Robert Mantran, Michel Camau and Pierre Agate, *Les régimes politiques arabes*, PUF, Paris, 1990.

Fukuyama, Francis, *The End of History and the Last Man*, The Free Press, New York, 1992.

Hassner, Pierre, *La violence et la paix, de la bombe atomique au nettoyage ethnique*, Edition Esprit, Paris, 1995.

Mackinder, Halford John, *The Geographical Pivot of History*, London, 1904.

Minassian, Gaïdz (Sous la direction), *Eurasie, au cœur de la sécurité mondiale*, Autrement, Paris, 2011.

Parsons, Talcott, *Le système des sociétés modernes*, Dunod, Paris, 1973.

Renouvin, Pierre, Jean-Baptiste Duroselle, *Introduction à l'histoire des relations internationales*, Armand Colin, Paris, 1991.

Political Sciences

Ideas, organizations and ideologies

Ansart, Pierre, *Les idéologies politiques*, PUF, Paris, 1974.

Arendt, Hannah, *Le système totalitaire*, Edition du Seuil, Paris, 1972.

Avril, Pierre, *Essais sur les partis*, Editions LGDJ, Paris, 1986.

Baynac, Jacques, *Les Socialistes-révolutionnaires*, Robert Laffont, Paris, 1979.

Candar, Gilles, Vincent Duclert, *Jean Jaurès*, Fayard, Paris, 2014.

Duclert, Vincent, *Jaurès, 1859–1914, La politique et la légende*, Autrement, Paris, 2013.

Durkheim, Emile, *Le socialisme*, Quadrige/PUF, 1992.

Duverger, Maurice, *Les partis politiques*, Armand Colin, Paris, 1951.

Furet, François, *Inventaires du communisme*, EHESS, Paris, 2012.

Haupt, Georges, *Le congrès manqué, l'Internationale à la veille de la première guerre mondiale*, F. Maspero, Paris, 1965.

Haupt, Georges, Madeleine Reberioux, *La IIe Internationale et l'Orient*, Edition Cujas, Paris, 1967.

Heller, Michel, *La machine et les rouages*, Gallimard, Paris, 1985.

Hoare, George, Nathan Sperber, *Introduction à Antonio Gramsci*, Le Découverte, Paris, 2013.

Muhlmann, Géraldine, Evelyne Pisier, François Châtelet, Olivier Duhamel, *Histoire des idées politiques*, PUF, Paris, 2e édition, 2012.

Mannheim, Karl, *Idéologie et utopie*, Libraire M. Rivière, Parios, 1956.

Michels, Robert, *Les partis politiques*, Flammarion, Paris, 1914.

Offerlé, Michel, *Les partis politiques*, PUF, Que Sais-Je?, Paris, 1987.

Individual and individualism

Birnbaum, Pierre, Jean Leca, *Sur l'individualisme: théorie et méthode*, PFNSP, Paris, 1986.

Bourricaud, François *L'individualisme institutionnel: essai sur la sociologie de Talcott Parsons*, PUF, Paris, 1977.

Caillé, Alain (Sous la direction), *La quête de reconnaissance, nouveau phénomène social total*, La Découverte, Paris, 2007.

Elias, Norbert *La société et les individus*, Fayard, Paris, 1991.

Guéguen, Haud and Guillaume Malochet, *Les théories de la reconnaissance*, La Découverte, Paris, 2012.

Molénat, Xavier (Sous la direction), *L'Individu contemporain*, Editions Sciences Humaines, Auxerre, 2014.

Ricoeur, Paul *Parcours de la reconnaissance*, Gallimard, Paris, 2009 (première édition, Stock, 2004).

Sociology, system, structure

Bobineau, Olivier, Sébastien Tank-Storper, *Sociologie des religions*, 2e édition, Armand Colin, Paris, 2006.

Boudon, Raymond, *A quoi sert la notion de structure*, Gallimard, Paris, 1967.

Bourdieu, Pierre, *Propos sur le champ politique*, Presses Universitaires de Lyon, Lyon, 2000.

Bourdieu, Pierre, *Le sens pratique*, Editions de Minuit, Paris, 1980.

Braud, Philippe, *Sociologie politique*, LGDJ, Lextenso éditions, Paris, 2011.

Braud, Philippe, *La science politique*, PUF, Paris, 1990.

Déloye, Yves, *Sociologie historique du politique*, La Découverte, Paris, 2003.

Dobry, Michel, *Sociologie des crises politiques*, PFNSP, Paris, 1992.

Dosse, François, *Histoire du structuralisme*, 2 tomes, La Découverte, Paris, 2012.

Duby, Georges, *Les trois ordres, ou l'imaginaire du féodalisme*, Gallimard, Paris, 1978.

Durkheim, Emile, *Les règles de la méthode sociologique*, PUF, Paris, 1983.

Durkheim, Emile, *Leçons de sociologie*, PUF, Paris, 1970.

Durkheim, Emile, Education et sociologie, Alcan, Paris, 1966.

Lagroye, Jacques, *Sociologie politique*, PFNSP et Dalloz, Paris, 1993.

Levi-Strauss, Claude, *L'identité*, Quadrige-PUF, Paris, 1987.

Merton, Robert King, *Eléments de théorie et de méthode sociologique*, Plon, Paris, 1965.

Modernity

Elias, Norbert, *La dynamique de l'Occident*, Calmann-Levy, Paris, 1976.

Gauchet, Marcel, *La révolution moderne, l'avènement de la démocratie*, Folio Essais, Gallimard, Paris, 2007.

Habermas, Jürgen, *L'espace public*, Payot, Paris, 1978.

Lacroix, Bernard, *L'utopie communautaire*, PUF, Paris, 1981.

Talmonn, Jacob L, *Les origines de la démocratie totalitaire*, Calmann-Levy, Paris, 1970.

Tilly, Charles, *Les révolutions européennes, 1492–1992*, Editions du Seuil, Paris, 1993.

Touraine, Alain, *Qu'est-ce que la démocratie?*, Fayard, Paris, 1994.

Touraine, Alain, *Critique de la modernité*, Fayard, Paris, 1992.

Weber, Max, *Economie et Société*, Plon, Paris, 1971, réédité en 1995.

Weber, Max, *L'éthique protestante et l'esprit du capitalisme*, Plon, Paris, 1985.

Strategy of Actors and Forces

Bourdieu, Pierre, *La noblesse d'Etat*, Editions de Minuit, Paris, 1989.

Levi, Jacques, *L'espace légitime, sur la dimension géographique de la fonction politique*, PFNSP, Paris, 1994.

Weber, Max, *Le savant et le politique*, Plon, Paris, 1959.

Crettiez, Xavier, *Les formes de violence*, La Découverte, Paris, 2008.

Durkheim, Emile, *Les formes élémentaires de la vie religieuse*, PUF, Paris, 1985.

Social Sciences

Caillé, Alain and Stéphane Dufoix (Sous la direction), *Le tournant global des sciences sociales*, La Découverte, Paris, 2013.

Corcuff, Philippe, *Où est passée la critique sociale?, Penser le global au croisement des savoirs*, La Découverte, Paris, 2012.

War and Warfare

Becker, Annette Stéphane Audoin-Rouzeau, *14–18 retrouver la Guerre*, Gallimard, Paris, 2000.

Horne, John (Sous la direction), *Vers la guerre totale, le tournant de 1914–1915*, Tallandier, 2010.

Tse-Toung, Mao, *La guerre révolutionnaire*, Editions Sociales, Paris, 1955.
Winter, Jay (Sous la direction), *La première guerre mondiale*, Combats, Fayard, Paris, 2013.

States and Nations

Badie, Bertrand, *Les deux Etats, Pouvoir et société en Occident et en terre d'Islam*, Fayard, Paris, 1986.
Badie, Bertrand, Pierre Birnbaum, *Sociologie de l'Etat*, Grasset, Paris, 1979.
Bayart, Jean-François, *L'illusion identitaire*, Fayard, Paris, 1996.
Birnbaum, Pierre, (Sous la direction), *Sociologie des nationalismes*, PUF, Paris, 1997.
Caron, Jean-Claude and Michel Vernus, *L'Europe au XIXᵉ siècle, des nations aux nationalismes, 1815–1914*, Armand Colin, Paris, 1996.
Carré, Olivier, *Le nationalisme arabe*, Fayard, Paris, 1993.
Chaliand, Gérard, *Repenser le tiers-monde*, Editions Complexe, Bruxelles, 1987.
Clastres, Pierre, La société contre l'Etat, Les Editions de Minuit, Paris, 1974.
Crozier, Michel, *Etat modeste, Etat moderne, Stratégies pour un autre changement*, Fayard, Paris, 1987.
Gellner, Ernest, *Nations and Nationalism*, Payot, Paris, 1989.
Gellner, Ernest, *Thought and Change*, Weidenfeld and Nicholson, Londres, 1964.
Hobsbawm, Eric, *Nations et nationalisme depuis 1780*, Gallimard, Paris, 1992.
Minassian, Gaïdz, *Zones grises, quand les Etats perdent le contrôle*, Autrement, Paris, 2011.

Ottman Empire, Turkey, Islam and the Middle East

Belfiore, Jean-Claude, *Moi, Azil Kémal, j'ai tué des Arméniens, Carnets d'un officier de l'armée ottomane*, Editions Parenthèses, Marseille, 2013.
Bozarslan, Hamit, *Le luxe et la violence, domination et contestation chez Ibn Khaldûn*, CNRS, Paris, 2014.
Bozarslan, Hamit, *Histoire de la Turquie, de l'Empire à nos jours*, Tallandier, Paris, 2013.
Bozarslan, Hamit, *Sociologie politique du Moyen-Orient*, La Découverte, Paris, 2011.
Bozarslan, Hamit, *Conflit kurde : le brasier oublié du Moyen-Orient*, Autrement, Paris, 2009.
Bozarslan, Hamit, *Une histoire de la violence au Moyen-Orient, de la fin de l'Empire ottoman à Al-Qaida*, La Découverte, Paris, 2008.
Bozarslan, Hamit, *La question kurde, problèmes politiques et sociaux*, La Documentation française, n°709, 20 août 1993.
Cetin, Fethiye, *Le livre de ma grand-mère*, Editions Parenthèses, Marseille, 2013.
Duclert, Vincent, *L'Europe a-t-elle besoin des intellectuels turcs?*, Eléments de réponse, Armand Colin, Paris, 2010.
Lewis, Bernard, *La formation du Moyen-Orient moderne*, Aubier, Paris, 1995.
Lewis, Bernard, *Islam et laïcité, la naissance de la Turquie moderne*, Fayard, Paris, 1988.
Mantran, Robert, *Histoire de l'Empire Ottoman*, Fayard, 1992.
Rondot, Pierre, *Les Chrétiens d'Orient, Cahiers d'Afrique et d'Asie*, J Peyronnet & Cie, Paris, 1955.

Russia and the USSR

Baechler, Christian, *L'Aigle et l'Ours, la politique russe de l'Allemagne de Bismarck à Hitler*, Peter Lang, Bruxelles, 2001.

Grousset, René, *L'empire des steppes, Attila, Gengis-Khan, Tamerlan*, Bibliothèque historique Payot, Paris, 1965.

Guetta, Bernard, *Eloge de la tortue, l'URSS de Gorbatchev, 1985-1991*, Edition Le Monde, Paris, 1991.

Heller, Michel and Aleksandr Nekrich, *L'utopie au pouvoir, Histoire de l'URSS de 1917 à nos jours*, Calmann-Levy, Paris, 1982.

Marcou, Lilly, *Les défis de Gorbatchev*, Plon, Paris, 1988.

Marcou, Lilly, *L'Internationale après Staline*, Grasset, Paris, 1979.

Nahaylo, Bohdan and Victor Swoboda, *Après l'Union Soviétique, les peuples de l'espace post-soviétique*, PUF, Paris, 1994.

Sebag Montefiore, Simon, *Young Stalin*, Phoenix, 2008.

Sebag Montefiore, Simon, *Staline: la cour du Tsar rouge*, Edition des Syrtes, 2005.

Suny, Ronald Grigor, *The Revenge of the Past, Nationalism, Revolution and the Collapse of the Soviet Union*, Stanford University Press, Stanford, California, 1993.

Thom, Francçoise, *Beria : Le Janus du Kremlin*, Cerf, Paris, 2013.

Thom, Francçoise, *Les fins du communisme*, Critérion, Paris, 1994.

Thom, Francçoise, *Le moment Gorbatchev*, Hachette, Paris, 1991.

Terrorism

Chaliand, Gérard, *Terrorismes et guérillas*, Flammarion, Paris, 1985.

Chaliand, Gérard, *Mythes révolutionnaires du tiers-monde*, Edition du Seuil, Paris, 1976.

Hyland, Francis P, *Armenian Terrorism: The Past, the Present, the Prospects*, Westview Press, Boulder, San Francisco, Oxford, 1991.

Wieworka, Michel, *Sociétés et terrorisme*, Fayard, Paris, 1989.

History and Memory

Baruch, Marc Olivier, *Des lois indignes? Les historiens, la politique et le droit*, Tallandier, Paris, 2013.

Charle, Christophe, *Homo Historicus, réflexions sur l'histoire les historiens et les sciences sociales*, Armand Colin, Paris, 2013.

Delacroix, Christian, François Dosse and Patrick Garcia, *Les courants historiques en France, XIXᵉ-XXᵉ siècle*, Gallimard, Paris, 2009 (première édition Armand Colin, 1999).

Delacroix, Christian, François Dosse, Patrick Garcia and Nicholas Offenstadt, *Historiographies I et II, concepts et débats*, Gallimard, Paris, 2010.

Dosse, François, *Paul Ricoeur, Les sens d'une vie (1913–2005)*, La Découverte, Paris, 2001, 2008.

Dosse, François, *L'histoire en miettes, Des Annales à la 'nouvelle histoire'*, La Découverte, Paris, 2010.

Duclert, Vincent, *L'avenir de l'histoire*, Armand Colin, Paris, 2010.

Favreau, Bertrand, (Sous la direction), *La loi peut-elle dire l'histoire? Droit, Justice, Histoire*, Bruylant, Bruxelles, 2012.

Granger, Christophe, (Sous la direction), *A quoi pensent les historiens?*, Autrement, Paris, 2013.

Hartog, François, *Croire en l'histoire*, Flammarion, Paris, 2013.

Joutard, Philippe, *Histoire et mémoires, conflits et alliance*, La Découverte, Paris, 2013.

Kipman, Simon-Daniel, *L'oubli et ses vertus*, Albin Michel, Paris, 2013.

Laurentin, Emmanuel, (Sous la direction), *A quoi sert l'Histoire?, La fabrique de l'Histoire*, Bayard, Montrouge, 2010.

Le Goff, Jacques, Pierre Nora (Sous la direction), *Faire de l'histoire*, Gallimard, Paris, 1974.

Le Goff, Jacques, *Faut-il vraiment découper l'histoire en tranches?*, Seuil, 2014.

Le Goff, Jacques, (Sous la direction), *La Nouvelle Histoire*, Editions complexe, Bruxelles, 2006.

Meyer, Michel, *Qu'est-ce que l'Histoire? Progrès ou déclin?*, PUF, Paris, 2013.

Nora, Pierre François Chandernagor, *Liberté pour l'histoire*, CNRS Editions, Paris, 2008.

Nichanian, Marc, *La perversion historiographique, une réflexion arménienne*, Editions Lignes & Manifestes, Fécamp, 2006.

Offenstadt, Nicolas, *L'Historiographie*, PUF, Que Sais-Je, Paris, 2011.

Revel, Jacques and Fernand Braudel et l'Histoire, *Pluriel Inédit*, Hachette, 1999.

Sirinelli, Jean-François, *Désenclaver l'histoire, nouveaux regards sur le XXe siècle français*, CNRS Editions, Paris, 2013.

History of Armenia and the Armenians

In Armenian

General

de Hratchia, Adjarian, *Un Dictionnaire prosopographique arméniens*, jusqu'au XVIIe siècle.

Eremian, S, P Arakelian, MS Hasratian, *Histoire du peuple arménien*, Erevan, 1956. Première édition en russe co-écrite par P Arakelian, M Hasratian, A Hovanessian (1951). Troisième édition, publiée en huit volumes à partir de 1967 co-rédigée par Tz Aghayan, P Arakelian, G Galoyan, S Yérémian, L Khatchikian, A Hakobian and M Nerseian.

Manandian, Hakob, *Théorie critique de l'histoire du peuple arménien*, Erevan, 1945–1952.

Ormanian, Malachia, *L'Eglise arménienne*, Imprimerie du Catholicossat arménien de Cilicie, Antélias, 1954.

Salmaslian, Armenag, *Bibliographie de l'Arménie*, Erevan, 1969.

Tchamtchian, Mikael, *Histoire des Arméniens des origines du monde à l'année 1784*, Imprimerie Venise, Saint-Lazare, 1786

Antiquity and Middle Ages

Abeghian, Manoug, *Histoire de l'ancienne littérature arménienne*, Erevan, 1946.

Adonts, Nicolas, *Etudes historiques*, Paris, 1948.

Aïrivanetsi, Mekhitar, *l'Histoire d'Arménie*, Edition K. Patkanian, Saint-Pétersbourg, 1867.

d'Ani, Samuel, *Extraits des oeuvres historiques pour fixer la chronologie depuis les temps anciens jusqu'à ce jour*, Edition Valarsapat, 1893.

Ayrivantec'i, Mxitar, *Histoire de l'Arménie*, Moscou, 1960.

Lastivert, Arestakes, de *Malheurs de la nation arménienne (1071)*, H. Berbérian, 1973.

Chirak, Anania de, *Géographie*, édition traduite par Robert H Hewsen, 1992.

(Lewond), Ghewond, *Histoire de la manifestation de Mahomet et de ses successeurs: comment et de quelle manière ils dominèrent l'univers, et spécialement notre nation arménienne*, Matenagirk' Hayoc', t. 6, Erevan, 2007.

Mekhitar, Goch, *Catholicos et événements du pays d'Aghvanie*, in Alichan, Hayabadoum, II, Venise, 1901.

Goriun, *La vie de St Mesrop*, Imprimerie Venise, Saint-Lazare, 1833.

Hadjian, Bedros, *Les grandes figures de la culture arménienne du Ve au XVe siècles*, Imprimerie Vahé Setian, Beyrouth, 1979.

Movsès Kalankatuac'i, *Histoire des Albaniens*, Matenadaran, Erevan, 1983.

Khatchikyan, L, *Colophons des manuscrits arméniens du XIVe siècle*, Erevan, 1950.

Khatchikyan, L, *Colophons des manuscrits arméniens du XVe siècle*, trois volumes, Erevan, 1955, 1958, 1967.

Korykos Héthoum de and Hayton, *Fleur des Histoires de la Terre d'Orient*, 1307, traduction, Venise, 1842.

Mecop'ec'i, Thomas, *Histoire de Tamerlan et de ses successeurs*, Paris, 1860.

Matevosyan, A, *Colophons des manuscrits arméniens des Ve–XIIe siècles*, Erevan, 1988.

Matevosyan, A, *Colophons des manuscrits arméniens du XIIIe siècle*, Erevan, 1984.

Mikaëlian, G, *Histoire de l'Etat arménien de Cilicie*, Erevan, 1952.

Nalbandyan, H, *Sources arabes sur l'Arménie et les Arméniens*, Académie d'Erevan, Erevan, 1965.

Nersês, Chnorhali, *Composition en poésie homérique sur l'histoire d'Arménie*, Imprimerie, Venise, Saint-Lazare, 1830.

Tarawnac'i, Stepanos Asolik, *Chronique universelle*, Matenagirk Hayoc', t. 15, 2012.

Ter-Minasean, Eruand, Elise, *Sur la guerre de Vardan et des Arméniens*, Matenadaran, Erevan, 1957.

Ter-Petrosyan, Levon *Les Croisés et les Arméniens*, 2 tomes, Erevan (Gulbenkian), 2007.

Uxtanes, *Histoire de l'Arménie*, Matenagirk' Hayoc', t. 15, 2012.

Yovhannes, Drasxanakertc'i, *Histoire d'Arménie*, CSCO 605, Peeters, Louvain, 2004.

Yuzbasyan, Karen, *De la bataille d'Awarayr au traité de Nuarsak*, Académie d'Erevan, Erevan, 1989.

Modern history

Alichan, *Sissagan*, Venise, Saint-Lazare, 1893.

Alichan, *Hay-Vened*, Venise, Saint-Lazare, 1896.

Alichan, *Hayapatum*, Venise, 1901.

Anasyan, Hakob, *Les mouvements de libération en Arménie occidentale au XVIIe siècle*, Erevan, 1961.

de Tabriz, Arakel, *Histoire de son temps*, Imprimerie, Amsterdam, 1669.

Hakobyan, V, A. Hovhannisyan, *Colophons des manuscrits arméniens du XVIIe siècle*, Erevan, 1974, 1978, Hakobyan (1984).

Sahamirean, Sahamir, *Principes de gouvernement (. . .)*, Madras, 1784.

Sahamirean, Sahamir, *Le Piège pour les ambitieux, Madras (. . .)*, 1773.

Siruni, Hagop, *Constantinople et son rôle*, tome 1 (1453–1800), Beyrouth, 1965.

Contemporary History

Adjemian, Haïg, *Hayotz Haïrig*, tome 1, Tabriz, 1929.

Babakhanian, Arakel ou "Léo", *Histoire de l'Arménie*, 10 volumes, Erevan, 1917–1949 (édition Erevan, 1967).

Badalian, Kh, *Le problème arménien du traité de San Stefano au congrès de Berlin, 1878*, Erevan, 1965.

Bakalian, Anny, *Armenian-American: From being to feeling Armenian*, Transaction Publishers, New Brunswick, 1993.

Kdridj Sardaryan, *Les normes du temps actuel et la pensée politique arménienne*, Edition Amaras, Erevan, 1997.

Sassouni, Garo, *La guerre arméno-tatare de 1920*, Publication Hamaskaïne, Beyrouth, 1969.

Simonyan, Hratchig, *Histoire des relations turco-arméniennes*, Publication Haïastan, Erevan, 1991.

Stepaniantz, S, *L'Eglise apostolique arménienne sous Staline*, Edition Apollon, Erevan, 1994.

Tchormissian, Levon, *Les partis politiques et la patrie*, Paris, 1946 (réédition en 1994).

Teoleolian, Minas, *La lutte contre la FRA*, Publication Haïrenik, Boston, 1962.

Non-Armenian

General

Dédéyan, V (Sous la direction), *Histoire des Arméniens*, Privat, Toulouse, 2ᵉ édition, 2007.

de Morgan, Jacques, *Histoire du peuple arménien*, Catholicossat arménien de Cilicie, Antelias, édition 2004.

Hovannisian, Richard G and Simon Payaslian, (Sous la direction), *Armenian Constantinople*, Mazda Publishers, Costa Mesa, California, 2010.

Hovannisian, Richard G (Sous la direction), *Armenian Tigranakert/Diarbekir and Edessa/Urfa*, Mazda Publishers, Costa Mesa, California, 2006.

Hovannisian, Richard G (Sous la direction), *Armenian Tsopk/Kharpert*, Mazda Publishers, Costa Mesa, California, 2002.

Hovannisian, Richard G (Sous la direction), *Armenian Van/Vaspurakan*, Mazda Publishers, Costa Mesa, California, 1980.

Mahé, Annie et Jean-Pierre, *Histoire de l'Arménie, des origines à nos jours*, Perrin, Paris, 2012.

Mahé, Annie et Jean-Pierre, *L'Arménie à l'épreuve des siècles*, Découverte-Gallimard, Paris, 2005.

Mouradian, Claire, *L'Arménie*, PUF, Que Sais-Je, Paris, 2014.

Pastermadjian, Hrant, *Histoire de l'Arménie depuis les origines jusqu'au Traité de Lausanne*, Libraire Samuelian, Paris, 1971.

Antiquity and the Middle Ages

Adontz, Nicolas, *Armenia in the Period of Justinian. The Political Conditions Based on the Naxarar System*, Lisbonne (Gulbenkian), 1970.

Adontz, Nicolas, *Histoire d'Arménie, Les origines du Xᵉ siècle au VIᵉ (Av. J.C.)*, Pais, 1946.

Adontz, Nicolas, *Etudes arméno-byzantines*, Lisbonne (Gulbenkian), 1965.

Agathange, *Histoire de l'Arménie*, RW Thomson, 1976.

Augé, Isabelle and Gérard Dédéyan, *L'Eglise arménienne entre Grecs et Latins, fin XIᵉ – milieu XVᵉ siècle*, Geuthner, Paris, 2009.

d'Edesse, Mathieu, *Chronographie*, (traduction d'Edouard Dulaurier), Paris, 1958.

de Khorène, Moïse, *Histoire de l'Arménie*, nouvelle traduction de l'arménien classique Annie et Jean-Pierre Mahé, L'Aube des peuples, Gallimard, Paris, 1993.

de Nareg, Grégoire *Paroles à Dieu*, Introduction, traduction et notes par Annie et Jean-Pierre Mahé, Peeters, 2007.

Dédéyan, Gérard, *Les Arméniens entre Grecs, Musulmans et Croisés*, deux tomes, *Bibliothèque Arménologique de la Fondation Calouste Gulbenkian*, Lisbonne, 2003.

Dulaurier, Edouard, *Recherches sur la Chronologie arménienne, technique et historique*, Imprimerie Impériale, Paris, 1859.

Dulaurier, Edouard, *Choix des principaux historiens arméniens*, Publication A Durand, 1858.

Feydit, Frédéric, *David de Sassoun*, traduction, Gallimard, Paris, 1964.

Garsoïan, Nina, Jean-Pierre Mahé, *Des Parthes au Califat, quatre leçons sur la formation de l'identité arménienne*, De Boccard, Paris, 1997.

Garsoïan, Nina, *The Epic Histories (Buzandaran Patmut'iwnk)*, Harvard University Press, Cambridge MA, 1989.

Grousset, René, *Histoire de l'Arménie, des origines à 1071*, Editions Payot & Rivages, Paris, 1995.

Khatchadourian, Hrant, *L'histoire de l'historiographie arménienne, Ve siècle*, 1979, Université du Michigan, Etats-Unis.

Kouymjian, Dickran (Sous la direction), *Movsès Xorenac'i et l'historiographie arménienne des origines*, Catholicossat arménien de Cilicie, Antelias, Liban, 2000.

Langlois, Victor, *Collection des historiens anciens et modernes de l'Arménie*, 2e édition, Lisbonne, 2001.

Macler, Frédéric, *Histoire universelle par Etienne Asolik de Tarôn* (2e partie) (la première partie de cette chronique a été traduite par Edouard Dulaurier), Paris, 1917.

Manandian, Hakob, *The Trade and Cities of Armenia in Relation to Ancient World*, Trade, Lisbonne (Gulbenkian), 1965.

Manandian, Hakob, *Tigrane II et Rome*, Lisbonne (Gulbenkian), 1963.

Mardirossian, Aram, *Le Livre des canons arméniens de Yovhannes Awjnec'i, Eglise, droit et société en Arménie du IVe au VIIIe siècle*, CSCO 606, Peeters, Louvain, 2004.

Mutafian, Claude, *L'Arménie du Levant, XIe-XIVe siècle*, Les Belles Lettres, Paris, 2012.

Mutafian, Claude, (Sous la direction), *La magie de l'écrit*, Sogomy, Paris, 2007.

Mutafian, Claude, *Le Royaume arménien de Cilicie (XIIe-XIVe)*, 1993.

Mutafian, Claude, *La Cilicie au carrefour des empires*, 2 volumes, Les Belles Lettres, Paris, 1988.

Mutafian, Claude and Eric van Lauwe, *Atlas historique de l'Arménie. Proche-Orient et Sud-Caucase du VIIIe siècle avant J.-C. au XXIe siècle*, Autrement, Paris, 2001.

Piotrovsky, Boris B, *Ourartou*, Les Editions Nagel Genève, Paris, Munich, 1970.

Reclus, Elisée, *Les Arméniens*, Magellan & Cie, dernière édition, Paris, 2006.

Roaf, Michael, *Atlas de la Mésopotamie et du Proche-Orient ancien*, Brepols, 1991 (première édition en anglais, 1990).

Russell, James R, *Zoroastrianism in Armenia*, Harvard Iranian Series 5, Harvard University Press, Cambridge MA, 1987.

Saint-Martin, Jean, *Histoire d'Arménie par le Patriarche Jean VI dit Jean Caholicos*, Traduction, Paris, 1841.

Sanders, Seth L (Sous la direction), *Margins of Writing Origins of Cultures*, The Oriental Institute of the University of Chicago, Numéro 2, Chicago, Illinois, 2007.

Ter Ghevondyan, Aram, *The Arab Emirates in Bagratid Armenia*, Lisbonne (Gulbenkian), 1976.

Thomson, Robert, *The Lives of St Gregory*, Caravan Books, Michigan, 2010.

Thomson, Robert, *Nerse of Lambron, Commentary on the Revelation of Saint John*, Hebrew University Armenian Studies 9, Peeters, Louvain, 2007.

Thomson, Robert, *The Lawcode of Mxit'ar Gos*, Dutch Studies in Armenian Language and Literature 6, Amsterdam (Rodopi), 2000.

Thomson, Robert, *The History of Lazar P'arpec'i*, Scholard Press, Atlanta GA, 1991.

Thomson, Robert, *Thomas Arstruni. History of the House of the Artsrunik*, Wayne State University Press, Detroit, 1985.

Thomson, Robert, *Elise, History of Vardan and the Armenian War*, Cambridge MA, 1982.

Thomson, Robert, *Moses Khorenats'i, History of the Armenians*, Harvard University Press, Cambridge MA, 1978.

Thomson, Robert, *Agathangelos. History of the Armenians*, Albany NY (SUNY), 1976.

Thomson, Robert, James Howard-Johnston and Tim Greenwood, *The Armenian History attributed to Sebeos*, 2 volumes, University Press, Liverpool, 1999.

Toumanoff, Cyril, *Les Dynasties de la Caucasie chrétienne de l'Antiquité jusqu'au XIXᵉ siècle. Tables généalogiques et chronologiques*, Rome, 1990.

Toumanoff, Cyril, *Studies in Christian Caucasian History*, Georgetown University Press, Washington, 1963.

Modern History

Hovannisian, Richard G and David N Myers, *Enlightenment and diaspora, the Armenian and Jewish Cases*, Scholars Press, Atlanta GA, 1999.

Jamgocyan, Onnik, *Les Banquiers des Sultans, Juifs, Grecs, Français et Arméniens*, Constantinople, 1650–1850, Les Editions du Bosphore, Paris, 2013.

Panossian, Razmik, *The Armenians: From Kings and Priests to Merchants and Commissars*, Columbia University Press, New York, 2006.

Contemporary History

Afanasyan, Serge, *La victoire de Sardarabad*, L'Harmattan, Paris, 1985.

Arlen, Michael, *Embarquement pour l'Ararat*, Gallimard, 1977.

Bakounts, Axel, *Mtnadzor*, Editions Parenthèses, Marseille, 1990.

Beledian, Krikor, *Seuils*, Editions Parenthèses, Marseille, 2011.

Beledian, Krikor, *Cinquante ans de littérature arménienne en France, Du même à l'autre*, CNRS Editions, Paris, 2001.

Beria, Lavrenti, *Histoire du Parti Bolchevik en Transcaucasie*, Moscou-Tbilissi, 1935.

Beylerian, Arthur, *Les Grandes puissances l'Empire ottoman et les Arméniens dans les archives françaises (1914–1918)*, recueil de documents, Publications de la Sorbonne, Paris, 1983.

Boudjikanian, Aïda, *Les Arméniens de l'agglomération de Beyrouth: étude humaine et économique*, 2e partie, HASK, Beyrouth, 1983–1984.

Derogy, Jacques, *Opération Némésis, les vengeurs arméniens*, Fayard, Paris, 1986.

Dink, Hrant, *Etre Arménien en Turquie*, Fradet, Paris, 2007.

Donabedian, Patrick and Claude Mutafian, *Le Karabakh une terre arménienne en Azerbaïdjan*, Groupement pour les droits des minorités, Paris, 1989.

Hakobyan, Tatul, *Armenians and Turks, From War to Cold War to Diplomacy*, Erevan, 2013.

Hovannisian, Richard G, *The Armenian People from Ancient to Modern Times*, 2 volumes, Palgrave Macmillan, New York, 1997.

Hovannisian, Richard G, *The Republic of Armenian*, vol 4, University of California Press, Berkeley, Los Angeles, 1996.

Hovannisian, Richard G, *The Republic of Armenia*, vol 3, University of California Press, Berkeley, Los Angeles, 1996.

Hovannisian, Richard G, *The Republic of Armenia*, vol 2, University of California Press, Berkeley, Los Angeles, 1982.

Hovannisian, Richard G, *The Republic of Armenia*, vol 1, University of California Press, Berkeley, Los Angeles, 1971.

Hovanessian, Martine, *Le Lien communautaire, Trois générations d'Arméniens*, Armand Colin, Paris, 1992.

Kevonian, Dzovinar, *Réfugiés et diplomatie humanitaire. Les acteurs européens et la scène proche-orientale pendant l'entre-deux-guerres*, Sorbonne, Paris, 2004.

Khatissian, Alexandre, *Eclosion et développement de la République d'Arménie*, Publication de la FRA Dachnakstoutioun, Athènes, 1989.

Khayadjian, Edmond, *Archag Tchobanian et le mouvement arménophile en France*, Centre national de documentation pédagogique, Marseille, 1986.

Libaridian, Gérard, *L'Arménie moderne, Histoire des hommes et de la nation*, Karthala, Paris, 2008.

Libaridian, Gérard, *La construction de l'Etat en Arménie, un enjeu caucasien*, Khartala, Paris, 2000.

Libaridian, Gérard, *Armenia at the Crossroads, Democracy and Nationhood in the Post-Soviet Era*, Blue Crane Books, Watertown, Massachusetts, 1991.

Loris-Melicof, Jean, *La révolution russe et les Républiques de Transcaucasie*, Librairie Félix Alcan, Paris, 1920.

Lubin, Armen (Chahan Chahnour), *La retraite sans fanfare, histoire illustrée des Arméniens, à leur arrivée à Paris suite au génocide de 1915–1916*, L'Actmem, Chambery, 2009.

Macler, Frédéric, *Quatre conférences sur l'Arménie*, Librairie d'Amérique et d'Orient, Paris, 1932.

Mahakian, Charles, *History of Armenians in California*, University of California Press, réédité en 1974.

Mandelstam, André, *La société des nations et les puissances devant le problème arménien*, Edition Hamaskaïne, Beyrouth, 1970.

Marienstras, Richard, *Etre un peuple en diaspora*, Les Prairies ordinaires, Paris, 2014.

Melkonian, Monté, *Histoire de l'ASALA*, Lausanne, 1990.

Messerlian, Zaven, *Sur le problème arménien*, Publication de l'Union culturelle Tekeyan, Beyrouth, 1978.

Messerlian, Zaven, *Armenian Representation in the Lebanese Parliament*, American University of Beirut, Beyrouth, 1963.

Messerlian, Zaven, *Armenians in Lebanon*, American University of Beirut, Beyrouth, 1959.

Minassian, Baghdig, *Arménie, peuple arménien et la cause arménienne*, Imprimerie Vahé Setian de Hamaskaïne, Beyrouth, 1979.

Minassian, Gaïdz, *Caucase du Sud, la nouvelle guerre froide*, Arménie, Azerbaïdjan, Géorgie, Autrement, Paris, 2007.

Minassian, Gaïdz, *Géopolitique de l'Arménie*, Ellipses, Paris, 2005.

Minassian, Gaïdz, *Guerre et terrorisme arméniens*, PUF, Paris, 2002.

Morganthau, Henry, *Vingt-quatre mois en Turquie*, Paris, 1919.

Mouradian, Claire, *Arménie, une passion française. Le mouvement arménophile en France (1878–1923)*, Magellan, Paris, 2007.

Mouradian, Claire, *De Staline à Gorbatchev, histoire d'une république soviétique, l'Arménie*, Ramsay, Paris, 1990.

Mouradian, Claire and Anouche Kunth, *Les Arméniens en France, du chaos à la reconnaissance*, Editions de l'Attribut, Toulouse, 2010.

Natalie, Shahan, *The Turks and Us*, Punik Publishing, 2002.

Nichanian, Marc, *Ages et usage de la langue arménienne*, Edition Entente, Paris, 1989.

Oskanian, Vartan, *Sur la route de l'indépendance, petit Etat, grands défis*, Editions Civilitas, Erevan, 2013.

Ritter, Laurence, *La longue marche des Arméniens, Histoire et devenir d'une diaspora*, Robert Laffont, Paris, 2007.

Sévak, Parouïr, *Que la lumière soit!*, Editions Parenthèses, Marseille, 1988.

Suny, Ronald Grigor, *Looking toward Ararat, Armenian in the Modern History*, Indiana University Press, Bloomington IND, 1993.

Suny, Ronald Grigor, *Armenian in the Twentieth Century*, Scholars Press, Chico, California 1983.

Tcharents, Yeghiché, *La maison de rééducation*, Editions Parenthèses, Marseille, 1992.

Ter Minassian, Anahide, *La République d'Arménie*, Editions Complexe, Bruxelles, 1989.

Ter Minassian, Taline *Erevan: la construction d'une capitale à l'époque soviétique*, Presses Universitaires de Rennes, Rennes, 2007.

Toriguian, Shavarch, *The Armenian Question and International Law*, Hamaskaïne Press, Beirut, 1973.

Walker, Christopher, *Oliver Baldwin, A Life of Dissent*, Londres, 2003.

Walker, Christopher, *Armenia, The Survival of a Nation*, Londres, Croom Helm, 1980.

Zarevand, *Touranie unifiée et indépendante*, Publication de la FRA Dachnaktsoutioun, Athènes, 1989.

The Armenian Genocide and Genocides

Akçam, Taner, *The Young Turk's Crime against Humanity, The Armenian Gencoide and Ethnic Cleansing in the Ottoman Empire*, Princeton University Press, Princeton and Oxford, 2012.

Akçam, Taner, *Un acte honteux, le génocide arménien et la question de la responsabilité turque*, Denoël, 2008.

Altounian, Janine, *Ouvrez-moi seulement les chemins d'Arménie, un génocide aux déserts de l'inconscient*, Les Belles Lettres, Paris, 1990.

Attarian, Varoujan, *Le génocide des Arméniens devant l'ONU*, Editions Complexe, Bruxelles, 1997.

Berdjouhi, *Jours de cendres à Istanbul*, Editions Parenthèses, Marseille, 2004 (première édition Boston, 1938–1939, deuxième édition, Paris, 2003).

Bruneteau, Bernard, *Le siècle des génocides*, Armand Colin, Paris, 2004.

Carzou, Jean-Marie, *Un génocide exemplaire: Arménie 1915*, Flammarion, Paris, 1975.

Chaliand, Gérard and Yves Ternon, *1915, le génocide des Arméniens*, Editions Complexe, dernière édition, Bruxelles, 2006.

Chiragian, Archavir, *La dette de sang, un Arménien traque les responsables du génocide, 1921–1922*, Editions Ramsay, Paris, 1982.

Dadrian, Vahakn, *Histoire du génocide arménien*, Stock, Paris, 1996.

Fuat, Dündar, *Crime of Numbers: The Rôle of Statistics in the Armenian Question (1878–1918)*, New Brunswick, Transaction Publishers, 2010.

Insel, Ahmet and Michel Marian, *Dialogue sur le tabou arménien*, Liana Levi, Paris, 2009.

Kevorkian, Raymond, *Le Génocide arménien*, Odile Jacob, Paris, 2006.

Kevorkian, Raymond, Paul B Paboudjian, *Les Arméniens dans l'Empire Ottoman à la veille du génocide*, Les Editions Arts et Histoire, Paris, 1992.

Kieser, Hans-Lukas, Dominik J Schaller, *Der Völkermord an den Armeniern und die Shoah, The Armenian Genocide and the Shoah*, Chronos Verlag, Zürich, 2002.

Gust, Wolfgang, *The Armenian Genocide: Evidence from the German Foreign Office Archives, 1915–1916*, Berghahn Books, New York, Oxford, 2013.

Hilsenrath, Edgar, *Le conte de la pensée dernière*, Albin Michel, Paris, 1992.

Marchand, Laure and Guillaume Perrier, *La Turquie et le fantôme arménien, sur les traces du génocide*, Solin, Actes Sud, Paris, 2013.

Lepsius, Johannes, *Rapports secrets sur les massacres d'Arméniens*, Payot, 1918, réédité en 1987.

Morganthau, Henry, *Ambassador Morganthau's Story*, New York, 1918 traduction en français sous le titre *Mémoires de l'Ambassadeur Morgenthau*, Paris, 1919.

Odian, Yervant, *Journal de déportation*, Editions Parenthèses, Marseille, 2010.

Pacha, Djemal, *Memories of a Turkish statesman, 1913–1919*, London, Hutchinson & Co, Paternoster Row, ouvrage non-daté.

Piralian, Hélène, *Génocide et transmission*, L'Harmattan, Paris, 1994.

Powers, Samantha, *A Problem from Hell, America and the Age of Genocide*, New York, Harper, Collins, 2003.

Racine, Jean-Baptiste, *Le génocide des Arméniens, origine et permanence du crime contre l'humanité*, Dalloz, Paris, 2006.

Sémelin, Jacques, Claire Andrieu, Sarah Gensburger (Sous la direction), *La résistance aux génocides, de la pluralité des actes de sauvetage*, Presses de la Fondation nationale des Sciences Politiques, Paris, 2008.

Tehlirian, Soghomon, *Mes mémoires*, Publications Houssaper, Le Caire, 1953.

Ternon, Yves, *Empire ottoman. Le déclin, la chute, l'effacement*, Editions du Félin, éditions Michel de Maule, Paris, 2002.

Ternon, Yves, *Du négationnisme mémoire et tabou*, Desclée de Brouwer, Paris, 1999.

Ternon, Yves, *L'Etat criminel, les Génocides au XXe siècle*, Editions du Seuil, Paris, 1995.

Ternon, Yves, *Enquête sur la négation d'un génocide*, Editions Parenthèses, Marseille, 1989.

Ternon, Yves, *La Cause Arménienne*, Seuil, Paris 1983.

Ternon, Yves, *Les Arméniens histoire d'un génocide*, Seuil, Paris, 1977.

Missak Torlakian, *Avec mes jours*, Imprimerie Haïg, Beyrouth, 1963.

Toynbee, Arnold, *Les massacres des Arméniens*, Payot, Paris, 1987.

Toynbee, Arnold, *Le traitement des Arméniens dans l'Empire Ottoman*, Payot, Paris, 1987.

Werfel, Franz, *Les quarante jours du Musa Dagh*, Albin Michel, Paris, 1936.

Zürcher, Erik-Jan, *The Young Turk Legacy and Nation-Building: From the Ottoman Empire to Atatürk's Turkey*, IB Taurus, London and New York, 2010.

Testimonies about the Genocide

Andonian, Aram, *Sur la route de l'exil*, MétisPresse, Genève, 2013.

Nichanian, Marc, *Le roman de la catastrophe, entre l'art et le témoignage, littératures arméniennes au XXe siècle*, volume 3, MétisPresses, Genève, 2008.

Nichanian, Marc, *Le deuil de la philologie, entre l'art et le témoignage, littératures arméniennes au XXᵉ siècle*, volume 2, MétisPresses, Genève, 2007.

Nichanian, Marc, *La révolution nationale, entre l'art et le témoignage, littératures arméniennes au XXᵉ siècle*, volume 1, MétisPresses, Genève, 2006.

Odian, Yervant, *Journal de déportation*, dernière édition, Editions Parenthèses, Marseille, 2010.

Toroyan, Hayg, Zabel Essayan, *L'Agonie d'un peuple*, Classique Garnier, Paris, 2013.

Uluhogian, Gabriella Boghos Levon Zekiyan and Vartan Karapetian, *Impressions d'une civilisation*, Skira, 2011.

The Armenian Revolutionary Movement

In Armenian

Adom, *Notre conviction à propos du problème national*, Constantinople, 1910.

Aghayan, Tsadour, *La Révolution d'Octobre et la libération du peuple arménien*, Erevan, 1923.

Aharonian, Avedis and *Christapor Mikaelian*, Publication Haïrenik, Boston, 1926.

Aharonian, K, *Les impuretés à l'occasion d'un cinquantenaire*, Beyrouth, 1966.

Alboyadjian, Archag, *Impressions critiques*, Imprimerie Noubar, Le Caire, 1952.

Amourian, André, *La FRA en Iran*, Publication Alik, Téhéran, 1950.

Ananikian, P, *La guerre psychologique et le Dachnaktsoutioun*, Publication Haïastan, Erevan, 1986.

Arakelyan, Rouzanne, *Fumée*, Publication Haïastan, Erevan, 1993.

Avo, *Kevork Tchavouch*, édition Album révolutionnaire, Beyrouth, 1972.

Avo, *Nejteh*, édition Album révolutionnaire, Beyrouth, 1968.

Badalyan, Kh, *Le problème arménien du traité de San Stefano au congrès de Berlin, 1878*, Erevan, 1965.

Berberian, Nazareth, *Sarkis Zeitlian*, Publication Drochak, Imprimerie Vahé Setian de Hamaskaïne, Beyrouth, 1993.

Bogossyan, H, *L'histoire de Zeïtoun*, Erevan, 1969.

Chahbaz, Stéphan, *Arpiar Arpiarian*, Altapress, Beyrouth, 1988.

Chakhatounian, A., *Fédéralisme et démocratisme*, Publication Haratch, Tbilissi, 1907.

Dasnabedian, Hratch, *Qui est le dachnaktsagan?*, Imprimerie Mikael Varandian, Erevan, 1991.

Dasnabedian, Hratch, *Le mouvement révolutionnaire arménien avant la création de la FRA*, Bibliothèque Révolution, Athènes, n°7, 1990.

Dasnabedian, Hratch, *Evolution de la structure organisationnelle de la FRA*, Publication de la FRA, Imprimerie Vahé Setian de Hamaskaïne, Beyrouth, 1985.

Dasnabedian, Hratch, *Révolution*, Imprimerie Vahé Setian de Hamaskaïne, Beyrouth, 1978.

Krikorian, Khajak Der, *Aram*, Imprimerie Mikael Varandian, Erevan, 1991.

Djamalian, Archag, *La FRA et le socialisme*, Imprimerie Vahé Setian de Hamaskaïne, Beyrouth, 1979.

Donabedian, K, *La FRA en Amérique du Nord 1895–1909 et 1910–1923*, 2 tomes, Publication Haïrenik, Boston, 1993.

Douman, Nigol, *Projet d'autodéfense populaire*, Paris, 1907.

Eblightatian, M., *De l'exode au Parlement*, Publication Kilikia, Alep, 1998.

Frankian, Yervant, *Christapor Mikaelian*, Edition Gaïdzer, Hamaskaïne, Beyrouth, 1989.

Garo, Armen, *Jours vécus*, Editions Vosguetar, Beyrouth, 1986.

Guidour, Arsen, *Histoire du Parti Social-Démocrate Hentchaakian, 1887–1963*, Imprimerie Chirag, Beyrouth, 1963.

Hampartsoumyan, Raphaël, *Kerekin Nejteh*, Editions Nakhijevan, Erevan, 2003.

Hovannessian, A K, *Episodes de l'histoire de la pensée de lutte de libération arménienne*, Erevan, 1959.

Hovannesyan, Edik, *La philosophie de la politique nationale*, Imprimerie Vahé Setian de Hamaskaïne, Beyrouth, 1979.

Hovannesyan, RP, *Les mouvements de lutte de libération nationale des Arméniens de Turquie et l'organisation Les Défenseurs de la Patrie*, Erevan, 1965.

Khajak, Karekine, *Qu'est-ce qu'une classe?*, Publication Haratch, Tbilissi, 1913.

Khajak, Karekine, *Vers la Fédération*, Publication Haratch, Tbilissi, 1907.

Katchaznouni, Hovannes, *Post-mortem, histoire, mémoire, articles, lettres*, Imprimerie Mchag, Beyrouth, 1965.

Kevorkyan, Hamlet, *La stratégie de la lutte de libération et les pages des combats héroïques*, Erevan, 2012.

Kevorkyan, Hamlet, *Nigol Douman*, Erevan, 2002.

Kevorkyan, Hamlet, *Dro*, Publication Azad Khosk, Erevan, 1991.

Khutinyan, Kevork, *Histoire analytique de la FRA, des origines aux années 1895*, Publication FRA, Erevan, 2006.

Khutinyan, Kevork, *Le Ier congrès mondial de la FRA*, Publication FRA, Erevan, 1992.

Khourchoutyan, L, *Etapes chronologiques des partis arméniens de la diaspora*, Publication de l'Académie des Sciences d'Arménie, Erevan, 1964.

Haïrig, Khrimian, *Grand-père et petit-fils*, Imprimerie Edvan, Beyrouth, 1957 (première édition Etchmiadzine, 1894).

Kulkhatanian, Abraham, *Le premier programme de la FRA et ses rédacteurs*, Bibliothèque révolutionnaire, Athènes, 1987.

Kulkhatanian, Abraham, *Les affrontements arméno-tatars*, 2 tomes, Paris, 1933.

Kurkdjian, Haroutioun, *Idéologie de la FRA*, 3 tomes, Bibliothèques Révolution, Athèhes, 1997.

Kurkdjian, Haroutioun, *Historiographie de la FRA*, 4 tomes, Bibliothèques Révolution, n°8 à n°11, Athènes, 1990, 1991, 1992, 1995.

Kurkdjian, Haroutioun, *Aperçus sur l'histoire de la FRA de 1919 à 1924*, Bibliothèque Révolution, n°3, Athènes, 1988.

Kuzalian, K, *Le développement de la pensée politique arménienne et la FRA*, Edition FRA, Paris, 1927.

Kuzalian, K, *Problèmes historiques*, Société d'éditions 'Araz', Beyrouth, 1937.

Lazian, Gabriel, *L'Arménie et la Cause arménienne à la lumière des relations arméno-russes*, Edition Houssaper, Le Caire, 1957.

Lazian, Gabriel, *Figures du mouvement de libération nationale arménien*, Publication Houssaper, Le Caire, 1949.

Levinski, V, *Les Internationales socialistes et les peuples opprimés*, Publication FRA, Paris, 1929.

Malkhas, *Souvenirs*, tomes 1 et 2, Publication Hamaskaïne, Beyrouth, 1956.

Meliksetyan, K, *Les luttes héroïques de Zeitöun*, Erevan, 1960.

Melitinetzi, K, *Souvenirs*, tomes 1 et 2, Imprimerie Mchag, Beyrouth, 1963.

Léo, *Du passé*, dernière édition, Edition Chem, Erevan, 2009.

Mikaelian, Christapor, *Pensées révolutionnaires*, édition de la FRA, Athènes, 1931.

Mnatzaganyan, Aramaïs, *La Révolution en Transcaucasie et les envoyés de Russie (1917–1921)*, Erevan, 1965.

Mnatzaganyan, N, A Hagopyan, S Bordoumyan, Gh Dallakyan and V Kzartinyan, *La Grande Révolution socialiste et la victoire du pouvoir socialiste en Arménie*, Erevan, 1960.

Navassartian, Vahan, *L'âme des idées*, Publication Houssaper, Le Caire, 1951.

Navassartian, Vahan, *Le Bolchevisme et le Dachnaktsoutioun*, Publication Houssaper, Le Caire, 1949.

Navassartian, Vahan, *Le socialisme et le démocratisme*, Publication Houssaper, Le Caire, 1924.

Navassartian, Vahan, *Ce que n'est pas et ce que ne sera pas notre ligne*, Publication Houssaper, Le Caire, 1923.

Nercessian, MK, *La lutte de libération du peuple arménien contre la tyrannie turque (1850–1870)*, Erevan, 1955.

Nercisyan, Achot, *Garo Sassouni*, Centre caucasien d'iranologie, Erevan, 2009.

Nercisyan, Achot, *Histoire de la FRA*, 1898–1908, 2ᵉ tome, Erevan, 2008.

Nercisyan, Achot, *Roupen*, Erevan, 2007.

Nercisyan, Achot, *Général Sébouh*, Edik Print, Erevan, 2005.

Odian, Yervant, *Camarade Pantchouni*, "Haïastan", 1989.

Ouzounian, H, *L'idée de la lutte de libération de l'Arménie occidentale dans le Parti Armenagan*, G. Printing, Los Angeles, 1986.

Papazian, Vahan, *Mémoires*, trois tomes, Beyrouth, 1957.

Piroumian, Roubina, *L'Arménie au rythme des relations entre la FRA et les Bolcheviks, 1917–1921*, Université d'Erevan, Erevan, 1997.

Piroumian, Roubina, *Cause arménienne*, Publication de l'Eglise apostolique arménienne, diocèse de Californie, Los Angeles, 1990.

Raffi, *Gaïdzer*, Publication Mchag, Chouchi, 1880.

Roupen, *Arménie*, Beyrouth, 1948, réédition Teheran, 1991.

Roupen, *L'organisation de la FRA*, Erevan, 1991.

Roupen, *Le conflit arméno-turc*, Los Angeles, 1990. Editeur non connu, ni l'année de la première édition.

Roupen, *Mémoires d'un révolutionnaire arménien*, 7 tomes, 2ᵉ édition, Hamaskaïne, Beyrouth, 1972.

Sabah-Gulian, Stepanos, *Les responsables*, Publication Jeune Arménie, Providence, Etats-Unis, 1916.

Sassouni, Garo, *Kevork Tchavouch, le lion des neiges*, sans date ni éditeur.

Sassouni, Garo, *Les mouvements nationaux kurdes et les relations kurdo-arméniennes*, Beyrouth, 1969.

Simonyan, Hratchig, *Les voies de la lutte de libération*, 4 tomes, Edition Hayakidag, Erevan, 2003–2010.

Tachdjian, Vahé, *Ichkhan*, Publication Mikael Varandian, Erevan, 1994.

Tarpinian, Roupen, *Le Bolchevisme et l'Arménie*, Edition Kechichian, Izmyr, 1922.

Tchelebian, Antranig, *Général Antranik*, Publication Arevig, Erevan, 1990.

Tchobanian, Archag, *La nation arménienne n'est pas fautive*, Imprimeria H. Boghossian, Paris, 1926.

Varandian, Mikael, *Histoire de la FRA*, Publication de l'Université d'Erevan, 1992, (première édition, Paris, 1932).

Varandian, Mikael, *Communisme et révolution mondiale*, Publication Houssaper, Le Caire, 1926.

Varandian, Mikael, *Protestations*, Publication FRA, Genève, 1914.

Varandian, Mikael, *Histoire du mouvement arménien*, deux tomes, Publication FRA, Genève, 1912.

Varandian, Mikael, *Courants*, Publication FRA, Genève, 1910.

Varandian, Mikael, *La patrie renaissante et notre rôle*, deux tomes, Publication FRA, Genève, 1910.

Varandian, Mikael, *Le Dachnaktsoutioun et ses opposants*, Publication Haratch, Tbilissi, 1907.

Varandian, Mikael, *Philosophie, sociologie*, Publication Haratch, Tbilissi, 1907.

Varandian, Mikael, *L'idée de nation*, Publication FRA, Genève, 1904.

Vratsian, Simon, *Mémoires, faits, figures, souvenirs*, six tomes, Imprimerie Mchag, Beyrouth, 1965.

Vratsian, Simon, *Anciens manuscrits pour histoire nouvelle*, Imprimerie Mchag, Beyrouth, 1962.

Vratsian, Simon, *La République d'Arménie*, Imprimerie Alik, Téhéran, 1982 (première édition) Beyrouth, 1958.

Vratsian, Simon, *L'Arménie entre le marteau bolchevik et l'enclume turque*, Publication Hamaskaïne, Beyrouth, 1953.

Vratsian, Simon, *Soixantenaire de la FRA*, Publication Haïrenik, Boston, 1950.

Vratsian, Simon, *Soixantenaire de la FRA, 1890–1950*, Publication Haïrenik, Boston, 1950.

Non-Armenian

Aharonian, Avétis, *Sur le chemin de la liberté*, Editions Parenthèses, Marseille, 1978.

Caprielian, Ara, *The Armenian Revolutionary Federation: The Politics of a Party in Exile*, University of New York, New York, 1975.

Carlson, John Roy (Arthur Derounian), *The Armenian Revolutionary Federation Dashnagtzoutioun has nothing to do any more. The manifesto of Hovhannes Katchaznouni*, Armenian Information Service, New York, 1955.

Dasnabedian, Hratch, *Histoire de la Fédération révolutionnaire arménienne Dachnaktsoutioun, 1890–1924*, Oemme Edizioni, Milan, 1988.

Kaligian, Dikran Mesrob, *Armenian Organization and Ideology under Ottoman Rule 1908–1914*, London, 2009.

Mathossentz, Murad and Nikita Dastakian, *Il venait de la Ville Noire, Souvenirs d'un Arménien du Caucase*, L'inventaire Cres, Paris, Londres, 1988.

Raffi, *Le Fou*, Bleu Autour, Saint-Pourçain-sur-Sioule, 2007.

Rouben, *Mémoires d'un partisan arménien*, Editions de l'Aube, Paris, 1990.

Ter Minassian, Anahide, *Histoires croisées*, Editions Parenthèses, Marseille, 1997.

Ter Minassian, Anahide, *La question arménienne*, Edition Parenthèses, Marseille, 1983.

Ter Minassian, Rouben, *Mémoires d'un cadre révolutionnaire arménien*, Publication de la FRA Dachnakstoutioun, Athènes, 1994.

Ter Minassian, Taline, *Colporteurs du Komintern, L'Union soviétique et les minorités au Moyen-Orient*, Presses de Sciences Po, Paris, 1997.

Nalbandian, Louise, *The History of the Armenian Revolutionary Movement*, University of California, Berkeley, 1967.

Tunçay, Mete, Erik Jan Zürcher, *Socialism and Nationalism in the Ottoman Empire*, 1876–1923, British Academian Press, London, New York, The International Institute of Social History, Amsterdam, 1994.

Publications without a specific author

Arménie, impressions d'une civilisation, catalogue d'une exposition éponyme organisée en 2011–2012, Venise, Italie.

Encyclopédie du problème arménien, Erevan, 1996.

L'actualité du génocide des Arméniens, Comité de défense de la cause arménienne Edipol, Créteil, 1999.

'Rethinking Armenian Studies', (2003) VII(2) *The Journal of Armenian Studies*.

Actuel Marx, Histoire Globale, n°53, PUF, Paris, premier semestre 2013.

Saint Grégoire de Narek Théologien et Mystique, *Orientalia Christiana Analecta*, 275, Rome, 2006.

La reconnaissance, des revendications collectives à l'estime de soi, Editions Sciences Humaines, Auxerre, 2013.

Le génocide turc des Arméniens, La pensée et les hommes, 57ᵉ année, n°90, 2013.

Le livre arménien de la Renaissance aux Lumières : une culture de diaspora, Editions des cendres, Bibliothèque Mazarine, 2012.

Simon Zavarian, trois tomes, Publication de la FRA Dachnaktsoutioun, Edition Hamaskaïne, 1983, 1992, 1997.

Lettres de Christapor Mikaelian, Publication de la FRA Dachnaktsoutioun, Edition Hamaskaïne, 1993.

Justiciers du génocide arménien, le procès Telhirian, Diaspora, Bayeux, 1981.

Hovnan Tavtian, 2 tomes, Athènes, 1988 et Erevan, 2004.

Articles

Arakelyan, PN, 'A propos de certains problèmes de l'historiographie arménienne', *Revue d'Histoire et de Philologie*, n°2, 1989.

Augé, Isabelle, Marie-Anna Chevallier and Gérard Dédéyan, 'Congrès international, l'Arménologie aujourd'hui et ses perspectives de développement, Erevan, 15–20 septembre 2003', *Revue des Etudes Arméniennes*, n°29, 2003–2004.

Babayan, LH, 'Historiographie', *Revue d'Histoire et de Philologie*, n°4, 1970.

Balekjian, Wahe, 'The University of Dorpat and Armenian National Awakening in the Nineteenth Century', *Armenian Review*, volume 41, Hiver 1988.

Beledian, Krikor, 'Désastres conjugués', Arménie, aventure d'une nation, *Revue des Deux Mondes*, octobre–novembre 2006.

Calzolari, Valentina, 'Je ferai d'eux mon propre peuple, les Arméniens, peuple élu selon la littérature apocryphe chrétienne en langue arménienne', *Revue d'histoire et de Philosophie religieuses*, tome 90, n°2, 2010.

Calzolari, Valentina, 'La citation du PS 78 [77] 5–8 dans l'épilogue de L'Histoire de l'Arménie d'Agathange', Travaux et Mémoires, *Revue des Etudes Arméniennes*, XXIX, 2003–2004.

Dadrian, Vahakn, 'Structural-Functional Components of Genocide: A Victimological Approach to the Armenian Case' in *Drapkin*, Israel, ed, *Vicitimology*, vol III. Lexington, MA: DC Health and Co, 1974.

Danielyan, Edward, 'L'échec de la critique moderne de la branche Sissak-Aran dans la tradition de Moïse de Khorène', *Revue d'Histoire et de Philologie*, n°2, 2008.

Danielyan, Edward, 'Les problèmes de l'histoire ancienne de l'Arménie dans l'historiographie', *Revue d'Histoire et de Philologie*, n°3, 2003.

Dasnabedian, Hratch, 'The Hunchakian Party', *Armenian Review*, volume 41, hiver 1988.

Djamalian, Archag, 'H Katchaznouni et la FRA Dachnakstoutioun', *Mensuel Haïrenik*, n°3–9, janvier 1924, février 1924, mars 1924, juin 1924, juillet 1924.

Eldem, Edhem, 'Osmanlı Tarihini Türklerden Kurtarmak', *Cogito*, 73, Printemps 2013.

Garibian, Sévane 'La mémoire est-elle solule dans le droit?', *Droit et Cultures*, 66, 2013/2.

Garsoïan, Nina, 'L'Histoire attribuée à Movsès Xorenac'i: que reste-t-il à en dire?', *Revue des Etudes Arméniennes*, XXIX, 2003–2004.

Gharibdjanyan, Stépan, 'De l'histoire de l'organisation de l'Académie des sciences d'Arménie', *Revue d'Histoire et de Philologie*, n°3, 2003.

Hornus, J M, 'Chronique orientale, l'Eglise arménienne', *Verbum Caro*, 13, 1959.

Kharadyan, Albert, 'Les courants sociologiques arméniens dans les années 1850–1870', *Revue d'Histoire et de Philologie*, n°1, 2006.

Khutinyan, Kevork, 'Les voies méthodologiques de l'analyse de la pensée arménienne', *Vem*, n°4, 2012.

Mahé, Jean-Pierre, 'Norme écrite et droit coutumier en Arménie du V^{e}au XIIIe siècle', Travaux et Mémoires, *Revue des Etudes Arméniennes*, XIII, 2000.

Mahé, Jean-Pierre, 'Colophons arméniens: dialogue entre les siècles', *Ecole Pratique des Hautes Etudes, Section des sciences historiques et philologiques, Livret Annuaire*, 12, 1996–1997, Paris, 1998.

Mahé, Jean-Pierre, 'Inscriptions arméniennes: mode d'emploi', *Ecole Pratique des Hautes Etudes, Section des sciences historiques et philologiques, Livret Annuaire*, 12, 1995–1996, Paris, 1997.

Mahé, Jean-Pierre, 'Agathange et la destruction des sanctuaires païens', *Ecole Pratique des Hautes Etudes, Section des sciences historiques et philologiques, Livret Annuaire*, 10, 1994–1995, Paris, 1996.

Mahé, Jean-Pierre, 'Entre Moïse et Mahomet: réflexions sur l'historiographie arménienne', *Revue des Etudes Arméniennes*, Tome XXIII, Paris, 1992.

Mandalian, James 'Quelle est la pathologie du peuple arménien?', *Mensuel Haïrenik*, n°4, année 30, avril 1952.

Mardirossian, Aram, 'Lettre à la splendide et célèbre communauté de Kcaw. Grigor Narekac'i contre les Thondrakiens', *Revue des Etudes Arméniennes*, XXIX, 2003–2004.

Muyldermans, Joseph, 'L'historiographie arménienne', *Le Muséon, Revue d'études orientales*, Louvain, 1963.

Parkhoutaryan, V P, 'A propos des problèmes soulevés par l'historiographie soviéto-arménienne', *Revue d'Histoire et de Philologie*, n°4, 1990.

Sarksyan, K, 'Mosvès Xorenac'i et la liste des maisons dynastiques', *Revue d'Histoire et de Philologie*, n°1–2, 1996.

Sarksyan, K, 'Mosvès Xorenac'i et son Histoire de l'Arménie', *Revue d'Histoire et de Philologie*, n°2, 1973.

Sarksyan, K, 'L'historiographie de l'époque pré-mesrobienne', *Revue d'Histoire et de Philologie*, n°1, 1969.

Shmavonan, Sarkis, 'Mikayel Nalbandian and Non-Territorial Armenian Nationalism', *Armenian Review*, automne 1983.

Ter-Martirosov, Felix, 'From the State of Urartu to the formation of the Armenian Kingdom, 2012' in Biainili-Urartu, *The Proceedings of the Symposium Held in Munich 12–14 October 2007*, eds S Kroll, C Gruber, U Hellwg, M Roaf and P Zimansky, série Acta Iranica, vol 51. Peeters, Louvain, 2012.

Toumarkine, Alexandre, Historiographie turque de la Première Guerre mondiale sur les fronts ottomans: problèmes, enjeux et tendances, *Histoire@Politique. Politique, culture, sociéte*, n° 22, janvier–avril 2014.

Youzbachian, KN, 'L'héritage scientifique de Nicolas Adontz', *Revue d'Histoire et de Philologie*, n°4, 1962.

Reviews and Journals

'Vem' (Arménie), '*Mensuel Haïrenik*' (Etats-Unis), '*Armenian Review*' (Etats-Unis), '*Socio*' (France), '*Revue d'histoire arménienne contemporaine*' (France), '*Drochak*' (Arménie), '*Le Débat*' (France), '*Journal of Armenian Studies*' (Etats-Unis), '*Esprit*' (France), '*Vingtième Siècle*' (France), '*Politique Etrangère*' (France), '*Politique Internationale*' (France), '*Questions Internationales*' (France), '*Hérodote*' (France), '*Revue d'Etudes Arméniennes*' (France), '*Revue d'Histoire et de Philologie*' (Arménie soviétique).

Index

www.ingramcontent.com/pod-product-compliance
Lightning Source LLC
Chambersburg PA
CBHW071845270326
41929CB00013B/2111